Peter Biddlecombe is a travel-ha... acclaimed first book, *French Lessons in Africa*, which has now been in print for over a decade, describes his travels through French-speaking Africa. It has been followed by nine gloriously funny accounts of Peter's further misadventures, all of which are published by Abacus, plus this one, making eleven in total.

Also by Peter Biddlecombe

French Lessons in Africa
Travels with My Briefcase
Around the World – on Expenses
I Came, I Saw, I Lost My Luggage
Very Funny – Now Change Me Back
Faster, They're Gaining
A Nice Time Being Had by All
Never Feel a Stranger
The United Burger States of America
Always Feel a Friend

Ireland
~In a Glass of its Own~

PETER BIDDLECOMBE

First published in Great Britain as a paperback original in
December 2005 by Abacus

A CIP catalogue record for this book is available from
the British Library.

ISBN 0 349 11694 6

Typeset in Garamond Light by Palimpsest Book Production Limited,
Polmont, Stirlingshire

Printed and bound in Great Britain by
Clays Ltd, St Ives plc

Abacus
An imprint of
Time Warner Book Group UK
Brettenham House
Lancaster Place
London WC2E 7EN

www.twbg.co.uk

Contents

Intro-hic-duction

Glory be to God. I'm not going to bottle out of it. Isn't it the finest, most glorious ting in the whole wide world whether ye are blue mouldy for the want of a pint or whether ye jest fancy a drop taken. 'Tis the mighty black stuff itself, the glorious black wine of Ireland, I want to be talking to ye about.

And isn't Ireland itself almost the like of it?

'Tis no lie, I'm telling ye. If those United States of America are a super finger-lickin' hamburger; if Italy, the home of the Pope himself as well as the scarlet-coated bishops of Rome, is a giant pizza; Germany, the grosse Wiener schnitzel in der ganzen velt and France, one giant uncontrolled ratatouille with in the centre a giant, err, Paris, hasn't t' ould country of saints and scholars, tinkers and drinkers just got to be the most singular, uncompromising pint of Guinness of them all. Deep. Dark. Rich. Smooth. Creamy. By the saints of God, I swear 'tis unlike anyting else in not only the history of the world but in the history of the world to come as well.

First, not that I'm too much of an expert on the subject – I have only a passing acquaintance with it – 'tis the water itself. Without the water I'm certain Ireland/Guinness Guinness/Ireland is nothing. The water, of course, is the Counties Waterford and Wexford. Beautiful, God-fearing counties. Beautiful, God-fearing cities. Even in the great rains. Which, they say, come soddenly. Then there is County Cavan. With so many lakes. God save us, they have hardly any soil at all. County Down and all those desperate seaside towns. It was in the county town Downpatrick, they say, that so reluctant was St Patrick to leave the land of Erin, dead though he was, they had to keep pleading with him to lie down so they could bury him. Then there is County Donegal, bleak, unkept, the place for thinking deep thoughts in the wet mist. And, of course, County Fermanagh, the land of the lakes. You'd not see the like of any of them anywhere in the world.

The roasted malted barley. That comes from the farming counties, God bless the lot of them: County Wicklow, home of the best barley in the world – 'tis far more important than all those great old Anglo-Irish mansions of unhappy memory where inside you'd be entertained with a sup of tea while outside everybody would be poaching everything in sight; County Kilkenny, itself named after a famous beer; and County Meath, mighty good farming country where they have a grand eye for a dumb beast.

Hops, of course, are County Kildare, where great hands they are with horses, they run off with all the world's top races, although the horses, of course, do more than hop. I tell you there's not a three-year-old in the world that would not give its hind legs to hop across to the famous green, green grass of Kildare for the thrill of the race.

Yeast, of course, is a spelling mistake for Yeats, the poet William and the painter Jack, both sons of County Sligo while the King Congs, the Guinness clan itself Mayo or may not come from County Mayo depending on who is buying the drinks.

After the roasted malted barley, the hops and the yeast come the proteins, the queer, wonderful things that I'm thinking do their all and their utmost to contain our needs: County Kerry, with all that soft, dreamy, delicious milk and butter. I tell you I'm drunk on the thought of it. County Westmeath, the damp land famous for its beef cattle. Droves of them they have. County Tyrone, whose proteins seem to have done more for the US than for Ireland.

Carbohydrates, like a horse fair in County Wicklow, are important but often overlooked. Why I don't know. But for the like of them the Guinness would be severely wanting. The sugar must come from County Carlow, the sweetest sweet tooth in the country on account of their mountains of sugar beet. The Counties Laois, Monaghan, Leitrim, Roscommon, and, of course, Louth, the smallest county of them all, about the size of a quick, small pint, make up the rest.

No pint is worth its weight in gold without that most important ingredient of all, Alc O'Hall, as it was always spelt in church schools throughout the land before they suffered the impact of European Union finance. Soon as anyone anywhere in the world gets any of the most famous Irish Alc O'Hall inside them it's not long before the famous County Tipperary isn't on their lips. Then there is County Limerick. County Limerick, however, is different. There they've only got to look at two glasses, not even two full glasses, and they start raving but definitely not singing the praises of someone whose name I can't quite recall at the moment but who they claim made a game of them, wrote about them, and libelled and slandered and destroyed their good name for ever. Talking of the authentic spirit of Ireland, God bless you, there's County Longford named, of course, after the good Lord himself to whom, it is said, the good St Patrick came to do worship although people do say it took some arranging. At first they say the good Lord Longford refused to meet him because he wasn't a member of the criminal fraternity: he wasn't in prison and he couldn't guarantee to write an article immediately afterwards for the *Guardian* revealing full details of their secret meeting. But holy man that he was even St Patrick himself didn't have the courage to go across to either County Derry or County Armagh, the shame on him. They say it's because he never knew when to call Londonderry Londonderry and Derry Derry. Armagh is one of the oldest cities in Ireland and sometimes, the Lord have mercy on us, it must be said it looks and feels like it. Then around 10 o'clock at night it's the same as the rest of them.

Now we come to the finings in other words the finest counties in Ireland which for my money are Galway and Connemara. But seeing as Connemara is not a county although Heaven only knows it deserves to be, it must be Galway alone. But whatever you do don't tell Connemara.

Nitrogen, all those little bubbles, has got to be County Offaly if only because it's offaly full of all those bogs and from every one a million little bubbles are surely escaping every day and night of the year.

Ireland: In a Glass of its Own

Guinness doesn't have a cork. But the nearest thing is the widget. So the widget has got to be Cork if that's not too Irish for you.

The crowning glory, that soft, white, creamy, frothy head has just got to be County Dublin, which is Dublin and County Antrim, which is Belfast. Glory be to God, if only I could remember all the good times I've forgotten I've had in Dublin and Belfast. But the crowning glory of the crowning glory, those glorious times the barmaids pour the Guinness itself and at the same time gently, delicately inscribe for that fleeting second their telephone number in the froth, that's just got to be County Clare, which I reckon I've walked across backwards and forwards on my own two feet, travelled by ass and cart and forgotten the times I've driven and been driven over. I reckon I know it better than I know myself. That's to be sure.

Oh go on with you then. The night is still young. Another? Mine's a Guinness. Thank God they don't believe in half measures.

Peter O'Biddlecombe

The Water Counties

Co. Waterford
Co. Wexford
Co. Cavan
Co. Down
Co. Donegal
Co. Fermanagh

Ireland is unlike any other country in the world. So too its history is unlike any other history in the world. In England, history is divided up into different periods, Henry VIII, Blackadder, Charles Dickens and *Pop Idol*. In France, it's divided up into soupe à l'oignon, Château Lynch Bages, Dom Pérignon and Je ne regrette rien. In Italy, it's the Pope, shoes, Versace and huge mountains of pasta. In Ireland, just as the country itself is divided up into a pint of Guinness, so too is its history.

In the beginning, at the very start of the process, there is what is known as the Water period, a period in their history of which perhaps not surprisingly they are none too proud.

It began precisely at opening time, the morning of 4004 BC when the first prehistoric human was washed up in the auld country to find out for himself if this thing called Guinness was as good as everybody grunted it was. He decided to stay. Before long because the last thing he wanted was to stay at home with the wife, moaning and complaining all the time like a howling banshee about his drinking and enjoying himself and making animal sacrifices to the gods with the lads at the Portmarnock Golf Club, Co. Dublin – even in those days women were barred from the Club – he took up hunting and gathering. Hunting for reasons to go out and have another Guinness. Gathering so he could collect all the excuses he could find to stay out with the lads as long as he possibly could. After all there was no way he was going to even

<1>1</1>

attempt to hunt the Great Irish Elk. First of all because it was more the size of an elephant than an elk. Second, if he'd been successful there would have been no point trying to gather it up on his shoulders and take it back home to herself for dinner because she would only complain it wasn't a vegetable, she didn't know how many chemicals it had been sprayed with and it wasn't listed in her *Sensible Woman's Guide to E-numbers and How Not to Tell the Doctor You Want a Caesarean Section for Cosmetic Reasons Only*.

In the Aran Islands they have a different version. They say the first person to ever land in Ireland was Noah's granddaughter, Caesar, which I suppose makes the Aran Islands the first Caesarean section of Ireland. Her granddaddy, they say, warned her the flood was coming. Completely contrary to everything that is said in the Bible, she immediately upped and made for Ireland on the assumption that any country that was completely desolate and therefore without sin need never fear the vengeance of the Good Lord. Mainland historians dismiss the idea out of hand. They say it's as likely as Bob Geldof looking as if he is enjoying himself.

Either way, our first prehistoric Irish human had no sooner settled into his routine – in those days it took thousands of years to settle into a routine, much the same amount of time it used to take to brew a decent cup of tea on a peat fire – along rolled the new Blarney Stone Age people with their newfangled moss-covered Blarney Stone shillelaghs, Blarney Stone fiddles and Blarney Stone bagpipes. Some say they came from southern Europe, Ibiza, where they were known as the Blarney Stoned people. Others say they were more likely from the Middle East which is one reason especially in and around the Gaza Strip why there are few stones left in the roads.

Their passion was mega: dirty great megaliths of stone. They scattered them all over the place. On hillsides. In the middle of fields. Somehow or other they even built one in the middle of Shannon Airport although how they got it behind the plate-glass window has been the subject of intensive debate for generations of Irish archaeologists. Having exhausted themselves with hauling megaliths all over the place, they decided to concentrate on building piles of blarney stones which was much simpler, lighter work. Instead of just calling it a pile of blarney stones they decided to call it a cairn. This they thought would sound much better as the subject of future doctoral theses than Pile of Blarney Stones, Under the Pile of Blarney Stones or simply Piles.

Some say Limerick was a favourite spot for the Blarney Stone Age Irishman and point to the piles of stones all over the city even today. Others are not so sure. They think the piles of stones might just be the results of yet another gang fight.

How do you tell the difference between a genuine Blarney Stone Age stone and an ordinary stone? Pick up a genuine Blarney Stone Age stone. Underneath will be a genuine Blarney Stone Age message, 'A kiss will release its magic,' 'Rub it and your thirst will disappear,' 'Put me down. You haven't paid for me yet. You thievin' English bastard.' Pick up an ordinary stone and underneath you'll find something you'll have to scrape off pretty quickly if you don't want methylphenidate coming out of your ears.

After the new Blarney Stone Age people came the new Copper Age people. Because they had now invented copper, this meant they could now build ring forts all over the country instead of the traditional piles of blarney stones.

Inside the ring forts there was always a royal enclosure with its royal house and royal seat. Around the royal enclosure were always non-royal houses and non-royal seats. Then, because the royal royals didn't want any non-royals wandering around their royal pad and leaving dirty non-royal footprints from their non-royal wellington boots all over their royal carpets, there is a banqueting hall where the whole ring fort and somebody else's wife could make merry without worrying about dropping any food on the floor. Outside the ring fort is usually a huge mound. Some people say it was a way of rating the success of the banquets. The better the banquet, the more food and drink was put away, the more people crashed out afterwards, the higher the mound. Others say it's a mass grave site. It's the result of what happened when the wives found out what the husbands had been up to while they had been at home doing the washing and ironing in as it was known at the time, the Iron Age.

3

Ireland: In a Glass of its Own

One of the best ring forts in Ireland is at Tara in Co. Meath. From here the builders thought they would spread across the country, building forts wherever they went. But it was not to be. Hence the early Irish phrase 'Tara Boom Delay'.

Another is in Dun Aengus on the Aran Islands which is still surrounded by sharp stone spikes to prevent outsiders getting in. But that's always been the traditional attitude of the Aran Islanders to visitors. Inside a fort in Navan in County Armagh archaeologists discovered the skeleton of a Barbary ape dating back to 200 BC which they claim came from Spain or Portugal for a stag night, had too much of the happy stuff and never made it back to the airport on time.

After the new Copper Age people came the new Bronze Age people. They created Ireland's first and greatest industry: tourism. All they did was lie around all day hoping to get bronzed.

After the new Bronze Age people nobody bothered to come any more. The Irish now had all the necessary skills to make all the weapons they wanted to stop themselves from being overrun and killed by too many new Bronze Age people who had drunk too much Guinness and couldn't take it. They also knew how to make gold and bronze jewellery, which resulted in another round of killing. Those who got gold wanted bronze and killed the poor guy giving it to them – or, at least, trying to. Similarly those who got bronze and wanted gold. Any who were left standing were then killed by the owners of those who got either gold or bronze because they thought they had no business giving gold or bronze away in the first place.

Inevitably this means there is gold and bronze lying around all over Ireland. I once asked a typical old Paddy I met in Dooleys overlooking the harbour in Waterford the best way of finding buried treasure.

'Simple,' he says. 'Eat a full bowl of warm, delicious tasty mouse soup. 'Tis the only way. I'll be having a glass of Guinness with you, sir, for the information provided.'

In the end, what with the killing and no doubt the mouse soup there was hardly anybody left in the bottom of the glass. Apart from the dregs.

Thus ended the Water period of Irish history.

Co. Waterford
A big splash of a county

Famous local resident
Donna Say A Word

Favourite food
Breakfast, Granville Hotel, Waterford

Favourite drink
Guinness

Favourite pub
The one in Dungarvan with the big door and the windows

Favourite restaurant
Cistercian Monastery, Mount Melleray
Speciality: You have to help with the washing-up afterwards

What to say
Where are you from?

What not to say
You're from Co. Cork

Waterford, which is Irish for water you have to ford across as opposed to water you have to live in, die in, clamber over stone walls in, chase cattle in and go to bars in, is as you would expect a big splash of a county. A dirty, muddy splash. Which I suppose is not surprising as it is situated on the banks of a river called Suir.

Compared to the likes of County Carlow and County Louth, which are about the size of a beer mat, it's a serious spread. Around 1800 square kilometres. About the size of London.

It also means serious business. It has serious ports which take serious large modern ships. At one time the quays which stretch for practically a mile along the River Suir were said to be the best in Europe. Not any more. Today they're the best in County Waterford.

It has an airport or rather Ryanair has an airport there. For this is where they started all those years ago when Michael O'Leary was taking swearing lessons from Gordon Ramsay. Today, of course, it's so busy you couldn't hear them if they tried to tell you how quiet it is. I'm only sorry they called it Ryanair. They should have called it Eirelift. After all, it's been home to some major world-beating industries in its time. It witnessed the birth of the bacon rasher, the cream cracker and blaa, blaa, blaa, those tiny loaves of bread you dip into your Guinness for breakfast. Before that huge Irish fry-up.

Today it's reduced to virtually three: Fishing. Glassmaking. Tourism.

Fishing, I can understand. They're on what they call the snot-green or scrotumtightening sea. It's in their blood. Everything they do involves the sea. Even going to church. I once went to mass in Waterford on a Sunday morning when a young innocent priest from, I think, Co. Mayo who looked as though he'd drunk nothing but the purest milk of human innocence all his life, beseeched us all to pray for seamen, good, honest Irish seamen. Ireland being Ireland at the time, one half of the congregation, largely I will admit the half crowded around the back door of the church and spilling out on to the street outside, immediately dropped to their knees.

> Englishman, Scotsman and an Irishman go into a bar. They order three pints of Guinness. The barman gives them the three pints. Just at that moment three flies land in each of the three glasses.
>
> The Englishman pushes his glass away.
>
> The Scotsman drinks the Guinness. Including the fly.
>
> The Irishman picks the fly out of his pint of Guinness, thumps it up and down on the bar yelling, 'Spititout ya bastard, will ya spit it out.'

'The more seamen we have in this country the better. Strong. Pure. Fearless. Prepared to go to places to which seamen the world over are dedicated,' declared the priest.

The other half of the congregation, those inside the church, veils drawn tightly around their heads, then also dropped to their knees and began fervently praying for all their worth for no doubt other reasons.

Glassmaking, I don't understand. I know they have all the raw materials they need: the unknown millions of Sir Anthony Heinz-57-Varieties O'Reilly, who seems to own every big company in Ireland apart from the ones he doesn't own. But it's not crystal clear. I can't see your typical, wild, impetuous Irishman having the time or the patience to fashion a delicate, fragile wisp of glass. I know they do and enormously successfully but I can't see it. It's like watching an Irish farmer play the Moonlight Sonata with his boots.

Tourism, I thought, was a natural. Until I checked into a hotel on the waterfront. There was no Top of the morning. 'Tis a soft day. Tanksamillion. The receptionist was the most miserable I've come across in the whole of Ireland. I asked if there were any rooms. She gave me a form to fill in. I filled it in. She took the form. She gave me the key. Not a grunt. Not a murmur. Not a word. If you're not careful you're going to grow up to become, as they say, a poor wilderness of a woman. Next time I stay at the Waterford Manor Inn.

On the other hand breakfasts at the waterfront hotel are unforgettable. The following morning the waitress couldn't stop talking. She was young. She was blonde. Her Irish accent was perfect. But not quite.

'You're not from Ireland,' I said as she brought me my third helping of black pudding.

'I am not,' she says the way the Irish do. 'So where would you be thinking I'm from?'

I took a guess. She pronounced her 'l's funny.

'Russia,' I said.

It was right. She was stunned. I got two extra eggs on my plate. On top of the four I already had.

'Now,' she says. 'Ye can't be telling me which part of Russia I'm from.'

Well it obviously wasn't Moscow or St Petersburg or any obvious town otherwise she wouldn't have asked me. I took another guess, Ekaterinburg. In the Urals. Yeltsin's home town. Where Tsar Nicholas and his family were murdered. She burst into tears. I was right. She was from Ekaterinburg. I had the best breakfast of my life. Very appreciative these Russian girls. Especially the ones from Ekaterinburg.

As far as the local countryside is concerned, it's dim and dismal. Even miserable. The Knockmealdown Mountains do not knock me down even though everyone goes on about the spectacular views, especially through the famous Vee. Maybe it's because I'm usually racing through them early on Monday mornings to get to Shannon Airport to get back to London to get to the office so I can put in a full day's work by 5 o'clock. Maybe it's because whenever I drive through them I can't help but remember it was here that they shot the last wolf in Ireland in 1786. As well as in Carlow in 1886. And in Monaghan in 1986. It's the same with the Comeragh Mountains. They always seem to be just a blur in the distant rain.

Waterford town, I always think should be a big, bustling place. It's in a beautiful setting. However you reach it, by boat, by air, by road, by rail, it should be at least as exciting as Cork or Galway City. But it's not. It doesn't have that buzz, that flaithiúlacht or excitement. Why on earth it is twinned with St John's, Newfoundland, I have no idea. There's nothing new found land about it unless, of course, years ago lots of people left Waterford for New York and ended up in Newfoundland thinking the skyscrapers were few and far between and decided to stay. People say it's like Kilkenny. Tiny streets. Narrow alleyways. Some even say it's like a tiny hilltop medieval city. Maybe it's because of its history.

The Vikings were here. Their legacy: fair haired children and a nasal drone which sounds a bit like my old rusty, broken-down Volvo when it is out of synch. They say it dates back to an ancient Viking custom: If you didn't pay them the taxes you owed them they cut off your nose. So many people refused to pay them the nasal drone became part of their heritage.

Apart from their own special sound they've also got their own special words. An eejit is not an eejit he's a rowdlamaun. Old girls don't chatter, they chitter whereas up in the North chitter means shiver as in, I suppose, my teeth were chittering. If you want the salt you don't say as we do, 'Oi. Giss it 'ere.' You say, 'Please to be so kind as to teach me the salt.'

After the Vikings came the Normans. They had an even worse way of trying to quell the local population. For every year you didn't pay them their money they stayed another year. For some reason everybody paid up on the dot.

Co. Waterford

Finally came the English and the good King John. In no time at all Waterford was the biggest, fastest-growing, most powerful city in the land. It could have become the capital. Cromwell, however, ruined everything. Or rather Cromwell's barber ruined everything. Before attacking Waterford in 1650 Cromwell summoned the local barber from Kilmacthomas for a shave and a short back and sides.

'Jesus, Mary and Joseph,' an old Waterford farmer once told me, as we were sharing a glass in a wonderful old Tea Room and Select Bar in Kilmacthomas close to where the barber shop was burnt down. 'Just imagine what a blessed island this would be if the good barber of Kilmacthomas had not been such a good barber. God rest his soul. I'll be having another one with ye, sir, if ye don't mind. Just to keep ye company.'

But as it has received so it has given. Waterford gave the Americans two things: Thomas Francis Meagher, one of the founders of the Irish Confederation, who was captured, sentenced to death, his death sentence commuted, transported to Australia, escaped, ended up in the US, fought in the Civil War and was made governor of Montana. They also for some reason which is not crystal clear to me gave them the idea for the chandelier in Philadelphia's Independence Hall. Now who thought of that, I wonder.

But no matter how many times I've been to Waterford, it always seems bleak and dismal. Even grimy. It's got some grand bars and hotels. Even clubs which for some reason they insist on calling Knight Clubs.

I've never been there for their International Festival of Light Opera which attracts visitors from all over the world but few locals. They apparently can't understand why 'Molly Malone', 'Fields of Athenry' and 'I'll Tell Me Ma' are never on the programme.

And I've never been there when they have their annual Spraoi Festival, which is Irish for Special People Return And Oinoy Inyone who's around when, I'm told, you can hardly move for Brazilian acrobats, Japanese drummers and Ecuadorian contortionists all trying to work out what the hell they're doing in Waterford when they should be annoying people in somewhere far more exciting.

But I was there once at Christmas. It was just the same. Dismal. Damp. The odd tree. A handful of lights. Telegraph poles had been chopped down and sawn up for firewood. Kids were literally falling 30 foot from a third-floor window on to the pavement below and surviving unhurt. Twenty-two-year-old whangers were taking their uncle's car, driving it through the city, refusing to stop when ordered by the Gardai or police, colliding with taxis, mounting a footpath, hitting a bollard and speeding out on to the Cork Road where they were finally stopped and arrested, a local policeman announced formally on television, 'on suspicion of drink driving'.

If it was true and the driver had been drinking I admire him. He had more courage than me. The bars, restaurants and Knight Clubs I went in all looked as though they had been designed by Serbs for Albanians.

The town, as they say, was 'walking with people'. Everybody was plodding around with their heads down. Maybe it was the constant rain and drizzle. But there was no Christmas spirit. Maybe it was out of embarrassment because they had been caught by one of Waterford's favourite con tricks. Park your car. Go off and do whatever. While you're gone a local chickenhead either lets down your tyres, smashes a side window or if they can get under the bonnet does something or other to the engine. You return, discover what's been done, start to go bananas or I suppose sham-rocks when there just happens to come along this nice young man who for the price of a couple of pints of Guinness will put every-thing right and see you on your way. Maybe it's the fact that for centuries they've been overlooked. Millions of people have come to Waterford. But millions of people have taken one look at the place and immediately made off for more exciting parts. It is bound to affect them. In fact so desperate are people to get out that four Waterford city councillors and their wives even agreed to go to Istanbul for of all things the Eurovision Song Contest. Their excuse? Local singer Chris Doran was representing Ireland. Local ratepayers didn't mind the expense. They'd do anything to help anyone escape for a couple of days. Whatever the cost.

For all that, it's still worth the visit.

I usually come in by train or bus from either Dublin or Limerick to Plunkett Station on the water's edge. Come in on the wrong day and you'll find pigs' heads nailed to stakes all over the place. People will tell you it's a publicity stunt. Don't you believe it. It's an old Viking trick to keep out illegal immigrants. In the old days it was simple. You arrived by ship. Jarveys, horses and carts to you, would be lining the quayside. A discreet word from the captain to the customs officer and straight through. No questions. No forms. No searches.

Today I have to tramp across Rice Bridge to O'Connell Street, across the City Square and into the wide Eighteenth-Century Mall which, however much they keep on about it, never strikes me as being very imposing or very eighteenth-century come to that. At the north end is their so-called famous Reginald's Tower which they say was built by the Normans in the twelfth century on the site of a Viking wooden tower. Which I don't believe. I ask you, if the Normans built a tower in the twelfth century in the far south-east corner of Ireland on the site of an old Viking wooden tower would they then have called it Reginald? Of course not. At the south end is, well, the south end.

The Cathedral is great fun for any student of the Irish body politic. It contains the tomb of a typical Irish politician: James Rise, seven times Lord Mayor of Waterford in the fifteenth century. It not only shows the body in an advanced state of decay, but it is so decomposed you can see all the frogs and worms getting out of it as well.

The Waterford Crystal factory, the biggest crystal glass factory in the world, I never bother with. I'm more interested in what goes in the crystal than the crystal itself.

But if there's anything that will make you appreciate the delights of Waterford it's a drive along the coast in a bitter gale, the rain lashing the windscreen, the tyres ploughing through seas six foot deep to Youghal pronounced Yowl, which is in either County Waterford or County Cork depending on who you talk to. I know I've done it many times. Sometimes non-stop. Sometimes stopping practically every inch of the way and being forced to take shelter in one bar or restaurant after another.

Start at Tramore, Irish for We used to attract tramore upper-class

13

Ireland: In a Glass of its Own

people than we do today. George III used to come here. So too the Prince Regent. Even the Lake poets who must have felt at home given the weather. Today it's known as the Margate of Ireland although to me it's more the Las Vegas of Ireland. There's gambling everywhere. Not your roulette, James Bond, smooth-dinner-jacket gambling but more old-fashioned, cloth-cap fairground gambling. They even gamble on the biggest gamble of all. At the end of Domeraile Walk there are three white pillars. On one of the pillars is a statue of an old sailor pointing out to sea. Any woman who hops around it three times on one foot, so the story goes, will be married within the year. Clockwise or anticlockwise nobody could tell me. As for the poor man who gets lumbered with such a super-stitious, one-legged hopper, he'll end up like the sailor. A block of stone. Unable to speak. Unable to move. The life drained out of him.

But I can forgive the perpetrators of such unhappiness. The bay is spectacular. They've got a lovely little racecourse, the smallest racecourse in Ireland. In fact, it's so small the winning post is in County Tipperary. There's also a million great bars and restaurants, which even not in a howling gale are fantastic.

The only thing I can't forgive are the speed ramps. They're everywhere. You can hardly drive two paces without hitting a speed ramp. Or maybe I just had too much to eat and drink. I noticed them more than I normally do.

At one time when, don't laugh, I was thinking of being a serious author, I dragged myself backwards and forwards along the coast at Bunmahon, an old copper-mining area, researching the early days of John Wheatley, the only really successful minister in the first Labour government of 1924. He was one of ten children. The family emigrated to Scotland. At the age of eleven he left school to work down the mines. At 24 he saved enough money to open his own grocery shop. Within three years he had married the daughter of a Glasgow publisher. He worked as a reporter on the *Glasgow Herald* and then the *Catholic Herald*. He then launched his own business, publishing calendars for shopkeepers. It gave him the security and financial independence he had been seeking all his life. At 39, a Roman Catholic businessman on the brink of

14

middle age, he threw himself into politics. He joined the strug-
gling Independent Labour Party. He became founder and chairman
of the Catholic Socialist Society and a member of Lanarkshire
County Council. He was very quickly elected leader of the Labour
Group on Glasgow Town Council.

Immediately his extremist views, violent language and ruthless
debating logic outraged everyone from his political opponents to
the Church authorities.

'If there is one set of humbugs in the world, if there is one
group of unadulterated hypocrites, it is the British ruling class,'
he told the Tories on one occasion. 'I do not believe in your honesty
at all. You are either knaves or fools. You are the greatest enemies
of the human race. I can see no hope for this country unless we
can get the people to overthrow your system.'

He was elected Member of Parliament in 1922. Within two years
he was Minister of Health. Within three years he was an alternative leader and a growing threat to MacDonald and the whole
façade of consensus politics.

Wheatley masterminded the first peacetime cooperation
between Government and industry. He was also the first minister
to tackle housing as a long-term problem. Subsidies were increased.
The responsibility was placed firmly and squarely on local authorities. As a result, he was the first minister to build a record 100,000
houses a year for letting at controlled rents. His Housing Act, said
John Strachey, was the 'most substantial measure of social reform
enacted during the 1920s'. Emmanuel Shinwell, a fellow Clydesider,
has described it as 'easily the best piece of legislation to reach the
Statute Book in 1924' and hailed it 'a triumph for the Independent
Labour Party'. A.J.P. Taylor calls it 'the greatest success of the first
Labour Government'.

Wheatley was also the most realistic – and the most far-sighted
– Labour member of the day. He prophesied the economic crisis
for the national government. He warned against the humiliations,
the savage reductions of wages and unemployment pay. He was
convinced the government would do nothing for the workers and
that the shock would set the party back twenty years.

Wheatley also exposed what he called the weakness at the heart of capitalism and remodelled his Marxism to meet the changing situation. Before Keynes or Beveridge, he realised mass unemployment was caused by the appalling lack of demand caused by capitalist production, deflation, balanced budgets and the gold standard.

Today his theories are remembered. But he is forgotten. He died in July 1930, an outcast. He refused office in the second Labour government out of loyalty to the Independent Labour Party. His company was involved in a sordid financial scandal. He fought and lost an unsavoury libel case. His tough, resilient nerve was giving way.

'I am beginning to think,' he said just before he died, 'that we politicians are all flies on the wheel.'

Michael Foot was also a big fan of his.

'He was the only one member of that Government who stirred enthusiasm among militant Socialists,' he wrote. 'John Wheatley looked a man of a different fibre from the others and his Housing Act left its mark when all else was forgotten.'

I trudged all over Bunmahon looking for clues of John Wheatley, his family, his family's families. Went to visit the local church. Looked up the records. Wrote a million background notes. Move over Roy Jenkins. This was going to be one of the greatest political biographies of all time.

But then I seem to remember somebody rang me up, offered to buy me a drink and it was goodbye to Wheatley.

Further along the coast Dungarvan is famous, Ireland being Ireland, because this is where in the old days women desperate to cross the River Colligan at its lowest point had to lift their skirts the height of their thick old-fashioned wellington boots and wade across. Not that there was the slightest risk of anything untoward. Most Irish men even today would think nothing of stepping over twelve naked women sprawled across the floor in all kinds of positions to get to their beloved pint of Guinness.

What nobody mentions is that Dungarvan was home to Ernest Walton, who with John Cockcroft was the first to split the atom. The son of the local Methodist minister, he went to school at Methody College, Belfast, where it was recognised immediately that he had a brilliant mind. He was made to study woodwork and metalwork. But it was enough to help him prove Einstein's theory $E=mc^2$ was true and, therefore, usher in nuclear energy, nuclear power and, of course, the nuclear bomb. We can only be grateful Methody College didn't teach him anything serious. God knows where we would have been then.

To many people, Dungarvan has gone to the dogs. At one time it was a busy little place. Then the harbour started silting up. The big ships began moving elsewhere. Other ports along the coast started modernising and making it easier for the local farmers to ship out their produce through them than through Dungarvan. Things began to slip further away. Today the whole place looks as though it needs a lick of paint. Well, two licks of paint. Trouble is the harbour is so silted up there's no way of bringing them in.

To the select few, however, going to the dogs was the best thing that ever happened to Dungarvan, especially if Master McGrath was running. The greatest greyhound of all time. Only beaten once in 37 appearances. Winner of all the big trophies. They've even got a statue to him in the centre of town.

Horse-lovers, yes. But I never realised that the Irish were also great dog-lovers until I went to Dungarvan.

'The Irish. Dog-lovers. We were dog-lovers before we were horse-lovers,' an old boy who looked as though he was covered in caterpillar fungus told me one evening in the bar at Lawlor's Hotel.

'The Irish wolfhound. Big. Tall. Proud. Great hunters. They hunted the wolf to extinction. The Irish greyhound. They're not all as great as the great Master McGrath but they're great. Every one of them.'

His enthusiasm was catching. As it happened, that was all that was catching. Luckily.

The only other real dog enthusiast I've met in Ireland, as opposed to people who keep dogs, was an old bag of spanners. It was about six o'clock in the morning. She was walking her dog up and down the middle of the new motorway between Limerick City and Ennis, Co. Clare. I say, met. I missed her by inches.

'What d'ye think ye are doin'?' she yells at me when I pull over to get my breath back.

'What am I doing?' I said slowly. 'What are you doing walking your dog up and down the middle of a motorway?'

'I've been walking my dogs up and down this stretch of land for over sixty years,' she says. 'And my father before me. And his father before him. And no new motorway or the likes of you are going to stop me. Good day to ye.'

Off she continued, straight down the middle of the overtaking lane.

Obviously barking mad.

Dungarvan, which was once owned by the Duke of Devonshire, also suffered because the Irish being the Irish never forgot how they welcomed Oliver Cromwell.

'Your good health,' cried a certain Mrs Nagle as the great Exterminator rode through town. It saved Dungarvan from being destroyed. But it didn't save its reputation.

It is also the perfect place to see how the English rig elections. No spin. No empty promises about education, education, education. The Act of Union in 1801 cut the number of Irish parliamentary seats by two-thirds. Those left were transferred to Westminster. An Irish parliamentary seat suddenly became worth having. Dungarven was one of the 33 seats which survived the cutbacks. The Duke of Devonshire was determined it should be under his control. The trouble was, apart from all the obvious handicaps, he was not a Tory. Hence the urban renewal trick, I mean decision to improve the quality of life for people, regardless of race or religion, living in the constituency. If his good constituents happened to identify him with such a good cause, so be it. First, he decided more housing was needed in the centre of town, Devonshire Square, Bridge Street, Cross Bridge Street and William Street which he just happened to own. Not only would the new owners be grateful to him, so too would all the local people responsible for building them.

What happened at the elections in 1806? Surprise, surprise. The Duke's candidate, General George Walpole, won the seat.

So it continued for the next twenty years. In 1810 work began on a new bridge. In 1815 the Duke donated the site for a new Catholic church. In 1820 he built new quays. In 1830 nearly 400

18

small houses on the edge of town suddenly appeared. Same kind of thing goes on today. Except they don't spend anywhere near as much money. In Bray, Co. Wicklow, the two opposing parties put up candidates with exactly the same name. In Co. Meath over 1000 people living outside Navan Town ended up on the Navan Town electoral register. Clerical errors, they said. Oh yeah. And Master McGrath ate my homework.

On the other side of Dungarvan Harbour is An Rinn, Aran Islands of the south-east because this is supposed to be one of the final authentic pockets of genuine Irish speakers in the country. All I can say is if they're authentic Irish speakers I'm a Chinese jackeen from Co. Cork.

Today Ardmore, as in It was here that St Declan ard more converts than St Patrick, is nothing but caravans. In the old days it was full of the old, the sick, the crippled and the deformed. They would come to try and cure their rheumatism. On the beach was the stone on which St Declan first set foot in Ireland. Crawl underneath it, the saying went, and you would be cured of your rheumatism. Trouble was if you were old and sick and crippled and deformed you didn't stand a hope in hell of crawling underneath it and, therefore, getting your rheumatism cured. Which is presumably why nobody talks about St Declan any more.

Inland, providing you don't stumble into a Continuity IRA training camp, Lismore is a must, if only to see the castle built by King John on a cliff above the River Blackwater. I don't usually rave about anything, especially castles – it doesn't do my ruptured spleen any good – but this is seriously spectacular. Best of all, like most things, is to stumble across it at night. Lighted lamps lead you across the bridge. Then suddenly there it is. Rock solid. Impregnable. What a castle should be.

As a thank-you present for defeating the Desmonds in Munster, Queen Elizabeth I gave it to Sir Walter Raleigh with 42,000 acres not of land belonging to her but of land belonging to the Irish people. Generous lady the Queen. But that was not all. There were strings attached. She only gave him somebody else's land so long as he filled it full of 'well affected Englishmen'. Which he did. Once a week he used to have the boys round, Sir Franky Drake, Eddie

Spenser of Faerie fame, Kit Marlowe and others too famous to mention when it is said they all used to dress up in black and do all kinds of strange things at Waterford Abbey. There were also rumours at the time that it wasn't Raleigh himself who discovered what made things smoke but Thomas Harriot, his scientific adviser, which is why when the Good Queen Bess gave Sir Walter Lismore Castle Sir Walter gave Harriot Molanna Abbey. And who died of cancer? Harriot. Not Raleigh.

Not that that is Lismore Castle's only claim to fame. Robert Boyle was born there. The man who knew everything about nothing. Nature abhors a vacuum, said everybody. No it doesn't, said Boyle, who with the aid of a lamb's bladder and a candle went on to prove it. The fact he also believed in faeries and allowed the wind to dictate his diet perhaps accounts for the fact he's not as well known as, say, Wolfgang Pauli, who did much the same thing in quantum mechanics. Boyle, however, was buried in St Martin-in-the-Fields in London. But he's no longer there. He was there when it burnt down in 1720. But he's now part of the vacuum that was left afterwards.

Many's the time I've tried to get inside the castle but every time something happens. I'm too late. It's closed for the winter. Last time I thought I'd made it. Then some dinky nebbish with a black-thorn stick waved me down. His dog had just been hit by a car. Would I take him to the vet. What could I say? I told him all about Master McGrath. He was so grateful he didn't offer to pay for the petrol.

But I'm not too worried about getting inside the castle. Another man who never got inside was the gardener, a certain Jimmy Paxton, who went on to design the Crystal Palace. Not many prospects for a gardener working in Lismore Castle then. Unlike the builder and decorators. One of them, Archie Pugin, ended up doing something or other with churches.

Lismore itself is nowhere near as exciting. Usually I stay at the Lismore Hotel, which is Lismore or less OK. More poor man in the local pub than rich man in his castle.

From Lismore I drive backwards and forwards to Cappoquin all the time. Every time I mean to take a look at the River Blackwater which is supposed to turn left there when it should go right – or the other way round. Something to do with parallel ridges, east–west valleys and which way the sun is shining. But I keep forgetting. Maybe one day I'll remember.

In Cappoquin I like to head up into the mountains behind the town and check myself into the Cistercian monastery there for a couple of days' peace and quiet. Peace and quiet. I was hoping it was going to be as quiet as a bunch of Irish policemen doing a spelling test. The first time I was there I got so many calls on my mobile phone for notes, reports, proposals and everything under the sun that I practically commandeered the only fax machine in the place. Apparently whatever I sent came out the other end in Gothic type. The last time I was there the place was full of roaring drunks, well, maybe quietly roaring drunks, trying to dry themselves out.

'The Lord says we must love our enemies.' I got trapped at the back of the church one evening by one slobbering hulk who looked as though he washed his face in a cement mixer. 'The drink is my enemy. I love it. Will ye tell me, for the Lord's sake, what I'm doing wrong?'

Thackeray stayed there during his travels through Ireland. But he didn't reckon it. What's the point, he sneered, 'of seeing shoes made or fields tilled by reverend amateurs, we can find cobblers and ploughboys to do the work better'.

Maybe it'll be better next time. Up at 3.45 a.m. Prayers at 4.00 a.m. Breakfast at 5.15 a.m. Prayers again at 7.15 a.m. Mass at 7.45 a.m. Reading and study at 8.30 a.m. And so on through the day.

If they'll have me, of course. Otherwise if the silent order of monks turn me down, I suppose, it will be back to miserable old receptionist at the waterfront hotel. God help me.

Co. Wexford
Sunny but damp

Famous local resident
John F. Kennedy's cousin, Mary Ryan

Favourite food
American apple pie and Irish-American fatherhood

Favourite drink
Guinness

Favourite pub
Anything but the R— P— H—, E—

Favourite restaurant
The Lobster Pot, Carne. Great seafood

What to say
Goddamnit. I prefer this to the White House

What not to say
Who's John F. Kennedy?

Wexford is a downmarket Waterford. Where Waterford is damp and dismal, Wexford is very damp and very dismal. Which is odd because Wexford, the harbour of the mudflats, lying low on the River Slaney, is in the sunniest and driest part of the country, the sunny south-east, which is supposed to have practically five hours of sunshine on average every day. More than enough to cheer anyone up, you would have thought. But not the Wexfordonians.

At first I used to think it was because they'd never got over the fact all their oyster beds – they had over 20 miles of them – were destroyed by the French. Deliberately, say the Irish. Accidentally, say the French. It wasn't them. It was a virus. Which, of course, is what they would say, n'est-ce pas, mon vieux? Then I discovered that Wexford was the birthplace of Commodore John Barry, 'Father of the American Navy'. That must be some burden to bear. Everything the American navy has done and not done throughout the world. All the responsibility of a man from Co. Wexford.

On the other hand, it was also home of one of my great heroes, Robert McClure, who discovered the North-West Passage between the Atlantic and the Pacific. The British gave him a knighthood. But as far as I'm concerned he deserved much, much more. Because when you think about it he was the first man to work out a way of getting to the Pacific without having to go to America first. Obviously he also had problems trying to get even a transit visa to get into the US. At least he did something about it. All I can do is queue up, wait and hope to God they don't lock me up, dress me in a red boiler suit and throw away the key because I did as I was told at the US embassy in London and filled in the wrong form.

Then I thought maybe it was the effect of the annual Wexford Festival when for two weeks of the year no end of French, German, Italian, Dutch and even one or two Americans posing as Canadians pack into The Barn behind White's Hotel by day to hear unknowns with unpronounceable names from Central Europe belting out the pop classics accompanied by a single piano and in the evenings squeeze into the tiny 440-seater Theatre Royal in the High Street to hear operas nobody has ever heard of. *Mirandolina* by Martinu? *Il giuramento* by Mercadante?!? Auber's *Manon Lescaut*?!!? I'm

---

Four Catholic mothers are having coffee.

The first Catholic mother says, 'My son is a priest. When he walks into a room everyone says, Father.'

The second Catholic mother says, 'My son is a bishop. When he walks into a room everyone says, Your Grace.'

The third Catholic mother says, 'My son is a cardinal. Whenever he walks into a room everybody says, Your Eminence.'

The fourth Catholic mother says, 'My son is a fantastic six-foot-two hard-bodied stripper. Whenever he walks into a room everyone says, My God.'

---

waiting for the day some poor, innocent Irish girl has to announce something by Chopin and Fokine. Once I was at a concert in Dublin and some pompous old lard-butt with apple-catcher knickers announced excerpts from *Die Fledermaus* except she pronounced it *Die! Fledermaus*. I swear to this day she still doesn't realise why the whole place fell apart, the proceedings had to be suspended and half the audience didn't have the courage to come back when play resumed.

Not that the Irish are interested in any of the operas known or unknown. They don't enjoy anything they cannot chat or talk through or sing along with. And opera is definitely not something you can chat or talk through or sing along with. There's so much yelling and screaming going on you can hardly hear yourself think.

I landed in Wexford one year just after the Festival was over. The talk was of a particular attractive soprano from somewhere in Central Europe who seemed to have wowed everyone with her smile, her fantasy hair, and what an old Irishman told me was 'her constant, positive curvature'.

An old blobject dressed up like the cat's meow sitting up at the bar tells me to ignore them.

'Don't you listen to them,' she says, 'The barreltones, 'twas lovely, 'twas lovely.'

I asked the barman if there was anything to eat.

'Have the flute salad,' she butts in again. ''Tis lovely. 'Tis lovely.'

Then, of course, I realised. Wexford is Wexford because they are gamblers. Secret gamblers. And not particularly successful gamblers either.

One lonely Saturday afternoon just before lunch, I set out on my usual crawl, a church crawl. I wanted to see St Doologue's Church, the smallest parish in the world. It's about the size of a collection plate. An empty collection plate. I also wanted to have a look at two nineteenth-century Gothic churches, The Immaculate Conception and The Assumption, known as The Twins. Their foundation stones were laid the same day. Their exteriors are the same. Their spires the same height, 230 feet. If there was time, I also fancied a quick trip to the birthplace of William Cody, father of Buffalo Bill Cody and the home of Dr Arthur Leared who invented – cough, cough – the stethoscope. A busy day ahead.

But you know what it's like. It was hot. It was one of those warm, sunny, south-east days. I was thirsty. I ended up in this bar down near the port. A couple of pints of the black stuff. Why I don't know but suddenly there I was in one of the houses practically overlooking the port. It was a mini-casino Las Vegas style.

In the front room, which was thick with smoke, was the poker school. Two tables. Hardly room to play your cards. It was packed with what looked like the jobless oblige. Old men who looked like country undertakers. Very old men who looked like very old country undertakers. A few young guys. The kind who look as though they live with their mother, work in insurance offices and play the piano but are desperate to improve their blingbling image. There were also a couple of boogaloos who looked as though they had turned up at the wrong party. But it was conventional poker. Not Texas Hold 'Em, Alabama Grope 'Em, Florida Recount 'Em, Arkansas Geld 'Em, New York Kvetch 'Em or even Indian poker in which everyone holds their cards up against their forehead so everybody can see what they've got except them. Not that I know anything about poker.

Dodging from the poker school in the front room to the betting shop in the back room, I met a guy in overalls all covered in grease. He told me he worked in a garage.

'Are you a mechanic?' I asked.

'No,' he says. 'I'm a McCarthy.'

I asked him where I could find the tiny St Doologue's Church. He didn't know. He told me he was a complete stranger to the place. He'd only been there twenty years.

Another of the punters, a big galoot from the fields, was going on about the killing of foxes. It was wrong. It was barbaric. Gunmen should not be allowed to scour the countryside in the middle of the night with the aid of powerful lighting equipment to try and shoot foxes. They should be killed quietly and humanely. By the hunt.

In the back room, which had a bank of television sets on one wall, they were betting on horses. All around the world. In the kitchen they were betting on everything else under the sun. Football. Rugby. Golf. Who could down a can of Guinness faster. With one hand behind their back. With two hands behind their back.

Racing from room to room to room like a footballer on performance-enhancing drugs was a young middle-aged man, keen, alert. He looked as though he had more balls than Wimbledon. He was gambling on everything. Someone told me he was a priest. If he was he was making more money much faster than he would passing the plate round on a Sunday morning.

'He's as good a right to be here as the rest of us,' says one of the punters watching the television screen. ''Tis a grand thing to see them enjoyin' themselves, God help the lot of them.'

His horse fell at the last fence.

'May the Lord save us. 'Tis nothing but bad luck they bring you. They should stay where they belong. Not coming in here ruining everything for the likes of us.'

I don't gamble – I only gambled once in my life. Never again – but I will admit I decided to flutter myself. I did have a go on the horses. Being in Ireland, being in an obviously unlicensed gambling den, it seemed the thing to do. I lost. I always do. Nobody else seemed to be winning either. Or, at least, if they were they were keeping mighty quiet about it. There was no whooping it up and punching the air. Not even the priest was letting loose an occasional alleluia.

Upstairs? Not a thing. This is Ireland don't forget. Your typical Irishman still thinks a brothel is a soup with vegetables in it. It was also Wexford. On a Saturday afternoon.

Another reason for Wexford's damp and dismal attitude could, of course, be that it was home to the suicide boats, the coffin ships, those vast, creaking, wooden famine ships that transported over 2.5 million starving Irish people to the land of the fat, the United States between 1845 and 1880, the greatest mass emigration of people experienced by any country in Europe before or since. It wasn't just individuals and families, sometimes whole villages just upped and staggered slowly down to the ships. There was no alternative: death or America. What a choice. It must therefore be a bit like living in Auschwitz or Buchenwald. You're constantly reminded of the horrors, the hunger, all those lives so needlessly lost. It wasn't your fault. You would have been against it. You've done everything you can to make certain nothing like it happens again. But it's still there. You can't forget it.

I get the same hang-dog vibrations in Tralee, Co. Kerry. At first I thought it was all that cream and all that cheese. Then I realised. It's the hangover from the famine. Tralee was also a big builder of coffin ships.

See a full-size, fully working replica of one of the emigrant ships today like *Dunbrody* moored alongside the quay in New Ross, and you get an idea of the terrors passengers had to suffer just to be able to survive. I've been on board enough old ships in my time to make Sir Walter look like a reject from a Mirror dinghy trial but I'm still amazed at how small they were, how filthy the conditions were and, of course, how vulnerable they were. That's just going backwards and forwards from Holyhead to Dun Laoghaire. The famine ships must have been hell on water.

It's strange. I've come across no end of books and descriptions of the famine itself – Trollope was convinced the Great Famine was sent by God to get the Irish to pull their socks up and get out there and earn a living – but few describing the plight of the famine victims actually crossing the Atlantic.

I can vaguely remember one book about the number of women who were forced to emigrate, the conditions they had to endure, the struggle to survive. I also read, I think, a book about Castlebar, Co. Mayo, about how half the population fled, the wailing and screaming when they left and how those left behind very quickly got over it and carried on the same as usual. But that's all. Nothing about the journey itself.

I tried to find somebody who could tell me more about the ships, why they were called famine ships. Were the passengers on board suffering from famine? Were they trying to escape the threat of famine? Did more die trying to escape than if they had stayed at home?

''Tis a famine ship it is,' I kept being told. 'A famine ship.'

'Yes. But . . .'

'If "the divil was going to collect his own" in a ship it would be in a ship like this.'

In Fenit down in Co. Kerry they do things differently. They've made it show business. There they have a famine ship which is used for parties and receptions and whatever. Where people used to huddle together below decks starving, terrified, at death's door people are wandering around eating, drinking, smoking big fat cigars. They also do trips to New York. Which, to me, is all a bit sick. At least in Wexford, it is as it is.

Not that Wexford doesn't have its fans and supporters. I know one group of Guinness fans in Dublin who've been round a few corners of Ireland in their time. Every Christmas Day they spend in Wexford. They all bundle into a coach Christmas morning, drive the two and a half hours to Wexford, spend the day stumbling from pub to pub before collapsing back into the coach for the long drive home. Far, far better, they claim, than spending the day with the family.

The other side of the county, New Ross with its tall, thin Dutch houses along the waterfront, gave me quite a turn when I first stumbled across it. I thought I was back in Old Holland. I expected everyone to start waiting for me to buy them a drink, offer me a choice of the very best spliffs that euros can buy and point me in the direction of a row of shop windows down by the edge of the water.

In the seventeenth and early eighteenth centuries New Ross was big business. It was shipping out beer, timber, livestock to as far as the US and Russia.

Today one of their biggest employers is Albatross Fertilisers.

Head north out of Wexford and you hit Enniscorthy. Locals say wherever you are in Enniscorthy you are either going up a hill, down a hill or at the top or the bottom of a hill. In the old days, not surprisingly, it used to be an Elizabethan command and control centre. From there they pushed back the Gaels of North Wexford and whoever else even thought of clambering up a hill.

It also used to be nothing but oak forest. The oaks were, however, cut down and shipped out as ship's timber and anything else that could cause havoc to peace-loving people around the world. Huge swaths of the forest went towards helping English entrepreneurs build Ireland's first ironworks which boomed until coal came along and made wood-burning ironworks uneconomical. The biggest wheeler-dealer? Henry Wallop. The odd one or two trunks were turned into paper on which was printed some poem called *The Faerie Queene* by a local lad called Edmund Spenser.

Today the only reason to go to Enniscorthy is not to go to the Riverside Park Hotel. It's like a cross between a holiday camp and a maternity ward. It's full of young families and kids popping up all over the place. Not my idea of Ireland. On the other hand it makes you realise what a great comfort children are in your old age. You won't be sorry to leave them.

Instead of the Riverside Park Hotel try the National 1798 Visitor Centre, which is fantastic. It shows how even in Ireland the French were forever being the French and having a l'Arc de Triomphe and stirring up trouble whenever they got the chance. They were behind the first moves for an independent Ireland. They wanted to overthrow the old order and establish a republic. What they were not behind was sensible, long-term, strategic planning and never fighting a war unless you stood a fair chance of winning. Which, I suppose, is obviously why they haven't fought many wars let alone won many.

Just as the British have turned Dunkirk into a victory so too has Enniscorthy turned the Battle of Vinegar Hill into a triumph when, in fact, all it left behind was a bitter taste in the mouth.

On 23 May 1798 Irish rebel forces seize control of Co. Kildare. In Enniscorthy led by Father John Murphy they also attack local troops and install themselves in the castle. Now what would you do in their position? Dig in, sit tight, man the barricades and perhaps raid the wine cellars or walk out, leave it behind and set up your headquarters at the top of a hill which could be completely surrounded? You got it. They leave the comfort and security of the castle and sit on top of a hill which could be completely surrounded. Father Murphy may have been able to fight and win spiritual battles but he was obviously no good at the temporal side of things. Over 20,000 English troops, surprise, surprise, surrounded the good Father's hilltop headquarters and for thirty days hacked his poor deluded parishioners to pieces.

Talk to anybody of Enniscorthy, however, and it's one of the greatest triumphs of the human spirit.

But, history apart, Enniscorthy is also home to one of the most in-your-face Roman Catholic evangelical groups I've ever come across, run not by some ecclesiastical worthy but by a self-confessed ex-East London gangster.

I don't know about you but I'm one of those back-row, heads-down, keep-quiet Catholics. Pronounce Amen let alone Deo Gratias a millisecond longer than you should and I begin to squirm. This group are the exact opposite. They don't just believe, they act and behave as if they believe. Even more amazing they're practically all teenagers, boys and girls. They spend their time going to schools, visiting churches, meeting people, being in the front line, doing the active positive things priests used to do.

I've met them a number of times. But while I admire them and their enthusiasm they somehow make me feel uncomfortable.

Whenever I'm in Co. Wexford I prefer to try and find some time for the slobs, the local name for their vast sprawling mudflats, the home of Ireland's mussels industry. But beware the geese. Why I don't know but half of the world's population of Greenland white-fronted geese spend their winter in Wexford. The other half are off enjoying themselves.

Head south-east of Wexford towards Bannow and Carnsore Point. This used to be known as Forth and Bargy. It was here that the Anglo-Normans first settled in Ireland in order to go forth and bargy. It was also here that until around fifty years ago they spoke their own Anglo-Norman dialect, Yola. A drink for the road was 'a bang of the latch'. A woman who was a cross between Mrs Thatcher and your mother-in-law, they called a bawshuk of a woman. For some reason or other 28 December, Holy Innocents Day, the day Herod first raised the question of child security, they call Childermass Day. Not that you can blame them. Even today they have such typical Irish names as Devereaux, Lambert and even Parle.

My favourite spot in Co. Wexford after all my other favourite spots, however, is Kennedy country, Dunganstown, the home of the great grandfather of John F. Kennedy. Here they play the Kennedy for all it's worth. Kennedy Bar, I can accept. But Martha's Vineyard. Come on.

The Kennedy Memorial Park contains over 500 trees donated by countries all over the world. Thank goodness Bill Clinton wasn't assassinated. They'd never know where to put all the trailers.

The Kennedy homestead is miles out of town, miles up a tiny lane that is about as crooked as his policies over Cuba and there it is. The most ordinary-looking farmhouse you could imagine, a two-room cottage with a galvanised roof in which is living a poor farmer who believes in keeping his fortune in turnips judging by the piles of them all over the place.

JFK's father, however, tried to deny everything. He not only moved the family out of their traditionally Irish area of Boston, he also gave up the booze so that he would be thought American as opposed to Irish. Greater hatred could no man have of his native Ireland than to deny himself the black stuff. His local relations are apparently just as keen to deny any contact with their famous, rich American cousins or whatever. The most I was told they would do is show the most persistent enquirer after knowledge their most precious possession: the JFK presidential dog tag.

What do I do? I head out not to Horetown – not because of the hores, but to the Courtyard Pub in Ferns where after presiding over his daily masses, weddings and funerals the local priest, Father James Fitzpatrick, is not only part-owner but one of the barmen as well. A true man of the spirit.

Cheers.

Co. Cavan
A lake for every day of the year

Famous local resident
The man who could drink five bottles of claret a night followed by a bottle of Maraschino as a chaser

Favourite food
Stodge. Anything that soaks up five bottles of claret and a Bottle of Maraschino

Favourite drink
Guinness

Favourite pub
The bar at the back of the Cavan horse sales

Favourite restaurant
Farnham Arms Hotel, Cavan. Especially the night before the horse sales

What to say
That's a fine young filly ye have there

What not to say
Does her husband know she's over here with you?

Forget the 365 lakes – one for every drinking day of the year – all the endless rivers and streams, the source of the mighty River Shannon, 250 kilometres from one end to the other, and all the brown trout fighting for their life in Lough Sheelin, Co. Cavan is horse country. Buying and selling horse country. Or at least to me it is.

Others prefer Ballinasloe in Co. Galway, where they have been buying and selling horses the Sunday before the first Tuesday in October every year since 1722, the Dublin Horse Show or wherever anyone has or knows of a horse to be sold anywhere in the country.

Just outside Cavan town which is not really a town – it's two parallel high streets surrounded by lots of houses – is one of the biggest horse buying and selling operations I've seen anywhere, from Mongolia all the way round the world and back again to Mongolia. There are two huge sheds the size of aircraft hangars where the buying and selling is done. Surrounding them is enough runway to accommodate a US invasion force about to make another pre-emptive strike on a sovereign, independent country, strip everybody naked and put dog leads around their neck. This is where the horses are delivered and collected.

From God knows when in the morning to late at night nonstop they are selling horses. All types. Tubby little Thelwell ponies covered in mud and brambles. Graceful, thermodynamic showjumpers. Huge enormous hunters the size of a battleship. Take one of them hunting you'd go all the way from Co. Cavan to the Giant's Causeway. Non-stop. In a straight line. Whatever was in the way. Some are sprightly, bouncy young things with years of love and attention ahead of them. Some are in their prime. Smooth. Sleek. Elegant. And they know it. Some look as though they've left their cart outside. A few look so old and broken down that if their mother and father saw them they would turn in their glue bottle. Business proper, however, begins the previous evening. In every bar within driving distance. Scruffy old Irish farmers.

Man is driving along country lane. Car breaks down. He gets out of the car, lifts up the bonnet, looks at the engine.

He hears a voice. 'It's the fan belt.'

He turns round. There is a white horse looking over a fence.

He adjusts the fan belt, slams down the bonnet and drives on. He comes to a bar. He stops the car and goes into the bar.

He tells the barman the story.

'Praise be to God,' says the barman. 'It was the white horse. The black horse doesn't know anything about cars.'

Dishevelled, rich old Irish farmers. Mysterious Irish millionaires who look even scruffier than the scruffiest old Irish farmer. Horse dealers of all shapes and sizes of wallet. Big breeders. Small breeders. The one-man breeder, who enjoys breeding horses and bringing them along for the pleasure. Blackmailed fathers who have finally given in and decided out of the kindness of their hearts to buy their daughter a pony of her own not mentioning the fact they'll be able to pick up a hefty government grant in the process because southern Ireland, in spite of its untold wealth, is still in what the European Union calls a 'disadvantaged area'.

Some in old, battered, bruised riding breeches. Some in brand-new multicoloured jodhpurs. Some in greasy old tweed coats and hats. Some in smart peak caps and Burberry-reject sweaters. Some in old raincoats held together with bits of twine. Some who look as though they have just stepped out of an advertisement in *Horse and Hound*.

Cavan people, they say, are mean. Not the night before the horse sales they are not. Not unless they've all left the county and gone off on round-the-world cruises on their government grants for the duration and the bars are full of foreigners.

The traditionalists are knocking back the Guinness. Non-traditionalists are knocking back non-traditional pints of Heineken with non-traditional double vodka chasers. A few old hunters are gulping back huge glasses of cherry brandy and vodka.

The craic was in full swing.

''Tis a fine horse. The best I've had.'

'. . . should do well, very well, as well as . . .'

'. . . throw him out on the scruff of the hill. That's all he's good for. I'll be . . .'

'A fine, sound horse he is. Serious. Lots of room in him. Jump the moon he would. Of course you'd have to give him a good roar first.'

'Horses. They're like women. You spend all your time and money on them. Then when you want them there is always something wrong with them.'

From all over Ireland they come for the sales. The professionals: Hugh from Co. Limerick, Michael from Co. Tipperary, Himself from the Scarteen. The not-so-professionals: accountants from Co. Roscommon; hotel keepers from Co. Kerry; part-time barmen from Dublin; hi-tech electronic whizzes with bulletproof jackets from Limerick; fishermen from Donegal. There's even the odd priest, if that's the right phrase, like Father Jack Stewart from Hollywood in Co. Down who buys and sells horses, trains them, enters them in the big races and occasionally obtains his just reward.

There are also the superstitious. They're the ones who usually feed their horses bananas.

I met one broken-down old stallion, who looked as though he spent all his nights out poaching rabbits. He told me he was there because he saw a horseshoe in the road.

'A horseshoe,' I wondered. 'Why does that . . . ?'

'And 'twas facing towards me.'

'Towards you?'

'Good luck. It means good luck. Facing away from me, you wouldn't see me here for dust.'

'You'll be buying then?'

'I'll be buying.'

I met another superstitious buyer. He was there, he told me, because New Year's Day he went out across the fields with his dog. The first thing he saw was a horse with its head turned towards him.

'Turned towards you?'

'Turned towards me, it was.'

'But why . . . ?'

'Good luck. If on New Year's Day you're crossing the fields, you see a horse, its head is turned towards you it means good luck. See its rear end, bad luck, the Lord have mercy on us.'

And, of course, there is also present around the rings, the bar, everywhere, every horse dealer under the pale Irish sun. But whoever they are, wherever they come from, they have their own terms and expressions. They don't have horses. They take to them. If they don't take to them, they follow them. A jet-black horse is not a jet-black horse. He is a brown because for the Irish a black horse is an evil horse that roams the countryside offering people lifts and then throwing them off its back into the sea. And a strollop? It's a lazy, couldn't-care-less horse that lollops around in the show ring. Which, of course, I knew all along.

I was in a bar in the centre of Cavan town one evening before a sale. It was a bit like the old Arkle bar at Cheltenham but without the wax jackets. The talk was of the Waterford Foxhounds in Tramore. Over sixty of them had turned out as was their custom in what the Irish call St Stephen's Day, Boxing Day, outside the

Majestic Hotel. Instead of being greeted with the traditional warm welcome they found themselves surrounded by around thirty protesters, blowing their whistles and hunting horns. I thought the old farmer I was with was going to go apoplectic. Instead he started telling me about two horses he once had which he could never tell apart until one day he realised the black horse was two hands taller than the white one.

The craic continues into breakfast. In the old days breakfast was two raw duck eggs and a drop of milk in a cup downed in one go. Not today it isn't. It's an enormous mixed grill, the works, everything, including liver and kidneys and a mug of tea stewed until, as they say, it's strong enough for a mouse to trot across the top of it.

Rush my breakfast or take my time, whatever time I get to the sales, it has already started.

In England buying and selling horses is worse than filling in your tax forms in Chinese. The horse is supposed to have a passport and a vaccination certificate. If it's a registered horse you need another bit of paper from the breeder or the stud or the breeding organisation that produced him. Most people also insist on a vet's report. Some even go as far as demanding blood samples.

Not in Ireland. In Ireland, or at least in Cavan, it's much more casual, more like a party. There are horses everywhere. Horses being unloaded. Horses being loaded. Horses being led across the miles of open runway. Oops. Mind the US bomber. Horses in the various show rings, walking, trotting, cantering, jumping or even refusing to jump. Queue up for a mug of tea there are even horses in the queue. Stop for a chat. The person you talk to is bound to be leading a horse. And all the time they are being patted, smoothed, given a Polo, another Polo, another Polo . . . Their ears are being tugged. Their eyes are being checked. Their legs are being given the once-over. Is its back straight? Is that a bruise? Look at the way it's holding that back leg. Watch it when it walks up and down. Now over there. Quick. That's a horse with presence. Real presence.

Then, of course, there is the non-stop line of horses going into the different rings to be sold. Tubby little ponies. Pretty little dressage ponies that look as though they learnt their lessons in Germany. Horses, top-class eventers, floating paces, beautifully marked. Obviously destined for the Dublin Horse Show one day. Racehorses. Steeplechasers. Showjumpers. Good temperaments. Well schooled. No vices. Good to shoe, box and clip. Hunters. Go over anything. Non-stop. Day after day after day. Horses outgrown by their riders. Horse being sold because owners can no longer afford to keep them. Horses being sold to pay off gambling debts, drinking debts, any kind of debt. Horses being sold to pay off the alimony. Some horses, it must be said, also being sold because they've been injured, they've turned nasty, they've lost their nerve. They're usually the ones with glazed eyes standing staring at brick walls. Some horses look beautiful, gleaming and shining, inside and out. Some look as though they've spent three days in a slurry. Most look as though they've been ridden through a stream on the way to clean them up ready for the big day.

For every pony, horse, hunter, clapped-out old bag of bones there are a million opinions each one a joy to the naked ear.

'He's an old spavindy ass.'

'They say he's hunted. To be sure. The only thing he's hunted is . . .'

'He's a mighty spirit in him.'

'No stable vices. Believe that you believe . . .'

'Sound on her legs as a three-year-old.'

''Tis a fearful old ting.'

'Poor hocks.'

'Turns his off fore out.'

'Had a horse once, a mighty fine horse. Wife said it kept biting her.'

'No scope.'

'Wondering whether I should get rid of it and get another one.'

'Not the greatest walker in the world.'

'You mean wife.'

'Lovely colt.'

'You bet your life, I do.'

'Good walker.'

'Lovely horse.'

'Bloody gave it away.'

'Stolen. You've stolen it. That's what you've done.'

'He'll break your heart – and your wallet.'

''Tis a fine horse.'

''Tis a fine horse indeed. He'd break the back of ye before ye got him out of the stable.'

'The divil take you.'

I once had an Irish Hunter. He was 17.2, a giant of a horse, practically the height of Nelson's Column. At least that's what it felt like when I was up there on the back of him. He started going weak on his back legs. The vets opened him up to find out the reason. His bones were crumbling inside. He'd grown too quickly for the bones to keep up. He had to be put down there and then. There was nothing anyone could do for him. He didn't come from Cavan. I got him from a farm in Worthing. Maybe that's the reason.

And, of course, there are even more opinions about the people doing the selling and the buying.

'He'd steal the cross off an ass's back.'

'A lovely man, he is. A real lovely man.'

'Not him. I wouldn't trust him to cross the road.'

'He looks as though he could zonk a mule, he does.'

'Have ye heard about the grooms party afterwards? Promises to be the greatest. They've brought some lads over, they say, from the King's Troop. Going to have a stripping competition with the local lads.'

'I'll tell me mother. We'll be there. Wouldn't miss it for the world. Tanksamillion. God bless.'

Outside the horse sales Co. Cavan is the price Ireland has to pay for having Co. Kerry, Co. Galway, and all the other beauty spots. It's bleak. It's desolate. It's practically deserted. The so-called Cavan panhandle is a bit like Dartmoor without the thrill of the chase. Even the Cuilcagh Mountains, the source of the River Shannon, look no more than a hill.

How the Shannon was created is itself a much taller story. It's all the fault of not St Patrick but a woman. Once upon a time there was a tiny rock pool on Cuilcagh Mountain. From there the ancient druids gained all their eternal knowledge and wisdom. Around the pool were seven hazel trees. Into these trees they transferred all their eternal knowledge and wisdom. But, they warned, the trees were for them. Nobody was to touch the trees. Then one day along comes a daughter of Eve. Zap. That's it. Instead of eternal knowledge and wisdom we've got the River Shannon and some mardy old bag who's obviously been supping with the divil who claims she didn't do a thing, she didn't touch anything, it must have come away in her hand. You know the type.

But on the other hand when seen through the bottom of a glass of Guinness, Co. Cavan does have its attractions. Virginia being one of them. Nobody ever complains of spending any time in Virginia. In Cuilcagh House in the 1720s a Dublin clergyman came calling on the Sheridans. There must have been something in the water or perhaps a bit too much magic in the mushrooms because before long the poor clergyman must have started hallucinating and dreaming of little men tying up big men hand and foot and staking them to the ground so that other men could crawl all over them. The Dublin clergyman: Jonathan Swift. The man staked to the ground? Lemuel Gulliver. Richard Brinsley stuck to the booze. As much as five bottles of claret at dinner followed by a bottle of Maraschino as a chaser. One evening during dinner he was told Drury Lane Theatre was on fire. It was the scene of many of his triumphs. He faced financial ruin. His reaction? He called for a bottle of wine.

'But sir,' screamed a bystander. 'You face financial ruin. How can you remain so calm?'

To which Richard Brinsley replied, 'A man may surely take a glass of wine by his own fireside.'

Brilliant. A true Irishman and native of Co. Cavan.

As far as I'm concerned I like being in Virginia because of the accent. Most Irish accents are soft and lilting. The Virginia accent seems somehow stronger and sharper. Like a bottle of Maraschino without the previous five bottles of claret to soften it up.

Henry William James, the grandfather of Henry, the novelist and William James, the philosopher, lived nearby in Ballyjamesduff. In their case they didn't dream of tying anybody up. Instead their readers dream of tying them up and staking them out in the sun rather than suffer the eternal boredom of reading any more nonsense about Great-Grandma America trying to rescue Little Miss Innocent America from the evil clutches of dashing, handsome young Mr Europe.

Ballyjamesduff was also home to Marcus Daly who went on to become one of the biggest American mining tycoons of all time. Thanks to Thomas Edison. Daly was sitting on top of an enormous copper mine in Montana. But nobody wanted copper. Then Edison invented electricity. The rest, as they say, made him decide never to go back home to Ballyjamesduff although he did throw a couple of dollars in the plate when they were looking around for funds to build the local church.

Killeshandra, home to the ancestors of Edgar Allen Poe, is more fun. Not because of the ravens. But because of the horseless, driverless carriage which, they say, trundles through the village in the dead of night to the Protestant church on the Ballyconnell Road collecting either victims to be sacrificed or bodies to be buried.

You have been warned.

Stranger still, however, is the story of Black Pigs Dyke which wiggles its way across the county. Take a look at the strange-looking earthworks. What is it famous for? For burying ancient Irish kings. For dividing one ancient territory from another. For teaching horses how to jump. No way. This is where the Irish invented the sauna, although being the romantic, poetic types that they are they called it the sweathouse. Being Irish, they also used it not for easing the aches and pains of everyday living but to sweat away the booze. Being Irish, they kept it strictly segregated. Being Irish, they also apparently kept their clothes firmly on even when they rushed outside and threw themselves into the nearest freezing stream, or rather bog.

If that's not enough ancient history for you there is the famous stone head at Corleck. Like everything in Ireland, there's always a big debate about it. Is it a man or is it a woman? As far as I'm concerned, it's obvious. It's a woman. First, it's stone. Second, it's got three faces, two of which have been lifted. The third looks as though it would have been if they hadn't run out of money and just let the whole thing drop. If you want to see and decide for yourself go quickly. Because it is bound to disappear from view before long.

Dublin, 75 miles away, has started sending all its domestic rubbish to Co. Cavan because its own dumps in Ballcally outside Lusk were declared illegal. The Environmental Protection Agency refused to license them and closed them down. That's the official story. My theory is that the grand O'panjandrums in Dublin were looking for a reason to go to the horse sales and getting the city council to pick up the tab. You never know with the Irish.

The evening following the horse sales, I was coming out of the Cavan Book Centre which is run by a nice, gentle, white-haired old lady. Coming along the street was the horseshoe man.

'So did your luck hold?' I asked him.

'It did indeed, thanks be to God. It did indeed,' he says. 'I got a beauty. A real beauty.'

'A good price?'

'More than I should have paid, Lord have mercy on me. But less than he was asking.'

Co. Down
Northern Ireland's sunny seaside

Famous local resident
St Patrick

Favourite food
Soap for flot wey toes

Favourite drink
Guinness

Favourite pub
Grace Neill's, Donaghadee (say John Keats sent you)

Favourite restaurant
Lobster Pot, Strangford

What to say
Down Patrick. Down Patrick

What not to say
Where's Carol O'Vorderman?

Co. Down, let me say straight away, is not as some people say the name of a quiz show on Irish television with Richard O'Whiteley and Carol O'Vorderman. It's a county of untold depths, unfathomable mysteries, impenetrable accents and people forever singing about the Mountains of Mourne sweeping down to the sea.

It is also the first county I visited in that strange, strange country known, where I half come from, as The North. Not that I mentioned it to anyone in the South. Good heavens above. I would have been as welcome as a Panzer division in Poland or I suppose the Americans in Iraq.

Now to the uninitiated, idiot-friendly hoople-heads and those who still think America is the land of the free I will explain what people in the South mean when they say the North. No I won't. I still enjoy hobbling around on two legs. Instead let me explain what people in the North mean when they say the North. No I won't. I still enjoy hobbling around on two legs and seeing what I am doing at the same time. I'm not saying it's complicated. All I'm saying is it's the only place in the world where it's safe to be a Jew. You think I'm kidding. Let me tell you even RTE, the Republic's answer to the BBC, doesn't understand the North. I was in Dublin just before the big EU enlargement celebrations. They were telling everyone who wanted to know what was happening in Belfast to log on to their website discovernorthernisland.com. No wonder many people think Ireland is the Land of Ire.

OK. Let's try it this way. I'm stupid. I know nothing. If I make a mistake who cares? My name is George Bush, I live in that place that is not called the Black House, I can't ride a bike and I think all foreigners come from overseas and this is what I mean by the North.

Compared to the South, the North is D-DAFTA, I mean six counties, Derry, Down, Antrim, Fermanagh, Tyrone and Armagh. It covers 5500 square miles. It's half the size of Wales. It has 200 miles of coastline, contains the largest lake in the UK, Lough Neagh, 153 square miles and one hell of a place to go for a shooting holiday. At one stage it looked as though it was going to be nine counties. Also in the running were Cavan, Donegal and Monaghan but the whole idea fell through when someone realised that taken together the whole thing would spell VASTER DIS GREEN EATER.

Irishman sees a man standing on top of St Patrick's Cathedral.

'Don't jump. Don't jump,' he shouts. 'Think of your wife and children.'

'I haven't got any wife or children.'

'Think of your parents.'

'I haven't got any parents.'

'Think of St Patrick.'

'Who's St Patrick?'

'Jump. You bastard.'

'Northern Ireland,' says the local tourist board. 'You will want to stay forever.' Say the wrong word and you will stay there for ever. It's more than a riddle wrapped in a puzzle in an enigma. It's that and more multiplied by an Armalite rifle and the Bible and divided by everything you can possibly think of.

In the old days when Ireland was divided up into four old provinces, it was simpler: Ulster for a soldier; Connacht for a thief; Munster for learning; and Leinster for beef. Not any more.

Wander around Catholic areas in Northern Ireland. There are as many signs saying 'Brits Out' as there are saying 'Manchester United 4 Ever'. Telephone Allied Irish Bank. Get put on hold. What music do they play to help you while away the hours? 'Land of Hope and Glory'. Listen to the local politicians. Instead of having one roundabout in town they want two. One for the Catholics and one for the Protestants. The Catholic one going the right way round. No. I didn't mean that. I meant . . . What the hell. There probably are some Northern Ireland politicians who believe there should be separate roundabouts for Catholics and Protestants.

Wander around the Protestant areas. There are signs everywhere saying Orange Hall. I couldn't find one. Dirty, grey, yellowy, dusty halls, yes I could find plenty of them. Go inside one if you dare. It's like turning back the clock to the days of O'Jurassic Park when politicians spent more time in Parliament than in the Circuit Criminal Court in Dublin. They are either complaining that government departments deliberately shirk their responsibility, fail to show due respect and consideration and are deliberately trying to eliminate every trace of Britishness from public life by not flying the Union Jack on the birthday of the Countess of Wessex; or, yet again, they are insisting on telling you the story of the Red Hand of Ulster. Thousands of years ago a pirate chief and his two sons were sailing along the beautiful, lush green coast. Says the chief to his two sons, It's yours. Whichever one of you first lays his hand upon it. Out with his sword comes the first son, chops off his hand and throws it on to the land. Hence the Red Hand of Ulster. Now I ask you. Is it any wonder it's difficult to deal with a people prepared to do that to get a patch of land? The other son, I like to think, went off to become a dairy farmer in County Clare and apart from marrying the wrong woman lived happily ever after.

Some people blame the English. Ireland was Ireland they should never have moved in all those Scots. Drapers to Draperstown. Planners to Newtown Stewart, postmen to Letterkenny, bakers to Buncrana, merchant bankers to Hornhead, politicians to – where else? – Downhill. Everywhere you go it's wee this or wee that. 'Will yah haf a wee glass of wather?' 'There's the wee menu.' 'A wee slice of dry bread.' They don't go anywhere. They have a wee wander to the wee shop. God help us, they even go to a wee toilet.

I blame the Vikings. Originally it was called Uladh, an old Irish word for Change my name and you will live to regret it. The Vikings changed the name to Ulster. Everyone has regretted it ever since.

The only good thing about it is it's slowly disappearing. Into the sea. Around 750 acres of land a year, according to the Coastal Research Group at Ulster University. The Protestants blame too many performances of *Riverdance*. The constant thumping, they say, has shattered the compaction of the soil, shifted a couple of tectonic plates and caused the Giant's Causeway to burst a few more hexagonal piles.

The Catholics blame Ian Paisley. They say that because of the Big Man even Northern Ireland wants to leave Northern Ireland.

I know who I believe. But if it's got to go I hope the last to go will be my favourite, Co. Down as well as the other five counties. See what I mean about the dangers of taking sides on anything to do with the North? I mean the bit that isn't the South . . . No I don't mean the bit, I mean the strong, vibrant, independent . . . No I didn't mean independent. Independent means independent and it's not. What it is is . . . Bejaysus. Why has life got to be so complicated? Can't they just hate each other peacefully?

Why am I so worried about Co. Down? Because if it wasn't for Co. Down the world would be a poorer place.

To start with we wouldn't have, in the best Co. Down tradition, SOAP FOR FLOT WEY TOES. In other words those soft, flowery potatoes from Comber. We wouldn't have SUB SHIRTI MMEU, SPINALMMERS let alone SCRAT ROT. In other words the British Museum, miners' lamps or tractors.

Sir Hans Sloane, a doctor from Killyleagh, a fishing village on Strangford Lough with a fancy castle which is all turrets and battlements, was surgeon to the West Indies fleet. He drank the local cocoa drink, decided it needed something extra, added milk, the rest as they say is a large decaf triple grandé, skimmed, no whip, wet mocha, Costa Rica La Laguna filter. If that's not enough to ensure he would live on for ever in what's left of the mind of every caffeine-addled chucklehead when he died he left his whole lifetime's collection of books and plants and gemstones to the nation providing everything was kept together. It was the birth of the British Museum.

Another local doctor, this time from Bangor, William Clanny, invented the miners' lamp. A farmer's son from, appropriately enough, Growell, Harry Ferguson, designed and built the first modern tractor. For which shire-horses the world over are duly grateful.

I won't mention that other famous Co. Down engineer and designer, Thomas Andrews. He designed the IT CAINT. If it hits an iceberg, it'll sink.

It goes on. If it wasn't for Co. Down we wouldn't have the Suez Canal.

The way the English keep on about canals you'd have thought they were building them before Venice was invented. Not so. Newry which sits uneasy in the Gap of the North, the Mountains of Mourne to the east, the Slieve Gullion to the west – in those days it was called Oldry – had one a full 20 years before Manchester. Not only that, it was one of the new hi-tech canals. With the help of nine different locks it climbed over 25 metres above sea level from Oldry up to Poyntzpass and the coalfields in Co. Tyrone. So busy was the canal – it used to export, among other things, all the Irish potatoes to England – at one time Oldry was the biggest port in the whole of the north of Ireland.

In fact canals are in Co. Down's blood. Even big ones like the Suez Canal. Napoleon said it wasn't possible. The British said it wasn't possible. There was no way they could build a canal that ran from the Mediterranean to the Red Sea via the Foreign Office in Whitehall. Francis Chesney from Annalong said it was possible. It was his survey the French used to build it. They also christened him The Father of the Suez Canal. The English showed their appreciation by sending him off to fight the Chinese during the Opium Wars. Because of his unique skills as a surveyor, they put him in charge of the artillery. You couldn't make it up, could you?

Go to new Newry today, it's still all canals and locks. One of them is even named after James Bond's dewy-eyed old scrunch, Moneypenny. Why? I have no idea.

The town hall is built on a bridge over the River Clanrye that runs through the middle of the town. Which means half of it is in Co. Down and the other half in Co. Armagh. Go there to complain that your Co. Down dustbins have not been emptied, they'll tell you you're in Co. Armagh. Tell them your Co. Armagh driveway has been blocked by an abandoned car, they'll tell you you're in Co. Down. As if town halls don't create enough problems already.

The centre is nothing but bars, restaurants, coffee shops, bus station, a fancy newly built hotel. I was there once during the Royal County Down, some big golf match attended by all the big names. At least I was told they were big names. Although to me most of them looked as though they spent more time in the bunker than Eva Braun. I was in the bar reading the riveting prose of the *Newry Telegraph*: 'When they stood up to sing, there was not an empty seat in the whole sacred building.' Around me all the talk was about top golfer Vijay Singh playing at the Royal County Down and how he had fallen in love with his caddy, Fanny Malone, how he couldn't wait to marry her and I forget the rest.

Up to recent years Newry used to have what they called hiring fairs which were more like modern-day slave markets. Apprentices, labourers, farm workers, maids, servant girls would stand around offering their services to any passing employer. If both sides agreed the price or rather the wages, the deed was done. If not both sides went off in search of a better deal elsewhere. Today, of course, it's the other way round. Companies are desperate to get into Newry. They are the ones being looked over and checked out. The old slave market has been replaced by graduate recruitment fairs.

Newry is one of the hottest property hot spots in the North. It's pleasant. All those canals and bars. It's safe. It's becoming more mixed. Protestants are no longer as dominant as they used to be. It's halfway between Belfast and Dublin. Ask a Protestant how to get to anywhere and he'll say, Take the Belfast Road. Ask a Catholic, he'll say, Take the Dublin Road. The veteran Maltese problem solver and father of lateral thinking, Dr Edward de Bono, has also told them to Think Big. Big deal. Was he going to tell them to Think Small? I could have told them that and for half the fee.

Chances are, therefore, Newry will soon be busy pumping new blood into the area. Which would not be surprising because it was two local men, Harry Martin and Joseph, later Sir Joseph, Barcroft, who discovered how blood circulates around the body in the first place. Martin did it with the help of a living, breathing, pumping dog's heart. He cut the heart out of the dog but still left it connected to the body. The antivivisectionists, of course, went bananas. They made his life such a misery that he turned to drink, then morphine and died of drugs. Which just shows you how irresponsible and uncaring antivivisectionists are. Barcroft suffered an even worse fate. He ended up in California. He became a world expert on blood, wrote a number of books on the subject which were hailed by the Americans as classics largely because they were made up of words of more than one syllable and then when the University of California opened a high-altitude research centre he suffered the final indignity. Instead of naming the research centre after him they named the hill it was built on after him: Mount Barcroft. Wonderful people. So sensitive. The Iraqis don't know how lucky they are.

Planners of the new Newry, you have been warned.

So it goes on. If it wasn't for Co. Down we wouldn't have one of the greatest inventions of all time, BUPS, PUBS. Pubs were invented in Co. Down. Hence the phrase, Will ye down another one, Michael? The first one, Grace Neill's, is still there today. In Donaghadee, Irish for *I will indeed Patrick. A glass of the black stuff, God bless you*. It's small. It's dark. It's cosy. It's what a pub should be. They've all been there. Daniel Defoe on a Friday where he suddenly got the idea for one of the greatest characters in fiction, Robinson Crusoe; Peter the Great to buy horses and no doubt collect dwarfs to put in wheelbarrows to run along the top of hedges; John Keats with friend Charles Brown. They were determined to walk hand-in-hand all the way to the Giant's Causeway over fifty miles away. They set off, reached Belfast, decided enough was enough, turned round, came back to the pub where after a nightingale sandwich, a couple of Irish urns of the black stuff and a quick turn with a local belle dame sans merci, Keats was inspired to write some of his most famous poems. Charles went upstairs and started planning a new career which would involve meeting lots of top British politicians. He decided to emigrate to Brazil.

I was in the pub one evening with the modern-day Daniel

Defoes, Peter the Greats and John Keatses. Daniel Defoe was telling me the story of St Comgall, who in the sixth century built an abbey up the road on the lough just outside Bangor.

'His spit could shatter a rock,' says Daniel Defoe.

''Tis a holy man, he was,' says Peter the Great. 'Baptised a mermaid as well, he did. She was so holy she went on to become a saint.'

'And is it any wonder?' says John Keats. 'She couldn't open her legs.'

Always lowers the tone does John Keats.

My God, if it wasn't for Co. Down we wouldn't have had the good St Patrick himself. They say he landed along the coast, close to the A2 Strangford Road around 432 if not 5 o'clock one evening, built his first church at Saul, and made his first convert, O'Dichu, the local chief, by 433 if not 5.15 p.m. He was so successful and so enthusiastic he decided he wanted to convert the whole county into a land of saints and scholars. More serious, sober souls urged caution.

'Down Patrick. Down Patrick,' they would say. 'You've done more than enough for the Good Lord already. Why burn yourself up? Have a drink.'

The name stuck.

They had much the same trouble when they buried him. He just wouldn't stay there.

'Down Patrick. Down Patrick,' they kept telling him.

The only way they thought they could keep him there was with a slab of rock. You can see it today in the grounds of the cathedral with his name on top: Patric. Obviously the work of an Irish stonemason. But even the slab of rock was not enough. Other places claim to be the burial place of St Patrick: Glastonbury, Kentish Town, Molly Casey's four-acre field at the back of Newmarket on Fergus.

A professor of Old Irish at University College, Galway once came up with the solution to the problem: There were four St Patricks. Four dead bodies. Four burial places. Which surprised everybody. Up until then everyone assumed there were two, one from Battersea, London, one from Wales. But then most Irish people see two of everything in any case. Especially after lunch.

The odds, however, have got to be on Down not just because the shops sell what they call 'Authentic Photos of St Patrick.' When he died, they say, angels came from across the border and told his supporters to put the body in the back of an ox cart. Where the ox cart came to rest, there they should bury him. Thank goodness the oxen were old and broken down. Just imagine what would have happened if they came to a rest outside Ian Paisley's front door.

Years ago I went to Saul, which I would have thought, precedent being precedent, would have been renamed Paul by now. I wanted to try and establish contact with the spirit of the place. But I didn't get far. Everybody wanted to tell me about the spirits of Finnebrogue House. The stone pillars holding up the gates to the House, they say, are haunted. They came from the ruins of Inch Abbey, on the banks of the Quoile. As a result not a horse will set foot in the place. The only way to get them in is for the rider to dismount and throw a cloak over their heads.

That's not the only crazy story I've heard. Once I was in Belfast. I had to go to Dublin. Instead of shooting, I mean driving down the main Belfast–Dublin road I took the scenic route. I drove out to Bangor. I couldn't get into the car park. It was closed. Some local road safety enthusiasts had poured oil all over it in the dead of night so that they could practise their wheel spins. At least that's what I was told. I couldn't drive through the centre of town either. Queen's Parade, Bridge Street, High Street and Gray's Hill were all blocked. Cars that had got into the car park then spread the oil all over the surrounding roads, turning the whole place into one vast oil slick. Not only the road safety enthusiasts had practice doing their wheel spins that day I can tell you. If they were road safety enthusiasts.

From then on heading south was no problem although I must admit, as a whole, I have little experience of anything heading south. Co. Down says it's their sunny seaside. To me it seemed to be nothing but fun parks, beaches, adventure playgrounds, fish 'n' chips and kids. To me that's not sunny. That's, I've got work to do in the office. I'll have to cancel my holiday.

Strangford, however, I thought, was fun. I popped into the Lobster Pot for a glass after I'd come across on the ferry from Portaferry. Two seconds I was buttonholed by this leprechaun who even though he was dressed all in black looked as though he couldn't organise a two-car funeral.

He insisted on telling me the story of Con O'Neill of Clandeboye who escaped from the castle because his wife had very cleverly hidden a rope inside a lump of cheese she brought in and gave him for lunch. A lump of cheese? A rope inside it? A wife doing something to help her husband? Come on. Does he think I'm stupid? He must do. I bought him a glass on the strength of it.

Downpatrick itself is a nice, pleasant, safe little town. It should be. It's got something for everybody. There is an Irish Street, an English Street and even a Scotch Street.

Irish Street is rather grand. A touch gentry. It was home to the Cromwells. No relation to Oliver. Well they would say that wouldn't they?

English Street is full of eighteenth- and early-nineteenth century town houses and Denvir's Hotel, which used to be the bus or rather stagecoach station of the day with stagecoaches leaving daily to Dublin and Belfast.

Scotch Street leads to Gallows Hill. They probably make you pay for the privilege as well.

Every time I go to Downpatrick I try and stay there. But there's hardly anywhere to stay. A couple of b. & b.s and that's it. And they're always full. Probably Big Ian and his supporters hiding up, planning to protest against horse racing on Sundays at Downpatrick racecourse. If I was him I'd forget the protesting and move the pillars holding up the gates at Finnebrogue House to the entrance to the racecourse. That would do the trick. Far more effective than a couple of verses of 'All creatures great and small'. Although I shouldn't joke. Co. Down takes its religion seriously. The local paper, the *Spectator*, once printed a photograph of a crucified Barbie doll. There was uproar. They were deluged with protests. In the end they had to apologise 'sincerely for the offence caused . . . It was never our intention to cause hurt or offence and we deeply regret the incident.' What? Over a Barbie doll? I'd have hammered in the nails myself.

On the other hand in spite of all the 'ups', Co. Down does have its downs.

Co. Down

First of all, that accent. It sounds like minced chicken anuses pulled backwards through a galvanised steel funnel. My God, where do they get it from? They say it's Lowland Scots whereas in Co. Antrim next door, it's Highland Scots. To me they are both equally and totally incomprehensible. Until I have what they call a small ball of whiskey. Then it begins to make sense. But only begins. It takes a good few balls before I can really understand them. Why on earth or rather why in heaven St Patrick landed here I have no idea. The poor man must have wondered where he was and what language they were speaking. In Co. Donegale abundance is a dance in the farm building, a boycott is a cot for boys. Me, I have no problems. I just assume whoever I'm talking to, whatever we're talking about, they're telling me to go to Portaferry it's the best place for miles around. From the top of the hill just outside of town you can see everything in the world worth seeing so long as it's the Isle of Man and beyond that, on a clear day, the Arndale Centre in the centre of Manchester.

I went into a bar once just outside Dundrum where for some reason everybody was going on about battery-powered trains as if they hadn't better things to do.

A wee boogaloo at the wee bar was holding wee court.

'Hltmskt umphlacto yormch,' he says.

'Portaferry,' I said. 'I will indeed. A good idea.'

'Fshmt klomgdos hlmzochoi,' he says.

As if the accent isn't bad enough there is Percy French and his Mountains of Mourne sweeping down to the sea. I wish they'd sweep right down into the middle of it. I mean, they're OK. Not half a patch on, say, the mountains in Co. Kerry or Co. Galway. But nowhere near the song and dance they make about them. I mean they're hardly big-time. They stretch 25 km from Newcastle to Rostrevor and at Slieve Donard rise as high as 850 metres. Wowee. That's over 30 times smaller than Mount Everest. Nobody has ever written a song about Mount Everest. Geologically speaking they're teenagers compared to say the Wicklow Mountains which are a good 400 million years old. They're also dangerous. Buzzard's Roost in the Annalong Valley has been rated one of the toughest and most dangerous climbs in the world. That's hardly sing-song material.

What also gets me is the whole Percy French 'Mountains of Mourne' industry. There are Percy French fine bone china loving cups, Percy French decorated plates, Percy French tea towels to wash them up with. There are Percy French books, tapes, videos. There is even a Percy French Society which has Percy French dinners where they sing Percy French songs. Not just the Mountains of Bloody Mourne but other famous classics such as 'Ballyjamesduff', 'Are Ye Right There Michael' and 'Come Back Paddy Reilly'. Not if you've got any sense you wouldn't.

And he's a Frenchman as well. What would they have done if he was an Irishman?

The amazing thing is the Brontës also come from Co. Down. Patrick, the father of the three closet lust bunnies, Charlotte, Emily and Anne, was born at Emdale. He taught at the local school before hitting the downward slope to Cambridge and then the fun palace that was Haworth Parsonage. But they are not rated anywhere near as important as Percy French. They've been swept right into the sea. Probably because they didn't write anything you can sing. *Wuthering Heights* may be a tear-jerker but it's hardly likely to raise the rafters at 10 o'clock on a Saturday night in Harry Afrika's opposite the bus station in Downpatrick.

But I must say, in spite of the accent, Percy and the Brontës, who have been plunged to the wuthering depths, I find time flies whenever I'm in Co. Down. Especially from 28 February to 1 March.

Thanks to the lateral Dr de Bono, Newry Council were thinking so BIG they forgot to include 29 February on their calendar for 2004. The sad, lonely spinsters of the parish were as understanding and reasonable as any sad, lonely spinsters anywhere in the world would be who had waited four years to get their claws into some poor, innocent, hard-working, downtrodden, pathetic bastard who's never done any harm to anyone in his life. There were letters in the newspaper, telephone calls to the radio stations. They even complained to their local councillors. One of them, a certain Pat McGinn, told the press, 'My phone has not stopped ringing with women demanding to know if they can go ahead and ask their partners to marry them.'

I wasn't too happy either. It meant I got home a day early.

Co. Donegal
The Donegale capital of Ireland

Famous local resident
Whoosh. He's gone

Favourite food
Whoosh. It's gone

Favourite drink
Guinness

Favourite pub
The one with the roof on

Favourite restaurant
The one with the roof half on

What to say
Windy? Never

What not to say
Where – Where – Where's the roof?

Co. Donegal or rather Co. Donegale is rough seas, rough winds not to mention some pretty rough seaside towns. The Irish, of course, say, To be sure, but the green hills and mountains of Donegal are greener and brighter and more vivid than they are anywhere else in the whole wide world. So much so that, they claim, old men always want to be carried outside the house and propped up against the wall when they are about to die so that they can die watching the green fields, the long narrow glens, the huge towering mountains and the rainbows which in Co. Donegale are made up of different shades of black and white and grizzly grey. Don't you believe it. They'd be blown away by the wind before their loving wives could get their hands on the bundle of insurance policies hidden behind a brick inside the chimney let alone call in the estate agent so they can sell the lot and be off to Copacabana beach with the local Playboy of the Western World.

People also say Co. Donegale, tucked away in the top left-hand corner, is nothing but potato, tweed and fish. Don't you believe that either. The potatoes are chips. The tweed is for the tourists. And the fish is covered an inch thick in batter although I'll grant them one thing. You don't have to put any salt on it. The seas are so rough, the winds are so strong that from the grey of dawn to the black of night everything is covered in salt. Sea salt. Even the local lamb. It's the only lamb in the world that is already salted when it's still huddled under a dry-stone wall in a 160 mph force 231/2 gale.

It's not surprising the Beaufort Wind Scale was invented by an Irishman, Francis Beaufort. What is surprising is he wasn't born in

Co. Donegale. The wind was so strong his poor mother ended up doing the deed in Navan, Co. Meath, the other side of the country. Which is just as well. Had he been born in Co. Donegale he wouldn't have seen the light of day until he was seven. When his mother took him to Dublin to meet the relations. He wouldn't have got round to inventing the wind scale either. That would have been much too exciting for Co. Donegale.

I'm not saying there's anything foisy about the good wind-blown Donegals and guys even though you keep hearing rumours they go around borrowing their little sister's sweaters to keep warm but they're not exactly, let's say, at the cutting edge of fashion. More the windy edge. They always seem to be more old-fashioned than the rest of Ireland, even when the rest of Ireland was

---

Irishman out in a storm with his friend. He collapses by the side of the road.

'Quick. Quick,' he says to his friend. 'I'm dying. Get me a rabbi.'

'A rabbi?' says the friend. 'I thought you were a Catholic.'

'I am,' he says. 'But I couldn't call poor Father Reilly out on a night like this.'

---

old-fashioned. Their faces seem to be more weather-beaten, their clothes older and shinier, their walk more miching and slower and as if they have spent their lives battling against the wind and the rain. Which they probably have. In fact if it wasn't for the wind and the rain they would never have got round to inventing tweed hats, tweed coats, tweed ties, tweed everything you can think of. Because the storms, the howling gales, the freezing cold forced them to look for an inside job. Everything to do with tweed is an inside job. The wool is spun and weaved and made up into lengths sometimes 70 yards long. Inside. In the dry and the warm. Over 70 yards it's too long for the barn or the shed and you're out in the storms again. Then it is cleaned, shrunk – back in the warm again – and sold on to the final manufacturer who sends his truck around to collect it.

The idea of spending as much time as you can locked up in your house in Donegal persists even to today. Gerry Robinson, who was one of the biggest financial wheeler-dealers of the last ten years and boasts a string of chairmanships and directorships including the likes of Granada, Allied Domecq, Compass as well as being chairman of the Arts Council, leaves his home in Co. Donegale on a Monday morning for a full week's work and is back again on Wednesday evening in case he gets caught in another storm.

In fact, if it wasn't for the cold there wouldn't be anyone in Co. Donegale at all. Years ago on Midsummer Night's Eve to keep warm they would light huge open fires everywhere. On hilltops. In the middle of fields. Even at crossroads. Young girls would jump through the fires hoping to marry young and have huge families. Old women would hobble round them on their knees regretting the day they leapt through the fire hoping to marry young and have huge families. When the fire was over, everybody would take a burning stick home with them. Before going in they would then walk around their home three times, hoping to goodness it would not burn the place down. Nowadays young girls have found easier ways of marrying young and having huge families than jumping through open fires.

The local water board, however, is foisy, very foisy although I have heard it described as many other things. I was in Rathmullen one Easter. The winds were howling. The rain was lashing down. It was so damp that every morning I found fish in the mousetrap in my room. I turn on the tap. No water. You'll never believe the inconvenience. For four days I had to drink Guinness out of the same glass. Not that I'm complaining. I swear the price of a pint in Rathmullen is the cheapest in the country: €2.80 compared to anything between €5 and €10 in any of the big bars in Dublin.

In the rest of Ireland when they talk about the weather they invariably refer to it being a soft day. The streets, they say, shine with rain. Not in Co. Donegale they don't. They say they are deadened with rain. In Co. Donegale it's always a hefty day. That is a good day. A bad day they say is as black as a tinker's ass or maybe it was something else. In the rest of Ireland it rains suddenly. In Co. Donegale it rains soddenly. In the rest of Ireland it rains three or four times a month. In Co. Donegale it rains twice. Once for three weeks. Once for four weeks. In the rest of Ireland when the sun comes out they say it is shy in the sky. In Co. Donegale it doesn't bother to come at all. Even the television weather forecasters have difficulty finding a new way of saying the same old thing. I once heard one forecaster say Co. Donegale would be in for 'heavy showers and occasional sunshine, weather permitting'.

On one of those days of occasional not so shy sunshine I was in a bar in the far north of Co. Donegale. The winds had been so strong they had blown one of the local council's giant gritters off the Frosses to Kilrane road. While it was practically full of grit. It had not only gone off the road, it had then rolled several feet down an embankment and finally come to rest on its side. Not only that but the local thieves were on the rampage again. They had been out stealing oil burners and stoves. See what I mean about Co. Donegale. Anywhere else it would have been gold, diamonds, old masters. The police, however, said they were hoping to catch them red-handed.

Says one of the old gorks sitting up at the bar with his cap pulled down over his face, 'We're lucky with it.'

''Tis an Indian summer,' says another.

'An Indian summer?' I had to ask why, didn't I?

'Because,' he says 'they'll be Apache fine weather before the rain begins again.'

Rain or shine, in spite of all the talk about the vivid green fields and mountains, Co. Donegale is not the greatest county in the country. It is desolate. It's so bad they can't even grow their own rye to thatch their own houses. It has to be imported from that haven of sunshine and warmth, Poland.

It's mountainous.

'There are mountains there to break the back of ye,' a retired schoolteacher turned professional rambler told me once while I was hanging around waiting for a bus somewhere between Bundoran and Malin Head.

It's even dangerous.

Go near Glenade Lake and a huge monster is likely to creep out of the lake when you least expect it, attack the nearest unsuspecting individual, preferably a young, innocent girl, and drag her back to his lair. So it's not an Irish monster then. An Irish monster would pass up any young, innocent girl and go straight for the Guinness.

If you think that's dangerous, don't even think of going anywhere near Lough Derg. The Spanish go to Santiago de Compostela. The French go to Lourdes. The Irish go to an island on Lough Derg where St Patrick spent 40 days and nights in a cave praying and fasting for what they call desperate penance. The cave, they say, is the gates of hell. Stumble in there by mistake and suddenly Christmas with the family will not seem so bad after all. Other caves have other, maybe not so dangerous dangers. Wander into the caves at Dunmore, Co. Kilkenny, I was told, and you'll be attacked by a huge cat. Go into the one at Rathcroghan in Co. Roscommon and you'll be trampled on by no end of hideous creatures. I've even come across serious, sane, sensible people who swear that all the caves all over the country lead down into a complete underground Ireland inhabited by fairies. In Youghal, Co. Cork, a young priest who looked as though he spent all his spare time watching underwater women's rugby once assured me that it was in this underground world that all the Catholics hid from Cromwell when he was busy destroying everything there was to destroy on the ground above.

'Ye must believe it,' he says. ''Tis as true as I'm standing here talking to ye.'

We were sitting at the back of a church at the time.

Today, however, there's no danger of anyone stumbling into the gates of hell. Everything on the original island was, they say, destroyed by the local Protestants because of all the attention it was getting. The Catholics did as you would expect. They moved everything that was left to another island and started up in business all over again. If anything, it's worse that St Patrick's original island and that was called Purgatory. While the French are in their cosy little pensions knocking back the foie gras and Cheval Blanc '47, the Spanish are in their haciendas eating their way from one end of the tapas counter to the other with the aid of a couple of gallons of Rioja, for the first 24 hours the poor Irish are having to survive on one slice of bread, a cup of tea and non-stop prayer. No sleep at all. After that things get better. There's another slice of bread, another cup of tea and as much sleep as you can get. For six hours. In a dormitory full of starving, thirsty strangers. The third day, yet another slice of bread and a cup of tea.

Some people even today still walk there barefoot. In total silence. Not a drink taken. Not just your so-called professional pilgrims with rucksacks and monotonous faces but also office workers, computer engineers, even, God save us, lawyers who you would have thought would have been more than prepared to get out of anything especially trudging around barefoot, in total silence and not earning a penny in the process. Unless, of course, of all people they felt they had more sins that needed forgiving than the poor innocents they lock up for life.

I went to mass once in Ennis, Co. Clare. The priest was doing a selling job on Lough Derg. Most sermons, I find, are a wonderful preparation for the next life. They go on and on and on and on for an eternity. Not this one.

'Everybody in this parish,' he thundered, 'is a sinner. Everybody must atone for their sins. Everybody must go to Lough Derg on pilgrimage.'

I didn't bother. I wasn't from that parish.

But those that do go say it's so rough and tough that at the end of three days they are in such a state they are looking forward to going home. Which tells you how bad it is.

In Sligo town I once met an old man on his way home after spending three days walking barefoot and praying non-stop on the island. He'd just finished a double mixed grill in the restaurant in the Southern Hotel by the bus station and was tanking himself up on Guinness.

'Body and Soul, they say. Come to Lough Derg for the good of your Body and Soul. It should be Body and Sole. I've got so many blisters on the soles of my feet, it'll take a year for them to heal before I'm back there again next year,' he told me.

The Coast of Co. Donegale, now that's something else again. But don't go mid-summer. It's boring. It's full of happy, sun-seeking holidaymakers. From Northern Ireland. If you're expecting to see, as they say, any red petticoat come swinging over the hills forget it. Around, here, they also say, the girls have the Pope's permission to wear the fat end of their legs below the knee.

Instead go in the depths of winter. The winds are howling. The seas are lashing the coast. There's torrential rain. One thunderstorm after another. Roads are flooded. The fields are flooded. It's freezing cold. So cold you wouldn't expect to meet a Christian out of doors. To stop their roofs being blown halfway across the Atlantic every other day, they have to lash them with rope and anchor them to the ground. Nobody even thinks of going coshering, visiting each other's houses. Open your front door a fraction, you could be standing in the middle of Times Square.

But it's not only the roof that gets blown away. Barns, sheds, bus shelters, road signs, even shop signs are at the mercy of the elements. Many's the time I've been driving through a tiny village or a town and I've seen signs like -ARS—ROOM, lob— POT, -HARM— or -ORNER -AR -EWSAGENT which I thought was something to do with Irish sheep.

I was in a bar once, I mean, in a -ar once somewhere near the Bluestack Mountains.

'It's destroyed, ye must be hearing the winds and the rain,' Ireland's answer to Old Father O'Time said to me as he shuffled up to the bar. 'Roaring all night like a banshee it was.'

'Ye are right there,' the barman said to him. 'The holy statues. They're soaked to the skin, they are, the poor, holy craters.'

The old man ordered a brandy, waited until he was given the brandy and then – the old trick – asked for a drop of port. That way he would only have to pay for the brandy. If he ordered them both together he would have to pay for both. There are few barmen in Ireland who would be mean enough to ask a poor old man to pay for a drop of port, especially after he'd just ordered a brandy.

'The drink,' he says, 'it improves with age. The older I get, the more I enjoy it.'

We talked about the weather.

'Is there ever a day here when it's not raining or blowing?' I asked.

'Glory be to God how would I know,' he says. 'I'm only 83.'

I asked him if it rained all the time, how could they tell when it was summer?

'Sure to goodness is that a question you're asking me?'

'It is,' I said.

'Then your question deserves an answer. Ye can tell it's summer . . .' – he pauses, obviously, for effect – 'when the rain gets warmer.'

We bought each other a Guinness.

Then it was time for him to leave. He downed his Guinness, left a dribble in the bottom of the glass, the sign of a proper Guinness drinker. We shook hands.

'We'll meet again in Heaven,' he said as he shut the door behind him and disappeared into the night.

Bundoran, the very south of Co. Donegale, is the Irish Blackpool. It's black whereas the other is black surrounded by a million lights. It's a pool whereas the other is a lake. Imagine a small Irish county town. Throw in a thousand amusement arcades, a couple of hundred tacky bars that proudly proclaim, 'We serve food ALL DAY From 1pm–4pm,' a clutch of flashy Nite Clubs and a bit of a beach and you have it. I've been there a million times but whenever I go there it never seems to be crowded.

'So how do we survive?' a well-dressed young man who looks like a cross between a bishop and a bouncer asks me one evening in the Bridge Bar.

'Amusement arcades,' I said.

'Yes,' he says.

'Slot machines,' I said.

'Yes,' he says.

'The place is full of Catholics from Belfast.'

'Yes,' he says.

'Well,' I said.

He laughed.

'Glory be to God.' He slapped the bar. 'You're as ignorant as a string of double ditches. Money laundering. It's money laundering. That's how they get the money back into the economy.'

The rest of the night we spent singing or trying to sing rebel Irish songs and buying each other pints of Guinness – in cash.

I got back to my hotel. The manager was still there. We treated each other to more Guinness. Everything was all right now, he tells me, but in the old days it was different.

'I remember once,' he says. 'This old Irish farmer arrives for a week's holiday. He brings all his furniture with him. Bed. Table. Chair. Cooker. Everything. So why are ye bringing everything with ye? I says to him. Because, he says, ye only charged me for the room. Everything else I thought I had to bring with me.'

The following day, mid-morning, I'm in Ballyshannon which has got nothing to do with the Shannon, bally or otherwise. It sits on a hill overlooking the River Erne. In summer it's a bit like, say, Hove, quiet, reserved, respectable. In winter, I couldn't tell you. I'm scared to leave Fergie's Pub down by the river. I only go there because I feel sorry for anyone forced to live with the British royal family. It must have been hell. They deserve all the support we can give them. Another pint please, Michael.

Donegal town at the top of Donegal Bay would have been blown away years ago if it wasn't for the coaches. Whenever I go there, winter or summer, there are so many I reckon they keep it firmly anchored on the ground. While that may be a good thing for business there are always so many of them you can't see anything of Donegal town itself.

Mention Donegal to an Irishman of a certain age and character and he'll tell you that unlike Bundoran which was almost wholly Catholic in the old days Donegal had Catholic hotels and Protestant hotels and Catholic bars and Protestant bars. Not that every Catholic hotel and bar was run by Catholics or every Protestant hotel and bar was run by Protestants. It was business. No matter what their principles, nobody was going to lose any business for anyone.

Mention Donegal to an Irishwoman. She'll tell you to go and see the Diamond.

''Tis as big as a square.'

That's because in Ireland diamond is their word for village or town square. Not that I've ever seen it. Too many coaches.

I'm a great believer in faminism so I went to see the famine cemetery next to a travellers' camp almost opposite the school. But I wish I hadn't. It was all overgrown, covered in weeds and brambles. Which didn't strike me as commemorating the memory of those who suffered and died from starvation. More an extension of the travellers' camp.

It's the same virtually wherever you go.

The first time I went to the famine graveyard in Kilkenny I almost missed it. There was a tiny sign. No plaque. No explanation. No commemoration. It was almost as if they were as irrelevant in death as they were in life.

In Sligo the famine graveyard on the Bundoran Road was unbelievable. Like all the others it was impossible to find. I almost gave up. Then it was there, tucked away behind a car park. I don't know whether I'm glad I found it or not. It was like a rubbish dump. Literally. Opposite the entrance was a sculpture of a single tree battling against the wind. Hanging on the branches were car floor mats. The cemetery itself was divided up into adults and children. Hanging across the adults section was a line of dirty washing. Piled up on the graves in the children section were broken-down tables, chairs and three piece-suites.

In Ballingarry in Co. Limerick I tried to find the Knockfierna Heritage Centre. In Adare in the tourist centre some twisted lycanthropic oddball told me it was devoted to telling the story of the famine, its causes, the suffering and the deaths it created.

I drove along the road outside Ballingarry for ages. Eventually I saw a tiny sign pointing up a muddy track between the fields. I skidded and splashed my way up the track. I passed a farm gate on the right. There was a sign warning that it was a farm. To me it looked more like the entrance to a quarry. Further up, I skidded and splashed in the red mud. I came to another farm gate blocking the path. Nothing.

I turned round and skidded and splashed my way down to the bottom. I knocked on the doors of a couple of houses close to the sign. No answers. Obviously nobody wanted to even entertain the idea of talking to anyone covered in red mud who was ruining their precious Spanish-style bungalow by his presence.

I went back to the sign. There was an old squasho in a battered old trilby and a greasy raincoat tottering past on a bicycle. I asked him where I could find the Knockfierna Heritage Centre. He pointed to the sign. I told him I'd followed the sign, splashed and skidded my way to the top but found nothing.

'Well that's it,' he says. 'Nothing. Nothing was left after the famine. Nothing is what ye've seen.'

He got back on his bicycle and cycled slowly on down the road.

Around one million people died. The lasting impact it had on families, on communities, on the country – you would have thought the famine cemeteries would at least all be identified, signposted, marked, cleaned up and given the standing and recognition they deserve. Look at all the time and money the Irish government spend on identifying, signposting, checking, licensing and author-ising bed and breakfast bugfests. They should do the same for the famine cemeteries.

On the other hand when they do commemorate the famine they seem to go over the top. I was in Cashel, Co. Tipperary, when the local Heritage Society commemorated the 150th anniversary of the famine, 'this dark period of our past', with five days of 'a colourful pageant of music, song, dance and drama'. What can you say?

On around the coast, if you're not blown away, you hit Killybegs, a natural harbour if ever there was one, which I reckon should be called Smellybegs. Everyone tells you it's the biggest fishing port in Ireland. There's no need. The smell tells you that. And the millions of screaming, shrieking seagulls. There are so many they look as though they were trained by Hitchcock for some film he planned and then forgot about. The fish, however, is fantastic provided, of course, you can fight the seagulls off. I lived on fish and chips the whole time I was there. When I left I took away with me many happy memories of some glorious meals as well as the smell of fish. Not to mention a few souvenirs which seemed to just drop out of the sky.

From Killybegs I headed out to Malinbeg, the far, far west corner hoping the windscreen wipers could withstand the winds. Just passed Kilcart where I think I saw a beach or it could have been a pile of sand washed up on the street, I glimpsed something that Co. Donegale is obviously trying to keep up its sleeve: cliffs that could be serious rivals to Beachy Head if you weren't killed in the attempt of getting to them. It was probably appropriately named Slieve League, nearly 2000 feet high, the highest cliffs in Donegale.

Malinmore must be the Irish for Suffermore. In winter, it's desolate. In summer, it's desperate. The further west you go the worse it gets. The only way people can manage to survive is by walking around in fancy black rubber suits, a mask over their face with tanks of oxygen strapped to their backs. Some of them even carry spears in order to catch fish swimming down the street.

Just down the road is Glencolumbcille which is a couple of houses and a church. The rest have been blown away by the winds. Every year at midnight on 9 June, I was told, in order to commemorate St Glencolumbcille the whole village turns out and walks the length and breadth of the village.

'Why midnight?' I asked a big, fat, jolly lard-butt huddled inside what looked like the remains of an old thatched cottage just outside of the village or it could have been yet another traditional folk museum.

'That way,' she says, 'if it's so black and cold we can stay inside in the warm. The poor priest would never be able to see whether we were there or not.'

'You mean 9 June. Practically the middle of summer.'

'Has been known,' her three and a half teeth chattered away like mad.

Everybody raves about Ardara. Why I don't know. Maybe it's the relief of getting away from howling 200 mph winds and back to mere 150 mph winds. Which probably accounts for the fact that all the road signs look as though they've swung round in the wind. Going into town there was a sign saying No Speed Limit. Leaving town there was a sign saying 30 mph.

Now whether you like it or not, you're trapped. There are signs inland to Glenties but the road is so bad, the potholes the size of loughs, you've got no alternative but to stick with the coast road. Not that there's much happening in Glenties especially since the knitwear industry collapsed in the 1990s and the likes of Fruit of the Loom withered away to nothing. Night-time, however, I'm told it's a different matter. That's presumably when the fruit is hung out to dry.

Follow the coast road. Dawros Head is nothing but camping and caravan sites. Narin has a beach. Dungloe is the start of Rosses country. It's bleak. It's desolate. It's windy. In fact it's so windy the only thing that can grow here are those giant electronic wind-mills. They're all over the place. And it's going to get worse. I was told – I beg your pardon – that there are plans – What did you say? – to build as many as two hundred and fifty of them – You'll have to shout – on the Tunes Plateau – What yer say? – out near Lough Foyle. What'll you have? – A pint of Guinness, God bless you.

The Greens think they're fantastic. They're clean. They're safe.

Sensible people are in two minds. Sure there are benefits but look at the sight of them. Wherever you put them they're an eyesore not to mention an earsore. They're expensive. Two maybe three times more expensive than alternatives. And how come if they're so fantastic all those lovey-dovey green countries like Holland, Denmark and Germany are drastically cutting back on them? What's more I can't for the life of me understand why they are painted white. They should be green. I'd have thought if the whole point of them was to ensure we didn't damage the environment, they should be painted a more environmentally friendly colour. But then I know nothing.

About the only time Dungloe lives up to its name and Dungloes is during its so-called ten-day Mary from Dungloe International Festival. I say so-called because it's about as international as the American World Baseball League. The only international pop group I heard came from Ballyshannon, just down the road. The range of international cultural events covered everything from raft-building races on the pier to egg-throwing competitions in Main Street. As for the Mary from Dungloe beauty competition they were so short of local candidates the only way they could have a competition was by opening it up to any Mary from anywhere in the world.

In Sweeneys Hotel, the night I was there, the betting was on a local beauty called Mary from Bayonne, New Jersey.

Gweedore is a tiny Irish-speaking enclave about the size of a beer mat, the ideal place you would have thought for the headquarters of Foras na Gaeilge, the main Irish language organisation. No way. The government wants to move them there. They want to stay in Dublin where Irish is one of the least spoken languages you're likely to hear there. I expected it to be even more bleak and desolate and windy. Not so. The place looked like a building site. Practically wherever you looked people were building: tiny bungalows, medium-size cottages and the occasional full-size manor. But nothing that looked like a headquarters building. All the buildings, which looked as though they were flushed with pride, had one thing in common. The roofs were all lashed to the ground.

I stopped at Bunbeg House by the harbour.

Over dinner I was talking to someone's best mate who was well into a Slieve League of sausage and chips.

'The scenery around here,' I mumbled. 'Is this as spectacular as it gets?'

'Why don't you go out to the Bloody Foreland and see for yourself,' he says.

Well thank you, I thought. I can tell which part of Northern Ireland you're from.

The following morning the locals are trying to convince me the Bloody Foreland is really the Bloody Foreland because of the blood red of the sunsets. No way. It's because all the Tories on nearby Tory Island are like Tories all over the world and bloody everything in sight that does not agree with them.

The local council came up with a plan to develop the island. The interests of the people they said should come first. They wanted to move everybody off the island and into fancy bungalows on the mainland and turn the island into an army firing range. The local Tories told the council where to go. They turned themselves into their own kingdom and elected their own king, an accordion player, painter and one-time pig farmer, Patsy Dan Rogers. His priority, he said, when he was elected was education, education, education. The amazing thing for a politician is that he's actually done something about it. For the first time ever they have their own secondary school. Seven teachers. Twenty-one children. The best teacher–pupil ratio in the country. Galway University is planning to open a campus for adults and visitors. Painting. Archaeology. That kind of thing. But surprisingly nothing to do with the weather or weather forecasting.

A Donegale woman I was told had tried to become the first woman to swim the 10 miles from Tory Island to the mainland. She was hoping to do it in six hours. But because – you've guessed – of the storms, the torrential rains, the strong currents it took her 8 hours 15 minutes. That's how desperate people are to leave the Tories behind.

At the far top left-hand corner of the county and I suppose the country I thought I was going to be in for some peace and quiet. One small town after another. The sea to the left of me, the Muckish Mountains to the right. I should be so lucky.

Dunfanaghy was Northern Ireland comes to Donegal.

Overnight a local businessman had slapped a sign up on one of the buildings he owns in the middle of town proclaiming, 'A Protestant town for a Protestant people.' Across the face of the building he was painting a huge Union Jack. But he had denied it was anything to do with religion. 'A Protestant town for a Protestant people.' Of course, it's got nothing to do with religion. Whatever gave anyone that idea? The whole town was up in arms. The Catholics were saying there was no way it was going to affect their attitude to the Protestants. They would continue to regard them the way they always had. All I know is as I zoomed past, the sign and the giant flag were still there.

Although strangely enough I was told by an old grockle with a pipe when I stopped for some refreshment in, I think it was the Stonecutters Rest in Creeslough, that nobody made a fuss whenever a fire engine from Northern Ireland crossed the border into Donegal to put a fire out. Neither did anyone make a fuss when the Northern Ireland fire service was on strike and the British army itself was driving across the border to put out the fires.

Letterkenny at the top of Lough Swilly is the biggest town in County Donegal. In terms of shops, it's probably the biggest in the country. It's supposed to have the longest high street in the known universe *pace* Stephen Hawking. But I'm not interested in shops – as far as I'm concerned the devil is in the retail – so I didn't bother even trying to throw the anchors out of the car to try and make it stop in the winds and the gales.

I did, however, try to get into the Holiday Inn. But it was full. Over a thousand Republicans had turned up for a dinner to celebrate the twentieth anniversary of Britain's biggest jailbreak when almost 40 of them escaped from the Maze prison near Belfast in which one prison officer was shot and one died.

First course was a reconstruction of the escape using videos, maps and photographs. Main course was a description of the escape by the three leaders, Gerry Kelly, Bobby Storey and Brendan 'Bic' McFarlane. Final course: the jokes. Says Bobby Storey, 'All the guns we had we made of wood. We make them in the prison workshop. You could tell. When we went to fire them they wooden work.'

Funny Storey.

From Letterkenny there's two sights to see, Lough Swilly and the Grianan of Aileach. Lough Swilly is supposed to have a man-eating monster, Suilach.

'Sensible monster,' the voice of local experience told me. 'He wouldn't dare go for any of the women around here. They're too tough.'

The Grianan of Aileach or the Grianan Ailigh is Irish for *It's another spaceship church like Liverpool Cathedral but better*. First, because it's in Ireland. Second, it's all white and clean. Third, it's light whereas Liverpool always seems so dark and forbidding.

Looking down on the church – sorry, I'll rephrase that – above the church is an old Blarney Stone Age fort. Some historians say it's all to do with Tuatha De Danann. A good Celtic god he built it as a memorial to his son a British blow-in who ran off with the king's daughter. Others say it was the Egyptians although how the ancient Egyptians got to Donegale let alone saw the sign pointing to the fort on the N13 I have no idea. The Irish are much more straightforward. They say it looks like an upturned cooking pot. I wouldn't know. I wouldn't know what a cooking pot looks like upturned or not. You don't see cooking pots in the restaurants I eat in.

I prefer Buncrana up on the Inishowen Peninsula. They have more pubs than grains of sand on the beach. Fantastic. No wonder it's one of the most popular holiday resorts in the North.

Malin Head, way up at the top of the Peninsula, is the most northerly village in Ireland. I could tell. My car got frostbite. Another couple of miles and the exhaust would have dropped off. But it was worth it. I don't think I've seen scenery like it anywhere else in the world. It was nothing but rubbish. Not today's rubbish. Yesterday's rubbish. Even rubbish going back as much as 15 years. It's seeping out of the sand dunes on to the beach. The tide then comes in, breaks up the dunes even more and spreads the rubbish even further afield. Obviously somebody was illegally dumping something. The locals are thick-skinned about it. It's also one of Europe's largest commercial crab-fishing centres. The old railway station is now the crab-processing plant although I didn't realise it at first. There are just as many old crabs on my local station back home in East Sussex.

I came back through Moville down the western side of Lough Foyle, so called because stop and face the lough and you'll be foiled by what you see. Look south, you'll see north, Northern Island. Look north you'll see south, the Republic of Ireland. That's stone-cold sober.

By the time I got to civilisation the rains were back. The streets were deadened. The wind was howling. The black-and-white-and-grizzly-grey rainbows were casting their gloom all over the place. It was as cold as a three-day-old lump of marinated soya bean curd. I ignored all the big pubs. I raced into a small pub near a bridge, managed to slam the door shut against the wind and staggered up to the bar.

Two old, pathetic victims of chronic fatigue syndrome were sitting there, slowly sipping the black stuff.

'Big depression coming this way,' says the one with the hat. 'Massive icy cold fronts. A strong, bitter north wind coming up behind it.'

The one without the hat puts his pint down on the bar slooowly. He looks up.

'Tell me, Michael,' he says. 'Is it the wife you'd be talking about?'

Co. Fermanagh
The ideal jumping-off place

Famous local resident
Bill Clinton's thirteenth cousin's fourth brother's ninth nephew

Favourite food
Hamburgers

Favourite drink
Guinness

Favourite pub
The Clinton Peace Centre

Favourite restaurant
Central Bar, Irvinestown

What to say
Fancy a cigar?

What not to say
Monica sends her love

Probably more than any other county, Co. Fermanagh, pronounced Firm Manner as in, well, never mind, is almost nothing but pure water. Well, water. It's not a subject on which I'm much of an expert.

As the Irish say, it's a land of lakes. If such a thing is possible. Over one-third of the place is under water. In fact, there are so many lakes and islands – over 250 at the last count – it was the last part of the country to be surveyed and mapped. They had problems finding somewhere solid on which to install their equipment. The biggest lake of all is Lough Erne, an old Irish word for *Earn all the money you can from those suckers who want to act the sailor and play about in boats.* And suckers they think we are too. Beware Upper Lough Erne, they say. It was here on the slopes of Slieve Beagh mountain near Lisnaskea that Noah's grandson landed in his own personal ark.

During World War II it was home to the flying boats that used to patrol the Atlantic looking for German ships and submarines.

On Boa Island on Lower Lough Erne is the oldest cemetery in the UK, Caldreagh Cemetery which looks in better condition than many of the newer cemeteries. I asked one old friend of Yorrick why it was called Boa Island. He said it was because the island was so small, people had to be practically doubled over and battened down and constricted so much in order to get them into the smallest possible size coffins.

Ask an Irish gravedigger a sensible question, what do you get? A sensible answer.

Ulster calls Co. Fermanagh its very own Lake District. Water.

Boats. Fishing. Cars. Crowds of people. Screaming kids. To me it's a downmarket Co. Kerry. The land and the lakes are not as soft

---

Shy, innocent, young Irishman decides he wants to get married. He takes his bride-to-be home to meet his family.

Over cabbage and potatoes, his mother asks his bride-to-be what she does for a living.

'I'm a prostitute,' she says.

'I beg your pardon,' says the mother.

'A prostitute,' says the bride-to-be.

'Oh that's alright,' says the mother. 'I thought you said Protestant.'

---

and gentle. There's not the variety and the extremes. It doesn't have that sparkle or the bars or hotels or restaurants.

Similarly the people. God save us. That Plantation accent. I swear even the fish have a Plantation accent. Then there is the way they say things. Food that's gone off, for example, has not gone off. It is 'distasted'. If they can't remember something, it is 'disremembered'. Instead of correcting the wrong image, they 'shafter' the wrong image. Which literary skill may or may not have inspired Oscar Wilde who went to Portora Royal School where he, no doubt, had a distasted time. So too did Samuel Beckett. You've only got to read the theatre programme for *Waiting for Godot* to see how it affected him.

Another local schoolboy who was obviously inspired by all that water sloshing around doing nothing was James Gamble who went on to splash out and launch, with Mr Procter, Procter and Gamble, the giant multinational soap detergent company.

Not that he is the only Gamble in Co. Fermanagh. There are plenty of others.

There are the famous Marble Arch underground caves. You wouldn't catch me putting a foot in the cave. My time will come soon enough.

There is Castle Archdale and its ghost dog or should that be a dog ghost? Stay there and halfway through the night some almighty slathering bitch could suddenly leap on top of your bed and start slobbering all over you.

Go to Belleek, the pottery town at the mouth of Lough Erne which looks as though it has gone to pots. There by the side of the road is a war memorial. There are war memorials all over Ireland. Trouble is this is an unauthorised war memorial. Erected by Republicans in the middle of the night. To honour those killed, as the IRA say, 'in active service'. On the very same spot where two local Protestants were shot dead by the IRA. Say the wrong thing to the wrong person, you could end up having your own war memorial.

The biggest gamble of all is, of course, Enniskillen, on an island between the upper and lower Lough Ernes, a one-time Protestant stronghold, home of the – to some – legendary Royal Inniskilling Fusiliers as opposed to the Royal Innisnonkilling Fusiliers, scene of an IRA bomb attack on a Remembrance Day service. It's less Protestant than it used to be. It's also less dangerous. But there are still stories about the low-flying military helicopters, motorists being stopped and searched who are neither African nor Asian and occasional attacks along Forthill Street in the early hours of the morning. The worst things that happened to me, however, were a run-in with the local Aughakillymaude Strawmen, a weird bunch of mummers, in the town centre one Christmas and practically a punch-up with some diet-ravaged old bag of bones outside the library in Halls Lane who kept insisting I should go for what she called a 'Free Body Composition Analysis'. Oh yes and a full-body tattoo and piercing as well. Thank you very much.

Enniskillen Castle was, by comparison, peaceful although I didn't understand all the fuss they made about the flag of St George being 'the English national banner until 1606'. I thought it still was. If not English football fans will be surprised they've been supporting a team by waving a national banner that hasn't existed for practically 400 years. It also seemed odd that they went on and on about the regiment originally being called Tiffin's Regiment. Who's interested in a regiment named after a biscuit? Then I discovered that the heavy artillery in front of the castle keep are not theirs at all. They're on loan from the Tower of London.

The Museum, of course, put their spin on it. They said it was originally called the Tiffin regiment because it was founded by a Colonel Tiffin to defend Enniskillen from the 'dastardly, unpatriotic, disloyal Catholic forces of King James in 1689'. As for the heavy artillery, did I want my money back?

If I had time I would have raised the matter with the £3.5 million Clinton Peace Centre built on the site of the IRA bomb attack, which doesn't strike me as the most neutral, let's-be-friends site in the whole world.

Some say it was named after Bill Clinton because he has distant family nearby in Roslea; because of the part he played in the Northern Ireland peace process; because of what he got up to late at night in the Oval Office to establish peaceful relations with his wife, Hillary; because of the way he completely ignored the genocide in Rwanda which resulted in practically one million men, women and children being killed.

I asked one anonymous-looking fuzzpop in Blakes Bar, which was smart but not exactly Tyger! Tyger! burning bright, if he thought naming the peace centre after Clinton was a good idea or not. He said, No. It should have been named after everyone who had fought for peace. Directly or indirectly.

I didn't ask what 'Directly or indirectly' meant. I was in a hurry. My excuse. I had a meeting on an industrial estate called Templackaboy. I didn't ask what that meant either.

Co. Fermanagh is that kind of place. Ask too many questions, ask too many of the wrong questions, you could end up by being thrown in one of their thousands of lakes.

Directly or indirectly.

The Roasted Malted Barley Counties

Co. Wicklow
Co. Kilkenny
Co. Meath

Having studied the Water period of Irish history now we come to the Roasted Malted Barley period, which to some people means going against the grain.

This is when the Celts, the Gallis or the Keltois moved in, roasted everybody in sight, malted them down and used them as fertiliser on the fields of barley. Hence the phrase, How many ears are there in that field?

Some say they came from as far afield as France, which would account for their civilised behaviour.

Others say Belgium, Spain and Switzerland which is why Ryanair is so popular. The Irish are trying to get their own back.

But wherever they came from they came on sailing ships powered by nothing but the wind. Which is why even today any settler in Ireland whether he is a poor German multimillionaire buying up half of Co. Kerry or a rich cousin from a tenement block in Boston, Massachusetts is known as a blow-in.

To look at, the Celts all wore black suits, black ties, coloured shirts and cloth caps. Half of them were heavy drinkers. These are the ones responsible for all the big swirls and loops in Celtic designs. The other half never touched a drop. They all smoked 250 cigarettes a day and had red hair. The tradition continues up to today.

Wherever the Celts went they formed themselves into tribes. At the head of the tribe was the warrior chief. Big. Powerful. Unmovable. Whatever she said, the men did. They were known as the Celtic Cross. It was only the children who had the strength and the courage to do what they wanted. Attached to each tribe were the usual assortment of hangers-on: magicians, prophets, horse doctors, lawyers and Members of Parliament.

They lived in huge communities, usually hilltop settlements which looked remarkably like primitive Spanish haciendas. Low. Well decorated. With a huge front door so the master of the house could get his maracas in without any trouble.

Around the haciendas they cultivated their own crops and raised their own cattle. The more crops they grew, the more cattle they raised, the richer and more respected they became. Unlike in today's society when a farmer with a huge acreage under crops and fields full of cattle is more to be pitied than admired. Especially by European Celts who keep throwing money at him.

The exception was pig farmers. But that depended on how often they could lead their pigs backwards and forwards over other people's borders. The more times they drove them backwards and forwards the more money they made.

Evenings were given over to fighting and getting drunk or getting drunk and fighting. From time to time a rambling Gay Byrne would leave his summer camp at Dungloe in Co. Donnegale, turn up late in the evening and tell old stories about people spending their evenings fighting and getting drunk. Eventually, because he rambled so much and each time told the same story a different way, people decided to keep a record of what he said. To do this, they invented what they called O'Gham, writing, which left them and everybody else more confused than ever, especially when the first book published was *O'Finnegans Wake* which even today scholars are still trying to translate into English.

The only solution, they decided, was to do what the great rambler himself did: ramble. Because the railway system was so bad they decided the only way to ramble was in huge, slow-moving wheeled vehicles, buses. Because O'Gham had just been invented they didn't know which direction they were heading. Instead of saying north, south, east and west they said, Ulster, Munster, Leinster and Connacht.

The Romans got as far as Celtic Britain. But stopped there. They heard Michael O'Leary, the famously foul-mouthed boss of Ryanair, yelling and screaming and swearing, thought it sounded too much like home and decided to stay put. The result is Celtic Britain didn't last long before it was crushed and destroyed by the Romans. Celtic Ireland, however, lived on uninfluenced, unpersuaded and untamed by anybody. Especially the O'Learys.

Thus ended a unique cereal in Irish history. It obviously accounts for its unique Celtic Irish behaviour, its unique Celtic Irish folklore and its unique Celtic Irish attitude to life.

Co. Wicklow
The Garden of Ireland

Famous local resident
Sally Gap

Favourite food
Shillelagh sandwich

Favourite drink
Guinness

Favourite pub
Johnny Fox's

Favourite restaurant
Tinakilly Country House Hotel, Bray

What to say
Put that shillelagh down, I'm not a Protestant

What not to say
My old army boots are just as good today as
they were in 1917

Co. Wicklow, the source of the River Liffey, claims to be the Garden of Ireland. Forget it. It is roasted malted barley because unlike, say, Co. Donegale it's the sun. There's little rain, few storms and the sea never lashes the coast to smithereens. Or at least nowhere near as often as it does in Co. Donegale. It's also roasted because in the old days this was the land of huge estates, huge country mansions, huge dining rooms and huge roasted dinners. Where, it was said, the poor kept all the fasts and the rich kept all the feasts. This was the Ascendancy, the ascendancy of the Protestants over the Catholics when the Protestants held the reins and the Catholics did the mucking-out. Which, whatever way you look at it, was not going to be the ideal basis for a stable relationship.

Brenda Behan, Ireland's most famous drunken house painter, called the Ascendancy 'Protestants on horseback'. Wander around Co. Wicklow today, you can see the impact they made in the grand empty houses, the empty churches, the empty schools. Even the names of the towns remind you of Protestants: Bray, Wicklow, Arklow, Powerscourt. Where the names Glendalough and Sally Gap come from I have no idea.

Co. Wicklow was also home to the Hellfire Club, a gonzo Rotary Club without the pinstripe suits, which did so much roasting and malting they were thrown out of Dublin by the city fathers because of their 'licentious and blasphemous conduct and devil-worshipping'. Obviously a junior Rotary Club. The reason Co. Wicklow didn't throw them out? They could control them. Co. Wicklow, which has so many trees you can hardly see the shamrock, invented that most famous of all Irish means of persuasion: the shillelagh, or to be more precise – no, please don't hit me – it was invented in – surprise, surprise – the peaceful village of Shillelagh. Peaceful because of the number of shillelaghs around and the number of Sheilas in wigs, white stockings and buckled shoes, as they were affectionately known in Ascendancy circles, prepared to use them.

Trouble is, today they've forgotten how to use them. As a result the whole place, Shillelagh and the whole of Co. Wicklow, is being overrun. Unfortunately not by the likes of the Hellfire Club. But by their opposites. Walkers. Hikers. And bikers. Everyone a knee

> Irish priest to old Irish gardener:
>
> 'My goodness. What a wonderful garden yourself and the good Lord have created together.'
>
> Says the old gardener, 'You should have seen what it was like when the good Lord was looking after it Himself.'

fetishist. They pour in by the million in their enviro-extremist cargo pants, their oh-so-dainty one-strap Velcro designer rucksacks and those little tree-deodorisers hanging from the laces of their boots. From Dublin, for a few hours' stroll at weekends. From all over the country, for a couple of days. From all over the world, for a cultural experience. To hug trees that are no longer there because they were torn down to make shillelaghs. To sashay up and down hills which are no longer there. Because in Co. Wicklow they are called mountains.

In the old days people even came to Co. Wicklow for serious, grown-up reasons: gold. The Croghan Mountains were the scene of Ireland's one and only gold rush, which lasted barely six weeks largely because nobody could say, There's gold in that thar Aughatinavough River. Well, let's face it, it's a bit more complicated than Dead Man's Creek, the Yellow River or even Fort Knox. Even the Irish admit it. They decided to rename the Aughatin-

whatever-it-was River Gold Mines River. By the time they got round
to it, of course, there was no gold left and no gold miners either.
They'd all gone off to California. Thank goodness. You could now
get back into Lynham's Bar in Laragh once more. But it was not
to last. Even though there is no gold rush and no gold miners you
still can't get into the place. In fact, the last time I didn't even
bother to try. I knew it wouldn't do my anorakophobia any good.
Go in October and you can't even get into Laragh. It's trampled
in boots. It's the Wicklow Mountain Walking Festival. The whole
place is smeared in corn-fed chisel-jawed pretty boys and a whole
complaint of women who I'm sure are inspired by God. Because
they all move in mysterious ways.

'No. No. Start at the car park at Glendalough. Follow the signs
to the Wicklow Way. The Poulanass. Beautiful. Just beautiful.'

'As good as Powerscourt?'

'Better. Better. A million times better I tell ye. I also like the
Djouce Walk along the summit there . . .'

'Tell me what d'ye use for stopping the blisters . . .'

It's not just me. Even the authorities in charge of the place
think the walkers are stupid. All along the roads are signs warning
motorists to beware of walkers, ramblers and hikers. It's a picture
of a pretty nondescript fooleen sitting down at a bench talking to
a tree.

If it was up to me I'd larch the lot of them. If that's the right
term.

But don't worry. It's going to get worse. Last time I was there
there was talk of turning the whole area into a huge ski resort
complete with aquatic leisure centres, hotels and what they called
interpretive centres. Which can only be centres which will translate all the appropriate messages which could be conveyed to
anyone who even thinks of turning up in the area with a pair of
skis.

'Céad mile failte.'

'Push off. Leave us in peace. We want to have a drink.'

But if the shillelagh failed to do its job in Ireland, the British
judging by their actions around the world, soon learnt to make
the most of it. The trees that were not used for shillelaghs were

used to build the British sailing fleet in the eighteenth century so that the ships could transport even more shillelaghs around the world for the purposes for which they were intended. Judging by what you read in the history books, the number of countries that were subdued, a very good job they did too.

Those, of course, were the days when weapons could be sold freely all around the world without anyone saying or even thinking a word. Not that the Irish said a word. They were too busy mucking out the stables for the Protestants on their horses. In any case the Irish were pleased. With the trees out of the way they could at last see what Co. Wicklow looked like and, if a convenient ass and muck cart was available, go visit.

First stop was Bray, Ireland's first genuine tourist resort, so called because of the continuous braying of the landladies about wiping your feet on the welcome mat, if you're not back by five o'clock for tea you go without and no lady guests anywhere within a million miles of the town's famous old jail even though this is where in the 1760s that most disgusting, loathsome and lascivious practice began: swimming in the sea. Admittedly it was over 200 years later they realised it was much more comfortable and much more fun if they took their clothes off.

Today it is still called The Gateway to County Wicklow although it's more a Victorian all-metal twirly-bit gateway than a wooden garden gateway, the kind of town which always makes me nervous about using my electric razor. Plug it in the wrong time of day and all the trams stop.

The promenade is long, wide and handsome. The kind of promenade made for crinolines and top hats rather than skateboards and blast boxes.

The long terraces of Victorian hotels and boarding houses look something out of Jane Austen. A paperback version of Jane Austen.

There are bandstands, neat green lawns, emerald of course. On a hot, sunny afternoon, let yourself go, you could be in the south of France. I know it's happened to me many times. Once I even caught myself ordering a glass of champagne instead of my usual Guinness. Wash my mouth out and pray to St Patrick.

Mornings I go to mass. Back to the hotel. Scallops. Traditional

Irish breakfast. With white pudding. Read the newspapers. Couple of pots of coffee. Pint of Guinness.

Lunchtime. Seafood. Maybe smoked salmon. Roast lamb. Push the boat out in the fancy Victorian-Italian Tinakilly Country House Hotel, once home to Captain Robert Halpin who commanded Brunel's *Great Eastern*, at the time the largest ship in the world. The cost: about half a funnel and three-quarters of the ship's propeller. Another pint of Guinness.

In the afternoon, walk along the promenade to Bray Head where the oldest fossils in the world were discovered. Not slumped in armchairs in the hotels. Not tottering along the prom. But in some rocks by the beach. The man who discovered them, Thomas Oldham, went on to become director of the Geological Survey of Ireland. His son, Richard, also a geologist, was the first to come up with the idea that the world had a core. Being an Irishman, he was convinced it was liquid, black with a creamy white froth on top. Less informed geologists maintain it's a solid nickel-iron core surrounded by a liquid, black with a creamy white froth on top.

Evenings, sit down to a fine pint. Or two or three. Watch the happy commuters on their way back from Dublin. Happy because Bray helped to make the commuter's lot a touch more pleasant than it used to be. In the 1930s they saw the launch of battery-driven trains. For nearly twenty years special battery-driven trains ran daily between Bray and Dublin. Before then you couldn't move for ass carts loaded with turf.

All very civilised.

One evening I'm in a bar along the waterfront. I was chatting away to a singularly unoccupied old clunker covered in cobwebs who was definitely not your hair grower of the year. In fact, you'd be hard pushed to make him hair grower of the century.

'Top of the morning to ye, governor,' he says to me as soon as I go into the bar. 'Isn't it a soft day? Thanks be to God.'

For some reason or other he starts going on about women. Which surprised me. First, because most Irishmen prefer to talk about far more interesting subjects: horses, dogs, the weather, the match. Second, he looked as though he was interested in them much as you'd be interested in old churches. It's nice to know they're still around but you're not particularly interested in going in them.

In the end, it turned out he would never dream of letting a woman shave him or cut his hair. But when he did have a shave or a haircut, he told me, he insisted on all his hair being swept up and packed away in a little wooden box.

'To be kept in a little wooden box,' I repeated slowly.

'Lord help us,' he says. 'When the Day of Judgement comes and we all rise from the dead I want to have a full head of hair for the occasion.'

Well, of course, why didn't I think of that? It's obvious, isn't it?

Bray – it's not the Bray of Vicar fame, that's Bray, Berkshire – is also Ireland's answer to Hollywood. Not only do they have a big film production complex, it is also used for location shots for a whole string of famous film and television series I've never heard of.

The Devil's Own. Brad Pitt. Was filmed in an eighteenth-century farmhouse perched high on the sea just outside Arklow.

Braveheart. The story of Scotland, Scotland and Scotland. Was filmed in Co. Wicklow.

Ballykissangel. The saccharine-sweet story of everyday life in a typical Irish village. Was shot in Avoca.

Excuse me, Tristram, you've dropped your eyeliner in my pint of Guinness.

Through the all-metal twirly-bit gateway and there is everything from mountains and waterfalls to mountains and waterfalls.

The one everybody talks about is the Great Sugar Loaf Mountain, which is neither Great, Sugar, Loaf or a Mountain. It's really the remains of an ice-age hill.

The real challenge, however, is to make for the highest point of all, which Ireland being Ireland has been converted into a pub, Johnnie Fox's in Glencullen, just outside Enniskerry.

But don't go in October.

A few years' time, however, the highest point could well be at Dillonsdown close to the border with Co. Kildare. It is the biggest illegal rubbish dump in the country. The rate it is growing, it will soon rival Everest itself. Then the Irish being the Irish, they'll put a pub on top of it. God bless them.

One year, in the middle of winter, I tried to drive from Enniskerry over the mountains to Sally Gap then down to Blessington. Most people go there because it is Christmas tree country. Forget Germany. A traditional Christmas is not Christmas without an Irish Christmas tree. Most Christmas trees for sale in the UK, Holland, France, Switzerland and even Austria come from Ireland. And most of the Irish trees come from around Blessington. Why does everybody want an Irish Christmas tree? Because, I was told, they look almost as good as a real artificial one. Come Christmas, however, the place is full of fairies looking for somewhere to settle.

I wanted to have a look at Russborough House, which is supposed to be one of Ireland's grandest stately homes. I also wanted to check out the waterfall nearby which is supposed to be home to a mighty evil black horse with fire in its eyes that storms all over the country trampling everything in sight. Obviously a mare. I wondered if I could borrow her for a few days.

There was snow all around. Everything was white and grizzly grey like some old blob object before her monthly detox and dye. The road was thick with ice. I kept sliding and skidding all over the place. That was before I even got in the car. When I finally made it, it was so bad I couldn't even drive round the straight corners let alone the bent ones. Once I nearly ended up in a ditch. I gave up and went back to Enniskerry and the Powerscourt Arms. It wasn't that I was frightened of being buried alive under all that ice, it was the thought of not having any vodka to go with it.

Every time I go to Enniskerry I try and stay at the Powerscourt Arms which looks like a slightly run-down, busy but very friendly pub guaranteed to give everyone a powerful evening. But they're always full. Instead I stay in the Enniscree Lodge up the road overlooking the valley. The first time I was there the lady of the house was half dead with a cold. The only girl on duty, who did everything, was from Ghana. I was the only one staying there. It wasn't as much fun as the Powerscourt Arms. But at least I brushed up my Evé, the language they speak in the west of Ghana and across the border into Togo.

As for the Powerscourt Waterfall, to listen to the locals you'd think it out-Niagaraed Niagara. I hadn't the heart to tell them.

In between the mountain and the waterfall is everything else.

Wicklow town is on the mouth of the River Vartry. It was here once that St Patrick tried to convert the local chief to Christianity. Because he was getting on his Co. Wicklow, the chief knocked the hell out of one of the holy saint's companions. Friendly people in Co. Wicklow. Today it's a small town with a few teeth missing. But it was a Wicklow Town man who made it and the world seem an even smaller place: Robert Halpin. He was the man who connected the world together with telephone cable. From Newfoundland to France. From Suez to Bombay. From Madras to Singapore. From Indonesia to Australia. He died from gangrene. He jabbed himself while cutting his toenails. Let that be a lesson to you.

Roundwood is probably the most unusual, unique, historic place in the whole country. Not because the Roundwood Inn is famous for serving mountains of what they call Irish-Germanic food. Not because this is where Dublin Corporation built a huge reservoir to supply drinking water to the city. But because this is where an Irish politician, Sir John Gray, chairman of the city's Waterworks Committee, as soon as he heard the decision to go ahead rushed to buy up all the land he could in the area to be developed. To stop it being bought up by property developers. He then resold the land to the Corporation – and this is what makes him so unique – at the price he paid for it. They don't make them like that any more. God bless you, Sir John.

Glendalough is where the patron saint of Australia, Saint Kevin, built a monastery whose fame was to spread throughout Europe. To listen to the local Wicklowers you'd think it was the Sydney Opera House, Ayers Rock and Nicole Kidman all rolled into two. Two lakes. The imaginatively named Upper Lake and Lower Lake. Admittedly they're striking. But they're more Glenda Lakes than say Kerry Lakes or Connemara Lakes. Glenda Lake is more practical. Carved by glaciers. Surrounded by mountains of granite over 400 million years old. Once joined together. Now wrested asunder. Around the lakes St Kevin, who spent part of his life like a koala bear living up a tree – how Australian can you get? – built his monastery. The Kerry Lakes and the Connemara Lakes are more magical, dreamy, out of this world. They glow. They shimmer. I wander around the Glenda Lakes. All I can think of is the old six o'clock swill. There is one compensation, however: getting there. Whichever way you go the drive over the Wicklow Mountains, providing you can drive over the Wicklow Mountains, is spectacular.

I prefer the run from Rathdrum up through the Vale of Clara, which has more ups and downs and twists and turns than is good for her. But then on and up through the Wicklow Gap the scenery is spectacular. It's like half-time during the Clash of the Glaciers. You can see what it must have been like all those years ago. Huge volcanic convulsions. Tempests. Storms. Unbelievable chaos. And best of all, no walkers, hikers or bikers.

Co. Kilkenny
The best beer in the world

Famous local resident
The fastest pint drinker in the world

Favourite food
Kilkenny cat

Favourite drink
Guinness

Favourite pub
Every one of them

Favourite restaurant
The snack bar where you catch the bus to Wexford

What to say
You're slow

What not to say
Kilkenny. Why wouldn't I?

With all the roasting, malting and barleying going on, Kilkenny is not where people were taken to be killed. Neither were Kilbaha, Kilcar, Kilelief, Kilcolgan or all the other 3,371,523 other places called Kil-something or other. It was a lie got up by the people on horseback. Like One man one vote, Freedom for all, Long live democracy, Tony Blair is a man of peace. Kil is Irish for Kind, Endearing, Thirsty.

Co. Kilkenny is not just the malt in the roasted malted barley, it's the beer itself. In fact, after Guinness, Kilkenny is one of my favourite beers. Soft. Smooth. Fabulous. Especially on a hot summer's day. Horses grazing in the paddock. The wife away for the weekend. Half an ox in the oven for dinner. But I didn't discover it in Kilkenny. I discovered it in the upstairs bar in Moscow airport. I was waiting for a flight that never came. After a couple of pints of Kilkenny I couldn't have cared less. I was happy. I didn't have a problem in the world. All my roubles had disappeared.

Not surprisingly Co. Kilkenny is home to the fastest pint drinker in the world, Ned Prendergast, from Graiguenamanagh, who can sink four pints in seven seconds. It takes seven seconds to pronounce Graiguen-whatever-it-is. As if that wasn't enough, he then smashes the glass and eats it. How long that took nobody ever bothered to work out. Everyone was too busy trying to beat his record.

Another Co. Kilkenny man also holds a world record. For conkers. He smashed 306 in less than an hour. Nobody could tell me his name, where he comes from or the secret of his success. But I was told to look out for a giant bottle of vinegar.

Kilkenny's fortune, however, was not built on beer. It was built on wine. My Lord Ormond was chief butler to Henry II. He was responsible for collecting the duty on all wine imported not just into Ireland but England as well. Given the sober tastes of the Irish, it wasn't long before he became one of the richest and most powerful men in the land with huge estates and castles all over the place, including of course his home base, Kilkenny Castle, overlooking the River Nore. Can you imagine how much more important they would have been if Henry II had made them responsible for the beer as well? It's not surprising, therefore, that with so much drink in their blood it affects their judgement.

> Brenda O'Brien is at home doing what wives do all over the world. Moaning and complaining about her hard-working, long-suffering husband.
>
> There's a knock on the door.
>
> 'Brenda,' says Pat, 'I must tell ye about ye husband. He's dead. Fell into a giant vat of Kilkenny's and drowned.'
>
> 'Lord have mercy on him,' says Brenda. 'Tell me did he suffer, was he in pain, was it quick?'
>
> 'You're not to worry about him, the Lord have mercy on him,' says Pat. 'He got out three times to have a pee.'

Kilkenny town is Ireland's medieval capital. It has two cathedrals, five medieval churches, a Norman castle, odd bits of medieval wall, five fabulous restaurants plus many other not-so-fabulous restaurants, cafés, the snack bar where you catch the bus for Wexford and, of course, 80 bars. Of the 80 bars only 75 have those aluminium drums of lager, ale and stout outside. The others have been stolen. Once when I was there there was an outbreak of beer barrel theft. The police said they were looking for a gang of criminals with silly smiles on their faces, slumped in a corner, singing Irish rebel songs. The police were confident that sooner or later they'd have the gang behind bars.

What do they call Kilkenny? The Marble City. Why? I have no idea. I can't for the life of me see any marble anywhere. Limestone. I can see the local limestone rock through the bottom of a glass and, yes, it could look like marble. Not that there are many empty glasses for long in Kilkenny. In fact, in many ways the limestone is more grey than marble. Although that might just be early in the morning.

For my money, Kilkenny should be called Marshalkenny. William Marshal built the Black Abbey for the Dominicans in 1220, the city walls, most of Kilkenny Castle to be his Irish headquarters, went on any number of Crusades, jousted with Richard the Lionheart, refused to give in and helped push King John into signing the Magna Carta.

Kilkenny also has a language of its own. A loaf of bread is known as a 'bric'. Hence the phrase, Is that another bric you've dropped there Paddy? Nobody is exhausted after drinking four pints in seven seconds. They get 'foundered'. With or without the four pints everybody is a fricker this or a fricker that.

Kilkenny is also not surprisingly given the amount of booze inside them home to the famous Murphy's Cat Laughs Comedy Festival which for some reason attracts comedians from all over the world. The biggest laughs of all, however, are reserved for the infamous Statute of Kilkenny which vainly attempted to establish what it called the Pale, an English only area to keep the English English and the Irish Irish. Inside the Pale the English must speak English at all times, use only English names, marry only English women, ride the English way, use only English bows and arrows, keep only English servants, sell their horses only to Englishmen. Break any of the rules and the penalty was simple: England. You're on the next boat. At one time it even stopped the Irish from entering Kilkenny itself. Which must have been a bundle of laughs. I mean who would serve the beer?

107

I landed there one year a couple of months after the Festival was over and everybody in the bars was still howling about some American comedian's description of Kilkenny as 'Disneyland for alcoholics'.

''Tis great that. 'Tis great,' an old blattereen with a flat cap and a clay pipe kept telling me.

Not only did he look so white he was beyond the pale, he had a bit of string tied around the little finger of his left hand. He told me he had a nosebleed that morning and that was how he stopped it.

Kilkenny Arts Week, their annual music and poetry festival, is something else. I thought it was going to be laughs. No way. They were all weirdos. If it wasn't for the beer I'd have been out of there before the malt hit the barley.

When Cromwell came calling it affected his troops in a different way. To get their kicks they tied two cats together by their tails, set fire to their tails and let them fight it out. Hence the phrase 'fighting like Kilkenny cats'. Cromwell, who hated cats as well as cat-holics, was said to be amused.

Also amused by his stay in Kilkenny was Jonathan Swift who went to the local Kilkenny College together with William Congreve and Bishop George Berkeley. In fact when you think about it they probably had their own Murphy's Cat Laughs Comedy Festival. Jon would do a quick turn about eating children: 'I have been assured by a very knowing American of my acquaintance in London, that a young healthy child, well nursed, is at a year old a most delicious, nourishing, and wholesome food, whether stewed, roasted, baked, or boiled; and I make no doubt that it will equally serve in a fricassee or a ragout.' Notice how even in those days the Irish tailed the Americans. Bill would do his Old Bachelor routine. Bishop Berkeley – nobody ever called him anything but Bishop Berkeley, even when he was at school – would, however, be the star of the show. He would explain the Church's position on gay clergymen. That's always guaranteed to bring any church roof down. If not the whole church itself.

Wander around Kilkenny today and you can still see Swift and Congreve and Berkeley going willingly to school. The tiny medieval streets and Tudor architecture. Rothe House, one of the few old Elizabethan buildings left in Ireland that escaped Oliver Cromwell's attention. Probably had two cats sitting on the doorstep. It's also got what they call slips, tiny narrow passageways or alleys running from one street to the next.

In the middle of summer, the sun shining, the streets packed with people, you can see where the Disneyland gag comes from. But on a dark, dismal day towards the end of the year you get the feel for the real thing. A couple of glasses of Kilkenny or no glasses of Kilkenny, the whole place is medieval.

I start near John Bridge. The castle across the river. I wander up the High Street into Parliament Street. Up through Irishtown and into the rock-solid medieval St Canice's Cathedral where Oliver Cromwell stabled his horses, which ranks him in the Irish mind up there with Sellafield and English lawyers. Once when I went in for a look I was nearly bowled over by a rock-solid old twig, who smelt a bit mardy. She told me she had just heard ringing in her ear which meant one of the Holy Souls in Purgatory was in need of her prayers so, in the name of God, would I get out of her way? Fast. God only knows what she would have done if she had the full nuclear soundbox.

The way back usually takes longer. Much longer. I dodge up and down the side streets, in and out of the slips, take in a couple of bars, a few pints of Kilkenny. Fantastic.

It's not the busiest town in the world. But there's always something to do, somebody who'll tell you their life story. Kilkenny is also for some reason the only place in Ireland where I get into big heated discussions about hurling – and I know nothing about hurling except that a cousin of mine is said to be the greatest hurling champion to have ever come out of County Clare.

I normally check in to my hotel and wander down to the bar by John's Bridge, which looks like a rock-solid branch of a rock-solid bank. Four-square. Squat. Impregnable. Which it once was. There I have a glass of Kilkenny's and talk all night about the likes of Eddie Kefier the hurling legend who led Ireland to the six greatest matches of all time, who lives just up the road.

'The Joe DiMaggio of hurling,' everyone calls him.

'But I never married Marilyn Monroe,' he invariably replies.

Outside Ireland, nothing would possess me to go to a hurling match. It's rough. It's tough. It's bone-shatteringly dangerous. In fact, it's almost as dangerous as a girl's game of hockey. Two teams of 14 unhinged gorillas, who look as though they enjoy nothing better than to skin, joint and tenderise each other, line up across a field the size of a casualty department. Then for hours on end they smash a ball backwards and forwards with a three-foot length of solid ash. Which is your hurley. To the Irish, it's football, cricket, rugby combined. In the ould days they would walk ten miles to a match and ten miles back. Today they'll travel hundreds. To the outsider, it's rugby played with sticks. It's a painful way to break every bone in your body. It's no-holds-barred, all-out thermo-nuclear war. With fewer survivors than Hiroshima.

'Well tell me Patrick, how do ye actually play hurley? I mean are there any rules?'

'Well sure to goodness, there are rules. What d'ye think we are, eejits?'

'OK. So what are they?'

'I'll be telling ye. My throat's a bit dry though. I'll be needing some lubrication, if ye don't mind.'

I still don't know the rules.

The amazing thing is hurley is still an amateur game. The likes of Kefier and my cousin in Co. Clare would be multimillionaires if they were footballers. But Ireland being Ireland all they're interested in is the occasional pint, the craic and the joy of smashing each other to pieces trying to hit the ball 80 yards across a muddy field in a force 10 gale.

'When you're ready, Michael. Another couple of pints of Kilkenny's. God bless.'

Many people say Co. Kilkenny is similar to Co. Armagh. But I can't see it. Co. Kilkenny is nice and friendly. You can understand what people are saying. The country is more soft, green country-side than Co. Armagh. You can also wander around anywhere you like without any fear of being shot. In fact some parts of Co. Kilkenny, especially around Inistioge (Irish for In the movies is it ye are?) on the River Nore, are so soft and green you can hardly see it for huge cars, trucks and Hollywood producers because it's forever appearing . . . in the movies.

I wanted to stay at Cullintra House. I was told the lady of the house had a somewhat individual way of looking after her guests. Dinner at nine. An hour's wait between courses while she fed the fox. Breakfast whenever she feels like it. Which is not as bad as it sounds. I've stayed in some bed and breakfast places where you have to bring your own breakfast with you. But I gave up on the idea. I'd hardly set foot in the place when some psychedelic woppo with a fake Quentin Tarantino haircut is following me around asking me why I haven't got any straw in between my teeth.

Iverk is safer. It's supposed to be home to Ireland's oldest agricultural show which has been running since Adam realised he had to look after things himself.

I was in a bar once just outside of town. This accountant-turned-farmer comes in, all Burberry and bowler hat. We start talking horses. He tells me, Ireland being Ireland, years ago lots of little girls called their ponies religious names like Madonna. As the years went by and Ireland caught up with the rest of the world the ponies were gradually named after Madonna, the musclebound acrobat who, he says, does a bit of singing. Then they were named after her songs, 'Material Girl' being the favourite. The whole trend hit a giant bale of hay, however, when the little girls now quite grown up objected when they trotted into the show ring to the commentator announcing they were 'riding "Like a Virgin".'

I tell you, I'd kill for a day in Kilkenny.

'Paddy. Another round of the black stuff, God bless you.'

Co. Meath
Not to be missed

Famous local resident
Jim O'Connell. The Jim O'Connell in Crossakiel

Favourite food
Thandwicheth

Favourite drink
Guinness

Favourite pub
The one just outside Navan

Favourite restaurant
The one next to the post office in Tara

What to say
What's the bandage for?

What not to say
Where's the motorway?

With Co. Meath it's a case of hit or miss or meath, I was once told by a dried-up old mumblety-peg with a lisp I mean lithp.

On the hit side Co. Meath, or Royal Meath as it is sometimes called, is obvious roasted malting barley country. It is practically nothing but fields. The sod is rich. The farmers are richer still. It would be the ideal place for growing barley if the farmers were not paid so much more not to.

It is also, of course, great hunting country. The Fingal Harriers, the Louth Foxhounds, the Ward Union Staghounds. Any day of the week you can charge across country with them halloing and yarraping for all your life's worth.

In Fingal Harriers country I met one old, battered, bruised fox-hunter who looked as though he'd never left the saddle since he clambered on to his first pony on Laytown sands when St Patrick was still in short trousers. We were drinking whiskey to keep out the cold. He asked me to excuse him because he said when-ever he drank whiskey he had to drink it with his eyes closed because he was scared that if he looked at it his mouth would water and he would dilute it. Wonderful. He then launched into a grand attack on the English and their attitude to fox-hunting.

'By God, you're a funny country,' he says. 'The British govern-ment wants to ban fox-hunting right?'

'Right,' I said.

'Northern Ireland is part of the British government, right?'

'Right.'

'What does the Northern Ireland British government website say?'

Irishman driving the two hours from Dublin back
home to Co. Meath. He's falling asleep at the wheel.

A police car overtakes him and pulls him in.

A policeman gets out and goes up to him.

'Tired, sir?' he asks.

'I am,' he says.

'I don't know if you realise,' the policeman continues,
'but your wife fell out of the car about a mile back
down the road.'

'Oh thank God for that,' he says. 'I thought I'd gone
deaf.'

He took a greasy old wallet out of his pocket that looked as
though it had been in there since the day St Patrick organised his
first collection. He laid it on top of the bar. He opened it up and
took out a clean white sheet of paper.

'The Northern Ireland British government website says,' he
solemnly read from the piece of paper as if he was reading the
just-discovered Fifth Gospel, 'Hunting with hounds is an ancient
field sport which serves as a practical control of foxes as well as
the financial and productive advantages it creates for people in
the countryside. It is also an equestrian activity very much enjoyed
by many horses and riders alike.' He put the paper back in his
wallet, picked the wallet up and put it back in his pocket. 'Funny
country,' he says. 'Funny country.'

He closed his eyes and emptied the glass.

But if the soil is rich, Co. Meath's history is richer still.

Go to Ardbraccan. They'll tell you they have a tree there that has existed since the beginning of the world, an ash, which with three others holds the sky in place above the earth; that the place was once inhabited by giants and that it's a thirsty business talking about the true history of the world, their throats are a bit dry and they'd be pleased to join you in a drop of the Guinness.

Go to Newgrange. Sitting on top of a hill is what looks like a huge Irish prehistoric flying saucer. It's about as circular as a potato cake with about the same consistency. It contains over 200,000 tons of earth and rock. On top it's covered in turf. The Irish say it's the best prehistoric site in Europe, older than the pyramids which, of course, are not in Europe but to the Irish that's a detail; that to build such a site the builders needed mathematics that didn't exist at the time, that the Greeks had not yet got round to inventing and that it couldn't possibly have been built by Irish builders because the roof hasn't leaked for over five thousand years. On the other hand, there's no door and the toilets are outside. You pays your prehistoric money. You takes your pick, as the Irish labourers no doubt said when they were building the thing.

An Irish archaeologist, who looked as though her career was in ruins, told me that come the winter solstice the sun hits the entrance and lights up the whole of the inside of the flying saucer for the time it takes to down a couple of Guinnesses. She even tried to persuade me to enter some archaeological sweep stake so that if my name was inscribed on a coloured rock and pulled out of an ancient druid's hat I could witness the event for myself on the shortest day in 2035. Providing the sky was clear and there were no clouds blocking the sun. When I expressed some hesitation she turned quite prehistoric which made me feel her only hope of happiness would be to marry another archaeologist. He'd be the only person in the world who would be interested in her as she got older and older.

To me, the whole flying saucer thing is uncanny. First, because you don't associate prehistory, ancient mounds, pyramid-like structures with Ireland. My view is quite simple. It if hasn't got a bar, it can't be Irish. Prehistory never had bars. Second, okay they've got it but are the Irish actually interested in prehistory. St Patrick, De Valera, Roy Keane, Terry Wogan. I can understand them being interested in them. But a pile of stones, 300 feet in diameter, five thousand years old. Never. In fact, I'm amazed the whole thing wasn't knocked down and turned into a dry stone wall, 4999 years ago.

Inside the flying saucer, its even more bizarre. You squeeze in through a tiny passage way. Enormous rocks all over the place. Another pint of the black stuff at breakfast and I wouldn't have made it. Then in the centre were three tiny side chapels, each about the size of a pallet of Guinness. The prehistoric archaeologist kept on about them being passage tombs. Tribes fled the sunshine of the Mediterranean to the rain and mist and howling gales of Ireland. They no sooner arrived than they realised what the weather would do to their health. They started building tombs all over the place. So far archaeologists had discovered 39 of them not to mention no end of stones and bits of rock jutting out of the turf which they say once formed the biggest archaeological clock in the galaxy. Or something like that.

To imagine what it was like in those days she then turned off all the prehistoric electricity. It was prehistorically black. I didn't move. I didn't fancy the idea of my career being in ruins as well. After what seemed like five thousand years with the lights back on again, she kept on about me telling her what I thought all the circles and twiddy bits carved on the rocks really meant. I didn't dare. For much the same reason.

What I did tell her was my own theory about the prehistoric flying saucer. It's a prototype pyramid. The builders came from the Mediterranean. They had this big hang-up about burying the dead. The only materials they had were rocks. They used them to build a huge mound. Inside it they built tombs for the dead. Time went on. Building techniques improved. Mathematics developed. The younger sons returned home where, surprise, surprise, there was a remarkable lack of rocks. Only sand. They developed the pyramids instead.

She wasn't interested. All she wanted to do was to get in out of the rain. Which means my theory must be right otherwise, like all women, she would have tried to contradict me.

From Newgrange, go to Tara, the original Irish prehistoric roundabout. From all over the country, five roads met at Tara. Tailbacks would stretch all the way back to the Iron Age. For 1000 years this was the centre of things. This was the seat of the old Irish kings: Con O'Neill, Con O'Ryan and Con the Lot of Them. They're only tourists.

To me, however, the real king of Co. Meath is Eddie Macken, the great showjumper who transformed the legendary Boomerang from a reject and a stopper into the best horse in the world. He's buried under a tree on the main avenue at Rafeeham. Boomerang not Eddie Macken.

Some local archaeologists, however, claim they've even discovered the remains of a Roman temple at Tara. Which, if true, would mean some considerable rewriting of the already hastily rewritten Irish history books.

'But I thought the Romans never came to Ireland,' I remember asking one sad old digger who looked as though he saw everything in black and white, as we sat together in some bar in Tara. He was, he told me, an amateur archaeologist.

''Tis true,' he says. 'As true as I'm standing here.'

'But then there can't be any Roman remains here,' I said.

''Tis true,' he says. 'As true as I'm standing here.'

'But the archaeologists say there are.'

''Tis true,' he says again. 'As true as I'm standing here.'

'But then how can they both be right?' My logical hall-English blood is coming to the fore.

''Tis true,' he continues. 'As true as . . .'

'So who do you believe?'

'I believe them both,' he says. 'Let's drink to their health. I'll be joining you, sir, in a glass of the black stuff, praise be to God.'

If that's not enough, in the nineteenth century a bunch of antique English collar-studs were convinced that also buried here was the Ark of the Covenant.

For me, however, the big question about the Ark of the Covenant is not where it is buried but why the Jews, the Chosen People, lost it in the first place. I mean, think about it. God comes all the way to see you. You don't have to go to him. He gives you the Ark of the Covenent . . . You then lose it. Come on. These guys were not serious. They didn't deserve it in the first place. No wonder God gave them a patch of sand and told them it was the Promised Land. It's more than they deserved.

I only hope the Irish find the Ark of the Covenant. Can you imagine the trouble it would cause? It would be fantastic. The Americans would have to intervene to calm everything down, introduce peace and stability to the situation as they do wherever they go and bring as they say closure. I can hear George Bush even now talking about their solemn duty to restore the Hark of the Covent, which has been disremembered all these years, to its rightful authenticity of ownership, some two hamburger theme park in Crawford, Texas. But that's all in the future. I'm sure one day Tara will hit the big time. But at the moment, it's a case of – I've got to say it – Tara boom delayed.

From Tara the choice is either Trim or Slane. Trim is, well, a trim, little thing. Clean. Neat. Tidy. Even the remains of Trim Castle, the oldest medieval castle in Europe, the true Irish star of the Scottish film *Braveheart*, are spotless. Not a brick out of place. Slane, however, is nothing but spelling mistakes. Bearing in mind the amount of blood that has been shed there over the years from the days of St Patrick himself – this is where he pulled off the great shamrock trick to explain the Holy Trinity – to the Battle of the Boyne, to accidents on the N2 motorway which cuts through the middle of the town, it should obviously be called Slain not Slane. The Conynghams in Slain Castle, famous for Ireland's greatest outdoor rock concerts, should be Cunningham. The Ye Old Post House should be The Old Post House. And the acne-spattered scuzzbucket in the Cunningham Arms Hotel who told me the joke about the Irishman taking a harpoon to the Wailing Wall in Jerusalem should be very careful who he tells jokes to in future because he could be responsible for even more blood being shed in the area.

Kells is kompleathy difrent, I mean Kells is completely different. Forget the Railway Bar. It looks as though it's hit the buffers. This was the site of one of the most important, most cultural, most influential monasteries in the whole of Europe. Over a thousand years ago they produced the famous Book of Kells, a fantastically detailed illuminated manuscript, which was kept in the parish church in Kells till 1654 when Cromwell had it moved to Trinity College, Dublin where it has remained ever since.

The Irish, of course, say it was designed, written and produced by Irish monks. Some people say Scottish monks. They were fed up with being kicked around by the Vikings, moved out of Iona, came across to Kells, built themselves a new monastery and started scribbling, or rather illuminating. The surprising thing is in Ireland everybody talks about the Book of Kells. Nobody talks about the Bangor Antiphony, the oldest Irish manuscript still in existence. Probably because it's stuck in a library somewhere in Milan.

'Maybe because it tells you how the mermaids do it,' my friend, the amateur archaeologist, suggests.

Thereby, as they say, must hang a tale.

The monastery itself was destroyed by the Vikings based in Dublin. The monks were either killed or shipped out. Some, some people say, to Iceland and from Iceland to America. Others to a far, far worse fate, back home to Scotland.

The town itself is worth a book if not an illuminated medieval film. It's been attacked and plundered seven times, burnt to the ground over twenty times and threatened twice with a personal appearance by Bob Geldof. The Church of Ireland Church of St Columba at the top of the town is probably the site of the original great stone monastery church. Inside the churchyard are four High Crosses and one Round Tower. The High Crosses depict various religious scenes. ''Tis the most beautiful one in Ireland,' they say. The Round Tower is also said to be one of the most beautiful of all the 70 round church towers in Ireland built between the ninth and twelfth centuries. Trouble is nobody agrees what a Round Tower is for. A stone house? A watchtower? A minaret with attitude? An overground air-raid shelter? A safe hideaway from whatever's happening outside? The first sign of trouble the priest would rush up to the top, sound the alarm, everybody would rush inside, pull up the ladder, slam the door, keep quiet and hope to goodness the attackers, the American tourists or whoever they were, would forget the whole sorry thing and go home?

'So what's a Round Tower for?' I asked a wizened old leprechaun with a blackthorn stick who was following me around.

'Well it's certainly not for square people,' he cackled, then spat on the ground and vanished.

They also say walk along the streets near the top of the hill: Cross Street, Castle Street, Carrick Street. They form part of the great arc that once formed the outer enclosure of the monastery. I didn't bother. I thought I might meet some square people, I mean, hikers and ramblers. I wandered across to the other famous Round Tower in Kells, the restaurant in Farrell Street next to the post office. Much more fun.

That's the hit side of Co. Meath. Now the meath side, as my friend with the lithp thayth.

County Meath wath where that good King Jameth II wath defeated by bad King William III of Orange at the Battle of the Boyne.

Now ith jutht green fieldth. But in July 1690 they were red. King Jameth and hith forceth were camped out on the slopeth of Donoie Hill, jutht thouth of Oldbridge. King William and hith troopth were on the wetht of the town. They crothed the river near Thlane where Thaint Patrick lit with beacon and thet Ireland afire with the flame of Chrithtianity, and did a flanker. King Jameth retreated firtht to Dublin then Waterford. The Catholicth were cruthed. The Protethtantth triumphant. It wath, depending on who you talk to, the end, the end of the beginning, the beginning of the end, the end of the end, the beginning of the beginning.

Today, however, everybody is friendly. Everybody shakes hands with everybody else except with Brendan Momthey. He shook hands with 14,169 different people in just eight hours at the National Ploughing Championship at Ballinabrackey and established a new world handshaking record. It would have been 14,168 if it wasn't for me.

'Go on there. Shake the man's hand,' all the peaked caps and wellington boots kept shouting.

Naturally I obliged. But I have to admit it was no long, lingering clammy clasp like you get from some sad hooptieth. Two seconds. That was it. Thank goodness.

Another big minus for many people is its success. County Meath is booming. It is one of Ireland's fastest-growing and fastest-developing counties. They are spending money repairing and upgrading the roads. They are even planning to drive a motorway across the Hill of Tara complete with a huge 34-acre floodlit intersection. Is nothing sacred?

When people complained, when they accused the government of trying to destroy one of the most culturally and archaeologically significant places in the world with a special key to understanding the continuous progression of European civilisation, the Taoitheach, the Prime Minister, dismissed them all as 'swans, snails and people hanging out of trees'.

I went into a bar on the way to Navan, the county town, to try and find out what local people thought of the Taoitheach's deep concern for 4000 years of Irish history.

'Will the day hold?' one of the local 4000-year-old residents asked me as soon as I stumbled inside. He had a huge, dirty bandage wrapped around his head, from the top of his head to below his chin and back again. It was, he told me, because he had a headache. He'd banged his head the previous day, which he said put it out of shape. Hence the headache. The bandage was to squeeze it back into its proper shape again. Once it was back in its proper shape again, the headache would be gone.

He seemed the ideal person to ask about the Taoitheach's deep concern for Irish history.

'If it's history you're interested in,' he says, adjusting his bandage, 'ye must go and see the most important person in Co. Meath.'

I thought he was going to tell me about Amedeo Guillet, the man who led a Charge of the Light Brigade against British tanks in World War Eleven, as George W. Bush says.

An Italian, he was leading 350 horsemen drawn from tribes all over Eritrea and northern Ethiopia. Facing them was the advance guard of the British invasion of Italian East Africa. He did what any Italian cavalry officer would do in the circumstances. He charged them. They were cut to shreds. Guillet retired, moved to Ireland and settled in Kentstown, just outside Navan. Today he's in his nineties and still riding. Instead of British tanks he now hath to face British motorists.

But it wasn't Amedeo Guillet.

It was Jim O'Connell.

'Jim O'Connell?'

'The Jim O'Connell of Crossakiel.'

Of course. That Jim O'Connell.

'Crossakiel,' he repeated. 'Birthplace of Jim O'Connell, one of the greatest men who've ever lived. Jim O'Connell.'

And there, opposite Gary's Bar. Alongside the Crossakiel Handball Club. The most historic of all the historic sites in Co. Meath. The monument to Jim O'Connell. The man who wrote 'The Red Flag'. Born just down the road in 1852, he was a Communist before Karl Marx was a Communist. He left home as a lad, went to London, settled down in Lewisham, led the struggle for an eight-hour day and then in 1889 during the London Dock Strikes, inspired by none less than the glorious Battersea and Wandsworth Trades Union Council, wrote the workers' favourite song.

Trouble was, he was five thousand years too late. If they'd had 'The Red Flag' and an eight-hour day then there wouldn't be anywhere near as many prehistoric monuments in Co. Meath as there are today.

Up the prehistoric workers.

The Hops County
Co. Kildare

Most countries have a Great Trek period in their history. Half the population trek from one end of the country to the other to avoid the other half of the population, which is largely composed of their in-laws. Ireland not being a big country didn't have the space for anything like a Great Trek. They also, because of their size and the fact they had so many monks and holy men and VMAT2 God genes all over the place, didn't have so many in-laws to escape from. Instead they had what is known as the Hop period of history. People were hopping about all over the place.

The first and the greatest was, of course, St Patrick himself who hopped across the North Sea, shamrock at the ready, to drive all the snakes before him. About the only definite thing we know about him is that he wasn't Irish otherwise he wouldn't have landed around the year 400. He would have already been there. The other thing we know about him is that he didn't do his followers any favours. He was so successful with the blarney that none of the ancient authorities was against him. As a result none of his followers got the chance to be martyrs as early Christians did in other countries so they missed the chance of getting fast-track entry into the Heavenly Kingdom. Thanks, Pat. An extra thousand years in Purgatory, what do I care?

Not that his followers didn't try to make martyrs of themselves. St Columba hopped off to live on Iona and then in France. What greater sacrifice could any man make? St Brigid went to the dogs as well as the sheep and the goats. Which tells you what she thought of the Scots and the French. St Brendan was prepared to make the greatest sacrifice of all. He tried to hop over to America. Some say he did. The Irish certainly got to Iceland. You can tell by the number of Irish bars in Reykjavik. From Iceland to Boston would have been nothing.

Some say they didn't make it. Do the Americans look as though they have been civilised for over 1500 years? Either way, the Church authorities wanted to have another go at making martyrs. They called for more volunteers to try and reach America. Which created one of the most important and significant cultural and religious movements in European history: the birth of Irish monasticism. In order not to have to go to America anyone with any sense hopped off to the most remote monasteries they could find. Better the chill of a force 8 gale whistling around the bottom of a woolly habit than being stuck in a five-star restaurant on Cape Cod with a clapped-out menopausal trolly dolly wittering on about the joys of dolphin-assisted birth.

The fit, the well and the healthy headed for monasteries down in the Dingle peninsula jutting out into the Atlantic in the south-west, where there was a monastery shaped like an upturned boat, Skellig Michael, a 220-metre jagged rock in the Atlantic and, of course, the Aran Islands off the coast of Co. Galway.

The threat didn't recede. From the ninth to the twelfth century still more and greater monasteries were built to accommodate the rush of keen, sensible, serious, upright Irishmen desperate to do anything but go to America. Monasterboice, just off the N1 to Belfast, for those in the North. Glendalough, for those in and around Dublin. Clonmacnoise overlooking the River Shannon in Co. Offaly for those in the middle of the country.

Once safely inside the monasteries, the new monks had to find a way of staying there. Huge illuminated manuscripts. Of course. A two-page essay on where I didn't go in my Advent holiday would have taken a couple of days. The poor monks could have been on the high seas by teatime. A handwritten one-thousand-page intricate illuminated manuscript, each page the size of the dining-room table, they could be at it for years and still not finish. Irish illuminated manuscripts, as a result, are some of the greatest illuminated manuscripts known to man. To the Americans, of course, they are just something to wrap their freedom fries in.

But that's not all that came out of the monasteries. Irish monks, it is said, because they realised there was nothing anyone could do for America and the Americans, instead decided to educate Europe.

Which is enough history for the time being. Now hop it.

Co. Kildare
What the doctor ordered

Famous local resident
Arkle

Favourite food
Grass

Favourite drink
Guinness

Favourite pub
The Vatican, Kildare Town

Favourite restaurant
Silken Thomas, Kildare Town

What to say
What d'ye reckon in the 3.30 p.m.?

What not to say
Will the Pope be in the Vatican tonight?

Hops put the zing into Guinness.

Co. Kildare's calcium-rich, lush, springy green grass was created not for anything as common as sheep but to put the zing into the world's finest, sleekest and fastest racehorses. To the Irish, don't forget, racehorses are far more important than any wife, child or mother-in-law. Especially wife, child and mother-in-law. They are the reason for eating, sleeping and drinking, the three greatest things in an Irishman's life. Although not necessarily in that order. If a big, famous horse is running nobody goes to work. Until recently children wouldn't go to school either.

Sean O'Faolain, one of Ireland's greatest blathereens, maintains that 'from the age of reason upwards' boys 'discuss the hopes and weights of jockeys, the victories and defeats of the trainers. Later they will also discuss their loves, for Kildare is an alarming place for gossip and its tongue is scandalous . . .' This afternoon I over-heard two of them at it in Newbridge as they hurled their satchels to the ground and squared up to each other in a rivalry of scorn.

'I say, put your shirt on Joe Canty for a five furlong every time.'

'Joe Canty! For crying out loud! Morny Wing for the five furlong. Morny Wing? Morny Wing? God! You might as well put your money on an elephant!'

When a legendary racehorse dies like Arkle, who won the Cheltenham Gold Cup three years running in the 1960s, it's worse than the death of a pope. The whole country goes into mourning. Serious mourning. Not the black tie, a quick Hail Mary and a smoke outside the back of the church mourning. But the real thing. Deep. Solemn. Serious. Half pints of Guinness instead of full pints. That serious.

I was in a bar once in Co. Kildare somewhere. An old jockey, five foot nothing, red face, peaked cap, was telling me how important horses are in Ireland.

'There's this man. His wife dies. She appears to her husband in a dream. She tells him she will be riding along in a fairy procession. If he stabs to death the horse she is riding, she will come back to life. Off the husband goes to see the fairy procession.

> The owners are at the races. A burglar breaks into their house. He is creeping through the sitting room when he hears a voice, 'Jesus is watching.' He looks up.
>
> He creeps into the dining room. He hears a voice, 'Jesus is watching.' He looks up.
>
> He creeps into the hallway. He hears a voice, 'Jesus is watching.' He looks up.
>
> He creeps into the kitchen. There in the middle of the room is a fat old parrot, sitting on a perch.
>
> 'Was that you,' the burglar says to the parrot, 'saying Jesus is watching? It was very good. Really had me going.'
>
> 'Thank you very much,' says the parrot.
>
> 'What's your name?' says the burglar.
>
> 'Henry,' says the parrot.
>
> 'That's a pretty stupid name for a parrot,' says the burglar.
>
> 'Well, I suppose when you think about it,' says the parrot, 'Jesus is a pretty stupid name for a Dobermann.'

'Along comes the horse. He lifts up the knife to stab it. But he can't. He can't kill a horse.' Such, he declared, 'is the regard in which horses are held in County Kildare.'

On the other hand, of course, it could have meant the guy didn't want his wife back. But that's obviously post-revisionist nonsense.

I was in Ireland when Istabraq, the champion hurdler, everybody's hope for the big race on Boxing Day, fell at the last fence. It was front-page news. Nobody was talking about anything else. Least of all their wives, their children and their mothers-in-law. This was far more serious.

As for betting, everybody bets on the horses. A pony here. A monkey there. The week's housekeeping. It's in their blood. Kids know how to calculate the odds before they can read. Old people refuse to die if they've still got an outstanding ante-post voucher wager in their pocket. Even priests and nuns. What am I saying? Especially priests and nuns. Come the big races everybody knows a priest or a nun who has backed all Charlie Swann's winners the first day of the meeting as well as two on the last day.

Only one priest's gamble, however, is still considered shocking. He was Father Nicholas Callan. His gamble? Electricity would be a winner. The reason his activities were shocking? He was fascinated by the early days of electricity and used to experiment on innocent volunteers such as a future archbishop of Dublin who he completely knocked out. But it was worth it. He went on to invent things like the induction coil, dynamos, galvanisation. He developed low-cost batteries which were sold as the Maynooth battery. He also forecast the invention of electric lighting. But the Irish never talk about him. To them, he's a loser. He never backed Charlie Swann's winners the first day of any race meeting let alone two on the last day.

But maybe the good priest wasn't holy to blame.

'In the old days racing wasn't as modern as it is today,' another old racing priest once told me as we were trudging back across the fields after a funeral.

Everyone is also a tipster. Everybody knows somebody who

knows somebody who works in a racing stable, saw the horses out on the gallops, spoke to the wife of the brother-in-law of the second cousin of the sister of the vet who has only just got back from the stables. The great tipsters are almost as popular as St Patrick himself.

Years ago I knew a great champion tipster, Dare Wigan, who used to work for the *Financial Times*. Wherever he went, whatever racecourse he was on he was immediately recognised. People would be forever rushing up to him saying, 'Hullo, Dare.'

The money they make, it's not important. They give it away. To bars. To banks to pay off their gambling debts. To bookies for the big meeting on Saturday.

If races are fixed they take it in their stride. Give the horse too much to drink before the race, if he's a good horse he'll still win. A drop of croton oil, a secret purgative, he'll run twice as fast. A shot of ACP, acetylpromazine. He'll walk it in his sleep.

It's the fun. It's the racing. It's horses even though some of them are burdened with names that sound as though they were chosen halfway through a not particularly pleasant late-night chicken tikka at Paddy O'Reilly's Traditional O'Tandori Restaurant and Bar: Please Be Good, Adulteress, Geespot by Pursuit of Love out of My Discovery, Cleopatra, 'a tricky ride' and, of course, Knickers, 'Never looked like coming down.'

Because the grass is so rich and so lush and so springy, Co. Kildare is home to not only one world-famous racecourse but two: the Curragh and Punchestown. A third, Naas, is also world-famous. But only to locals.

The Curragh is the greatest show on turf. It's Epsom, Chantilly and Kentucky all rolled into one. From March to November it is host to some of the biggest flat-racing events in the world: the 1000 and 2000 Guineas, the Irish Derby, the Irish Oaks as well as the Irish St Leger. The Curragh itself is around 20 square kilometres of beautiful, springy, unfenced, vast open heath. In the distance the Wicklow hills or rather mountains. It's the perfect training ground for any racehorse as well as a playground for the Irish army. Many's the time I can remember driving through there and being stopped and searched by the army.

Once, I remember, in the middle of a raging Co. Donegale of a gale.

I stopped the car. The soldier, a fresh-faced young innocent who looked as though he should have become a nun, made me get out. He took everything apart. He even made me take my jacket off so he could search the pockets. I was soaked. As I climbed back in I asked if he knew the quickest way to Dalkey, south of Dublin.

'Are you going by car,' he says, 'or on foot?'

'By car,' I said slowly.

'Bedad,' he says. 'That's the quickest way.'

He then turned and fled back to his sentry box out of the rain.

Punchestown is the jumps, steeplechasing and home to the Irish National Hunt Festival, the SAS of the horse world. If these guys had been in the Charge of the Light Brigade they wouldn't have been worried by a bit of gunfire. They would have sailed right over the top of the cannons and been in Istanbul by the time the pubs opened.

As for Naas, it's the place to go for a winner. Especially if you're looking for a high-powered luxury sports car, like a BMW 530 TDI, a Fiat Leon or even a Mercedes Kompressor on the cheap. Know what I mean? But don't whatever you do say I sent you.

Huddled around the racecourses are all the top trainers apart from the top ones like Aiden O'Brien who is at Ballydoyle in Co. Tipperary, where he believes the grass is even richer, even lusher, even springier.

'Horses,' a tiny leprechaun of an ex-jockey once told me in a bar outside Newbridge. 'This has been horse country since forever.'

The Curragh even sent horses off to Napoleon to fight the British.

'Don't you believe it,' the barman says. 'If it's tomorrow's runners and riders ye are interested in don't come here. Take yeself down to the beaches of Kerry.'

I left them to fight it out.

They're probably still at it.

As if God's own horse country, two world-famous racecourses and one world-famous to the locals local racecourse is not enough,

Ireland: In a Glass of its Own

Co. Kildare is also home to a string of other world-famous horse institutions.

The Irish National Stud founded in 1900 by a Walker, Colonel Hall Walker of Johnnie Walker fame, is dedicated to the future, to breeding nothing but the very best, the fastest horseflesh-and-blood racing machines on earth.

The Irish Horse Museum is dedicated to the past. It's the holiest of holies. It's St Peter's, the Dome of the Rock and Vanessa Feltz all rolled into one. At the heart of it are the bare bones of Ireland's greatest racing legend, some say the greatest steeplechaser of all time, Arkle, who won the Cheltenham Gold Cup three years running in the 1960s – 1964, 1965, 1966. To say 'won' is to under-estimate him. He beat the competition into the ground. He pulped them. He blew them away. He annihilated them. His epic duels, every second of them, with archrival the great English horse Mill House, are still deeply embedded in the soul of every true race-goer.

When I was there, standing by the statue of Arkle in the museum wiping a tear from his eye was one of them.

'A wife is a wife,' he says. 'But glory be to God, I loved this horse.' He gulped hard. I thought he was going to go into a Co. Donegale of a blub.

'He also made me a lot of money, God bless him,' he goes on. 'More than that slattern of a wife of mine. Lost me every penny he made me.'

But to begin with Arkle was an ordinary horse. Owned by Anne, Duchess of Westminster, he was trained by Tom Dreaper at Greenogue in Co. Kildare. His first jockey, Pat Taaffe, always maintained 'he moved so terribly behind, you could drive a wheelbarrow right through between his legs'.

But before long he was winning race after race after race. In all, out of 27 races over fences, he won 24 of them. The last, the 1966 King George VI Chase, he came second even though he'd broken a bone in his leg. Reports of his recovery and treatment were front-page news not only in Ireland but in most of the racing world as well.

Stand and watch the homage, the reverence, the sheer eye-

134

watering devotion accorded the pile of bones and you'll never mock again the crowds queuing up to touch the big toe of St Peter in Rome, the tooth of the Holy Buddha in Kandy or even more important, Graceland, Elvis Presley's hang-out between hamburgers in Memphis, Tennessee.

On the way out, however, one of the attendants stopped me. He looked like a reformed alcoholic who'd gone back on the bottle.

''Tis not him ye know,' he whispered. 'I was there the night they buried him. Two hours later some young fellas came over and dug him up again, took him away on the back of their bike. 'Tis another one. But they had to have something for the visitors. TTTSHH. Ye didn't hear a word I said.'

Next to the museum is for some reason a Japanese garden. Not, I hope you understand, that I am in any way paranoiac but I thought it was because from there they could build a tunnel to get into the museum to steal all the secrets, take them back to Japan and build bigger and better racehorses with which to conquer the world. But it was not true. It's all down to a local horse owner and trainer, Lord Wavertree, who did everything by the stars. If a horse's horoscope was wrong he would refuse to train it. If the stars told him not to race a horse he wouldn't race it. The Japanese garden? The stars told him to do it.

That's what they say.

I didn't bother to go in. Taurus seemed to be in conjunction with Venus. Pluto didn't seem none too pleased about it either.

Instead, it seemed like the time had come to visit not an ordinary establishment, not a grand castle, not even a palace but the Vatican itself. No, not that Vatican. The other one. The important one. The scruffy, run-down bar in the middle of Kildare town. Not to pick up the latest on whether Cardinal Dionigi Tettamanzi, the archbishop of Genoa, would make a better pope than Cardinal Count Christoph Schoenborn, the archbishop of Vienna, or even Cardinal Dario Castrillon Hoyros, the head of the Congregation of the Clergy. But for a laugh, a drink, some gossip. Another drink. More gossip.

Many's an evening I've spent in the back room of the Vatican. Many's the drink I've taken. Many's the things I have learnt.

You want to train a jumper?

Put a pole in front of the stable door. Whenever they come out, whenever they go in, they have to jump over it. Gets them used to it.

Any of your cattle have problems?

Forget the vet. Blow cigarette smoke up their nose. The fairies can't stand smoke. Off they go. Your cattle will immediately get better.

Arthritis.

The only way to cure it is by singeing it with the flame of a burning newspaper. Preferably the *Irish Times*.

I even heard one old booze-hound lamenting the fact that 'there's people dying now that never died before'.

After my first visit, I remember, I came back home and happened to mention to our local priest that I had spent the previous Friday night at the Vatican. Poor man. For a split nanosecond of eternity a look flashed across his face: Hey, I've spent over 60 years of my life looking after this lot, how come you get the night out at the Vatican? When I told him – joke, joke – the Vatican was, in fact, a pub, his expression completely changed. He was even more annoyed.

Not that the Vatican is the only watering hole in town. The other one is St Brigid's Well. All over Ireland there are holy wells. Sometimes I think there are as many holy wells in Ireland as there are bars. They are everywhere. Usually in the ground. Most are fully official, fully authorised and fully patronised. Others are local, hidden, secret.

The official ones are grand. The big ones are like holy swimming pools. The smaller ones are like holy goldfish bowls.

Big or small they put the likes of Lourdes to shame. Morning, noon or night you can see people kneeling in front of them, standing saying their prayers or just crossing themselves quickly as they pass by.

'So what do people pray for when they go to a wishing well?' I once asked a father of ten children who looked as though he was looking forward to the thrill of garrotting himself.

'Single girls,' he says, 'wish for a husband. Married women wish they were single. Married men just hope for the best.' St Brigid's in Kildare town is supposed to be one of the best. Some say it's because St Brigid along with St Colmcille and the other one whose name I forget is one of the top three saints in the country. They say she proposed to St Patrick. But he bought her off by suggesting women should be officially allowed to propose marriage on 29 February. She agreed. Only to discover later that 29 February only comes round once every four years. Whether she's popular because people sympathise with her or with St Patrick I've never been able to find out.

I hate saying this but my sympathies are with St Brigid. Not only is she Irish she has an Irish view of heaven. Read the writings of most of the saints. It's all very, well, heavenly. St Brigid's are Irish.

> I would like to have the men of Heaven in my own house
> with vats of good cheer laid out before them.
>
> I would like them to be merry in their carousing
> I would like to have Jesus among them, too.
>
> I would like to have a great lake of beer for Christ the King
> I'd like to be watching the heavenly family drinking
> it down through all eternity.

St Brigid's well in Kildare town, however, is down there with the dregs. How do I know? When I was trying to get into the cathedral grounds an old lady, who looked as though she could have been St Brigid's sister, told me not to waste my time because she said the only way to know if a holy well was going to do its job was if there was a tiny white fish swimming around in the bottom of it.

'And that well,' she tosses her head towards the well, 'that well has no fish. It's a fraud. Take my word.'

I took her word.

Ireland: In a Glass of its Own

In spite of St Brigid's, I like Kildare town well enough. I always go out of my way to go there, have a quick couple of pints in the Vatican, wander around. Sometimes if I've got business in Dublin and even if there's no racing I'll still stay in Kildare and catch the train in the morning into Dublin like a regular commuter.

The gateway to this horse heaven is Newbridge which is not what the gateway to a horse heaven should be. In the old days the British cavalry used to be based here, the barracks running the length of one side of the road. Facing it, the town on the other side. Obviously not any more. Today it's more suburban Dublin. The talk in the bars is about wives and children – their own wives and children – the cost of living, what was on television yesterday evening. To tell you how different it is from the rest of Ireland, it's the only place where I don't mind staying in b. & b.s. Go anywhere else in Ireland and if it's cold they'll ask you if you would like your bed warmed. If you say yes they'll send one of the sons upstairs to warm it for you. Or worse still, as you climb the stairs you'll see a hunched figure in a candlewick dressing gown shuffling down the corridor. In Newbridge if all the b. & b.s are taken it's because they're packed with salesmen on the way to Dublin.

The rest of the county is pretty much the same. But then anything compared to the Curragh, horses, Kildare town, is bound to be pretty boring.

Kilkea, yawn, was Ernest Shackleton's home town. Ireland's stone-cold English heroic failure.

Maynooth, yawn, once used to be famous as far away as China for turning out thoroughbreds of its own who could tackle anything, overcome any obstacle and come racing home with the prizes. From 1795 St Patrick's College there has been turning out priests. Not just your ordinary local priests. But the top-class, smooth, championship priests destined for the toughest foreign mission assignments you can imagine. Move over, SAS. Here comes Father Reilly. Many of them were living and dying in China in the old days when to even be suspected of being a priest meant death. Today everything seems to be in second or perhaps even third gear. The challenges are not so dangerous. The priests are nowhere near as numerous. The town itself also looks like a chop suey that has gone off the boil.

Similarly Monasterevin. At one time when Luciano Pavarotti and the other tenors were only a fiver, this was a place of pilgrimage for fans of the legendary Irish tenor Count John McCormack, still regarded by many as the greatest tenor of all time.

'Sure, he must be,' one old boy who looked like a glamour-challenged New Age dustman says to me in the Vatican one evening, 'he's sold more records than them others.'

'Well,' I began nervously.

He put his glass down on the bar.

'So God help us,' he declares.

He was that kind of Irishman.

'Will ye tell me how many 78s have the others sold? John McCormack sold millions, I tell ye, millions. And these others . . .'

There was only one thing I could say.

'Willyebehavinganotherone?'

The Yeast Counties

Co. Sligo
Co. Mayo

Without yeast there would be no Guinness. Yeast is the big converter. It will take an ordinary liquid and turn it into pure gold. Today, according to many experts in the drinks business, whisper it not, the best yeast comes from Denmark. So too in Ireland. The best yeast was the Vikings even though, at the time, they couldn't affjord it.

Come the ninth century they were virtually everywhere. In Dublin where Oxmantown is derived from Ostman, Viking for Men from the East. In Waterford, which is of course derived from Waterfjord. In Nore Valley, Co. Kilkenny, which is derived from Norse Valley. Other parts of the country honoured their presence: Fair Head, Hook Head, Mizen Head, Clogherhead and, of course, Blacksod. Laytown, Co. Meath commemorates their principal activities; Devenish Island, Co. Fermanagh their homeland because people thought the furthest north they could have come from was Devon. The exception was Limerick town. The Vikings made little impression on it. Even in those days professional rapers, killers and pillagers were scared of the local Limerick gangs.

With the raping and the pillaging out of their system, the Vikings settled down. They made themselves at home in their coastal settlements. All the old stone shacks and bronze buildings they turned into proper little towns with houses, squares and streets lined with traffic cones. They opened shops but because business was slow they invented coins which made it easier to go bankrupt. They even began to export to the rest of Europe. One of the biggest exports being all the gold and bronze jewellery produced during the Gold and Bronze Age. The Vikings exported everything back home. You want to see the best of early Irish art. Forget Ireland. Go to Norway instead.

Ireland: In a Glass of its Own

Without the Vikings, Ireland would not be what it is today. The Vikings brought them into the modern world. They did for Ireland what the Romans did for the rest of Europe. They taught them trades and skills. They showed them how to build towns and cities. They showed them how to trade. They introduced them to the outside world.

With business booming in their coastal settlements, the Vikings decided to expand. They began to move inland. But they very quickly found they had problems opening up Volvo dealerships throughout the country. Many skirmishes had to be fought with local warlords much as they have today. One of the biggest was at Clontarf in 1014. The local warlord and Irish hero, Brian Boru, both won and lost. He won the war. But lost his life. Volvos continued to roll across the country. The only way Ireland could defend itself was by turning the clock back hundreds of thousands of years: to the Blarney Stone Age. Instead of building their houses, towns and monasteries in wood, they built them in stone. That way they couldn't be burnt down.

The Vikings liked what they saw. Even more. Instead of packing up and going back to the frozen wastes, Strindberg and Oslo on a Saturday night, they decided to stay. They threw away their helmets, gave up on the raping and pillaging and became Irishmen. The women, it is said, were not unhappy. A big, strapping, 6-foot-3-inch blond Viking made a change from a man in a black suit with a cloth cap who never took the pipe out of his mouth.

Co. Sligo
Yeast is best

Famous local resident
Yeast

Favourite food
Yeast

Favourite drink
Guinness

Favourite pub
Yeasts'

Favourite restaurant
Yeasts'

What to say
Yeast said soonest mended

What not to say
I must arise and go now

Co. Sligo, squeezed between south Donegale to the north and the mountains of north Mayo to the south, if that's not too Irish, is Yeast country personified. Although, the Irish being the Irish, they often misspell it and call it Yeats country. Either way as chintzy Sunday afternoon anthology lovers the world over know, Yeast or Yeats, the upper-class Irish Protestant snob with the designer-rumpled shock of grey hair falling carelessly over his forehead, the starched collar and tie, the fancy black ribbon tied around his glasses no doubt in the days before Sellotape was invented to keep them together, who accused lower-class Irish Catholics of forever fumbling 'in a greasy till', helped make Ireland what it is today. He gave it a style, a sparkle, a magical feel. The likes of Dromahair, Benbulben, Knocknarea, Cummeenn, Gencar, Drumcliffe, the Rosses and, of course, Innisfree would be no more than dull names on an unknown map if it wasn't for Yeast/Yeats. For which I will never forgive him. You can't get near them today for back-to-front-baseball-cap gutbuckets who think they're sophisticated because they drink nothing but Pepsi and Pabst Blue Ribbon and quote *Reader's Digest*.

But without Yeast or Yeats, I admit, Ireland would be duller, stodgier, not so, well, magical. More like, well, Wales. Which in many ways is amazing because Yeast or Yeats was no way your typical Irishman.

'Gaelic is my native language,' he once drawled in that languid manner of his, 'but it is not my mother tongue.' Much the same way I suppose he might have lounged back in his house in Dublin or his flat in London and said, 'Wife coming. Maud Gonne.'

Maud Gonne was, of course, his scrunch, his local mentally challenged bedutante. Why, I have not the slightest. She doesn't look as though she'd stick her mother tongue in your ear while you were finishing your pint of the black stuff. If she did she'd only make you feel you needed a couple more. Pints. Not tongues. Yeats and Maud, however, made one hell of a rhyming couplet.

> Protestant church next door to a Catholic church. The roof of the Protestant church is full of bats. The roof of the Catholic church has none.
>
> Vicar says to the parish priest, 'How come we've got nothing but bats in our church roof and you haven't got any?'
>
> 'Easy,' says the Catholic priest. 'We used to have nothing but bats. But I gave them confession, holy communion and confirmation. Never seen them again.'

He wasn't a drinker either. He maintained he only visited a bar once in his life. He preferred tea and the tea bags who served it up. He minced around in his fancy tweed suits, somebody once said, like one of his beloved swans at Coole. He spoke in a soft sing-song voice that made asking for a cup of tea seem like Keats's 'Ode to a Nightingale'.

He made a big deal out of 'We Irish', a phrase which he lifted from the good Bishop Berkeley of Co. Kilkenny, that Irish philosopher of vision, who couldn't even see through a glass darkly because his eyes told him it was clean. But he refused to shake hands with anybody, Irish or otherwise. In any case you can bet your next glass of Guinness that Yeats's 'We Irish' referred more to the Golden Age of eighteenth-century Ireland and the likes of Swift, Burke and Goldsmith rather than the desperate years of the famine, the mass exodus and the Troubles.

It's also amazing that Yeats is so closely associated with Co. Sligo. He probably spent more of his life in Dublin and London than he did in Co. Sligo.

> Boldly and openly to Dublin and London
> I go but to my scrunch I sly go.

He is said to have scribbled this on the back of a beer mat when he caught the midday train from Dublin. Which left at 1.36 p.m.

It might have been only a phrase he was passing through but it made such a powerful impression on his 'We Irish' neighbours, they decided to name the county after it. But as Dublin and London were already taken they were left only with Sly go. Such is the way great decisions are taken.

Yeats was born in Dublin, went to school in Dublin, as a senator he lived in Dublin. Oliver St John Gogarty called it his silk hat period. After he left the senate he settled down in, where? Dublin, where because he was so loved by his fellow Irish he was forced to live with an armed guard on his home in Merrion Square, after a disgruntled 'We Irish' no doubt evicted from his bee-loud glade on Innisfree because of gawping tourists took a pot-shot at him while he was working one day in the drawing room.

Another Co. Sligo writer, however, has had far more day-to-day influence on the world than Yeast/Yeats but nobody talks about him. William Higgins, who was born in Collooney, came up with the idea of rearranging the letters of the alphabet to fit different chemical elements: H Hydrogen + O Oxygen + G Guinness = One hell of a night out. He also came up with the fancy lines linking them all together.

Sligo town, however, is pre-Yeast/Yeats. It's better now than it was. In the old days it was dull and stodgy. It was difficult to see if there was any life in it at all. Today it's slightly less dull and stodgy. Not just because they've turned up the music in the local Tower Hotel so loud you can't hear yourself think about complaining about it but because of the fighting and the brawling that goes on all over the place.

Last time I was there it was like World War II meets Baghdad.

Ireland: In a Glass of its Own

Two brothers and their families practically wrecked the place or if they didn't it looked like it. The fighting started outside of town. Both sides, who lived up on a street in Granmore, were armed with pickaxe handles, hurley sticks and knives. There was talk of attacks at petrol stations, cars being driven at people, people being threatened with murder. Finally the fighting moved to the local police station. Fighting? One of the police inspectors told the local court it was 'mayhem'. The judge, however, let everybody off. No doubt aware that it didn't do any harm to liven up the place from time to time. That and the fact, I suppose, he didn't want his own house smashed to pieces.

Fighting in Sligo town is also said to have inspired Yeast/Yeats to write one of his famous poems. Staying with friends they say he heard so many of them say 'I will arise, put on my flax jacket and go now into town and trust I will be free' but because he was forever talking to the fairies he got the words all wrong and came up with something about arising and going off to a lake to escape the violence.

Sligo town is still, however, a filthy place to live or stay. There's so much rubbish all over the place it's known as Slugole town. Even Yeats's office, which has been re-created in the Yeats Memorial Building on Douglas Hyde Bridge, which every year organises a Yeats Summer School which in Yeats's honour teaches fairies to write like fairies about fairies, is a mess. Papers all over the place. Books everywhere. One of the old twigs in charge told me it wasn't Yeats's fault. It was all because of the totally insane, unreasonable, paranoid demands of his publisher. I didn't say a word. Well I couldn't could I? Publishers insane, unreasonable, paranoid? Never.

If that's not bad enough, there's the greatest insult of all. Those paragons of tidiness, cleanliness and order, those wonderful people who would never dream of letting their dog foul the footpath let alone have what they call a pee-pee in public, the French have offered to come over and help them clean the whole place up. Their first proposal: to get every kid in town to make little drawings about their feelings towards the environment. Where are all the drawings going to end up? Thrown on the streets. Wonderful people the French. Such a lot they have to teach us.

Local sociologists, however, blame the violence on the water. It's got a funny smell. It's supposed to be full of bacteria. Faecal bacteria. But nobody I spoke to was bothered. They never touched the stuff anyhow.

I'm not saying Slugole town is not fun, but the only laugh I had the whole time I was there was the name of the local firm of solicitors: Argue and Phibbs.

Some people put Slugole's problems down to being a crossroads town. On the coast, on the River Garavogue and behind it Lough Gill, it was founded by the Normans who thought from there they could control the rest of Ireland. Little did they know the Irish. Then it became an important link between the North and the South. Travellers could go whichever way they liked. But they had to cross the bridge at Slugole town. Inevitably, they say, this brought in the business but with the business it brought in problems.

Others, sane, sensible, rational men, dismiss this argument as being too simple. The reasons Slugole is a mess, they say, are far more complicated. It's the Protestants. There are too many of them around. It's more Ulster than Ireland. Many people, in fact, call it Little Belfast.

Way back in the early 1600s the English shipped in as many of them as they could. In the mid-1600s the locals tried to solve the problem. Many of the British newcomers were rounded up and thrown in jail. Irish mobs then attacked the jail killing practically everybody inside. At first many Brits, who had escaped, fled. But by the 1650s and the 1660s they were back again, old settlers returning, new settlers, soldiers who had served in the wars of the 1640s: they decided to stay.

By the nineteenth century the wealthiest landlord in Sligo was the British Prime Minister himself, Viscount Palmerston, of gunboat fame. A Brit threatened anywhere in the world by Johnny Foreigner, send out the gunboats. He was an absentee landlord, of course. Too busy trying to keep the world in order to worry about Slugole.

Depending on who you talk to some people say that today as much as half the population are Protestants. Others say that at least half the population are Catholics.

Ireland: In a Glass of its Own

In the bar in the Tower Hotel one evening – I was too scared to go into any of the local bars – a local eminent social philosopher, who was obviously to the spanner born, put it another way: The Catholics go to Killarney. The sly go to Yeast/Yeats country. Maybe the story about the poem was right after all.

A couple of pints later another leading local froleen blamed it all on a certain Tom Healey, a famous fiddler from Ballymote who could do with the fiddle the opposite of what the Pied Piper did with the pipes. In Tom Healey's case, if you crossed him, he would send a plague of rats to your home and that would be the end of you.

The surrounding countryside is everything Slugole town isn't: lively, exciting, peaceful. Some say better than even Killarney or Connemara. Which is why the Irish always refer to Yeast/Yeats country and never Yeast/Yeats town. Charles 'The Water-Babies' Kingsley, who also wrote a novel called Yeast, couldn't make up his mind either. One minute he was going on about it being 'a land of ruins and of the dead. It moves me to tears.' The next minute, this champion of the poor and oppressed was raving about the number of salmon waiting to be hooked: 'I had magnificent sport this morning. There is nothing like it. The excitement is maddening.' Some fisher of men.

Most people start their tour of Yeast/Yeats country at Lough Gill, which, of course, is named after a favourite measure of alcohol, and end up in the churchyard at Drumcliffe. Benbulben in the distance. If there were going to be any living sacrifices to the gods to try and save Yeats's soul this would be the place. A table-top mountain. A 1700-foot plunge to the ground below where himself is buried.

I decided to do it the other way. The Go-sly way. I wanted to be certain the man who believed it was only possible to 'educate Catholics mentally and Protestants emotionally', who believed in Home Rule for his own reasons, who was a politician who in 1917 invested in machines that received and amplified messages from the spirit world which he hailed as 'the greatest discovery of the modern world', was definitely dead and buried. The last thing I wanted was to suddenly turn round and see him, a bundle of horoscopes in one hand, Maud Gonne in the other, staring at me through his wonky glasses.

The first thing that surprised me about Drumcliffe was that he was buried there at all. I know his great-grandfather was rector there a million years ago, the fuss the Irish government made when he died in the south of France in 1939, how he was too important to be left there and how it took them practically ten years to arrange to bring the body home. I'd have thought he would have been enshrined in Dublin, outside the Abbey Theatre or maybe facing the post office, in the middle of a fairy circle or even at the bottom of Innisfree. The other thing that struck me was how conventional it all was. A grave like any other. A stone and surround like all the others. A simple epitaph he wrote for himself rather than pay a poor professional writer to come up with something inspiring:

> Cast a cold eye
> On life, on Death
> Horseman, pass by.

Me, I would have suggested something short, something meaningful, something that people would remember for ever like

> Here today. Gonne tomorrow.

Or better still:

> Gonne but not forgotten.

As it is it looks like the grave of someone important like the local auctioneer or even the local magistrate who gave his life to maintain law and order in Slugole town.

It's not as if the locals don't care about literature. This is after all where two saints, two holy men of God, went to war against each other over a book. In the left-hand corner of the monastic boxing ring, St Columba. In the right-hand corner, St Finian. St Columba borrows a prayer book from St Finian. He copies it. St

Finian demands back both the original prayer book and the copy. St Columba refuses. Both upright, honest, strict churchmen agree the matter should be decided by the state. King Diarmuid decides in typical Irish style 'To every cow its calf. To every book its copy.' St Columba disagrees. Both holy men come to blows. Their supporters come to blows. Battle. Blood. Killings. Then surrounded by blood and gore because he still hadn't won, St Columba sails off in a huff to the Scottish island of Iona, Irish for Iona the book but St Finian wants it back.

Yeats should have stayed in France. They'd have named no end of streets after him, thrown medals at him, made him an honorary member of every academy you can think of. They would have accorded him the status that rumpled shock of grey hair, the starched collar and tie and the wonky glasses deserved.

When I went to Drumcliffe the rain was lashing down so hard that I wouldn't have gone out in it to see my own grave. But I did to see Yeats's. The way he's been treated, I thought it was the least I could do. In France, of course, they would have arranged that no rain ever fell on the grave of such a great man.

As I was standing there looking at the grave a cruddy retired Mr O'Yorrick shuffled up to me.

'I wouldn't have that,' he says. 'I want to be alive when I die so I can make all my own arrangements. Good day to ye.'

He doffed his cap and was gone. Not, I would have thought, to Innisfree. More to where it costs about €2 a pint.

Maybe he was one of Yeats's fairies. A grave-protector fairy. Unable to use the magic machine linking the real world with the spirit world.

Maybe he was one of the people who believe Yeats is not buried there in the first place. Look at the facts, they say. The French agree to anything anyone else suggests even a request from the Irish government? Never. The French be able to find anything after ten years especially as after five years the body was dug up and moved to your typical French chamel house of old bones with hundreds of other bodies? Impossible.

Not so, say the true believers. It's the man himself. Yeats wore a truss probably as a result of his strenuous activities with Maud

Gonne. The bag of old bones sent back by the French contained a truss. The man in the box is, therefore, himself.

I don't know about about you but it seems to me which ever side you believe a great deal has to be taken on truss.

Having beaten my way to Drumcliffe I was now ready for the tour. Most people go by car. I thought I'd go by boat. It might be slower. But it was bound to be safer. There was also less chance of being buried by heavily French-accented rubbish.

Up from Sligo town we went along the River Garavogue into Lough Gill which they say is owned by Prince Charles and there's the Isle of Innisfree – or is it? The boatman couldn't make up his mind. First, it was. Then, bejasus, it wasn't. Then we didn't know whether we were looking at the same island twice. In the end I gave up. Not only did they all look the same, all the islands looked so covered in trees I couldn't for the life of me see how anyone could pitch a tent on any of them let alone build a small cabin of 'clay and wattles made'.

The boatman, however, gave me a tip: 'Whichever way the wind blows on Halloween it will blow for the whole of the winter.'

Who needs Michael Fish?

I didn't fancy going back to Slugole town with the rubbish swirling along the streets with grave accents and the bacteria starting to glow in the twilight. Instead I decided to go to somewhere much safer, Mullaghmore, which is a wonderful, tiny harbour. A solid harbour wall. A beach. Two hotels, the Beach Hotel and the Pier Head Hotel. The perfect hideaway. Providing, of course, you're not Dickie Mountbatten and the IRA are not after you, whether or not you're a left-wing royal, a Republican sympathiser, a lifelong friend of Noel Coward's or a regular reader of the *New Statesman*.

I also stopped off in Ballymote, a tiny village with a Church of Ireland church in the centre which was being refurbished and I swear a bar called The Fawlty Towers. I could be wrong. It was a long day. I had stopped once or twice on the way.

I was going to head for Strandhill, get a couple of buckets of cockles and mussels to take back to the hotel for dinner, but in the end I thought I'd better complete my Yeast tour of Yeats country or my Yeats tour of Yeast country. You never know what those fairies could do to you. Although I have my suspicions.

I made for Lissadell House, the childhood home of probably the greatest single inspiration of Yeats's life, the heroine of the Irish struggle for independence, the all-Irish Countess Markiewicz, who would have stuck her mother's tongue in anyone's ear. When she was released from jail in Britain, she travelled back to Ireland and finally when she arrived home they say she received a one-minute-long standing ovation. Which I would have thought was nothing to brag up. After all, think about it. She was arriving home. Most of the people doing the welcoming home were obviously staff and they were being paid for it. If she'd have been arriving back in the Polish home of her husband, the staff would have kept the ovation going for about three weeks just to avoid doing any work. And why a standing ovation? It all sounds too terribly English for somebody who was desperate to get rid of them. I'd have thought pints of Guinness all round with a shot of Wyborova would have been far more appropriate.

Yeats talks about visiting the house, how he was captivated by the baby Markiewicz and her sister, Eva, the surrounding landscape and how it influenced so much of his poetry. I thought it was going to be, well, Yeatsian. Dark. Forbidding. Long mysterious corridors. Huge twisting staircases. An overgrown garden. A terrible beauty. Long black ribbons holding everything together. The occasional fairy. No way. It's more Beckett – Samuel not Thomas – than Yeats. It's a soulless, grey, limestone Georgian mansion plonked down on a patch of grass on the northern shore of Sligo Bay. There's nothing interesting let alone exciting about it at all. Even the most enthusiastic Irish estate agent would have problems working himself into a lather over it. It's nothing but gch, gge, bedrooms and pot. for dev.

I also thought it was going to be chintz all over the place, zebra-skin rugs, cod psychobabble and – parked outside – an armour-plated 3x3 Robin Reliant. Not at all. Inside it's got about as much atmosphere as a Russian Ministry of Culture. The Great Hall is about as enticing as a doctor's waiting room. The decorations are sparse. The quality of most of the furniture is about on the same level as William McGonagall's 'Tay Bridge Disaster'. Yeats's so-called bedroom has a single bed and a modern duvet on top of it. How authentic is that?

Wandering around, however, did give me one idea. Maybe Yeast/Yeats country should not be in Sligo at all but in and around London. After all, true Irishman that he was, he went to school in Hammersmith; kept a flat in Woburn Buildings, Bloomsbury; was a member of the Savile Club where he used to talk to the mirrors telling them to adjust his image; ran away with Ezra Pound to a cottage in Ashdown Forest to study Norse sagas and no doubt one or two other things; married in the Harrow Road Registry Office; and boasted that 'everything I have has come to me through English'. Although I suppose if it was in London, the centre couldn't hold, the whole Yeast/Yeats thing would fall apart.

Getting into Lissadell House wasn't Innisfree either. It cost me a fortune. But at least I didn't get beaten up.

Co. Mayo
Mayo may not be the best

Famous local resident
Herself

Favourite food
Whatever goes with port

Favourite drink
Guinness and port

Favourite pub
Ashford Castle

Favourite restaurant
In the hotel I'm not telling you

What to say
Have you ever won any wars or are you French?

What not to say
Are you from around here?

Co. Mayo may not provide more yeast or sparkle to Ireland than Co. Sligo.

They've had the French come calling. They've got one of the best hotels in the world. It's where St Patrick himself came to banish all the snakes from Ireland. And if that's not enough to convince you, it's the only place in the country that's been visited by Herself, the Blessed Virgin, the Holy Mother of God. No, she didn't stay at Ashford Castle or even in the stables at Ashford Castle. She stayed at Knock, a tiny village in the middle of nowhere. On the west wall of the local church. And, if I haven't mentioned it before, Co. Mayo has got one of the other best hotels in the world. Because in every room they give you a free decanter of port.

The downside is the women are a touch independent. They all think they're related to Grace O'Malley, crook, bandit, pirate queen, plunderer, tribal chief who once visited Queen Elizabeth I in London but refused any gifts on the basis that she was her equal and equals did not patronise equals. It's also the wettest part of Ireland but, the Lord bless them and save them, if you've got a free decanter of port waiting for you when you get back to your hotel, who cares?

The French landed in August 1798 which is not bad when you think they had a good few million years to get ready for the great day. Three times the honourable leaders of Revolutionary France tried to invade. Twice they turned back. The third time they only succeeded because their three frigates sailed into Killala – Irish for 'Kill the Frogs' – Bay under General

Humbert. Humbert flying the English flag. A typical underhand French manoeuvre.

Some say it was to back the Irish rebels against the English. Others that it was to creep in through the back door to try and take England itself. A few even said they wanted to join the annual pilgrimage to Croagh Patrick, the oldest pilgrimage in the world, where for thousands of years people have been climbing the mountain in their bare feet to commemorate the day St Patrick banished snakes from Ireland. Don't you believe it. The French

---

Reverend Mother goes out behind the convent at Knock to talk to the chickens.

'OK,' she says. 'The Pope is coming next week. Lots of guests. I want you all to start laying five eggs a day from now on so that we can put on a good spread. If not, you're for the chop.'

The following morning she goes out into the yard.

The first chicken has laid five eggs.

'Very good,' she says.

The second chicken has laid five eggs.

'Very good,' she says.

The third chicken has laid only three eggs.

'OK,' she says. 'That's it. You're for the chop.'

'Typical Reverend Mother,' says the third chicken. 'You do your best. They're never satisfied. And I'm a cockerel as well.'

---

would never commemorate a thing as sacrilegious as that. They would never have banished them. They would have eaten them. A few have even claimed they were trying to get their hands on the formula for making Guinness which was hidden in the false bottom of a drawer in a desk in Ashford Castle, the Guinness family home in Cong, which stands for Carry On Nocking back the Guinness. But they failed.

Instead they took Killala and Ballina and marched on Castlebar. A young French bugler spotted English troops planning to attack, sounded the alarm and was promptly shot for his troubles. Well, what did he expect? An invitation to Buckingham Palace? Note to French buglers. If you see the enemy coming, get somebody else to blow the damn thing. The English, however, felt guilty about it and allowed themselves to be defeated. The French expressed their appreciation by proclaiming the town, in their endearing low-key way, the Provisional Republic of Connacht. It was about the last time the French army beat anything in their lives. Apart from maybe the occasional oeuf brouillé.

Tell you what. If you want a laugh log on to Google and type in "French military victories". Hit the 'I feel lucky' button. There's not a single French military victory on the whole World Wide Web. When we did it a message kept flashing up, 'Do you mean French military defeats?'

As for the French bugler he was buried on the hill of Turlough where even today they say on some summer nights you can still see and hear him sounding the alarm. I can never go to Turlough without thinking not of the French bugler but of a grand old Anglo-Irish patriarch I knew a million years ago called Turlough O'Brien. He was great company. Gossipy. Chatty. Indiscreet. Always good for a drink and a story. The kind of character you would find in a William Trevor novel. But with laughs. Turlough town, however, is the opposite. A bit staid. A touch serious. Which, I suppose, is not surprising when you think it is still trying to shake off the reputation of one of their local lords who ruled the place like a Genghis Khan/Mrs Thatcher/King Herod clone. He had his own army fully equipped with arms stolen from any number of local shipwrecks. He hunted by night, fought duels at the slightest hint of an insult and once threw his father in a cage with his pet bear for months on end. In the end he was arrested by somebody else's troops, the government's, tried and sentenced to death. He turned up for the hanging ceremony smashed out of his mind, clambered up the ladder, put the rope around his neck, took a flying leap into the crowd which had turned up to gloat – and broke the rope, the ladder, the gallows, the whole caboodle and escaped. To ruin a good story, he was eventually recaptured, sobered up and the job was done properly.

From Castlebar the French made for Sligo, crossed the Shannon and headed towards Dublin. The English decided one own goal at the hands of the French they could put up with but there was no way they were going to let them make a habit of it. They headed them off and sent them running at Ballinamuck near Longford.

But as anyone who knows the French knows, French influence lasts for ever. Like an overstrong string of garlic. There are signs and statues and discreet memorials to the French all over the place. Pick up an old Irish prayer book. Tufts of dry hair flavoured with Gauloise tumble out. Talk to anyone about anything, every other sentence they're beseeching the well-known French lady, St Fairy Anne.

A number of French memorials are also wandering around Co. Mayo today.

'Before the French came,' a serious schoolteacher type with rimless glasses told me, 'the middle of the night was known as the wee small hours. After they left they were known as the *oui* small hours.'

Well, he was drinking white wine, I admit.

One of the best hotels in the world is Ashford Castle, once the Guinness family pad, a huge, sprawling manor from heaven set in the middle of 25,000 acres down in the south of the county. Is it French or Irish? French. Everybody there drinks far more French wines and champagne than Irish. There is even an obelisk in the grounds inscribed in French, '*Rien n'est plus. Plus ne m'est rien,*' which roughly translated means, No Guinness. More wine. Me? Whenever I go there I drink Guinness. What's the point of going to Ireland and drinking French wine? It's stupid. I always drink local. I admit in some countries it doesn't work. But in Ireland, it's fantastic.

The Prince of Wales went there in 1905 for what he described as 'outstanding woodcock shooting'. One evening I asked the barman if there were still plenty of game birds in the area. Two caps off the top of a bottle of Guinness and a stamped addressed envelope, I'll send you the addresses.

I always try and go there out of season. That way I don't have to meet the likes of Bono or, God help me, Bob Geldof. That would be a bundle of laughs, that would. I don't have to keep avoiding Americans who keep on about how many innocent Iraqis they killed that day. And it's cheap. Don't tell them or they'll put the prices up. The last time I stayed there I paid less than I paid in some ordinary-looking shack with no restaurant in Co. Down. In any case I reckon I practically own the place. The amount of money I've spent on Guinness over the years I'd have thought just about covers everything. Well maybe not the ashtrays. Trouble is whenever I stay there I keep thinking: If I hadn't spent all that money on Guinness over the years maybe I could own a place like this.

Cong Abbey nearby is in ruins. The whole thing, it is said, collapsed of a broken heart when it realised the Guinnesses were leaving Cong for ever.

Talk to the auld tshilibuas in the local bar, who wouldn't know what a white wine was if they had to milk it, and they'll tell you they got their own back on the French. Every hour the post office at Blacksod Point used to phone their weather reports to London. On 4 June 1944 the Allies were poised to land in France and begin to roll back the Nazis all over Europe. The post office told London things were looking grim. A cold front was crossing the north-west coast. Heavy rains and force 7 winds were on their way. Operation Overlord was postponed.

'Serve 'em right,' one ould sod cries, wiping the tears from his eyes.

'But was it true?' I asked.

''Tis a pint of the black stuff I'll be having, godblessyesir.'

Cong – to the north, Lough Mask, to the south, Lough Corrib, short for Corribean because so many super-rich people live in and around the area who holiday at the Irish-owned luxury Sandy Lane Hotel in Barbados – is also *Quiet Man* country, the John Wayne classic about the killer Yank boxer going back to his roots to try and forget. You either love it or you hate it. John Wayne is John Wayne. Maureen O'Hara is Maureen O'Hara. Barry Fitzgerald is Barry Fitzgerald. The Irish are the Irish, nothing but boozers and brawlers. I love it. It's hammy. It's corny. It's nothing but the purest paddywhackery but I can watch it again and again and again. And I never watch films. The last time I went to the cinema the piano broke down.

But a couple of glasses in the local bar and you soon discover *The Quiet Man* had precious little to do with Cong. The cottage where the action or rather the lack of action takes place was in Maam, down the road. The railway station was at Tuam. The licentious, shocking, crude scene where Mary Kate takes off her stockings, causing heart attacks the length and breadth of Ireland, was in Thor Ballylee, once home to Co. Sligo's pin-up boy, W. B. Yeats. As for the bar, that's in Hollywood, although I was told there are plans to ship it back. You can bet your life it won't end up in Cong.

About the only genuine link Cong has with *The Quiet Man* is Pat Cohan's bar. Except it wasn't a bar then. It isn't a bar now. But that hasn't stopped them. After all why let the truth get in the way of a good story? There are *Quiet Man* postcards, *Quiet Man* books, *Quiet Man* anniversary celebrations. There is even a worldwide *Quiet Man* fan club. Cong today also has a *Quiet Man* Cottage Museum, a *Quiet Man* Coffee Shop, a *Quiet Man* Tour on a *Quiet Man* jaunting horse and cart. There is also a *Quiet Man* Heritage Centre dedicated to the men of Co. Mayo who were reduced to silence by the blatherings of the French and how it took the arrival of an American by the name of John Wayne to get them going again.

When was the film made? 1952. Still, over fifty years later, they can't keep quiet about it. And the amazing thing is most of the people going on about it look as though they couldn't tell whether a silent film had a soundtrack or not.

Poor St Patrick, by comparison, is practically ignored. Even in Killala he has to fight for attention and he founded the place.

Co. Mayo

You also have to look hard to find any mention of the fact that the site of the first Christian church in Ireland opened by St Patrick is today buried under the foundations of the local Church of Ireland cathedral.

But whenever I go there I always have other things on my mind. Like rain. It doesn't just pour with rain, it comes down like Co. Donegale stair rods. But I shouldn't complain. One year I was there, they told me down the road in Crossmolina it had just rained for over 110 days non-stop. They'd had over 25 inches of rain. There wasn't a wellington boot to be seen in the shops. Doctors' surgeries were full of young people complaining of rheumatism and arthritis. The only people who were celebrating were the fishermen. They hardly had to get out of bed let alone out of the house before they could land a big, juicy catch.

I blame St Patrick's Tower, which looks less like a tower and more like a French nuclear silo. It's so high it pierces the clouds. Which, I reckon, causes the non-stop rain.

In Ballina they say they speak with a French accent. I'm not surprised. It was the first town to allow itself to be captured when French troops landed in 1798. What's more even today they have their own Mardi Gras. Which, I admit, starts at 10 o'clock as dusk is falling, winds its way through the streets and ends up with a firework display. On the other hand the fact it takes place in July, drugs are kept to the minimum and everybody keeps their clothes on especially the ould messieurs suggests they haven't quite got the hang of it.

To me Ballina is a mini-Westport – the River Moy runs through the middle of it. Either side is a mall. It is also famous for its musical bridge on the road to Belmullet. Musical? Yeah. If you grab a big stone and run it up and down the metal railings. Another Irish con that has brought in millions of US dollars in its time.

In Ballinrobe, a busy little crossroad town, they don't make music or even speak at all. This is Captain Boycott country. Such was his long and lasting relationship with his boy tenants that they were so much in awe at his presence they were unable to even wish him good morning let alone goodbye. His girl tenants, however, would never agree to a girlcott. Lucky them.

Castlebar is different. They'll talk about anything. Trouble is you have to be careful who or what you're talking about. If you hear people talking about the Castlebar races or even inviting you to take part, beware. The Castlebar races were, in fact, a massacre. Of the English. By the Irish. Helped by the French. It all happened a long time ago. In 1798. But you know how the Irish love a good story. If, however, they're not talking about the Castlebar races they might very well be talking about the Charge of the Light Brigade. No not the wimps who rush up to a bar to order a lemonade shandy. The real thing. The Earl of Castlebar Castle, who was known as the Exterminator, was reckoned the most savage of all the savage English landlords during the famine. Not only did he evict tenants and their families dying of starvation, he brought in Scottish farmers to replace them, built a racecourse for his amusement and established his own personal criminal courts to try and convict his own tenants. Such a paragon of virtue had no problems later ordering the Charge of the Light Brigade.

If, however, you do get involved in a friendly bar-room discussion watch out for the quiet man sitting in the corner with his hat pulled down over his face. It could be one of the Earl's descendants, Lord Lucan, the one who murdered his children's nanny in London in 1974. Some people say he never disappeared. He just came home. It's just that after the way his great-great-great-great-old man behaved nobody took any notice of him.

As for Castlebar itself, it looks as though it stopped breathing about the same time Lord Lucan's nanny stopped breathing. They've got their share of run-down old buildings. They've got some smart modern buildings. A few bits of modern sculpture. But more than anything they've got more than their fair share of satellite dishes and hi-tech communications equipment all over the place. The communications mast in the backyard of the police station is about the same size as the Eiffel Tower. Which can only mean one thing. The Irish are expecting the French to invade again. All the communications equipment is to ensure that they can immediately double-check any Frenchman who turns up waving the English flag claiming to be English. Clever guys the Irish.

With all this illegal phone tapping and spying on other people's conversations going on, it's no wonder the confessional boxes in the churches in the area are so overloaded. Some of the priests, as a result, have introduced their own special sin-bins to speed up the whole process. In Islandeady Church, the local priest has installed no less than four sin-bins, an idea he cheerfully admits he got from chatting away one weekend with his nephews about rugby.

Other churches have gone the other way and cut down the number of sins. Many's the time I've been told an Irishman has gone to confession, admitted killing an English soldier only to be told by the priest it's not a serious offence so it's not worth confessing.

Some churches, however, are still churches. Every year over 1.5 million people come to Co. Mayo to visit the church at Knock which ranks alongside your other famous places of pilgrimage, Lourdes, Fatima, and Medjugorje.

Virgin might not fly into Knock but the Blessed Virgin herself does. On 21 August 1879 she appeared to no less than 15 local people on the west wall of the village church. In the background two unknown figures. Not a word was spoken. Some say that was because there was there was no way even the Blessed Virgin herself would understand the local Co. Mayo accent.

The Church investigated and confirmed it was for real. At first only local people came visiting. The sick were healed. The disabled walked again. Slowly its fame spread until the arrival of Father Horan who was more parish impresario than parish priest. He decided to put Knock on the map. Worldwide. He campaigned. He promoted. Because he knew Co. Mayo had the worst roads in the country, he built a local airport to handle the crowds he knew would one day come visiting. On schedule. On budget. Which argues for using parish priests to build airports in future rather than all these expensive, highly trained civil engineers and project managers.

Father Horan also got off his knees and practically insisted the Pope came visiting. That did it. They were made. Move over Lourdes and Fatima. Knock was up there with the best of them.

Ireland: In a Glass of its Own

So confident were they that people were going to be cured, they didn't even bother opening a chemist's shop in Knock to cater for coughs and headaches. It was only a couple of years ago the local Western Health Board caved in and gave the go-ahead. They were suffering from a perpetual migraine caused by all the local residents complaining about having to travel to Claremorris, Kiltimagh, Ballyhaunis or even Kilkelly for an Elastoplast or a cough sweet.

From all over Ireland people now head for Knock, admittedly with the help of some smart ecclesiastical marketing. One of my aunts in Ennis, Co. Clare, about 100 miles away, claims her children passed all their examinations thanks to Knock. She would catch the special Knock pilgrimage bus in Ennis in the evening after work, arrive in Knock around midnight, pray like mad until 4 o'clock. At 4 o'clock go to mass. Be on the coach at 5 o'clock. Fall asleep. Be back in Ennis again at 7 o'clock ready to go to work, tired, exhausted but confident that her children's future was secure.

From all over Europe people also come. The groupies who visit every shrine practically regardless. The 'Our Lady' fans who go to 'Our Lady' shrines. And, of course, those who can't resist the combination of a visit to a shrine, mass in the huge underground basilica and a pint of Guinness afterwards.

I haven't been to Lourdes or Fatima. But I've been to plenty of other shrines for all kinds of religions and non-religions but Knock is somehow different. If anything it's more practical, down to earth, even workmanlike. You're in. You're kneeling down. You're saying your prayers. You're giving money, as they say, to disabled children. You're up and you're out again. It's like a shrine run by men who spent their time at horse shows or cattle markets.

I went to mass once in the big circular church. Every two minutes, literally every two minutes, the priest was looking at his watch as if he had a miracle to catch and didn't want to be late. In the end I gave up bothering with anybody trying to pass any examination and went out and wandered around town, well, up and down the street outside. It was empty. No crowds. No people. No wheelchairs. It was either an off day or there were no examinations waiting to be passed.

I went into a bar. Why not? This is the religion whose leader turned water into wine. There in the far corner were a group of Nigerians huddled together trying not to be noticed.

An old boy, a parasite for sore eyes, puts his Guinness back on top of the bar.

'Blacker than a famine potato. That's what they are,' he whispers to me.

'They're here for the shrine?' I wondered 'Like everybody else?'

''Tis people smugglers they are,' he says. 'Knock. 'Tis a grand cover. Everybody says they're here for the shrine. They go to the shrine. They come here. They wait. They're collected. They disappear. See it all the time. I'll join ye in a Guinness if I may. 'Tis only the courteous thing to do, the Lord have mercy on us.'

Another old boy joined us. Old. Dishevelled. He looked as though he left a slug's trail behind him wherever he went.

''Tis false bank drafts they're into,' he whispers.

Yet another old boy joins in. He looks more gone to seed than disintegrated.

''Tis false/stolen credit cards,' he insists.

As far as the Nigerians were concerned, therefore, it was a case of Opportunity Knock.

Like the Nigerians I'd been to the shrine. Now I had to get to the famous airport. I wanted a taxi. My friend at the bar said they were all out of town.

'Collecting people to come to the shrine?' I wondered.

'Not at all,' he says. 'Taking ye friends to secret addresses all over the country. 'Tis making a fortune they are. That's why nobody's reporting it. 'Tis good business, thanks be to God.'

'So how do I get a taxi?'

'Try the newsagent,' he says.

Of course. Why didn't I think of that? The *Irish Times*, please, a packet of fags and a taxi to the airport. It's obvious isn't it? You want a drink, you go to the grocer's. You want a taxi, you go to the newsagent.

The taxi driver, tall, busy, an animated *Sunday Times Business News*, Irish edition, told me he'd lived there all his life. He'd been baptised in the local church, had his first communion there, had been an altar boy there for years. Even today at his grand old age helped out wherever he was needed.

'So you believe it?' I said.

'No,' he says. 'It's not possible.'

'So why do . . . ?' I began.

'Except,' he says, 'I've seen it happen. I've seen people get up off their stretchers and walk.'

As we hurtled down the lanes like a horse and cart on speed, he told me the story of a Dublin doctor. For 15 years he'd been bedridden. For 15 years his family had brought him to Knock, praying for a cure. For 15 years, the doctor told them it was a waste of time. He was a doctor. He knew his medical condition. He knew there was no way he could walk again.

'I was with the priest himself,' says the newsagent taxi driver part-time altar boy. 'He was going around blessing everybody. It was almost routine. He'd done it a million times before. Nothing had ever happened. It was as if he didn't believe what he was doing either. He comes up to the doctor. He didn't take any notice of him. It was routine. He splashes him with the holy water and walks on. The doctor, I swear to God, not a word of a lie, the doctor gets off his stretcher and stands up. The priest, he couldn't believe it. The hair on his neck stood up on end. Nobody could believe it. Nobody. Not even the doctor. But there he was after 15 years being in his bed, standing up and walking about. The poor priest. He nearly had a heart attack.'

'So you believe it?'

'No,' he says, ''Tis not possible.'

'And the doctor?'

'He comes back here every year on the anniversary of his cure. He helps in the church. He helps other people who are bedridden.'

'You've spoken to him.'

'A million times.'

'He told you he was cured. You saw it. You must believe it.'

'No.'

'Why?'

'Quick,' he says, 'there's your plane. You'll have to run or you'll miss it.'

Co. Mayo

On the plane on the way back, I sat next to a smart young accountant type with a neck brace.

'No luck then,' I said.

'Not at all,' he says. 'I only wear this thing for the up-grades.'

Turn up at a check-in, he told me, he not only gets up-grades, he gets a wheelchair. He is waved through security. The other end there is another wheelchair waiting for him. Straight through security. Right to the head of the taxi queue.

'You should try it,' he says. 'It's the greatest.'

No way. Knowing my luck if I wore one for over two minutes I'd trip up over a statue of the Virgin Mary, break my neck and end up by being in a wheelchair for the rest of my life. I've got enough problems as it is. Thank you.

The other famous miracle about Co. Mayo is Achill Island, so called because of the harsh Atlantic climate. Everybody who goes there catches a cold. It is the Aran Isles meets civilisation. It's bleak but friendly. Isolated but busy. Reasonable but expensive. In other words, the Achill heel of Co. Mayo.

The largest island off the west coast, it's surrounded by, they say, shark-infested waters. Although the only sharks I've ever seen there were in the Railway Hotel. All black jackets, black suits and earrings. Trouble is every time I go there I end up drenched in heavy rain or I suppose it could have been the spray from the Atlantic. It's not quite Co. Donegale. But it's getting there. The advantage is you never know how long you've stayed there. The sky is the same colour day and night. You can never tell whether you've been there three days or three weeks. It's so bad even the dogs are frightened to go out during the day. Nobody can see the foxes creeping across the new bridge linking it to the mainland in order to kill all the local chickens. Neither can the fishermen see the sharks when they go out fishing in their souped-up curraghs. My advice. Stand by the bridge and watch them swarming in. In BMWs. In camper vans. In enormous hiking boots.

In Aughness, a tiny village on the edge of the Atlantic itself, I found they were more concerned about salmon than sharks. Every year the fishermen face more and more restrictions. Every year they have lower and lower catches.

'In the old days we'd be landing 500 fish a day,' a battered old Captain Ahab with a cloth cap tells me. 'Now we're lucky if we get 500 fish a season.'

Westport, I go to not for the free decanter of port – whatever gave you that idea? – but to visit the town where by chance the hotel happens to be, where the Carrowreagh River meets Clew Bay, which some say is as beautiful as Bantry Bay. With a free decanter of port thrown in.

To me Westport is vintage Georgian. Well Irish Georgian. It is laid out Georgian-style with two long malls either side of the river and two squares, one of which is called The Octagon, which is dominated by a statue of St Patrick.

'Peerless Westport,' said William Makepeace Thackeray when he dropped in.

Whether that was a warlike Yorkshire working-class joke or a description of its glories I've never been able to find out.

On the North Mall is The Olde Railway Hotel, which Thackeray thought was 'one of the prettiest, comfortablest inns in Ireland, in the last part of this pretty little town'. And so it is today. Except first thing in the morning, upstairs, the corridors are full of blokes wandering around in their underpants. Which, the first time I had the privilege, gave me quite a turn. I thought they were looking for a back passage. Then I realised. The Olde Railway Hotel is the only hotel I know in the world where they put the trouser presses outside the bedrooms instead of inside. That's Ireland for you.

The hotel I try to stay in is just outside of town. Not just for the free decanter but because I don't fancy wandering around with other blokes in their underpants first thing in the morning. Well, that and the fact the last time I stayed in The Olde Railway Hotel I couldn't get away from this Marley Tile salesman whose sole aim in life was to fold Irish banknotes into various letters of the alphabet which he then made up into all the filthiest words in the English language.

Maybe William Makepeace would have appreciated his turn of phrase. I just wanted to drink.

The name of the hotel which puts a free decanter of port in

every bedroom? I'm not telling you. If everybody starts going there they might change their mind. I get little excitement in my life as it is.

In the old, old days come 23 June everybody in Westport would dance around fires on Peter Street and Church Lane and elsewhere. In the background bands would be playing. Around the fire old women would be hobbling and dancing, saying their rosaries and throwing stones into the fire. Not any more. They ran out of stones. Now there are plans to throw the old women on to the fire.

Today on the last Sunday of July, which they call Garland Sunday, everybody sets out to climb to the top of Croagh Patrick, the Holy Mountain, which is always covered with either mist or pilgrims. Or both. It was here on the summit St Patrick fasted and prayed for forty days and nights. If the old shlimazls in the bar at the Olde Railway Hotel are to be believed, it was only after forty days and nights he was able to persuade God to make Ireland his own. Any other country, they said, it would probably only have taken a few minutes. Either St Patrick was a lousy salesman or Ireland was a difficult sell.

As if that was not enough to be going on with, afterwards St Patrick had a one-to-one with a certain evil Crom Dubh, who lived on a fort on the cliff. Crom Dubh hurled shafts of lightning at him. St Patrick, holy man that he was, returned the shafts of lightning but, because he was a holy man, below ground not above ground. The flames below created the Hole of the Ancient Fire, which even today is one of the most fantastic blowholes in the world. During the French invasion, locals hid down there for safety. Such is the way of the world they escaped both the French and the English but were drowned by the sea. Above ground, St Patrick, ever eager to love his enemy, hurled his crozier at Crom Dubh and cut off the lump of cliff on which his fort was built.

If you want to clamber to the top of the Holy Mountain and do the job properly you leave Westport at midnight, walk five miles to the foot of the mountain and start putting up the scaffolding there. No. No. That's a joke. You take your shoes and socks off and, still fasting, climb the 2500 feet to the top. Which, of course, some people also consider a joke.

Ireland: In a Glass of its Own

Those who are seriously dedicated to the life of the spirit do it from Gwen Campbell's pub at Murrisk. They start with a couple of pints, race up to the top in their Nikes and race back down again for another couple of dozen before it closes. I tried it once. But it didn't do my soul any good. Come to think of it, it pretty much ruined the rest of my shoes as well.

Real enthusiasts, however, forget the whole thing and tuck into a mountain of cakes and Swiss rolls washed down by barrels of Guinness in training for another famous Co. Mayo annual fixture, Roundy Roundfort, the search for the roundest, not necessarily the fattest person in the land. Every year two or three fat people used to roll into the village of Roundfort so that it became so overcrowded that the competition had to be moved to a field outside where there was more room.

Once I got within five miles of the place but I couldn't see anything for heavy lorries, fork-lift trucks and massive swaying mountains of flesh almost as big as Croagh Patrick itself.

The winner I discovered later weighed in at 32 stone, 6 stone ahead of his nearest rival. And to think 200,000 Mayo people died during the famine.

The ideal way of finishing up my trip to Co. Mayo was I thought a quick look at Moytura House near Cross, built in 1865 by Sir William Wilde, surgeon, author and father of Oscar. But everybody told me it was always known as a house of no importance. So I didn't bother. I went back to Gwen Campbell's pub instead.

I Mayo may not go back there again next time.

The Protein Counties

Co. Kerry
Co. Westmeath
Co. Tyrone

Proteins are body builders. They help to replace the parts of a body that have become run-down, weak or anaemic. They boost. They strengthen. They reinvigorate. Just as the arrival of the Normans boosted, strengthened and reinvigorated Ireland after the Vikings had gone native and soft and taken to the drink and telling silly stories all hours of the day and night. Once the Normans had conquered England and Wales, there was no stopping them. They saw the Vikings enjoying themselves in Ireland and decided to follow in their giant footsteps. But because they came with a cause, to civilise and not like the Vikings to rape and pillage, it was known as the giants cause way.

What's more they did it the French way. Like General Humbert Humbert sailing into Killala Bay, they denied they were French. Instead they said they were Northmen. They were related to the Vikings. They shared the same ancestors. They had both crossed the Bering Strait. Therefore, they were Northmen. They came from Northway.

The Vikings said, No way. They were pure Vikings. The French were impure. Which shows you how perceptive the Vikings still were even though they had gone soft.

The result was the French turned nasty. They got the English to do the dirty work for them. Their excuse, as ever: a woman, Dervorgilla, Irish for 'She smells like a gorilla'. She had just left King Tiernan O'Rourke and ran off with King Dermot MacMurrough, Irish for You're going to need more than a mac to survive this storm.

King Tiernan did what any Irishman would do if his wife ran off

175

with his best friend let alone his second-worst enemy. He went off for a couple of pints of Guinness with his mates. His courtiers, obviously at the mercy of their own wives, protested. Why should he have all the laughs when they were working day and night and still going home to a miserable old sack of potatoes? They forced him to drive King Mac out of Ireland. Which was a silly thing to do. It also proves how much the courtiers were at the mercy of their wives because only women could have come up with such a stupid idea.

King Mac immediately went to see Peter O'Toole who was playing Henry II at the time. He gave him permission to recruit an army in England and to return home and throw King Tiernan out of house, home and the local bar. The Earl of Pembroke, Richard Fitzgilbert de Clare, said he would back King Mac. He would recruit a bunch of English, Irish, Scandinavian and French mercenaries to fight for him. But on one condition. If they were successful, when King Mac died, he, the Earl of Pembroke, known to his friends as Strongbow on account of his liking for cider, would take over. The land of Guinness would become the land of Strongbow. King Mac agreed.

The two of them returned to Ireland. With them went all the upright, honest, God-fearing English, Irish, Scandinavian and French knights money and the promise of money could buy.

They landed at Banbow Bay, County Wexford at 11.69 precisely. To them it was a sordid matter of getting their own back on King Tiernan for stealing King Mac's wife and throwing him out. If they got his kingdom back they were happy. Nobody said a word about getting his wife back. That wasn't even on the winelist.

To Irish historians, however, it was – can you hear the roll of drums? – the start of 750 years of the English Jackboot Embedded Deep Into Their COUNTRY. It was only in 1922, with the establishment of the Irish Free State, that the jackboot was lifted and they could breathe again.

Objective Irish historians also cannot help but point out that the invasion was backed by the Pope. Who was the Pope? Adrian. Where did he come from? Yup. You got it. England. He was the only English pope in history. And what did the only English pope in history try to do to Ireland? He tried to crush it.

The Protein Counties

Give that man a pint of the black stuff and a BA in Irish Studies.

Before you could say the English pope gave the English king permission to do a Tony Blair in Iraq, the English jackboot was all over the place. The following year, 1170, the Irish-Anglo-Norman army landed at Baginbun Head on the Hook Peninsula, Co. Wexford, fought off a much larger Irish force and by August were whooping it up in Waterford. King Mac did the only decent thing he could. He gave his daughter Aoife to Strongbow who would have preferred a pint of the best. But that's life.

Having got the English to do their dirty work for them, not for the first or the last time in history, the French then moved in and took over. Churches and cathedrals were built. New religious orders were imported. Towns and cities were built each with their own lord mayors, town clerks and town councils. A proper legal system was introduced. Coins were minted. Oh yes and castles were thrown up all over the place in Dublin, in Kilkenny, in Cashel, in Limerick, in Clonfert to ensure Ireland stayed French and nobody else's.

But it wasn't all one-way. The French learnt a lot from the Irish, who they praised as 'a filthy people, wallowing in vice'. The men, they said, 'in many places in Ireland debauch the wives of their dead brothers'.

There you are. If it wasn't for the Irish, France wouldn't be the country it is today.

Co. Kerry
It's Kerry gold

Famous local resident
General de Gaulle

Favourite food
Killarney anything at all

Favourite drink
Guinness

Favourite pub
Killarney Grand

Favourite restaurant
The Great Southern

What to say
Bonjour, Mon Général

What not to say
Would you like me to bring you your letters, *Mon Général*?

In the old days, they said there were two heavenly kingdoms: the Kingdom of God and the Kingdom of Kerry.

Don't you believe it. Co. Kerry is no kingdom. It's almost pure protein. It's milk. It's butter. It's cheese. It's fish. It's also some of the most beautiful scenery in the world. Before or after you've had a pint of the black stuff. Still deep blue lakes. Gentle soaring mountains. Deep, rich valleys. Lush lowlands. Smooth beautiful fields. Wide open wetlands. Spectacular coastline. Long sandy beaches. Glorious bays. Forget Samuel Beckett. He said the fields of Co. Kerry were covered with nothing but 'uneaten sheep's placenta'. But then he would say that wouldn't he?

It's also got the rich, colourful language to match. Deep blue adjectives. Mountainous exaggerations. Lush adverbs. Spectacular overstatements. You think I'm exaggerating. Paidi O Se, manager of the Kerry football team once rounded on his own supporters: 'Being a Kerry manager is probably the hardest job in the world,' he declared, 'because Kerry people, I'd say, are the roughest type of f++++++ animals you could ever deal with. And you can print that.' Print that the Irish newspapers did. Which, of course, made him hastily backtrack.

'What I mean is,' he said, 'the Kerry supporters are very hard to please, always demanding the highest standards because they are a very proud race of people.'

Nice one Paidi. Nobody believes a f++++++ word of it. Stuff that in your deep blue lakes and smoke it.

Co. Kerry, however, is as Paidi O Se would say, f++++++ marvellous give or take a few football managers.

181

If you feel run down. If you want to be reinvigorated, remodelled, recharged in order to live another 1000 years it's the only place to go on earth. Apart from all the others. I declare to God, it's the

> Three nuns die and arrive at the Pearly Gates.
>
> St Peter says, 'I'm sorry. I don't know what's happened. But we're full. Go and wait over there.' He points to a bench. 'I'll sort things out. I'll come back to you in a minute.'
>
> The nuns wait for one thousand, two thousand, three thousand years. Eventually St Peter comes back to them.
>
> 'OK,' he says, 'All sorted. One quick question. Give me the correct answer and you're in.'
>
> To the first nun he says, 'What's the capital of France?' She says, 'Paris.' He says, 'OK. You're in.'
>
> To the second nun he says, 'What's the capital of Italy?' She says, 'Rome.' He says, 'OK. You're in.'
>
> The third nun is a Reverend Mother. She says, 'Now what's all this keeping me waiting all this time? Here am I, I've given you the whole of my life. This is not what I expected. It's not good enough. And to have to sit with the other nuns as well. For three thousand years. It's not good enough.'
>
> 'OK,' says St Peter. 'One quick question and you're in. What's the capital of Swaziland?'

land that adrenalin forgot. Fierce busy. They don't know the meaning of the words. Tinnitus. They've never heard of such a thing. Years ago, I was told, it was also known as the land of grey dresses. Dark blue was Co. Cork. Blue was Co. Galway. Today nobody is interested. Nostalgia isn't what it used to be.

You might also, of course, dramatically enrich your vocabulary. Half an hour in a bar anywhere in the county, you'd think you were in the Seamen's Return in Bangkok. And that's lunchtime. The evenings are even worse. That's when the women turn up.

Young people go to Co. Kerry for the scenery and the food. They have some spectacular restaurants. The first time I went to Killarney I can remember having a beautiful roast duck in a restaurant overlooking one of the lakes. It was magical. I can still see it and taste it. The duck not the restaurant.

Old people go there for the peace and quiet. General de Gaulle went there when old, broken, virtually crushed by the near-revolution of 1968 to, depending on who you talk to, either recharge his batteries and prepare for the fight back or disappear off the face of the earth. He said he liked the people. They were quiet, understanding and, something the French at the time were not, respectful. He would go into the local church. They would immediately turn their back on their God and the altar and salute and bow and even applaud him as he made his way to the front row which had been especially enlarged to take his height and size. Humble, modest man that he was he always maintained that such a display of respect and admiration was not for him personally. The Irish he maintained would react the same way in the presence of any Frenchman.

The only time de Gaulle ever spoke English was not to the likes of Churchill, Roosevelt or the Lord God Himself, none of whom he deemed worthy enough to be addressed in their own language because of the little they had done to help him over the years, but to the Irish. To the Irish president, Eamon de Valera, who practically looked like his younger brother. To the local people of Co. Kerry. And, of course, to the staff at the Great Southern Hotel at Parknasilla just up the road from Sneem who looked after him while he was there.

De Gaulle also felt at home in Co. Kerry because it was O'Connell country. The son of a shopkeeper and smuggler, Daniel O'Connell, the Liberator, was born near Cahirciveen at Carhen. To the French, he above anyone else liberated the Irish people from their detestable tyrants, the English. Balzac put him up there with Napoleon and Cuvier as one of the greatest European figures of his century because he 'incarnated in himself a whole people'.

From childhood O'Connell was one of de Gaulle's heroes. His grandmother wrote books about him. He was his shining example of a leader who freed his people from the yoke of slavery. But more than anything de Gaulle admired him because they both shared the same enemy, the English.

Today in Sneem, in the subtropical south-west corner of the county, de Gaulle's visit is commemorated with a huge circular stone inscribed in French paying tribute to the peace and security the Great Man enjoyed during his visit.

Inevitably, it's known locally as the Gaullestone.

I don't go to Co. Kerry like de Gaulle to hide away from the world, I go there for far more important reasons. For the fairies, the wine-cellar fairies. Co. Kerry is the only place in the world which believes in fairies who haunt only wine cellars. Now if you're going to be a fairy, which is something I admit I have never even vaguely considered before, being a fairy condemned to spend your eternity haunting wine cellars is not that bad an option. I can think of worse things some fairies I know tell me they have to do. Trouble is if you're looking for them, you have to spend all your time in wine cellars, checking the bottles, seeing if they're inside and if they are, opening the bottles and releasing them. Then, of course, there's the problem of what to do with all those open wine bottles ... Suggestions, please, inside a bottle of Guinness left at the bottom of the Gaullestone in Sneem.

Fairies apart, the whole world and their wife go to Co. Kerry – even General de Gaulle took Mrs General de Gaulle with him. But only two people in the history of the world have willingly left Co. Kerry. The first was a monk, St Brendan the Navigator. He discovered America. All I can say is, It serves him right. He should have stayed at home. It would also have saved us all a great deal of time and trouble over the years. Can you imagine no McDonald's, no

Cokes, no pre-emptive strikes, no friendly fire, no George Dubya? The list is endless. On the other hand St Brendan obviously didn't like what he saw which is why he kept quiet about it unlike our friend Christopher so I suppose he wasn't all bad.

The other deserter was Tom Crean, a farmer's son who went three times to the Antarctic with both Captain Scott who died there in 1912 and Ernest Shackleton who died going back there ten years later in 1922. The reason he went? The reason all great explorers leave home and risk their lives against the unknown. To get away from the wife.

Poor Tom Crean, one of the greatest Antarctic explorers of all time – when Evans was on the verge of dying, he walked 30 miles across the ice with only three biscuits in his pocket, to get help – was so dominated by his wife, Nell, that he was never allowed to talk about his adventures. He wasn't even allowed to show anyone his souvenirs or mementoes of his adventures. Everything was put in a cardboard box and put out of sight on top of the wardrobe. Worse still, in the pub he bought when he came back home, the South Pole Inn, he wasn't even allowed a decent drink. All day and every day he would spend virtually sitting alone in the corner with half a pint of Guinness reading the newspaper. No wonder Tom Crean called her Eskimo Nell. Or was it Eskimo Hell?

Go to the pub today. Her evil influence lives on. The fuss and bother to get some ice for your drink. If truth was told, I felt like going outside for a long walk.

If you haven't the courage and I wouldn't blame you, try and find it on the map. While you're looking, you'll also notice that Co. Kerry is like three fat frostbitten butter fingers desperately holding on to a glass waiting for some ice in the South Pole Inn.

The lower one, the strip of land between Bantry Bay and Kenmare Bay, the Beara Peninsula.

Next, between Kenmare Bay and Dingle Bay, the Iveragh Peninsula, which is Ring of Kerry territory.

Finally, the top one, between Dingle and the Atlantic, the Dingle Peninsula.

The Beara is ordinary to medium. Wild and rugged. Bronze Top. The Iveragh is fantastic to even more fantastic. Gold Top. The

Dingle is medium to rocky to a bit wild in places. Silver Top. If that's not too technical.

The starting point for all three is Killarney. In fact Killarney is the ideal starting place for anything anywhere in the world. It's also the ideal place to which to return. The trip from Killarney to home will, of course, add another three days on your trip. Another advantage.

Some people sneer at it. They say it's too touristy. It's full of nothing but leprechaun tea towels, jaunting carts and a never-ending stream of coaches. What's more it rains all the time. Nonsense. Paris is full of French people but it's still great fun. Rome is full of Italians. New York is full of . . . I see what they mean.

I was there once when everybody was talking about some local o'bigwig who said Killarney was getting like New York City.

'We are going up and up and up,' he apparently said.

The o'bigwig is crazy. It's not going up and up. It's small. It's pleasant. It's friendly. The hotels are delightful. Delightful being the operative word. I stayed in one hotel once which had just installed one of those fancy key sockets by the door. Put the key in, all the lights come on. Take the key out, all the lights go off. Except they'd wired the wall safe into the same circuit. I'd leave the room, take the key out of the socket, the safe would spring open. But bad hotels, there is no such thing. As for the bars, they're fantastic. Fantastic atmosphere. Fantastic characters. Fantastic talk. They also have the right sense of priorities. Go to church on Sunday morning. They are collecting not for the poor, the hungry, the suffering. They are collecting for the Killarney Salmon and Trout Angling Club. I even like the jaunting carts. They are a darn sight better than London buses. On top of all that, it's in a beautiful setting. On not one but three lakes. Mountains in the background. Pure genius. As for the rain, either it's just another rumour or I've been dead lucky. I've been there a million times. But I can't once remember it raining. Cold, yes. Bitterly cold, even more. But that was January.

They say that in 1938 when Hitler marched into Austria the whole of Salzburg wanted to up and move to Killarney. They thought it was the only place in the world they would feel at home. The only thing, they say, that put them off was what they heard about the Cork Great Southern Ladies Day at the Killarney Races. They decided instead to stay at home and suffer the wrath of Adolf Hitler. My own theory is that they thought the Ring of Kerry had something to do with Wagner. When they discovered it wasn't, they called the whole thing off. But you decide.

Most people who land in Killarney, the Irish for Cill Arne, a sloe tree – A sloe tree! That's much too fast for Killarney – rush off to the Museum of Irish Transport in Scotts Gardens, opposite the railway station with its authentic 1930s garage complete with 1930s calendar; make for the Killarney Model Railway which has more trains and more track than the real-life full-size Irish railway; or even the Coolwood Wildlife Sanctuary with its rooks and squirrels. Or, Heaven help me, the Aqua Dome, Ireland's largest indoor water leisure centre. Even though the outdoors is far, far better. In any case, I'm no Latin scholar, not like the monks of Ireland of old, but shouldn't that be either Aqua Doma or Water Dome?

Not me. I shuffle out of the Great Southern which must be one of the best hotels in the country apart from all the others and head for The Laurels on Main Street or any of the other bars that takes my fancy for a chat and a laugh.

The craic, they say, in Kerry is the best in the world and the best craic in Kerry is in Killarney or to be precise just outside, in Gneeveguilla where they've even erected a statue to the King of Craic, Eamon Kelly. I never met Eamon Kelly. But apparently he was such a great storyteller he talked himself into going commercial. He did stand-ups or rather fireside sit-downs before stand-ups were invented and toured the country telling his stories. He also had his own fireside radio show.

I've known and sat and listened to a good many storytellers in my time. One of the best was one of my old uncles, Tomo, who could not only tell story after story after story about the old days, about farming, about the weather, about how he found his wife. He had the matchmaker have her walk up and down the street outside the bar so he could check whether she had knock knees. He could talk about everything and anything and quite often about nothing at all. He could also lilt the night away. Many's the time I've seen him sit beside the big open peat fire in his old black suit, collarless shirt, big boots, his hat perched on top of his head and lilt away to any jig, reel or dance that had ever been invented. Sometimes he'd be accompanied by Dessie from up the lane on his penny whistle. More often he'd do it all by himself.

Once I remember he came to London. We took him out to a fancy fish-and-chip restaurant in Baker Street complete with sawdust and pianist. I was no sooner into my first pile of chips than he was gently lilting away with the piano. Then slowly he got louder and louder and the piano quieter and quieter until he took over the place. It was a real blast from the past.

After the bars and the craic in Killarney there are the restaurants. In the old days when a Big Mac was a filthy old waterproof, two sizes too big for you, covered in mud and smelling of dead rats, the Irish were famous for their food. Dishsot and pottage ragwort stew. Giant hog weed dumplings. They could take anything in the world and cook it until it tasted of nothing. Or, at least, nothing edible. Restaurants were so bad you'd order your meal and the last rites at the same time. Not any more. Irish restaurants are now out of this world.

In the old days people would eat buckets of potatoes without giving them a second thought. Now, God help us, they discuss them as if for all the world they were discussing a book, an opera or even a racehorse. Caras, they're practically trouble-free, blight-resistant, high-yielding. Charlottes. Ideal for salads. Best served undressed. Maris Piper, perfect for chips. Especially if cooked three times. Pink Apple Fir. Perfect with salmon. Roosters, they're soft, light, floury. King Edwards, they're rougher, tougher. A British Queen. Well now. It depends which part of Ireland you're from. I once spent an evening with a bunch of Irish potatoholics who even discussed ways of cooking them. Chips. Don't use potatoes with a high sugar content. They will caramelise and burn the cooking oil. I couldn't believe it. In the old days we had far more important things to talk about. Horses. Horses. Horses.

In Killarney I like Gaby's, the near-legendary seafood restaurant, which seems to have more plaques and certificates on the wall than they have plates on the tables. Putting plaques up on the wall of a church or even taking one down is much more complicated. The insides of the city's churches are protected. Move a candlestick from one side of the altar to the other and you practically have to get planning permission.

After Killarney the other starting point for any spin around Kerry is Tralee on the River Lee, which is no river at all, hardly even a stream. That's Ireland for you. But be warned. There are dangers. Depending which bar you go in, who you talk to and what you are drinking the coast around Tralee is either the German coast, the IRA coast or one of the most historic areas in the country.

The German coast because along here on Banna Strand was where Sir Roger Casement landed from a German submarine on Good Friday in April 1916 after trying to recruit Irish prisoners of war to fight for the Germans, was captured, taken to London and executed for treason on 3 August 1916.

The IRA coast because along here, it is said, the IRA used to land most of their weapons.

Historic because this is where William Pembroke Mulchinock composed the most important song in the history of the world, 'The Rose of Tralee', to commemorate all the thorny problems that have been created by women since time began. To hammer home the point they've even created a Rose of Tralee International Festival. The race meeting is grand. But the rest of it is neither one thing nor the other. It's not a beauty contest. Neither is it a fashion contest. The winning girl, they say, is selected for 'the truth in her eyes'. Which is obviously where it stays. If she's anything like the rest of them, the last thing she'll ever do in her life is think of speaking it.

When I first went to Tralee, when the Imperial Hotel was still a hotel, it was all very innocent and very Irish and very embarrassing. The girl with the red hair and the fattest ankles always seemed to win. Now I'm not so sure. The last time I was there various thorny issues had arisen. The shops were full of 'Rose of Tralee' yo-yos, 'Rose of Tralee' pencils. And, dare I say it, 'Rose of Tralee' rubbers. There was even talk of – my God, what is Ireland coming to? – sexing it up in order to stop the whole thing from wilting.

They'll be calling it the Tarts of Tralee 'and getting them to dance a jig around a pole in the middle of the stage,' one old-timer told me one evening in Paddy Mac's.

If they do, it'll bring the town crumbling down around them. Already I find the place dull and slow and somehow out of touch. They go on about their Georgian heritage but for the life of me I can't see it. Denny Street, a formal mall laid out in the nineteenth century, is way past its prime.

''Twas our pride and joy,' my friend told me.

No more. Today it's practically nothing but cheap hotels and b&bs which I was assured come up to scratch. Scratch being the operative word if they're anything like the b&bs I've stayed in over the years. The rest of the place seems to be nothing but Late Nite Music, Tonite Big Mike and 'Ye canna park there. That's a free parking space.' As for the people they're no longer as relaxed and friendly and chatty as I remember apart, of course, from my friend who, in any case, told me he was from Limerick. Somehow it seems to have lost its fun and its sparkle.

About the last time anything exciting happened in and around Tralee was when the father of Lord Kitchener of Khartoum was publicly horsewhipped at Tralee races by his next-door neighbour, the arch-Catholic Knight of Glin for threatening some of his tenants with eviction. The event obviously had a deep effect on the young Horatio Herbert. He spent his whole life horsewhipping everyone from the Dervishes at Omdurman to Asquith not to mention the Boers, the Indians, the Egyptians, the government and at least half the British people, forcing them to join up and die for him at the front in the First World War.

From Tralee if I've got time I like to head north to Listowel. It's the opposite direction to the Ring of Kerry but was home to the legendary Irish writer John B. Keane who owned and ran a bar there. He had more of the Ring of Kerry about him, they say, than the Ring itself. Read his books. He is not your Samuel Beckett. He is relaxed and chatty and friendly. A landlord, I suppose, leaning across the bar, gossiping away about this person and that, what the weather is like, the price of cattle, who the bishop had to tea the other day. Whenever I used to go in his bar he immediately recognised me as a fellow writer. He completely ignored me. I had to fight to get a drink. Obviously because being a writer I looked so poor none of the staff thought I had enough money to be able to afford one. He's gone now. But his books are still great fun.

The town itself lives up to its reputation for having one of the country's greatest writers living in its midst. There are more bars and pubs and even upmarket off-licences selling some pretty expensive wines than there are bookshops. There's even an Americano Pub although to be fair it does have eight Complete Works of Shakespeare in the window so I suppose it can't be too bad. I went in there one evening for some literary conversation. The only thing people wanted to talk about was Listowel Town Council's decision to sell what they called pooper-scoopers. I threw in the Listowel and left.

If I'm not heading for Listowel and literary conversations about pooper-scoopers, I make for Ballybunion which I always think is well named. It's a bally bunion on the coast of Co. Kerry. It's Margate and Clacton and Southend. Not the beautiful, wonderful, splendid County Kerry we all know and love. But I don't mind. All those bally amusements and crowded beaches make me appreciate the rest of the county even more.

The Dingle Peninsula. One of the longest continuously inhabited places in the world. Over six thousand years and still drinking. Running the length of it, the Slieve Mish Mountains. Drive through there, you still see donkeys being ridden, pulling carts, refusing to move. You also experience the rain where they say it rains every other day and if it doesn't, next time it rains it makes up for it.

I got soaked once just filling the car up with petrol.

'Rain at seven, sun by eleven,' the ould boy grinned through his rusty skin when I ran inside the office to pay.

'But it's 11.30,' I said.

'Eleven at night,' he says.

The best way in is through Stradbally, Kilcummin and turn left through Connor Pass, which is spectacular. But spectacular. From there you can see practically the whole of southern Kerry as well as across to Co. Clare and even on to the Aran Islands. On a clear day, fabulous. On a not so clear day, almost as fabulous.

Ireland: In a Glass of its Own

Dingle town, the most westerly town in Europe, was once so remote they had to produce their own coinage. Nobody else bothered to go there. Willingly. The only way to get there was to be shipwrecked. I'm not saying a word, but they say the locals have a lighter, sallower complexion than people a few miles down the road. Come St Stephen's Day – Boxing Day, to you – they also used to have this strange ceremony. They used to round up all the goats they could find, put them in little painted carts and parade them through the town. The fact that Dingle town was full of French and Spanish traders may or may not have had something to do with it.

Today it's a boozer's delight, a drinker's dream come true. It has more pubs than any other town in Ireland. I started to count them, got as far as nine then decided to give up and go and have a drink. There were ten other people in the bar like me so we assumed that meant there must be over a hundred pubs in the town. Trouble is whichever pub you go in they're still going on about that God-forsaken film *Ryan's Daughter* which was about as close to life in Ireland as that desert queen Lawrence was to the Seven Pillars of Wisdom. There's even regular bus trips out to see the beach where the film was shot, the place where the typical Irish village was built because no typical Irish village existed at the time. When was the film made? 1971. A word of advice. If you want to go to Dingle go there. Don't think about it. When things began to heat up a bit in Paris Marie Antoinette planned to escape to Dingle. She had second thoughts. Then look what happened to her.

From Dingle don't drive back along the north side of the peninsula. It will only depress you. Whether you've been doing the bars or not.

Brandon Bay is where St Brendan at the grand old age of 59 made the biggest mistake of his and everybody else's life. When he should have put his feet up and started taking it easy, for some reason or other he started his wanderings. To the Shetland Isles after getting them confused with the back of a whale. It was only when he dug in the flag to claim it for the ould country did he realise the difference. To Iceland where it was so cold he couldn't stick anything in anything. Then to Newfoundland or Labrador and back via Miami. If only he'd kept quiet about it. Think of all the trouble he would have saved us. The amazing thing about St Brendan is that of all the places he discovered and visited, of all the food and drink he had, it was in France, in Brittany that he got food poisoning and died at the grand old age of 93. It is because of his heroic achievements and his unique standing as the first and the greatest of all Irish explorers that the authorities spelt his name incorrectly when they came to name his home town Brandon Bay.

Today all Ireland's sailing heroes discover is mackerel, bass, plaice and cod and that gets fewer and fewer every year. But if you're tempted to check on the fishing: Don't. The whole area is full of dead bodies. Not fish dead bodies. Men dead bodies. Wander along the coast and you're likely to see washed up on the beach, floating in the sea, bones, skulls, whole skeletons of sailors ship-wrecked centuries ago as well as the remains of Irishmen and women, eighty Spaniards, 600 Italians and a papal nuncio tortured and massacred by the English including Sir Walter Raleigh himself in the siege of Smerwick Harbour in 1580. After they had surrendered. Some say it's all the fault of soil erosion. The bodies were properly buried. But the sea is eroding the graves. The bones, the skulls, the whole bodies are breaking loose and floating out to sea. Others blame local amateur archaeologists. They dig away wherever they want. Their diggings loosen up the soil. The bodies float free. One or two people even say the bones and skulls and bodies should all be gathered together and given a proper funeral. Although, I must say, not too many people agree.

Back to Killarney, a couple of pints of Guinness in O'Connors, another fantastic meal, this time in Foley's and I'm heading out to the Iveragh Peninsula, the Ring of Kerry, a 100-mile circular drive through literally heaven on earth. Think of a glass of Guinness. Think of the Dublin Horse Show. Think of a brand new hunter standing in the stables. It's all that and a thousand times more. Every time I go there it's the same. No cars. No parking meters. No road rage. Peace and quiet. Beautiful countryside. Some people, mostly men, say it's better to do it clockwise. Some, mostly women, of course, say anticlockwise. I usually go clockwise because that's the sensible thing to do.

First stop Kenmare where the Irish are forever singing about a gap in the hedge there. Kenmare itself is small, quiet, sleepy. But a riot of colour. God only knows what it would have been like today if the town's founder, a Sir William Petty, had got his way. He wanted to ship in 20,000 doughty maidens, I think he called them, rounded up from the streets of Manchester to make whoopee with the local Protestant landowners to ensure the place remained Protestant for ever. Obviously what's known as a Petty idea.

I stop. It's so quiet. It's so still. It's so ... Then I get a heart attack. Suddenly in the back of my car is this sound of scurrying and fluttering. For the first time in my life I have a bird trapped in the back. Somehow the poor thing had managed to get in and was hurling itself at the rear window desperately trying to escape.

I did the decent thing. You would have been proud of me.

I drive on to Parknasilla which is almost subtropical. It's sheltered from the north-east winds. The vegetation is lush. There are palm trees all over the place. I stop the car. I get out. Three steps, I'm covered in mosquitoes. It's Ireland's very own Riviera. The grand hotel there, once the home of the Church of Ireland's Bishop of Limerick, Dr Charles Graves, grandfather of the poet, Robert, is the grandest there is. GBS used to stay there and scribble away in a sitting room of an afternoon. The result: *St Joan*. If only writing travel books was as easy. I have to spend hours in the bar before I even put pen to paper.

The road now twists and turns. More scenery. More subtropical plants. More Irish mosquito bites.

Now we're into Daniel O'Connell country.

Caherdaniel was the home of General de Gaulle's hero, Daniel O'Connell, the man who smashed the Penal Code on Catholics, which banned them from owning land, swords or horses, voting, education not just in Ireland but anywhere in the known universe and taking any part in government.

Yeats labelled O'Connell 'The Great Comedian of the Irish race', which tells you how Irish the great Irish poet was.

Co. Kerry

To the north is Cahirciveen where the Great Man was born. Today it's covered in shops. In the nineteenth century, however, it was covered in academics from Trinity College, Dublin, which practically owned the place. The Protestant academics were trying to teach the Catholic Kerrymen how to sow potatoes of all things. Which must be the biggest Kerryman joke of all time. The Kerrymen, however, had the last laugh. They didn't tell the academics anything about rent reviews, inflation or how to manage an estate. As a result many families until recently were still paying as much as 1s 6d a year ground rent to their masters in Dublin.

In the old days it was easier and quicker for people living here to get their post from America than from Dublin. American politicians even campaigned here for re-election. They said it was because they hoped by influencing the locals they would influence their friends and relatives living in the States. I don't believe it. I believe the Americans thought it was part of America. You know what they're like.

Bearing everything in mind, it seems odd, if that's the correct word, that the Memorial Church in Cahirciveen to Daniel O'Connell, which opened in 1888 has still not, over 100 years later, been completed. The body of the church is there. Black limestone from local quarries. Granite from Newry up in the North. But the tower is still waiting for the builders. Which is either a calculated insult to his memory or another example of Irish builders starting a job and never finishing it. The heritage centre nearby, however, has been fully built and completed. Maybe they used different builders. Or the letter with the cheque arrived by post.

It also seems odd, Co. Kerry being Co. Kerry, that down by the pier is an old, rusty, broken-down, graffiti-covered Irish fisheries patrol boat. Some say it's there to stop the Germans from invading. Others that it's to stop the IRA from landing more arms. I think it's there to remind people what other parts of Ireland look like.

In the Cahirciveen Park Hotel, which is more Park than Hotel, a smooth old frightwig who looked like a bishop on holiday told me the boat was known as the Olympic Flame. Because it never went out.

Waterville I like. It was a favourite in Victorian and Edwardian times. You can see why.

Now, if the weather is not too bad I dodge off from the Ring to Ballinskelligs to see the Skellig Rocks. The larger, Skellig Michael, 700 feet high, was home one thousand years ago to a group of monks who believed in anything but the easy life. Winds and gales apart, they carved 600 steps out of the solid rock so that they could build their church and monastery on top.

The old boatman who took me out for a look told me his mother-in-law had been marooned there already for 300 years but they were rushing around doing their best to rescue her as quickly as possible.

Little Skellig is covered in puffins. I think.

Back to the Ring and on to Valentia Island, which has two claims to fame. It was the place from where the first transatlantic cable was sent in 1858: 'St Brendan was wrong. You don't exist.' More important, without Valentia nobody would be able to play billiards or snooker anywhere in the world. They used to supply the slates that made up the green baize table tops.

Now the Ring turns rough. The Kenmare Bay side is all soft and green and chocolate boxy. The Dingle Bay side is rough, rugged, tough.

Glenbeigh was home to Rowland Winn who sued his architect for exceeding both budget and the acceptable number of leaks to the roof. The architect wasn't worried. He had other things on his, err, mind. He'd just run off with Ellen Terry. Winn's heir inherited the pile, promptly turned Muslim, headed off for Mecca, came back insisting he was called Al O'Hadji Winn and turned down the chance of being King of Albania because, he claimed, 'there is no salary attached to it'. Oh the innocence of the Irish. There was no salary for the job because whoever landed it was expected to generate their own. If you see what I mean.

Killorglin is the place to go, especially mid-August, if you are of a nervous disposition, a vegetarian and an animal lover. That's when they hold their annual three-day Puck Fair when the biggest billy goat they can find – those French and Spaniards again – is led through the town or more usually nowadays transported in a cage on the back of a lorry to be hoisted to the top of the highest tower and there to preside over the nearest the Irish get to three days and nights of debauchery.

'Why a goat?' I asked an old doo rag I met in the bar in Bianconi's Hotel, who looked as though he was forever experiencing unwanted bowel movements.

''Tis the goat that warned us of Cromwell and his men,' he says.

'And to show your appreciation you stick him on top of a tower for three days.'

'We do. We do,' he says, he says.

'So what would you have done if he hadn't warned you?'

He cackled like an old hen.

'I'll be having another one, I thankee sir,' he says and heads for the back door.

'Why a goat?' I asked another old drinker in the bar. He looked as though he was suffering from a complete absence of bowel movements.

''Twas certainly the fault of Mr Cromwell,' he says. 'Mr Cromwell is in Killorglin. He is having lunch with his wife and an old goat. He says to one of his men, "Will ye throw the old goat out of the window?" When he realises they've thrown the wrong one out of the window, he says, "Puck." We've been commemorating the event ever since. I'll also be joining my friend with ye in another one if I may, sir.'

Back to Killarney along the banks of the River Laune, a couple of pints at McSorleys, a meal at Linden House and I'm heading off to the Beara Peninsula which is nothing like the Ring. Nothing like the Dingle. Or maybe I've just been spoilt.

Anyhow it's back again to Killarney, a couple of pints in the Killarney Grand, a meal in the Malton Rooms at the Great Southern.

'Finished your travels, have you, sir?' says the waiter who looks so grand he probably owns the place.

'I have,' I say.

'And what if I may ask is your favourite memory?' he says.

'Easy,' I say. 'One Saturday afternoon in Parknasilla, I'm talking to some of the staff who were around when General de Gaulle was staying next door. They were telling me what a privilege it was to serve such a great man, a world figure, a living legend. One of the old porters says to me, "It was a privilege. Every morning the mail would come to the hotel for the General. Every morning I'd go across and take the great man his French letters . . .""

I got free drinks for the rest of my stay.

Co. Westmeath
+++++++++ ++++++++++

Famous local resident
Michael +++++++ O'Leary

Favourite food
Anything but +++++++ airline food

Favourite drink
Guinness, +++++++ marvellous

Favourite pub
Gigginstown +++++++ House

Favourite restaurant
Gigginstown House's ++++++++ kitchen

What to say
I love Michael +++++++ O'Leary

What not to say
Who the ++++ is Michael O'Leary?

If County Kerry is all the soft, green beautiful proteins that do you nothing but good, Co. Westmeath is all the rough, tough, hard-nosed, hard-edged proteins that do you nothing but harm. Or at least your eardrums harm. For just as Co. Kerry is Daniel O'Connell, the great Liberator, Co. Westmeath is Michael +++++++ O'Leary, the fast-talking, foul-mouthed, mega-rich boss of Ryanair, the great Liberator of low-cost air travel for the masses. Not that he is from Co. Westmeath. He's from Co. Cork, the land of the Blarney Stone. It's just that his house, or rather sumptuous Georgian pile, Gigginstown, is not just in Co. Westmeath, it is practically the size of Co. Westmeath. But that's not the amazing thing. The amazing thing is the great arch-critic of government subsidies got a government subsidy to do it up.

The result is wherever you go in Co. Westmeath, wherever you turn, there is Michael +++++++ O'Leary or Biggles as he is known to his neighbours.

Go into a bar anywhere within earshot of him, which is practically half of the county, and they'll be talking about him.

'A holy living terror. That's what he is I tell you.'

'... had the name of money ...'

'... made his weight in gold ...'

'The Lord be good to him. He'll need all the help he can get.'

Go to mass on Sunday in the Cathedral of Christ the King, they're even singing hymns on his behalf: 'O God, Our Help in Wages Vast'.

Head into Dublin, 50 miles away. You're overtaken by a black

201

Mercedes speeding down the bus lane. It's Michael + + + + + + +
O'Leary. Rather than risk going in by train which runs over a bog

> Old Irish woman lands at Dublin airport on her way
> back from Lourdes.
>
> 'Anything to declare?' asks the customs officer.
>
> 'Not a ting,' she says.
>
> He opens her suitcase. Inside is a bottle.
>
> 'Holy water,' she says.
>
> He opens the bottle, sniffs it.
>
> 'It's whiskey,' he says.
>
> 'Glory be to God,' she cries. 'Another miracle.'

which in places is up to 20 metres deep, he paid £4000 for a taxi
licence so his big black Mercedes could hurtle down the bus
lanes and get him to and from work in the time it takes to load
a disabled passenger on to a Ryanair flight at Stansted airport.

Why he doesn't go by the Royal Canal I don't know. It practically runs along the bottom of his garden. A fast speedboat, jet
foils, a pair of skis, he could be in Dublin in no time at all.

Pick up Ryanair's annual report. There he is again not in anything
as boring as a suit and collar and tie but dressed as a French maid,
a frilly apron around his waist and a green fluffy feather duster
gripped coyly between his teeth.

If that's how he appears in his annual report, God alone knows
what he turns up in at parties in Gigginstown Mansions. I shudder
to think.

In the old days loving, caring parents in Co. Westmeath who

wanted nothing more than bringing up their children without any hang-ups used to terrify the life out of them with stories of the Babow, a wild woman who liked nothing better than to feast on dead bodies. Now they show them photographs of Michael +++++++ O'Leary. In fact, come to think of it, the whole county looks as though it's been shown a picture of Michael +++++++ O'Leary. With or without the green fluffy feather duster. Although to be fair to him he wasn't responsible for what the Irish Advertising Standards Authority considered the 'most grossly suggestive and offensive' advertisement since St Patrick cast out the snakes: an enormous outdoor advertisement proclaiming, Roger More.

Maybe that's why whenever I go to Mullingar, it always looks empty. Drive past the water tower, down the hill, across the canal, along by the shops, over the canal again and out. There's hardly any traffic. Hardly any people. Bars are practically empty. Hotels are easy to check in to. Dining rooms are virtually deserted. Nobody is around for breakfast.

There are two theories. First, someone heard a rumour Michael +++++++ O'Leary was coming into town.

Second, don't tell a soul, they've all gone off to the local cock-fight.

'Cockfighting? I thought it was illegal.' I was in Canton Casey's one evening in the middle of what looked like a chickenpox party.

'It is,' an old farmer who looked as though he had mange rather than chickenpox told me. 'But they can't stop it. It's in the blood.'

Now as it happens, I'm an expert on cockfighting. I've seen cockfighting all over the Far East. I even got close to a cockfight once in the US. Did I get to see one in Co. Westmeath? I didn't. But I met a man who did. He was an enthusiast. He went to so many he looked as though he spent all his life in empty barns and remote farmhouses.

From what he told me – don't say a word to anyone, otherwise I shall have to kill myself, that's the Irish way of keeping secrets – Irish cockfighting is small Guinness compared to cockfighting in the Far East. In Ireland, it's illegal. Meetings are small. They are arranged at the last minute. What gambling there is is small-scale. In the Far East, especially in the Philippines, it's legal. Meetings take place in huge sports arenas. Sometimes they last for days on end. The gambling is big-time.

The one aspect where Ireland seems to score is the toughness and quality of the birds. In the Far East, most of the birds are small, lightweight, athletic, bred for speed of reaction. In Ireland they seem to prefer the slow, tough old birds. Their favourite: the Old English game cock. Which surprised me. You'd have thought every red-blooded Irishman would have been more than pleased to see every Old English game cock torn to shreds. Not just for Oliver Cromwell. Not just for the Troubles. But for everything virtually since the beginning of time.

But if cockfighting is a crime, stealing huge stones to build your own prehistoric monument is not. Some Irish historians maintain Britain was responsible for the biggest takeaway in Irish history. Huge stones from in and around Mullingar were used to build Stonehenge. English scientists, of course, say it's not true. The stones used to build Stonehenge came from the Prescelly Mountains in Wales.

I asked an old bot I met another evening in Canton Casey's, who looked as though he was there at the time, if it was true the stones for Stonehenge came from Mullingar. He took his hat off, put it on the bar, took a long drag of his pipe, looked me straight in the eye and said, 'It is and it isn't.'

The stones came from Mullingar. But they weren't Mullingar stones. They were African stones, brought to Ireland in the ice age, dumped in Mullingar, then somehow moved to England for the building of Stonehenge.

'Mullingar. 'Twas known as the land of the waters,' another old boy tells me.

'The waters brought the stones to Mullingar. The waters took them from Mullingar to Stonehenge.'

About five miles south of Mullingar is another puzzle: Belvedere House and its famous Jealous Wall. The Irish make a lot of fuss about it. Robert Rochfort, Earl of Belvedere, discovered his wife was having an affair with his brother. He tells her father. Her father says, 'So what? She's always been a bastard.' Poor distraught hubby, Robert, then locks her up and throws away the key. After he dies, she is released, old, broken, haggard, more of a pain than when she was first locked up. The house was later owned by Colonel Bury, the man who spent his life looking for the Abominable Snowman, inspired it is said by the Earl's wife.

A great story. A crowd puller. The place was empty. I felt as though I was there not so much for matters of historic interest, more for picking up advice and tips.

Ten miles to the west of Mullingar is the Hill of Uisneach. From the top of the hill I was told you could see not only the whole of Westmeath but practically the whole country as well. In the old days it was the meeting point for Ireland's five ancient provinces, Connacht, Leinster, Munster, Meath and Ulster. I went there. I couldn't see a soul.

On the way back to the car, I met an old man wandering around all over the place. He looked like a heart attack waiting to happen. He told me the top of the hill looked like a cat ready to pounce. I couldn't see that either.

His friend and drinking partner tells me that Co. Westmeath being the centre of Ireland, everything drains every which way.

'Take a look at Lough Lene,' he says. 'It drains both to the east, to the Irish Sea and to the west, to the Atlantic. 'Tis a rare sight.'

I'm sure it would be if I could see it. But I couldn't.

On the way back to O'Leary land, I stopped for a glass in a bar near Ballynafid.

Everyone I met had their story about the hill. It was the birthplace of the druids. It was where Halloween started. It was the seat of the high kings of Ireland. My favourite. It was the source of Lough Ennell, Lough Iron and Lough Owel. An ancient giant, Tuirill Picreo, hit the booze, had far, far too much to drink and vomited the three of them up. Now go there on a nice summer's day with the family and enjoy yourselves. Cheers.

An elderly schoolboy who looked like a defrocked schoolteacher told me that if it was booze I was looking for I should go and call on the Ginger Man himself, J. P. Donleavy, who lived to the manner prawn down the road in Levington Park, a broken-down spread with a couple of hundred acres, a herd of Hereford cattle and the only fossilised marble fireplace in the whole of Ireland. At first I was going to. Turn up with a couple of bottles of booze. Tell him we shared the same publishers. Ask him why his editors allowed him to say things in his books while mine didn't. He'd have to invite me in. We could then reminisce about the old days, the victories, the occasional defeats, how after the publication of *The Ginger Man*, he never had to worry about where the next drink was coming from.

I remembered his description of his encounter with Irish stout.

Bartenders with sleeves rolled back handed the glasses over the heads as the rounds of drinks were bought and the sound of mechanical corkscrews twisted their way down with a thump and pop into the necks of the bottles of stout. And it was the name of this dark brew, stout, which confounded me when I first encountered it in James Joyce's writings. This beverage, which pumped blood through the hearts of the citizens and fuelled the city and ended up flowing through pub latrines, sewers and back to the Liffey from whose headwaters it had first come.

I remembered reading somewhere that he had his own bar complete with a Guinness pump.

But then I remembered reading somewhere else about his cats, the Christmas cards that stay on the mantelpiece for ever and the lonely-hearts advert he put in one of his recent books: 'Slightly reclusive but anxious to get out more, gracefully older fit man . . . requires pleasantly attractive younger lady of principle.' Obviously the fireplace wasn't the only fossilised thing in the house. I decided to stay put and have another drink instead. It seemed more fun.

Somehow or other I always feel sorry for Athlone/Alth Luain/Luan's ford. It's a crossroads town. It's a garrison town. It's a big commercial centre, the biggest inland town in the country after Kilkenny. Trouble is it doesn't feel like it. It feels as if it's been passed by, overlooked, a stopping place on the way to somewhere more important. Whenever I go there the streets are empty. There's little traffic. Few people. No buzz. On the other hand a bunch of drunken Irish hurlers could have been in town smashing television sets, setting off fire extinguishers and generally making whoopee so that nobody was prepared to risk showing their head above the parapet.

Everybody I met, I expected to criticise and condemn their antics. Not at all. Everybody was in favour of them.

I met a retired Irish colonel in the bar at the Prince of Wales Hotel. He looked like the kind of colonel who goes into battle determined to see more of his own troops killed than the enemy's. A cross between Lord Cardigan and Lord Kitchener.

'Why not?' he barks at me. Most un-Irish. Obviously spent too much time with the British. 'The last time it happened the Royal Huey Hotel opened the bar and served free drinks until it was all over. Jesus, Mary and Joseph, am I going to complain about that? More power to them. More power to them.'

The following morning I saw him marching across Market Square. Everybody and everything was scurrying to get out of his way.

It was here in Athlone in 1691 the Irish Jacobites tried to stop William of Orange breaking through into Connaught. But in vain. He finally managed it. By using old Luan's ford. Bet he wouldn't have succeeded if there had been a couple of Irish hurlers in town.

Today, however, Athlone calls itself the Heart of Ireland. If it is, it's almost stopped beating. It's desperately in need of a transplant. It's scruffy. It's dirty. It's quiet. Very quiet. Even the bars are closing down because of lack of business. Can you imagine? In Ireland? Bars closing down for lack of business. They are in Athlone.

Dominating everything is an enormous water tower shaped like a spaceship. Practically underneath it is a shrine for people to pray for some signs of life. If they are, they'll be there a long time.

Athlone Castle looks like a blob that has come out of a spaceship. Trouble is it doesn't look as though it would scare anyone let alone stop them. Witness the way they let William of Orange go. Which doesn't say much for the Irish army's Western Command which is based there.

The only sign of any life is down on the banks of the River

Shannon which flows through the town. In fact, it was the lock, the dam and the quays in Athlone that virtually opened up the Shannon for tourists and those fancy, schlubby pleasure boats.

In the old days the Shannon was a major trade route. Special locks and canals had to be built. Steamships used to run from Athlone to Killaloe and on up to Carrick-on-Shannon. Dredging was a problem in some parts, trying to stop the river from silting up and keeping open the wider channels for the shipping. Today, of course, that's all gone. The SS *Shamrock* chugs up and down with Ma and Pa from Ohio not talking to each other and Grandma in the back falling asleep all the time.

Maybe that's why everyone is miserable. They've realised what they've done. They've flooded the country with American tourists, their baseball caps and their ten-gallon cans of Coke.

About the only place of note I could find in Athlone was the Bawn just off Mardyke Street, birthplace of Count John McCormack, who was a legendary Irish tenor before anyone had ever heard of a tenor let alone three.

One evening I wandered along Dublin Road, Church Street, Mardyke Street and Sean Costello Street, which they call the Golden Mile. It was practically deserted.

I wandered down the narrow streets leading to the bridge over the river. Deserted.

I went into a couple of bookshops. No *Ginger Man* in sight although I was offered a signed copy of Oscar Wilde's 'Ballad of Reading Gaol'. Price: €12,000. The story of how that turned up in a bookshop in a garrison town in the middle of Ireland would be a book in itself.

The only excitement seemed to be in the Strand Tackle Shop by the river. That was only because they were closing.

I walked back to the hotel with a local fisherman or as that unique travel writer Jan Morris would say, fisherperson, who knew the plaice well. He agreed the town felt empty. But, he told me, that was because property prices were so high – a two-bedroom flat overlooking the river was going for about €220,000/£175,000, as expensive as Dublin – everybody was frightened to go out in case somebody broke in and damaged everything. I invited him into the hotel bar for a drink. He said No. Which stunned me for a couple of days. He was the first Irishman I've ever met who turned down the offer of a free drink. But that's Athlone for you.

He told me he was after an early night. He was going to be up early the following morning and off to Big Meadow, about half a mile downriver from the Shannon Bridge in the centre of town. It was the breeding grounds for the local corncrake. Only in Athlone could that happen. Only in Athlone.

In desperation, I thought I'd try the Seven Wonders of Fore which are world-famous throughout Fore, a tiny village near Lough – it drains both ways – Lene. There's the famous Monastery in the Quaking Sod, the famous Mill Without a Race, the famous Water Which Flows Uphill, the famous Stone Raised by St Feichin and three others which are even more famous but I can't remember them. There was nobody at any of them.

North of Athlone is Lissoy, Oliver Goldsmith country, known to the Irish as Poet's Country because he was a failed doctor – he was even turned down for service in India – a failed usher, a moderately successful biographer, historian, novelist and play-wright. Admittedly he did write 'The Deserted Village', in which I'm convinced he immortalised Athlone as 'Sweet Auburn', but I would have thought that no more makes him a poet than writing 'The Ballad of Reading Gaol' makes Oscar Wilde a poet.

Why was the village deserted, especially when Co. Westmeath is the exact geographical centre of Ireland?

I think I know the reason why.

Co. Tyrone
The empty quarter

Famous local resident
None. They've all gone to America

Favourite food
Irish hamburgers

Favourite drink
Guinness

Favourite pub
Mellon Country Inn

Favourite restaurant
Glenavon House Hotel

What to say
Psst. How much is the booze?

What not to say
Rubbish

As proteins, Counties Kerry and Westmeath have worked wonders in Ireland. County Tyrone, Northern Ireland's largest county, has worked its wonders in America. If, that is, the Ulster American Folk Park outside Omagh is to be believed. For whatever little America has done to improve the peace and tranquillity of the world is because of one thing and one thing only: County Tyrone.

Business. Hugh and Robert Campbell. They both emigrated in the early 1800s. Hugh went to New York then on to Philadelphia where he became one of the big wheeler-dealers. Robert became a fur trapper, built Fort Laramie and ended up another big wheeler-dealer in St Louis.

Banking. Thomas Mellon emigrated around the same time. He went first to western Pennsylvania, lived in a two-room log cabin. Within four years because of his 'labour and privation' he had paid off the mortgage. Another year he had 'as fine a six room dwelling as the best of our neighbours and that Fall and Winter as good a square log double barn as was to be seen thereabouts'. He moved to Pittsburgh. He became a judge and built up a huge industrial and financial empire which survives up to today.

Publishing. John Dunlap, which I am sure is a printer's error, became the most important printer in the land. Without him there would be no America today. He printed the American Declaration of Independence. Seeing the power of the printed word and how quickly it could be ignored he went on to publish America's first daily newspaper, the *Pennsylvania Packet*, which went on to set the standard for American journalism because of the number of lies they could packet into each issue.

Religion. John Joseph Hughes emigrated in 1817. From a family that produced linen cloth, he became a man of the cloth and ended up the first Catholic Archbishop of New York. He laid the foundation stone of St Patrick's Cathedral.

Politics. James Wilson emigrated in 1807. His grandson Woodrow became president in 1913.

Irish border post.

Five Germans arrive in an Audi Quattro.

'Out. Out,' says the customs officer. 'Do you think I'm stupid. Quattro means Four. It's illegal to have five people in an Audi Quattro.'

'Nonsense,' says the driver. 'That's just the name of the car. Get me your supervisor. I'll sort it out.'

'I can't,' says the customs office. 'He's over there. He's arresting two Italians for being in a Fiat Uno.'

Why did they go? There are three theories. First, they were professional emigrants. Most of them had come from Scotland. So what's another country? Second, the local women were so ugly, they had no choice. The story goes that Harry Avery, a local O'Neil chief hanged nineteen men because they refused to marry his sister. The twentieth was blind. He didn't know any different. Third, David Blunkett was not running the US immigration service so they stood a good chance of getting in.

Go to the museum today, it's so American you begin to feel even more sorry for the poor emigrants. Famine. Emigration. America. Then to be commemorated in an American Folk Museum. As a waxwork. My God. Haven't they suffered enough? Are there no depths to the shame and misery they have to endure?

Whenever I go there it seems to be full of either strange American blobbies from Loserville trying to discover their ancestors or masses of scruffy blackheaded kids who look as if they won't live long enough to have any ancestors.

I was there once when this eye-bleedingly terrifying gang of whoopy-do Americans bundled into one of the restored traditional Irish cottages with all the enthusiasm of a high-class lump of Afghan. One of the sunbed-fricasseed jig-a-boos yells out, 'Hey. Get down off the gas oven, Granny, you're too old to be riding the range.'

In another cottage, there was a crucifix on the wall. Some snotty-nose schnickelf bawls out, 'Hey Ma. Who's that guy asleep on that bit of wood?'

To tell you the truth, the only satisfaction I get out of going there is to go around it the wrong way. That way I get all the American exhibits, the Pennsylvania Log Farmhouse, the Pennsylvania Log Barn, American Street and all the other Yankee Doodle Danders out of the way first. I've then got more time to concentrate on the important bits, the Irish bits, the Famine Cabin, the Weavers Cottage, the Tullyallen Mass House and the others.

The Americans try and stop me. Like they try and stop anything sensible in this world. Everybody, they insist, should do as they say. Oh yes. Since when have they been infallible?

Outside the museum, however, things are not so relaxed. For County Tyrone or the bushes as it is locally known because of the extent of woodland in the county, especially down towards its south-east corner, has had more than its unfair share of troubles.

Omagh. Market Street. August 1998. One of the worst-ever atrocities in Ireland. Thirty-one people killed. Over 200 people injured.

When I first went there shortly after the bomb went off everybody was uptight, tense. Everybody knew somebody who had been involved. I parked near the big three at the top of the hill: the double-spired Catholic cathedral, the single-spired Church of Ireland church and the spireless Methodist church. I walked down the High Street. Everybody was trying to avoid everybody else. There was none of the chatter, the craic you find in any high street in Ireland.

Those were the days when people still spoke in initials: CAC, Continuity Army Council; CCDC, Central Citizens Defence

Committee; CRA, Civil Rights Association; NICRA, Northern Ireland Civil Rights Association; CRIS, Crime Report Information System; FRU, Field Reconnaissance Unit; HOLMES, Home Office Large Major Enquiry Service; and, of course, IRA, INLA, RUC, SDLP, SOE, UDA, UVF. The huge murals, the size of houses, were still there. 'Remember the hunger strikers. We have not forgotten them.' So too the posters, '26+6=1', 'Brits out', 'Loose talk costs lives', 'No decommissioning' although according to some with the number of cement trucks criss-crossing the county from the Sperrin Mountains in the north to the Slieve Beag range in the south on the borders with Co. Fermanagh and Co. Monaghan it was as plain as the beard on Gerry Adams's face that some decommissioning or other was taking place.

I was there again during the World Cup 2002. The place was as divided as it is on anything. The Protestants were for England. The Catholics for Ireland – or for whoever was against England.

In Catholic areas, Irish flags were everywhere. On lamp-posts. On telegraph poles. Hanging out of bedroom windows. Tied down to roofs. Whenever Ireland was playing the place was deserted. The streets were empty. There was no traffic. Whenever England was playing it was the opposite. The streets were busy. Traffic was flowing. In the bars the tellies were on. But everybody was desperately trying to avoid watching. Unless, of course, things were going badly for England.

'My son. He's just come back from across,' a barmaid in the Mellon Country Inn tells me. 'He's got a David Beckham shirt. I daren't let him wear it. They'd kill me.'

'So what is he going to do?' I ask. 'Just wear it in the house?'

'No. Wait until the World Cup is over. Then it'll be all right. David Beckham is fine, when he plays for Manchester United. When he plays for England, he's Oliver Cromwell in football boots.'

I also met two strange fat, lardy gutbuckets who told me the reason Ireland would beat Spain and go on to reach the final was because the malachite crystals were for them.

'A Cameroon witch doctor has put a spell on our team,' the paler one tells me.

'But it didn't work,' I say.

'That's why he caused a big storm over the whole country,' she says.

Their solution: cover the Irish team's photograph with malachite crystals. That would break the negative energy being generated by the storm and allow the Irish to win. The more crystals on their photograph, the more chance they had to win.

Yeah. And a three-legged horse can win the Grand National.

In Protestant areas, it was the opposite. Union Jacks and St George's flags were everywhere. Whenever England was playing the streets were deserted. When England beat Argentina they went wild. Memories of Mrs Thatcher and the Falklands were too much for them. The whole place practically had a collective heart attack. Then when England lost, they didn't lose. They were, I was told again and again, 'goal-shy'. What's more, nobody mentioned malachite crystals.

Today things are more relaxed. The posters, the murals, the slogans are still there. But fading rapidly. Instead of empty streets, the place is buzzing.

Strabane, once Northern Ireland's biggest unemployment black spot, is a boom town. Thousands of euro-spending Irish families from the Republic are suddenly pouring in to take advantage of the lower sterling prices.

In the old days the only people who went there went there to see Gray Printers on the main street. John Dunlap used to work there. Today, I'm told, it's a museum. Inside everything looks the same as it did in the eighteenth century. Which is obviously why I failed to recognise it as a museum. It looked just like various printers I used to work for not so many years ago.

Now people who come there come from virtually all over. All seeking – what else? – the booze. It's cheaper, much cheaper in Strabane than in the South. A bottle of vodka, a litre, £11.99 or €19. In the South, the equivalent of €25 or maybe €30. A pack of 24 half-litre cans of Tennents, €15. In the South, at least double that. And so on.

Are the good Protestants of Strabane worried that most of their new-found high-spending shoppers are Catholics? What do you think? Their only worry is accidents. Road accidents.

Ireland: In a Glass of its Own

'You'd never believe it. The big problem is mini-roundabouts,' one strict God-fearing Protestant mushoshu told me. 'These Republicans act as if they've never seen them before. They don't know whether to ignore them and go straight over, whether to turn left as they should, whether to turn right or whether to do a three-point turn. It's amazing we've not all been wiped out by now.'

Another Protestant mushoshu who looked as though he couldn't tell his phospholipases from his guanine nucleotides told me the story of Paddy from the wilds of Co. Donegale. He comes to Co. Tyrone. There are so many people about, the local policeman keeps stopping the traffic, shouting out 'Pedestrians' so people can cross the road. After he's done this three or four times Paddy, who is still standing on the pavement, shouts out at the policeman, 'Lord have mercy on us, isn't it about time you let the Catholics have their turn?'

The locals, however, are still as cautious as ever.

'Round here we say, Never buy a rabbit without a head. It could be a cat,' a straight-up-and-down military barman in the Glenavon House Hotel, Cookstown told me.

The big dodge, of course, is petrol and diesel. Many people, farmers and businessmen, drive backwards and forwards across the border filling up with petrol and diesel. Except the cars are fitted with extra tanks behind the back seats, in the boot, under the floor. They fill up with as much as they can take without raising suspicions. Back home they either store it or sell it on to whoever.

A refinement is red diesel. Ordinary diesel is taxed. Red diesel is not. Buying red diesel when you are not entitled to it is another offence. Except the poor old Irish farmers know what to do.

'So how do you remove the red from the diesel?' I asked one old farmer, who looked like nobody's fuel, one evening over a couple of Guinnesses.

'By mixing it with the green from the Republic.' He downed his Guinness almost in one go. 'They cancel each other out.'

Some say it's of no consequence. Others say it's big-time. Over 400 out of 700 petrol stations in Northern Ireland are selling either illegal or mainly illegal fuel. The total cost of the fraud to the poor long-suffering British taxpayer: between £350 million and £450 million a year. Which, I suppose, is better than Tony Blair going off fighting another illegal war.

For one part of the population, however, the real scam is not petrol. But holy water. I was there once when a chain letter from a certain Marie de Notre Dame was doing the rounds. Enclosed with the letter, it said, were three drops of Lourdes holy water. Only £14. All cheques, postal orders, cash gratefully received. Please send the letter on to your friends. So many people were falling for it, the local priests had to issue a special warning. Lourdes holy water does not travel in envelopes. Even if it did it's not worth £14.

As for the Republicans, when they first started coming they didn't know what to expect. Whether it would be safe. Whether they'd be shouted at. Whether they'd be kidnapped and never heard of again. Even if they had been members of the All Ireland Gustaff Sub-Machine Gun winning team in both 1969 and 1971. It was a bit like East Germans venturing for the first time into West Berlin.

Now they're used to it. It's almost like home. They don't even bother saying a quick rosary any more as they cross over the border.

'It must be said in fairity that they do be welcoming us,' an old farmer from Letterkenny tells me.

You can also – don't tell Gordon Brown, he'd have a heart attack – spend your euros as freely in Strabane as you can in Paris, Frankfurt or Rome.

'We're the most euro-friendly town in the UK,' a very happy bank manager tells me over a glass in a bar outside Cookstown. 'If he wants to launch his campaign for the euro he should come here. We'll show him how to do it.'

Not that there weren't scares about the euro when it was first launched in the South. So many people told me I would be cheated. So many told me to beware of forgeries. Cheating and forgeries I discovered none. If anything I found shops and bars and hotels were more than eager to round down to the nearest round figure. A bundle of newspapers: instead of, say, €11.35 shops would round down to €10. Instead of, say, €22.73 bars would round down to €20. Hotels rounded down to either the €50, the €75 or the €100. One very nice barman even gave me five €5 notes when I asked for change for a €20 note.

As for forgeries, none either. Or at least none apart from a poor-quality €10 note somebody tried to pass in a shop in Straffan, Co. Kildare.

I went into a bar in Cavan town. I ordered my glass of the black stuff, a glass for two others, three rounds of bacon sandwiches. White bread. No lettuce or tomato. Just bacon.

'Sure. 'Tis near enough,' the old guy behind the bar said, sweeping up the notes without even looking at them.' 'Sure we'll all be euronating before long.'

In fact, I reckon everybody was disappointed at the smooth, efficient, very professional changeover from one currency to the other. None more so than the British who seemed to be stunned that such an operation could be successfully handled without their leadership.

Having cracked the cross-border trade in Strabane, I made for Dungannon, a typical hilltop Planters' town. To the British, it was the scene of the first modern civil rights protest by the Catholics against the Protestants in Northern Ireland, in 1969. To the Irish, it's a famous centre for hare coursing. Trouble is many's the year the hares are in short supply. Which may or may not have something to do with it being a famous centre for hare coursing.

I was there one year when there were so few hares around, they had to arrange one way or another to bring them in from the Republic. Not just two or three. But lorryloads for all the hare coursing events all over the county.

There were so many lorries going backwards and forwards across the border, I was told, it threatened to upset yet another booming cross-border business: rubbish. So strict are the rules in the South and so reluctant are they to have their own rubbish dumps, trucks will drive all the way from Wexford in the deep south-east to dump their rubbish in Co. Tyrone.

The pity of it is that if Hugh and Robert Campbell, Thomas Mellon, John Dunlap and all the others had stayed behind the likes of Co. Wexford would not be dumping their rubbish in Co. Tyrone. Co. Tyrone would probably be the centre of the world.

The Carbohydrate Counties

Co. Carlow
Co. Laois
Co. Monaghan
Co. Leitrim
Co. Roscommon
Co. Louth

Carbohydrates are the sugars and starches and bread and potatoes that some people say make us happy, other people say make
us fat. Hence phrases such as, Carb your activities, Carb your
appetite, Carb your enthusiasm. Either way they cause all kinds of
problems. Maybe not the massive, terminal problems other ingredients can cause. But enough to create a few heart-stopping beats.

Like the English caused Ireland throughout the Middle Ages.

Most of the time the English King Edwards or Potatoheads, as
they were known to the Irish, were too concerned with trying to
get the jackboot into the French and the Scots to worry much
about Ireland. The result was the influence of the English in Ireland
went off the boil from time to time. The big English families in
Ireland, however, went from strength to strength, especially the
three Irish musketeers, the earls of Kildare, Desmond and
Ormonde. They had enormous power and influence when in 1173
Henry landed at Waterford and declared it a 'royal city'. They
hardly took any notice and carried on much the same as usual.

Ireland itself also played its part. Because it was so spread out.
Because parts of it were impassable. Because whenever any English
soldiers asked the way to the nearest battlefield, they couldn't for
the life of them understand the directions they were given.

'Excuse me, could you tell me where the battlefield is?'

'Where it always has been.'

'Is this the quickest way to get there?'

'It would be quicker for you if you were the other side of the hill.'

'Is this the quickest way by chariot?'

''Tis quicker than walking.'

The situation continued for around 200 years when there were virtually two Irelands. The Ireland of the big English castles and the landowners, the likes of Prendergast, Fitzgerald, Costello and even Joyce. And the Ireland of the Irish outside the castles. Because the split continued so long without any effort to bridge the gap, each side developed its own culture. The Ireland of the big English castles, of course, sided with the English. The Ireland of the Irish sided with the Irish. Their churches were smaller; their doorways, more rounded; their arches, more pointed. More carbohydrate than protein.

Then came the Tudors. They wanted everything and they wanted it on their terms. Out went the cosy two-part them-and-us arrangement. In came 'If Ireland is English, it will be Tudor English' quickly followed by 'If Ireland supported the Yorkists during the Wars of the Roses, we'll make those bastards suffer.' English law was imposed. No excuses. No dodging. No choosing which bits you like and which bits you don't like. The Irish Parliament was made subservient to the English Parliament. The Irish Parliament couldn't even open for business unless the English gave permission.

Henry VIII turned the screw still further. Instead of being called Lord of Ireland, he made himself King of Ireland. He installed English troops on Irish soil. The English jackboot was firmly on the Irish windpipe. He also broke the power of the big local chiefs or kings as the forerunners of today's arch-Republicans called them. All 200 of them.

First, he was tactful. Give me everything you've got so I can register it in my name. Then I'll give it straight back to you. Tidying up. Administration. Keep the papers in order. He called it 'surrender and regrant'. Those who went along with him called it the longest night of their lives. Those who didn't were crushed, their lands split up among Henry's loyal supporters.

Then came women trouble. Henry not only wanted a new Church of England, he also wanted a new Church of Ireland. The

English Irish gave in. The Irish Irish were Irish about it. First, they said, Er, what was that you said? You only proclaim your laws in English and I don't speak in English so I didn't quite understand what you're saying. Then, they said, Hullo. Hullo. We can't hear you. If you want us to set up a new Church of Ireland you'd better come and tell us about it – knowing full well that by the time the royal train arrived wherever it was going it was probably going to be too late for anything. Then they had to get a bus or a taxi across the bog, up the side of a mountain or across one of the lakes of Killarney.

The result was the English grabbed their share of churches and monasteries in Ireland but nowhere near the number they grabbed back home in England. What Henry forgot, of course, was that the Irish Irish were Catholic Catholic. They were Catholic because they were Irish. They were also Catholic because they had been conquered by Normans admittedly in the pay of the English but they were still Normans. Where did the Normans come from? Was any English king going to be able to tell anyone with even the slightest drop of French blood in their veins what to do?

By the time the English got around to pushing the Church of Ireland in Ireland Ireland the fight back had begun. The Catholic Church was now not just the Catholic Church it was something with which to fight the English. Catholics v Protestants was the new game in town. The Tudor policy of making Ireland England was shattered. Not that the English gave up.

Elizabeth I pushed ahead with the Church of Ireland. She grabbed all the trees in the country for her navy. In return she built Trinity College in Dublin to be the bastion of Protestant learning in Ireland. She did everything she could to root out everything Irish from Ireland. But Ireland was not alone. Catholic Spain wanted to hit Protestant England. Where better than via Catholic Ireland? For two reasons. First, it was an easy target. To the Spanish, the Irish were brute beasts living in straw huts in the mountains. Large-bodied. Handsome features. As, err, active as the roe-deer. Perpetually at war with the English and each other or as Cuellar in his Narrative of the Spanish Armada graphically put it, they were forever going 'Santiago'.

He also made some other perceptive comments.

The women, he said, were very beautiful but badly dressed with a shawl forever doubled over their heads and tied in front. They were great workers and housekeepers. After their fashion.

The men wore short jackets and tight trousers made out of coarse goat's hair. Their hair came down to their eyes. They were great walkers.

As for food and drink, he said they ate everything half cooked and even though they had the best water in the world – are you ready? – they never drank it. They preferred sour milk. Obviously the forerunner of a milk stout.

The second reason the Spanish wanted to attack through the back door: the English Irish had massacred all the survivors of the Spanish Armada when they were washed up on the west coast of Ireland.

In 1601 the Spanish landed at Kinsale, Co. Cork. They were met by powerful Irish chiefs and their armies. All in their short jackets and tight trousers. But they didn't get very far. They were all cut to shreds by the English. The Queen's representative, Sir Humphrey Gilbert, accused the Irish of being nothing but filthy, subhuman, barbarous animals. To show that he was nowhere near as filthy, as subhuman and as barbarous as them, he then, upper-class English gentleman that he was, lined the path to his tent with the heads he ordered cut from the bodies of dead Irish soldiers.

Elizabeth now slightly changed tack. Instead of subjecting Ireland to a ruthless reign of terror she compromised. OK, she said in her best Glenda Jackson accent, you can believe whatever you want but you must be loyal to the English crown. Said the Irish, ''Tis a glass of the black stuff, I'll be having, God bless ye, Ma'am.'

Those who were not loyal and not even prepared to pretend they were loyal, she crushed. Their lands she gave to those who were prepared to be loyal: full-blooded English living in England. Instead of taking the country by force she was going to take it by stealth.

Which part of Ireland was more pro-Irish and anti-English than any other part of the country?

Which did more to attack and try to destroy the English?

Which did more to uphold the beliefs and influence and status of the Catholic Church?

Ulster.

Give that man a signed photograph of Ian Paisley. And a pair of earplugs.

But it was not to last. Under the Stuarts, Ulster did a U-for-Ulster-turn. All the anti-English, Catholic earls and major landowners in Ulster suddenly in 1607 upped and virtually overnight fled aboard a French ship for France. All their land, the Stuarts gave not only to English but also to Scottish Protestants. The Catholics, they squeezed on to smaller and smaller and poorer and poorer tracts of land. For the first time in Irish history, Irish towns began to have Irish quarters. A few even had five of them.

Then to speed up the process, Ulster was given the full colony treatment or colonic irrigation as it was known in the bars at the time. All the rubbish that nobody wanted was flushed out and dumped on Ulster. Companies were set up to find settlers to go out and establish plantations. The only qualification required: They were Protestant. Whisper it not but Derry only got its name Londonderry because it was settled by settlers sent out from London. God only knows what it would be called today if the settlers came from Mutch Itchin in the Crotch.

The more Protestants came, the more Catholics fled. Some went off as mercenaries. They fought for the French, the Spanish, the Austrians, the Poles, anybody with the necessary to pay them. Some went off as missionaries and monks. Some just followed families and friends to wherever. They were desperate to get as far away from the English as possible.

The irony, of course, was the more the Irish left because they couldn't stand the English the stronger the English became. Which, in turn, led to civil war. The Catholics that were left had enough. They rose up against their rulers, the Protestants. In Portadown in Co. Armagh Catholics rounded up over 100 Protestant men, women and children, robbed, stripped and raped them and threw them in the river. Similar events took place all over the country.

Charles I, who was already having problems of his own, pleaded with Parliament for more money to tackle the situation in Ireland.

Instead of deciding to fight the Catholics in Ireland, the Protestant Parliament decided to fight each other. All over Europe Protestant was fighting Catholic, Catholic was fighting Protestant. Not in England. The English Civil War consisted of Protestant fighting Protestant; Anglican fighting Puritan; High Church fighting Low Church.

There was little sweetness around. There were few people getting fat. The carbohydrates were winning.

Co. Carlow
The sweetest county

Famous local resident
Spiritual

Favourite food
Sugar lumps

Favourite drink
Guinness

Favourite pub
The old railway building next to Jacobethan Station, Carlow
town

Favourite restaurant
Teach Dolmain, Carlow town

What to say
Oooooh

What not to say
Yaaaaargh

Co. Carlow is well and truly a carbohydrate. It is sugar-beet country. It was home to the first sugar-beet factory in Ireland. Its golden brown Carlow sugar is famous throughout the world.

Years ago I was practically living in Istanbul. I was travelling all over the place. From Cyprus way up to the Karakum Desert in Central Asia. Istanbul was an ideal base. Central. Civilised. Plenty of good food and drink. Especially after the delights of desert living. One evening I'd just got back from visiting the Kurds up near the border with Iraq. I checked into a nice little hotel in Taksim in the centre of town overlooking the Bosporus. The room was about half the size of a flea's armpit. I know. There were plenty of them around to measure against the size of the room.

I wandered through the lounge on the way to the restaurant. What was on television? A story about a Carlow-based Irish coffee producer called Hot Irishman winning the World Young Business Achiever Award which had just been given in Istanbul. The winning ingredient? Not Irish whiskey. Not the dark roast Colombian coffee. But the golden brown Carlow sugar.

To celebrate their success I did what any other half-Irishman would do, I went and half finished the only bottle of Irish whiskey they had. Or, at least, the only bottle they had left of what they said was Irish whiskey. But, the Lord help me, am I going to complain if it's the only bottle they have left? It's not as if the odd bottle harm half to my system has done any.

Co. Carlow itself is tiny. Only about 350 square miles. The second-smallest county in the country. But, by the Saints of God, do they think they're the sweetest thing on earth! Which, in fact, they probably are. They have sugar with everything. A cold winter's morning. In the rest of the country, it's a huge fry-up and a couple of mugs of tea or coffee. In Co. Carlow, it's a glass of mulled Guinness with one, two or even three lumps of sugar in it. Depending on how many teeth you have left in your head. Then it's time to beat a retreat.

Holy nun dies. Goes to heaven. St Peter is waiting by the Pearly Gates.

'I'm sorry,' he says. 'I don't know what's gone wrong. But we're full. Would ye mind going down to hell for a few days? I'll sort things out. I'll give you a call.'

'Not at all. Not at all,' she says. 'Only too pleased to help out.'

The holy nun goes down to hell. After a week, no call from St Peter. She calls him.

'Quick,' she says. 'You've got to get me out of here. They've taught me how to smoke.'

St Peter says, 'Yes. Yes. Don't worry. I'll sort things out. I'll give you a call.'

Of course, he doesn't call.

A week goes by. The holy nun calls St Peter.

'Quick,' she says. 'You've got to get me out of here. They've taught me how to drink.'

St Peter says, 'Yes. Yes. Don't worry. I'll sort things out. I'll give you a call.'

> Of course, he doesn't.
>
> A week goes by. The holy nun calls St Peter.
>
> 'Forget it,' she says. 'I'm staying.'

Carlow town is also very snobby. A Carlow town address is like a Cheltenham, a Bath or a Gloucester address. People in Carlow town, who look as though they've said No to drugs but the drugs weren't listening say, 'How dare you talk to me about addresses? We haven't been introduced. Good day.'

Some people say it's bad manners. Others say they don't like talking to strangers because they are ashamed of how many teeth they have missing. I think it's all because they're embarrassed by what happened to their most famous son, John Tyndall, who was born in Leighlinbridge. His father was a policeman. He went to the local Ballinabranagh National School. He got a job with the Ordnance Survey. He studied physics under Dr Robert Bunsen of Bunsen burner fame. He went on to become one of the leading scientists, lecturers, writers of his day. He knew everybody. Darwin, Huxley, Faraday. He was the first to explain why the sky is blue. He helped prove germs existed and caused diseases. He developed a forerunner of the fibre-optic cable. He takes ill. He asks his loving wife, for whom he has worked so hard to keep her in the manner to which she has become accustomed, to give him his medicine. She gives him instead a killer overdose of sleeping tablets. By the evening he's dead. Now that's a caring Carlow wife for you.

They can't be too proud of their second-most famous son either.

Go to Carlow town, by all means. But don't whatever you do mention anything about dropping in on anybody. Because it was a Carlow-born Church of Ireland clergyman from a strict Quaker family, the Revd Samuel Haughton, who calculated the drop necessary to hang a man. Forget all those Wild West films. The posse captures the baddies. They string them up to the nearest tree. The leader of the posse then goes along kicking the boxes out from under the baddies' feet. It won't work. The good Reverend calculated that to hang the average man, it would take at least a 4.5-metre drop to break his neck outright. Anything less, the job would be half done. Anything more, things could get quite, err, messy. But that's not all the holy clergyman was famous for. He also calculated a novel way of measuring blood pressure. He would sever the main artery in a dog and measure the distance the blood spurted out. But I didn't tell you that. You know what people are like about dogs.

Instead mention the one subject they always like visitors to raise with them before they've even ordered the first pint, the highlight of Carlowlife: heroin addicts. At the last count they had practically a hundred of them scattered all over the place. Scattered being the right word. But these are not ordinary heroin addicts. Not even the ones with green and yellow elephants sitting beside them. These are Co. Carlow upmarket heroin addicts. A small fix: €25. A gram: €200. A week's supply, no questions asked: €700. A heroin salt lick for your horse: €1000. One reason why outsiders say Carlow town is so snobbish: the high price of heroin on the streets.

The other reason and the second Carlowlife subject they just love to discuss before the second pint is the annual August Fair Day in Borris.

'It's a great day is it?'

''Tis. 'Tis that indeed.'

'A tradition?'

''Tis. 'Tis that indeed.

'Going on for hundreds of years?'

'It has. It has.'

'A great day out?'

''Tis. 'Tis that indeed.'

'Then why do all the shops shut, why do they all put shutters up against the windows, why do all the pubs close? Why do the police surround the town, stop traffic from going in or out, why does it take weeks to clean up all the mess and rubbish afterwards, why . . . ?'

'Will ye be having another?'

'I will. I will.'

'God bless.'

'God bless.'

But even that I'll forgive them. Because, sugar apart, they're big on the drink. They don't only produce their own range of beers but a range of unique spirits as well.

The beers I found in Carlow town in an old railway building on the banks of the River Barrow. I had a go at a red ale called Mollings, a wheat beer called Curim and a Guinness lookalike called O'Hara's. My favourite: O'Hara's. It didn't have the round-ness and the depth of a Guinness. But it was close. A few more pints and I could have been an addict.

The spirits are of a more insubstantial nature. Half the people I met swore to me on the life of all they hold dear as well as that of their wife that they wouldn't tell a soul what they had told me. So I'm afraid I can't tell you that Clonegal or Huntingdon Castle on the River Derry down near the border with Wexford is haunted by Maeve, Queen of Connaught. Many's the night she can be seen by the holy bush in the grounds combing her hair in the moon-light. Sitting beside her, a white cat. Mary. Mother of God, now I've told you, you're going to have to kill the man who told me. And the white cat.

But that's not all. The other half of the people I met swore to me on all they don't hold dear including their wife that sometimes in the Red Bedroom of the castle you could see an apparition of a bishop; in the downstairs passage, a maid; in the Red Room, a nurse; and in the Yellow Room, a tiny hand drifting across the room. Which was obviously harmless.

It wasn't the first ghost story I've been told. Late at night in most Irish homes and even hotels the talk often turns to the resi-dent ghost.

In the depths of Co. Galway, I was once told of a hare which leaps around the bottom of the garden and then suddenly turns into a witch.

''Tis awful. 'Tis awful, may the Lord have mercy on them,' they say.

Ireland: In a Glass of its Own

In the fancy Shelbourne Hotel in Dublin, spiritual home of the o'glitterati, the talk is of a pale, sick child called Mary Masters who died of cholera, who haunts the wine cellars and basements.

''Tis awful. 'Tis awful, may the Lord have mercy on them,' they say.

Leap – as in Leap of the imagination – Castle, Co. Offaly, however, is the top of the spirit scale. They say it's the most haunted house in Western Europe. Bejasus. A monk prowls the grounds. Cloaked figures disappear around every corner. Children's screams are heard from the basement. Prisoners' moans filter through from the dungeons. And from behind the walls of the chapel, you can still hear the agonised screams from forty members of an Irish clan impaled on spikes and walled up for ever.

''Tis awful. 'Tis awful, may the Lord have mercy on them,' they say.

Co. Carlow is also the first place I've come across which believes in architectural ghosts. Strange buildings that don't exist and strange buildings that do exist.

One evening I was in The Castle Inn. It was coming up to closing time. The talk had turned to ghosts, which seemed odd as Carlow had done more than most towns to abolish them. It was the first town after Dublin to install electric street lighting.

An old boy with a serious face, a black hat and an empty glass told me to go and take a look at Bagenalstown on the River Barrow.

'It looks,' he says, 'like Versailles.'

'Versailles,' I wondered.

'Versailles,' he says.

'Versailles, France?'

'Versailles, France,' he says. 'You can tell. It's obvious. The Court House looks like the Parthenon.'

The following morning I'm in Bagenalstown. Why, I don't know. But for the life of me I couldn't find it.

I kept stopping and asking people where it was. Nobody knew what I was talking about.

'This is not the best place to look for it,' an old boy with a bicycle told me. 'Try somewhere else.'

With which he clambered back on his bicycle and cycled down the lane.

I stopped in a bar. Nobody had heard of it either.

'Are you sure?' the barman says to me. 'This is not France, y'know.'

Mon Dieu. Is that a fact? I wondered why nobody understood what I was saying.

Outside the bar I stopped an old lady. She looked as if she had just escaped from behind a chapel wall.

''Tis as gone as it'll be,' she says and races off down the road.

But I found something even more spooky.

Driving along country lanes in the middle of nowhere near the Blackstairs Mountains, where if you eat too much they say you are 'fog full', I suddenly saw in the distance the kind of gate you see outside a French church, behind the gate, the doors of a maharaja's palace.

I slammed on the brakes. Was I coming under the influence? Was I dreaming? Was the fairy juice finally getting to me? Were there really, really . . . I got out. I wandered through the gates. They were real enough. I opened the doors. As solid as a two-day-old naan sandwich with a cheap chicken vindaloo inside. Behind the doors, chandeliers. A Venetian room. A Moroccan room. And, of course, an Indian room.

I hurried back to what was called a music room. Music room! The place was full of thick swirling mist. Through the mist, I could see candles. Then – and, I can tell you, this really gave me a turn – I heard a harp, some singing . . .

It scared the bejesus out of me, I can tell you.

I turned and saw a big burly figure coming towards me. It could have been St Peter himself or a big buck Irish navvy.

'Excuse me,' I said to the cratur. 'I'm looking for the people who run this place.'

'You've come to the right place,' he says.

It was too much for me. I ran for the car, leapt in and roared back up the lane to the nearest bar.

'Jesus, Mary and Joseph,' said the barman. 'You look as though you could do with half a dozen drinks.'

I told him what I'd seen – or, at least, what I thought I'd seen.

'That's no architectural ghost,' he says. 'That's the bed and breakfast down the road. Run by Tony Crilly. He thinks it's unique. Take no notice.'

Unique. I'd say it was unique. Especially after all that talk about ghosts and witches.

'Now,' says the barman leaning across the bar to me, 'there's only one thing that will do the trick. What you need is a Hot Irishman inside you. Stay there. I'll go and get you one straight away.'

I tell you. I'm not going anywhere in Co. Carlow again. In body or in spirit. However many lumps of sugar they give me.

Co. Laois
A life behind bars

Famous local resident
Spud Murphy

Favourite food
Potatoes Potatoes Potatoes

Favourite drink
Guinness

Favourite pub
Egan's, Portlaoise

Favourite restaurant
The Castle Arms, Durrow

What to say
I demand to see your lawyer

What not to say
Honestly, he told me your name was Spud

If Co. Carlow is sugar, Co. Laois is potatoes. Small. Not large. Cheap. Not expensive. Ordinary. Not the best. In other words the ones full of carbohydrates.

Believe me, I know my potatoes. All 9,253 of them. I've even been to the earthquake-proof potato gene bank deep inside the International Potato Centre in Lima, Peru. Not many people can say that. Not, of course, that many people would want to. They've probably got far more interesting things to do with their life.

I've also done everything there is possible to do with a potato. Well, almost everything.

I've planted them in long, almost straight lines, heaped the soil on top of them, watched over them and watered them.

I've dug them up at my wife's instruction, shaken the earth off them and stored them away in dry sacks in a safe place where they've been totally forgotten. For ever.

I've eaten them every way you can think of: mashed, chipped, roasted, boiled, wedged, burnt to a cinder. That's when I visit my wife's mother.

But I must admit, more than anything I prefer my potatoes squashed, the juice distilled, three times filtered through charcoal, chilled and served in an up-right glass with a stack of ice and a slice of lemon. Almost as good as a pint of the black stuff. Cheers.

Come to think of it, Co. Laois, which used to be known as the Queen's County because it was there in Abbeyleix that the eighth Viscount Ashbrook, Robert Flower invented the latch-hook needle which, as all us girls know, made it so much easier to make rugs and carpets without so much as breaking a single nail, actually

239

looks like a potato. One of those gnarled, twisted ones, encrusted with lumps of mud, that are always for some reason reluctant to

> Policeman stops girl driving through Portalaoise. He gives her the Breathalyser. She blows into it.
>
> 'My goodness,' he says to her. 'You've had a couple of stiff ones.'
>
> 'Jesus, Mary and Joseph,' she exclaims. 'Does it tell you that as well?'

leave the warmth of the sod to rot slowly away, forgotten, ignored and overlooked inside a sack at the back of the boiler house.

The best part, like the best part of a potato, is the outside, the skin. The Slieve Bloom mountains up on the border with Co. Offaly are not the greatest mountains in the world. We are after all talking Co. Laois not Co. Kerry. But they're pleasant, work-manlike, everyday. The best thing about them is the description of them in an Irish book, *Long Distance Walks: A guide to the way-marked trails*. It suggests the best way to tackle them is with two cars.

Inside the potato skin, there are some pleasant towns. In a carbohydrate kind of way.

Portalington is unusual. It's a mixture of Irish, French and German, a three-chip town. Irish because, well, it's Irish. French because French Huguenots settled here. St Paul's Church is built on the site of the old French church although you'd never guess if it wasn't for a few old gravestones in the churchyard. German because Germans settled here after Cromwell had done his worst. The power station on the edge of the town has nothing to do with the Germans. It was built in the 1930s. It was the first power station in Ireland to generate electricity using peat. I turned up there once. Suddenly I thought the power station wasn't burning peat but cannabis. The police had just seized a massive 4.5 tonnes of the stuff, worth around £10 million, one of Ireland's largest drug seizures ever. It was all packed inside a consignment of doors from Durban, South Africa, shipped through Antwerp, Belgium and then Dublin. How they got to Portalington nobody was saying. I didn't dare look vaguely interested. Well, what would you do if your passport showed you had just got back from Colombia, Bolivia, Venezuela and, you know, that country in the mountains with all those poppies? There was no way I wanted to inject anything into the conversation.

Stradbally is not where famous Irish-made violins are produced. It's more O'More, the centre of O'More power and influence. In the good old days. Today it's no O'More. It is, however, famous for its old O'Boilers. There are more than enough of them at the Irish Steam Preservation Society museum. Still hissing. Still spitting. Still likely to blow their top. Which reminds me. Must post that postcard.

Mountmellick is also no O'More. Once a great linen centre. Once virtually a Quaker town. Today it's frayed at the edges, a bit tatty and O'More a sinker than a mere quaker.

Ballyhide, however, kept on the right lines. Come to think of it, it had no alternative. Because local-lad-made-great engineer William Dargan built most of Ireland's railway lines as well as roads, canals and practically the whole of Belfast harbour. He also built a railway that used to literally suck the trains uphill. Now, where he got that idea from, I have no idea. Dargan also established the Irish National Gallery of Art where no doubt he came across many, err, Queen's citizens.

Abbeyleix is the human face of the Irish famine. The local number one, Viscount de Vesci, not only went out of his way to help the suffering and the dying unlike most big farmers and landlords but when the famine was over he helped the survivors erect a fountain to himself in the village square as a thank you. Not many landlords did that for their tenants either.

Vicarstown is where the largest simultaneous Riverdance took place in the history of the world. Over 1,000 people. All along the banks of the canal. On 30 April 2000. You'll never know how much I regret not being there.

The centre of the potato, the heart of the spud, is Portlaoise. Not because it is a town with a heart. It hasn't got one as far as I could discover. It's bland. It's full of shops. Including, they boast, the best shopfront in the whole country. Wowee. Now that's something to boast about. What they don't boast about is that it is also home to one of the biggest prisons in the country. As a result, the place is full of wall-humping, hard-eyed, groiny prison officers. Half of them look as though they've been beaten up. The other half look as though they beat themselves up so as not to look any different. Go into a bar, casually mention while you're waiting for the Guinness to settle that you heard, maybe, perhaps, in a manner of speaking, there was a rumour that D Block was condemned 40 years ago as being unfit to hold prisoners but was still in business, that there was no full-time doctor in the hospital's 203-bed facility even though more and more prisoners had drug problems or try and tell a joke about prison officers or even the police, ranks close, doors are slammed shut, the whole place goes silent.

I was in Egan's once just after some prisoners had escaped. One of the wall-humpers was reading a report about it in the *Irish Independent*.

'Lads. Lads,' he bellows. 'Says here in the Independent the break-out was caused by unsuitable screws in the country's most modern prison.' He read the words slowly with his finger. 'But that can't be true,' he went on. 'That door was mended last week.'

There was not a sound.

I finished my glass and fled.

Some say they're the way they are because they are a proud, close-nit community who believe in what they are doing. I think it's because they are trying to understand what was being said.

In fact their whole view of the world is so back-to-front there were enormous street signs displayed back-to-front. More unnervingly nobody seemed to have noticed.

The good citizens of Co. Laois, every one of them chips off the old block or Potatoheads as they prefer to be called, like nothing better than to be continually reminded of their association with the Solanum tuberosum, which as every Latin scholar knows, means

Eat these and you'll end up with as many tubers as if you spent all day lying in the sun.

Go into a shop or supermarket. No matter how busy or crowded it is the shop assistants love nothing better than spending hours on end discussing the relative merits of one potato over another.

Go into a restaurant. The manager will be only too pleased to return your meal to the kitchens if the potatoes are not the variety you wanted or not cooked to your satisfaction.

Go into a bar. The barman likes nothing better than to be greeted as Spud. Or even Spud Murphy.

Believe me.

Have a nice stay in Co. Laois. Whether it's three days, three weeks or thirty-three years.

Co. Monaghan
You'd Monaghan if you got thrown out of your hotel

Famous local resident
Anyone but Sir John Leslie

Favourite food
Anything but a Big Macca Burger

Favourite drink
Guinness

Favourite pub
Any but Castle Leslie

Favourite restaurant
Farnham Arms Hotel, Cavan town

What to say
Please throw me out of my hotel room

What not to say
The best hotel in Co. Monaghan is in Co. Cavan

If Co. Carlow is sugar, if Co. Laois is potatoes, the stony grey soil of Co. Monaghan is a sweet potato. None more so than Sir John Leslie, the giddy owner of Castle Leslie, a rambling Victorian monstrosity in Glaslough, home to Winston Churchill's christening robe, and the first house in this part of the world to have a bathroom. Inside or out. Over 80 years old. A bit of a raver and freestyle dancer. And the last person in the world to keep a secret. He is the man who famously told the world's press that Paul McCartney was planning to get married there on Tuesday 11 June but he'd been told to keep it a secret.

I was there at the time. Quite by accident. Thanks to the good Sir John and his little secret I got thrown out of my hotel to make way for the wedding guests. So was everybody else staying anywhere in and around Monaghan town. Warm, welcoming, hospitable people that the Irish are, they obviously thought they could make more money out of the wedding guests and hangers-on than out of us poor, hard-working wage slaves. What made it worse was that I had already ordered and paid for my Continental Breakfast the following morning. Go anywhere in the world, hotels automatically serve a Continental Breakfast. Not Ireland. In Ireland everybody goes for the huge, greasy, Traditional Irish Breakfast. If you want Continental you have to order it and pay for it the night before. I only ordered it because I was leaving extra early otherwise I'd have gone for the Traditional as usual.

My only option, a Big Macca Burger, specially created to honour a lifelong vegetarian, and a desperate search for somewhere else to stay. Even the St Vincent de Paul night shelter for the poor and destitute of the parish was fully booked.

Thanksamillion, Sir John. Any time I can do you a favour and throw you out in the street because I've guests coming, let me know.

The nearest place I could find was the Farnham Arms Hotel in Cavan town, a million miles and two hours' drive away.

Then it was touch and go whether I got the last room or some antsy Australian sheephead who claimed he was digging for gold at Tullyback close to the border with Co. Antrim.

In Rockcorry there was another man who changed the shape of things: John Gregg. He was the inventor of one of the two modern forms of shorthand: Gregg. The other, of which I am the proud owner of a certificate for writing at 120 words per minute: Pitman. Pitman is small, neat, very precise. Gregg is huge and wild and scrawly.

Co. Monaghan, apart from when it's full of people going to weddings and drinking champagne, is more water than land. 'A charmful water-loose county,' someone told me. Nearly 200 lakes full of every kind of length of fish you can imagine. Most of them the grandest in the world.

The cats similarly are also the grandest and the biggest in the world. Some of them, the size of pumas. Fully armed police and the army are forever being called in to hunt and track them down. Special surveillance aircraft circle overhead. Huge areas of land in Rossmore Forest Park are sealed off. But in vain. The grandest cats are so full of the grandest fish they somehow always manage to outsmart the obviously less than grandest police and army Ireland has to offer.

What little land there is for the pumas, they don't call land but tiny hills, or as somebody once said, 'a basket of eggs', which may or may not have something to do with the fact there are chicken, duck and poultry farms all over the place. Which probably accounts for the fact everyone told me the local priest was a clucking guardian angel.

'Young girl goes to him for confession,' a failed gamekeeper whose reading was not up to the necessary calibre tells me while we're watching the great Irish puma hunt. 'Father, she says, 'tis ashamed I am, but I'm pregnant. Says the priest to her, Are you sure it's yours?'

The puma hunt over, I even discovered a quail farm in Emyvale. Doesn't that also prove that the grandest pumas in the world are gorging themselves on the grandest fish otherwise there wouldn't be a duck or a chicken or a quail in the whole county?

In the old days, especially around Carickmacross, Co. Monaghan was always known for lace making. Today it's known for trucks racing backwards and forwards to Derry. Try and cross the main road any time of the day or night, it's easier to get a hotel room in Monaghan during a McCartney wedding. What's in or not in the trucks is another matter.

One evening in the Shirley Arms as the roar of the traffic began to die down and I began to hear myself drink I fell in with a bunch of locals only too willing to spill the low-down on Sir John. One of them was your typical stage Irishman. Red face. Tufts of hair. An overcoat that looked as though it came over with St Patrick. A pair of old boots. He looked as though he was at the other side of a gallon of poteen. He told me he was a martyr for the drink. Every time his eyebrows started to twitch he knew somebody was going to buy him a drink.

His eyebrows were twitching.

I offered to buy him a drink.

'Whatellyehafftotink?'

Who says I don't speak the language?

'A shlarge Guinness,' he says. 'And a shlarge Jameson's. God bless hyou.'

He finished them one after the other. Zonk. Zonk.

'People shlop me in the shtreet,' he says. 'They shask me where ish the shnearest boozer. I shay, You're looking at him. And the shame again, shplease your worship. You're a shgood man. TanksbetoGod.'

Another old-timer, who was more National Theatre than small-town rep, red face, tufts of hair, raincoat and boots, joined us.

'Owareyenow?' he says.

'Wahyehavin?' I asked him.

He told me he was getting scared because he was getting

splotchy yellow marks all over his fingers which he said was a sign of death. The fact he smoked over 40 cigarettes a day didn't seem to have any bearing on the matter.

I didn't buy him a packet of cigarettes.

Nobody seemed surprised the old raver had spilled the beans. Known as The Disco King of Ireland, most weekends, apparently, the good Sir John can be found in any of the local discos whooping it up to what he calls 'the boom-boom music'.

I met one old lady with a dodgy ginger wig. She told me she handled all the dirty washing for the good lord himself.

'He claims he suffers from discoitis,' she tells me. 'He goes to Ibiza and says he dances until seven o'clock in the morning. That's probably because he can't do anything else.'

A descendant of Attila the Hun, apparently Sir John's only other claim to fame they told me was the fact his father was the man who famously thumped Bernard Levin on the old *That Was The Week That Was* about the same number of years ago.

Drink gave way to more drink.

I mentioned the traffic, the lorries ploughing backwards and forwards to Derry.

God help us, says the stage Irishman, 'I'm shnot shaying. Northerners are shsuspicious. They don't jusht want to shopen shup a vein in your arm to see the colour of your blood they want to know which shway it ish flowing as well.'

Monaghan town itself is a Rotary Club kind of town. Upright. Respectable. A couple of fancy buildings. Some interesting old ruins. Two small ponds or rather lakes. A couple of eggs. All a touch boring. Or maybe Scottish. I can't imagine anyone there having a riotous time. Especially when you're likely to be kicked out at a moment's notice and have to trudge the streets looking for a room.

Castleblayney, named after the castle built by the Blayney family – complicated, these Irish town names, like Mon, moan, Aghan, Irish for 'mother-in-law' – is much the same. Big. Busy. Serious. Respectable. Too much traffic. Too few places to park.

Just outside Castleblayney is Lough Muckno. A name like that I thought I just had to see it. Then somebody told me about the Lake Muckno Leisure Park so I didn't bother.

Co. Monaghan

Somebody else then told me that Co. Monaghan was famous for clones. The Lord save us. Thousands of Sir John Leslies stomping around all night to boom-boom music and getting people thrown out of their hotel rooms. It was too much. But, God is good to us, it turned out that clones was Clones, a pretty nondescript town on the border with Co. Fermanagh with some pretty nondescript remains of a nondescript abbey, a strange-looking round tower and something even stranger, Hilton Park, a fabulous out-of-this-world hotel set in the middle of rolling parklands three miles out of Clones on the Ballyhaise Road. Which did not throw its guests out on the streets whoever was coming to town. Everybody told me I couldn't miss it. Big green gates, they said. And, of course, I missed it. The gates were black.

I don't want to say too much about it because Clones is home to Barry McGuigan, a former world boxing champion. I know he was only a featherweight but he could still do me some damage. Well maybe not so much as Sir John did but it's not worth the risk.

Co. Leitrim
Leitrem alone. They're asleep

Famous local resident
Ireland's answer to Chekhov

Favourite food
New Year's Day salmon

Favourite drink
Guinness

Favourite pub
The one with the Zimmer frames

Favourite restaurant
The one that serves solid food

What to say
Thirty-nine, if a day

What not to say
But I'm shouting as loud as I can

Carbohydrates cause problems. In many cases heart-stopping problems. There's no better proof of this than Co. Leitrim, which is known as the poor heart of Ireland. The whole place looks as though it is suffering from a heart attack. If not, the consequences of one. For the first thing you notice when wandering around the empty streets and market places is how few people there are to notice. The second thing you notice, if you see anybody, is how old they are. Since it gave birth to the mighty River Shannon, 240 miles from beginning to end, Co. Leitrim doesn't look as if it's given birth to anything else. It must have not only the fewest but the oldest people of any county in the country. In fact it has so few and so old people that you hardly notice it is also the wettest county in the country.

I asked one heavily perspiring owner of an Irish-registered Zimmer frame if it was true Leitrim was Irish for 'Leitrem alone and they'll live for ever'.

'Will ye speak up?' he says. 'I canna, for the love of God, hear what ye are mumbling about.'

In fact so out of date are the doddery old residents of Co. Leitrim – all three and a half of them   that to them West Brit means Dublin. Something which my friends in Dublin really appreciate.

''Tis an advantage,' I was told by a doddery old kluk, who looked as though she'd been to the split ends of the earth and back. Twice. On a hospital trolley. 'We're an undeveloped area. We get more money from them people in Brussels than anywhere else . . .' She began to nod off. I chinked the glasses on the bar.

She woke up. 'More money. More help. Tanksbetogod. I'll have another one. And more zzzzzz.'

She was snoring so loudly, she woke up the only other drinker in the bar.

'By God, ye're right,' he says. 'A sparrow flies over Co. Leitrim. He brings his own lunchzzzzz.'

Old farmer goes to the doctor.

Doctor says, 'I'm sorry but I'm afraid you've not only got cancer you've also got Alzheimer's.'

Old farmer says, 'Thanks be to God, I haven't got Alzheimer's.'

Fans of Co. Leitrim, which looks as though it's being squeezed to a long, slow cot death by Co. Sligo on one side and Co. Donegal on the other, deny it.

'Look,' they say, adjusting the batteries in their hearing aids and wobbling their Zimmer frames in the air. 'Look at Carrick. Look at Rockin' Robin's night, whatdoyecall it, bar, pub or something. There's always plenty of zzzzz.'

Sure Rockin' Robin's is one of the biggest nightclubs in the west. Sure they can pack in up to 2000 people at a time. Sure they have more than their fair share of hen nights and stag parties. But – this will come as a shock to the old dodderers of Co. Leitrim – everybody comes from outside the county.

For the benefit of any readers from Co. Leitrim I'll not only repeat that but I'll repeat it in big bold capital letters. EVERYBODY COMES FROM OUTSIDE THE COUNTY.

Rule number one if you're planning to make whoopee in Ireland. Don't do it on your own doorstep. Do it on somebody else's. Rule number two: if you are going to do it, do it where the locals won't take any notice or even realise what you're doing: Co. Leitrim.

Such is its reputation that it attracts hen parties and stag nights not only from all over the country but from as far away as London itself. Dublin, Temple Bar used to be the number-one target for the London-drinking Irish lovers. Not any more. Too many people. Too many controls. Too high prices. Too many problems having a smoke. They have moved on to Carrick, Rockin' Robin's and anywhere else that provides the necessary. And lets them smoke. Whatever.

I know a group of farriers and young farmers from back in Sussex who regularly hit Co. Leitrim fishing for a good time. They take in a couple of races or a local hunt. Then they hit Rockin' Robin's or any one of a number of bars in the area for the full weekend before staggering back home on a Monday morning, hung-over, bleary and not having spent a penny on a hotel or a b. & b.

If you're living in Sussex, a word of advice. Never get your horse shod on a Monday morning. It could be lame for the week.

Or at least that used to be the case until Ireland introduced its ban on smoking in bars and clubs and restaurants. Now the crowds have moved north across the border where they can smoke away to their lungs' content. Those who can't move north have moved outside. There are now so many people outside pubs smoking I reckon that having banned smoking inside bars the government should now insist on special health warnings on the inside of pub doors, 'Government Health Warning. Smoking outside can damage your health and cause all kinds of pneumonia and even death.' Are they concerned about people's health or are they not? What's more there's more of the craic going on outside the bars and clubs than there is inside. In fact, the craic is so good outside I'm actually thinking of taking up smoking just so I can join in.

I was in Ireland just after the ban came in. A group of us went out to the local bar for a big reunion celebration. You know the kind of thing. Everybody talks about their failures, their disasters, the mistakes they've made. Then they talk about work.

I got the first round. The visitor returning from over. The usual thing. Then one by one everybody made their excuses and went outside for a smoke.

'If God did not want man to smoke he wouldn't have invented

chemotherapy,' says one old sludge trap with methylphenidate coming out of his ears as he gets up to go outside.

I spent practically the whole evening by myself, sitting at the bar, reading the menu a million times over and chatting away to an old boy who looked as though his clothes were a happy hunting ground for woolly bear larvae. He was sucking an empty pipe.

'Doctor just told me I've got cancer in the cheek,' he says. 'Says it comes from smoking the pipe in the same place all these years.'

'Did he tell you to stop smoking?' I wondered, the way you do.

'No,' he says. 'Told me to smoke the pipe the other side of my mouth.'

My grand evening out in smoke-free Ireland. I was back in my hotel by 8.30 p.m. Everybody else was off to spend the rest of the weekend with wives and girlfriends. Not necessarily their own. But, hey, I've got the clean pair of lungs.

The bars and clubs apart, plenty of other people go to Co. Leitrim also fishing for a good time. On New Year's Day. On the banks of the Dowes River where 22 years out of 25 they catch the first salmon of the year to be caught in the whole country.

I'm not hooked on fishing. It's a bit too hectic for me. But I was dragged there one year to see if I could stand the excitement. Excitement! It was one of the three years out of 25 they caught nothing. It was so bad that six days later the first salmon of the year had still not been caught. The whole place was left reeling. In more senses than one. It was worse than the death of Shergar, Joseph Locke and, when it comes, Terry Wogan all rolled into one.

Small groups gathered on street corners.

''Tis strange. 'Tis strange. Last year we had the first one caught and eaten by teatime.'

People sat in bars staring at their glass of Guinness.

''Tis the bad weather. 'Tis the high waters. Was the same in 1994. The first salmon wasn't caught then till January 15. 'Twill be the same again this year, the Lord have mercy on us.'

One old fisherman, huge waders, collar and tie, sports jacket and an old hat full of flies and feathers, had a far more rational explanation.

Global warning? Pollution? Drift-net fishing? Overfishing? Smaller spawning stocks?

''Tis the curse of the red-haired woman,' he says.

'Red-haired woman?' I wondered.

''Tis a fact. See a red-haired woman when ye go fishing and ye'll have a bad day of it.'

'Because she scares away the fish?'

'Because ye'd be thinkin' of her all the time, ye wouldn't be able to do ye job properly.'

Well that's it then. Ban all red-haired women and we'll be back to eating fresh salmon for lunch on New Year's Day.

All those in favour say, Scarlett O'Hara.

To look at Co. Leitrim, however, you'd never guess it had any unseen shallows even though in many places the soil is often no more than an inch deep. Beneath the soil is either gravel or thick, sticky, blue clay.

Carrick-on-Shannon, the big town in the county, or Carrick as it is known to the half-dozen locals who live there, is probably the most unIrish town in the country. Call me a traditionalist if you must, but to me Ireland is market towns, bars, squares, thatched cottages, horses, churches, maybe the occasional convent, a priest or a nun wandering down the street, a happy man slumped in a doorway, a couple or three empty cans beside him.

Carrick is none of them. It's a river. It's boats and pleasure cruises. A marina. Sweaters and boaters. There's no town square. Just a row of shops. Not even the church is a full-time church. It's only in business a couple of days a week. A leftover, no doubt, from the days when it was a Protestant stronghold.

At one time there was talk of opening up the Shannon so it could take boats to Carrick and then from Carrick on up to the lakes of Co. Fermanagh. No more. Every time they tried to have a meeting to discuss the idea everybody fell asleep.

Outside Carrick, it's the land that guidebooks forgot. Even Lonely Planet don't mention it on their map of the area.

Somebody told me about Mohill, home to Turlough O'Carolan, a wild, raving poet, blind harpist, composer and roaring drunk.

His greatest achievement: drinking whole bottles of whiskey one after another. His greatest shame: writing the music for 'The Star-Bannered Spangle' or some such tune, I can never remember. On his deathbed, he called for a large whiskey but couldn't drink it. Instead he kissed the glass.

'Two old friends,' he says, 'should never part without a kiss.'

What a way to go. Fantastic.

But I couldn't find Mohill. Not anywhere. Not even in my battered old copy of *Fodor's Ireland*, which looks as though it helped St Patrick himself find his way around. Maybe it's like 'The Star-Spangled Banner' itself. All hot air. No substance.

Somebody else told me about Dromahair. Something to do with the O'Rourkes and Lough Gill. Somebody else again recommended Carrigallen. Ideal spot for also hitting Counties Cavan and Fermanagh, they said.

Were they in the guidebooks? No way. Was the tourist office any good? All they gave me were leaflets on boats, boats and more bloody boats. I tried stopping and asking people the way. There was nobody to stop and ask. Or if there was most of them died before I got to them.

One old boy I managed to catch staggering into a bar somewhere near Drumshano.

'God bless ye,' he says. 'They ought to be thereabouts.' And disappears into the bar.

I stopped a few miles further down the road.

'Where am I?' I asked another old boy staggering into another bar.

'You've no problems,' he says. 'You're right here.'

'But where's here?'

He hobbles into the bar I assumed to ask somebody. Ten minutes later I am still waiting.

I drove on.

That evening I spent in a mysterious b. & b. up a lane, down a track, in the middle of a field run by a young couple. They were in their seventies.

I mentioned that Co. Leitrim was the big unknown.

'Not for much longer,' says the patriarch of the house. All white hair. Deep voice. Old suit. And rectal polyp. 'The council are having a local cinema.'

'A local cinema?' I wondered nervously.

'A local cinema,' he says again as if the polyp was beginning to throb. 'It will drive around the county.'

'But how will that help people find out about the place?'

Have I misunderstood? Am I missing something? Is being in Co. Leitrim beginning to affect me?

'You don't understand,' he says and he was dead right I didn't. 'The cinema will show films about the county. They've started making the films already.'

Oh now I understand. Co. Leitrim is going to make films about Co. Leitrim to be shown in a van driving around Co. Leitrim to Co. Leitrim people living in err, Co. Leitrim. Of course, it all makes sense now. And to think I didn't understand what he was saying. Must be the lack of smoke and fish.

Mrs Matriarch, who looked as though she took in the neighbours' washing when they weren't looking, said it was very cold. Would I like my bed warmed?

''Tis no trouble at all,' she says. 'I can get young Sean to go and lie in it for an hour. He'll warm it up a treat for ye.'

Sean was fifty years old, fat, unmarried and smelt like a steroid-addled pig.

Not only did I decline the lady's kind offer I piled every stick of furniture in my room up against the door that night. Just in case they took their hospitality to, perhaps, unreasonable extremes.

Well, you can never be too sure can you? Even in Ireland.

About the only good thing about Co. Leitrim or rather the only protein in a mass of carbohydrates is John McGahern, whom some hail as the Irish Chekhov. If he is, he is Chekhov on a bad day. A Lady without a Dog. Thirty-three Sisters. A Cherry Orchard that gives you the pip.

His books are pure Co. Leitrim. Slow. Plodding. Dull. Unexciting. His last, *That They May Face the Rising Sun*, would make anyone want to spend the rest of their days in Rockin' Robin's. Even if it was full of farriers from East Sussex. Smoking their lungs out.

Set on the edge of a lake somewhere in the middle of the

county, it tells the story of two ex-trendy London types who have come back to seek their roots. Their neighbours: Jamesie and Mary Murphy, who've practically never set foot off the land part-surrounding the lake.

'Have you any news?' says the ex-trendy London type.

'No news. Came looking for news,' says Jamesie.

Long Co. Leitrim silence.

'I'm sure I told it all before,' says Jamesie.

'Go ahead. There's nothing new in the world. And we forget. We'll hear it again,' sighs the ex-London trendy type.

It's spring.

'Everything will have started to grow,' says Jamesie.

'It's all going to be very interesting,' says ex-London trendy type.

He starts building a shed.

'How the rafters frame the sky,' exclaims the ex-London trendy type.

'As long as they hold the iron, lad, they'll do,' grunts the builder who sounds more like a blunt Yorkshireman than your lyrical Irishman.

By the Lord and all the holy angels they wonder why nobody, not even the salmon, goes to Co. Leitrim any more. If this is all there is on offer I might as well smoke a packet of 20 and throw myself in the lake now without waiting for them to finish the roof on the shed. It would be a blessed relief. But that's my opinion. Give it a try. It'll be good experience for the future. It'll give you an idea of what it's like being locked up in an old people's home.

Co. Roscommon
Travellers' heaven

Famous local resident
Brazilian theological student

Favourite food
Anything but a knuckle sandwich

Favourite drink
Guinness

Favourite pub
Any one. Providing it's empty

Favourite restaurant
Any one with a Brazilian theological student

What to say
What a nice caravan

What not to say
Move along there, please. Move along.

Co. Roscommon should be Co. Roughcommon. There are definitely no proteins here. This is 100 per cent carbohydrate country. They look as though they eat them all the time. From late in the morning when they get up. To early in the evening when they go to sleep.

The locals are slow, quiet, stolid. The last proteins they probably ever saw left with Oliver Cromwell all those years ago. They've been living off carbohydrates ever since. The last one to have any sparkle was Elizabeth Gunning, who with sister Mary lived at Hollywell House, just outside Roscommon town. But Roscommon they were not. At one time they were reckoned the most beautiful women in the whole of Ireland. Mary married the Earl of Coventry. Elizabeth married first, the sixth Duke of Hamilton and then the fifth Duke of Argyll, notching up four dukes-to-be in the process. Thackeray said she was double-Duchessed. The King asked her once what would give her the greatest pleasure. 'A coronation,' she replied.

The land is supposed to be rich pasture, ideal for cattle and sheep to develop massive hidden reserves of botulism, TB, listeria, mad cow disease or whatever it is they're supposed to be riddled with nowadays. If not, I'm not only rough but common as well.

The roads are unbelievable. Even the unbelievable roads are unbelievable. Drive out of Dublin with your eyes closed. Head south. The road signs are like that in Dublin. If you want to go west it's best to head south. If you want the airport you head for Belfast. You can easily tell when you're in Co. Roscommon. There are no motorways. No plans for one either. There are virtually no small or medium-size roads. No plans for any either. All they have are crow-infested farm tracks. Sometimes there are so many crows you can't tell where the crows end and the farm track begins. Get stuck behind a tractor anywhere else in the country you can over-take it in five, maybe ten minutes. Get stuck behind a tractor in Co. Roscommon you're there until harvest time.

Ask anyone what any road is like in Co. Roscommon from anywhere to anywhere they'll tell you, 'It's the sort of road I wouldn't like to have to praise.'

Farmer driving along road in his BMW. Sees a Traveller eating nettles and weeds by the side of the road.

'What are you doing?' he says.

'I'm a Traveller,' says the man. 'I can't get any work. I haven't got any money to buy food. All I can do is eat the nettles and the weeds.'

'That's crazy,' says the farmer. 'Come back to my place. You can have a decent meal.'

'Can I bring the family?' says the Traveller.

'The family?' says the farmer.

'Yes,' says the Traveller. 'The wife. Ten children. Two uncles. Six cousins. Four nieces . . .'

'That's crazy,' says the farmer. 'I've only got a small front lawn.'

I was once driving somewhere in the middle of the county, suddenly there was a sign, 'Improved Roadway Ends'. Oh yeah?

When was it improved? 6557 BC ready for the invention of the wheel.

The only good thing about it is that in Co. Roscommon you don't see any dogs stretched out by the side of the road, blood spurting out of their ears. The dogs can walk faster than the cars. Those that can't chase parked cars.

Trains? What trains? They have yet to arrive in Co. Roscommon. Co. Roscommon is still pre-Stephenson.

Telecommunications? They're still using baked bean tins and a bit of string.

I was there once when everybody was complaining that an American company which was originally planning to come to Co. Roscommon had changed their mind and decided to go to Co. Kerry instead. Why, they couldn't imagine.

'So what's Co. Kerry got that Co. Roscommon hasn't got?' a sleepy old bank manager asked me one evening in Down the Hatch, a bar in Roscommon town.

I nearly choked on my Guinness.

Co. Roscommon goes on about being the ancient capital of Connaught. The Gateway to the North-West. So, incidentally, does Co. Longford. They say they gave ancient Ireland its last king and modern Ireland its first modern president. The truth is because of the poor state of the roads, the trains, telecommunications and almost complete lack of any industrial development at all apart from the occasional halal meat factory, the place is deserted. No wonder Oliver Goldsmith called it the Deserted Village. He should know. He was born in Elphin. Which is about as sleepy and deserted as you can get. The cathedral was damaged by a storm in 1914. It was pulled down. They still haven't finished rebuilding it.

In fact the place is so deserted the only way the local tourist board can make it sound halfway interesting is by including in all its publicity material information about towns outside the county: Ballinasole, which is in Co. Galway, Lanesborough, which is in Co. Longford and Athlone, which is in Co. Westmeath.

You can see their point.

Castlerea was the birthplace of Sir William Wilde, father of

Oscar. But who's interested in the father? When was the last time anyone mentioned Shakespeare's old man?

Cloonequin was the birthplace of Percy French, the man who put the Irishness into Ireland. Trouble is all his famous Irish songs are about everywhere else but Co. Roscommon.

Ballintober was once home to the mighty O'Connor clan. All I can say is if I was an O'Connor, there are better places to make your kingdom than Ballintober. As for the Castle, it's so covered in weeds and creepers I swear in 1000 years' time it will be rediscovered like the temples of Angkor Wat and people will tell tales of the O'Connors and pay good money to sit and watch the sunset. But today, never.

Castleplunket. A name like that, I thought, has got to be a winner. Powdered wigs. Fancy boots. Spindly eyeglasses. Syphilitic fops in Regency costume. Complete with poodle perm. No way. It's a tiny place. Nothing there and half of that is a Honda dealership.

Strokestown has what must be the widest main street in Ireland. Twelve lanes. Maybe more. Depending on the number of lorries. But who wants to go somewhere where there are 12 lanes of lorries?

Tulsk. Every year hundreds of people recreate the famous Cattle Raid of Cooley, Queen Maeve's desperate bid to capture the famous bull of Cooley.

Day one, they trudge to Longford, Co. Longford.

Day two, they're in Kells, Co. Westmeath.

Day three, Drogheda, Co. Louth.

Day four, Carlingford.

Day five, Dundalk.

Day six, Ardee, where they re-enact the capture of the bull.

Ask yourself. Why would serious, sensible people want to put themselves through that kind of agony, 350 miles, six days, fording rivers, crossing mountains, sleeping rough just to commemorate some old Irish queen's bull fixation? It's got to be a cover. The real reason is to get out of Co. Roscommon.

Boyle, I thought, was going to be pretty hot. A garrison town. Between Lough Key and Lough Gara. In the distance the Curlew

Mountains. The famous Boyle Abbey that has been everything in its time. Even a dog kennel. Frybrook House that once used to ring its bell at 5 p.m. inviting everybody within hearing distance to drop in for a drink. Dinner as well if they wanted. But it's all cooled down a lot since then. Instead it's more like a weak, cold cup of tea. No. I tell a lie. There is King House which promotes itself as 'Home to Roscommon County Council's Steinway Concert Piano'. Woweeeee. My apologies all round.

Roscommon itself is a busy little town. Trouble is it's not a Co. Roscommon town. It's a Brazilian town. Practically everybody you see is Brazilian. In the streets. In the offices. In the bars. I went into one bar. The girl serving drinks was a Brazilian theology student. I went in there for a couple of glasses of the black stuff and ended up discussing quantum theory and what can and cannot be seen through a glass darkly.

I didn't have the same luck in the Bank of Ireland in the centre of the square. I waited there once for a full 20 minutes while the girl from Ipanema went to change some dollars for me into euros.

The Abbey Hotel is the sparkiest place to stay in town. Sparky that is if there is an electric cable hanging low off the bathroom ceiling with a sign on the door saying, 'Steam will activate fire alarm. Please close bathroom door.' All the time? Only when inside? Then what happens when you've had your bath? You stay there until all the steam has disappeared? You risk making a rush for the door, getting yourself entangled in that loose cable hanging from the ceiling and try to get out of the door, slamming it fast behind you before a puff of steam sets off the alarm? It was all too much for me. I decided to forget the bath and go and have a pint instead.

'The cable,' I said to the barman. 'It's dangerous, hanging down like that over the bath. Electricity. Water. That kind of thing.'

'Don't worry,' he says. 'It's not live. Just rip it down when you get back.'

Oh yeah. Stand in the bath. Rip an electric cable off the ceiling. That an Irish barman says is not live. What d'ye think I am? American?

The real shock, however, was the rubbish all over town. It's everywhere. They also seem to have more travellers than anywhere else in Ireland. Not just the one caravan. But long, long lines of them. By the railway station. Opposite the mart. Near the new arts centre.

Some of the caravans are sparkling clean and immaculate. Some are like mobile rubbish dumps. Some are surrounded by smart 4x4s. Some by broken-down old wrecks. Some of the kids are smart. Some filthy. Some caravans look neat and tidy. Some are practically buried by piles of rubbish, tin cans, lumps of old iron, bikes. Some even by cigarettes, tobacco and drugs. In huge quantities. Imported legally or illegally. Directly or indirectly through a secret network of Irish lorry drivers travelling backwards and forwards to Belgium, France, Holland or anywhere where the goodies are available.

It's virtually the same all over the country. Travellers. In lay-bys. Stretched out along country roads. Huddled together by farm gates. Scattered across huge open fields. On the front lawns outside bishops' private houses.

Some people say, It's nothing. It's a way of life. It's tradition. It's what helps to make Ireland Ireland. Others say, It's a shame. It's disgusting.

'They're filthy. They turn up in a town. Everything is a mess. They go into a bar. They order drinks. They don't pay. They take over the toilets. Do their washing there. Leave the place a mess. Then you can't get rid of them.'

'The council. Why should the council build houses for them? They cause nothing but trouble. They get a free house. I've worked hard all my life. I have to buy my own house. Where is the fairness in that?'

'It's money they're after. Nothing else. They turn up on your land. They refuse to go unless you pay them. How else d'ye think they keep going? They've not the money for it.'

'The Bishop of Killaloe should know better than letting travellers camp out on the front lawn of his palace. He'll be lucky to find his cross and crozier next time he needs them.'

'Extortion. That's what it is. You want to build a row of houses. The council objects. Local people object. You bring in the travellers. You pay them to stay there. Eventually the council and the local residents change their mind. They'll be imploring you to build your row of houses. It'll mean the travellers have to leave. You've got your row of houses. The travellers have money in their pockets. How else do you think they live?'

'Watch out. Give them half a chance, they'll steal the froth off the top of your Guinness.'

Not that Roscommon itself is not doing its best to solve the problem.

Plan A. They say they've had so many meetings of the County Council, the Chamber of Commerce and the local branches of the Tidy Towns Association not to mention the Irish Business Against Litter League to discuss the matter and generated so much paperwork that every day the mountains of waste paper get higher and higher until hopefully one day there'll be so much official paperwork it will completely smother all the mess created by the travellers.

Plan B. A number of local residents are trying to persuade one of their local judges to come out of retirement.

'A great man, he was, a great man,' one of the pillars of the community told me. 'Smart suit. Waistcoat. Dedicated Rotary Club enthusiast. Generous to a fault. The kind of man who would lay down his wife for a friend.

'Anybody come up before him, anybody, he would say, Twenty-four hours. You've twenty-four hours to be out of Roscommon. If you're still here in twenty-four hours I'll throw you in jail and throw away the key. No trouble. No trouble at all we had then.' He downed his Guinness. 'He'd soon sort the problem out. God bless you. I'll have another one. Tanksbetogod.'

The drink taken, I got up to stagger back to the hotel.

''Tis a word of advice I'll give you,' he says. ''Tis the voice of experience. Don't go near the travellers.'

Why? Are they going to attack me? Rob me? Follow me home and park on the front lawn?

'Don't go near them,' he says. 'Their bad luck might rub off on you.'

The only good thing about Co. Roscommon? I know a bar which

stays open until 4 a.m. Sometimes even later. Just knock on the window. Tell them you've come for the engagement party. They'll understand. It definitely won't be deserted. But don't tell them you're a traveller.

Co. Louth
We shan't remember him

Famous local resident
Lord Drogheda. It's true

Favourite food
Boyne salmon

Favourite drink
Guinness

Favourite pub
Any one in Carlingford

Favourite restaurant
Any one in Carlingford

What to say
But he did exist

What not to say
So who was he then?

Too many carbohydrates are not good for you. They upset your equilibrium. Make you fat. Even upset the balance of your mind. I can prove it. For years of my life I worked for Lord Drogheda, from the Irish *Droichead Atha*, Bridge of the Ford, which sounds typically Irish to me. If you've got a bridge who needs the ford? If you've got a ford who needs a bridge? Either way he was like something out of a limp *Brideshead Revisited*. A touch lah-di-dah. Terribly upper-class. To the manner born. But great fun. Awfully civilised. Terribly nice. Lunches and dinners with him were always just super.

But to the solid, down-to-earth, good people of Drogheda – an old, historic town on a bend in the River Boyne, once the third-largest city in the UK after London and Dublin, starting point of the Black Death in Ireland in 1348 thanks to its estuary and harbour, scene of the worst massacre carried out by Cromwell in the whole of Ireland, a hotbed of Republicanism between the official and the provisional Sinn Fein, those who wanted to play the game politically and those who wanted to play the game militarily – he never existed. He was hot air, a puff of wind, a figment of my diseased imagination.

'Drogheda. Lord Drogheda. The divil mind you. Ye are imagining it. There's no Lord Drogheda around here. It's too much of the black stuff, ye've been having,' the old biddy with a wobbly hip told me when I checked in to the Westcourt Hotel slap bang in the centre of town.

Drogheda was originally a walled city with ten gates. Only one survives today, the St Laurence Gate, which must be one of the best-preserved in the country. A tribute to the one-tenth of the Irish building community who actually put up things that last.

'Lord Drogheda. Lord Drogheda. Not at all. There's only one Lord that I know of, and its not a lie I'm telling ye,' a tiny man with a prayer book the size of a dining-room table told me. Admittedly we were chatting as we came out of St Peter's almost opposite the hotel.

> The Irish government send a peacekeeping force to Africa.
>
> The day they arrive the colonel in charge tells the troops, 'You're here on a peacekeeping mission. If any Africans tell you Africa is bigger than Ireland, I want you to agree. I don't want you to fight about it.'

I'd been in there to see the shrine containing the head of Oliver Plunkett, executed by the English in 1681. Shrine. It looked more like a Vatican spaceship. I tried to get into the other St Peter's, the Church of Ireland church, containing the tombstone of Oliver Goldsmith's uncle. But it was always closed. First, a deserted village. Now a deserted church. Outside traffic was crawling along the street. Armed military were delivering money to one of the banks.

'Not at all. Not at all. You've made a mistake. If there was a Lord Drogheda I would know. Believe me,' a wild young soap dodger with a shock of hair and a gammy leg was adamant when he stumbled into me on my way out of the local Millmount Museum.

'Are you sure?' I hesitated.

'Of course, I'm sure.' He was even more Louth-mouthed than before. 'I run the museum, I should know.'

Sure you should know and I'd believe you except the historic museum of Drogheda, built on an artificial hill overlooking the town, burial place to a Spanish-born warrior poet, scene of one of the worst, bloodiest sieges laid by Cromwell, a major player in the Battle of the Boyne, a key factor during the Civil War seemed to be full of nothing but kitchen utensils, a sofa bed and a heap of old telephone equipment.

'You've made a mistake,' he sneers. 'Believe me.'

Made a mistake! How could I make a mistake?

The 11th Earl of Drogheda (Charles Garrett Ponsonby Moore, KBE), Viscount Moore, of Drogheda, Baron Moore, of Mellefont, in Ireland, and Baron Moore of Cobham, Co. Surrey, in the UK, Capt. RA (TA) 1940, on Staff of Min. of Production 1942–5, Man. Dir. The Financial Times Ltd, Chm. Industrial and Trade Fairs Ltd, Dir. Economist Newspaper Ltd, Chm. Royal Opera House, Covent Garden Ltd, Chev. Legion of Honour (1961), OBE (1946), KBE (1964), b. 23 April 1910, educ. Eton, and Trin. Coll. Cambridge, S. his father 1957; m. 16 May 1935, Joan Eleanor, only daughter of late William Henry Carr, gave me my job on the *Financial Times*. My office was just down the corridor from his on the top floor of the old *Financial Times* building in Cannon Street in the City. I saw him, I spoke to him a million times every day. Occasionally he even gave me some leftover eggs from his farm somewhere out near Windsor Castle. He was real. He was flesh and blood. Blue blood. Very blue blood.

I carried my quest the length and breadth of the county, which luckily is the smallest in the country – the wee county – 317 square miles, about the size of Lord Drogheda's London pad in Lord North Street, Westminster to which at one time I was a regular visitor although nobody ever believes me.

With it being the smallest county I thought it wouldn't be too difficult to find someone who had heard of Lord Drogheda – after all small area, small groups of people, population around 100,000, somebody who was a household name in the highest households in the land would be bound to make some kind of impact in the much smaller, much more lowly household of Co. Louth.

From Collon in the south way up to Dundalk and Carlingford on the Cooley Peninsula in the north I searched for the unknown Lord.

Collon. A tiny village. Upmarket. I stopped at the Forge Gallery Restaurant. They told me there would be bound to be somebody at the monastery on the edge of town who could tell me all about

Lord Drogheda. They were famous not for their prayers but for their honey. If I asked nicely they'd be bound to sell me some.

'They produce so little, the best they keep for themselves and there's nothing left for anybody else,' a motherly type with arctic circles round her eyes tells me.

When I got there I discovered it was a Cistercian monastery. The monks are not allowed to speak. In any case it was late. They had all gone off to sleep. And there was no honey still for sale either.

Ardee. The people there had no Ardee about anything. They couldn't even tell me why they had two castles, one either end of the high street. Were they friendly castles? Were they enemy castles? Had they heard of Lord Drogheda? No Ardee.

Mellifont Abbey. Ireland's first Cistercian monastery. Once the most magnificent monastery in the country. Now one of the most magnificent monastery ruins in the country. Some say it's because the Irish and French monks didn't get on. Somebody said something. After all those years of silence, wham, that was it. No French monks. No monastery. Others blame age, decay, Oliver Cromwell, VAT. I know who I believe. Was there anyone there who could help me? I only met one old man hobbling around the place. He looked more Gothic than any of the arches. He also had a stutter.

'C-C-C-C-C-Cold. 'T-T-T-T-T-Tis c-c-c-c-c-cold,' he said as we hobbled the length of the church and back again.

'If-If-If-If-If i-i-i-i-i-it's g-g-g-g-g-going t-t-t-t-t-to b-b-b-b-b-be c-c-c-c-c-cold i-i-i-i-i-it's g-g-g-g-g-going t-t-t-t-t-to b-b-b-b-b-be . . .'

That trip I was going to be in Ireland for only two weeks. I didn't think I'd have the time to talk to him about L-L-L-L-L-Lord D-D-D-D-D-Drogheda. I left him to his d-d-, I mean deliberations.

Just outside Mellifont Abbey was a mud-splattered sign pointing left to Monasterboice. I followed the sign. I went left. I ended up on the Dublin–Belfast motorway, the most dangerous road in the country. I retraced my steps. There was the sign. Yes it said Monasterboice. Yes it pointed left. Yes I followed the sign. Again I ended up on the Dublin–Belfast motorway. Yes I stopped and asked people the way. Nobody had heard of Monasterboice. After all it's only been there since the fourth or fifth century. Founded by St Buithe, a follower of St Patrick. Again I tried. This time I took the opposite direction to which the signs were pointing. In ten minutes I was there. Was it worth getting cross about? Yes and no.

Yes because there was nobody there to talk to. I parked the car. Nobody. I walked across the road to the crosses. Nobody. I had a good look at them. One, 6.5 metres high, is one of the tallest in Ireland. The other two are more manageable. The interesting thing is they're not your ordinary, plain and simple crosses. They're more like stained-glass window crosses. They're covered in panels recounting different episodes from the Old and New Testaments. Here's Adam and Eve. There's Moses and Aaron. Up there is the Last Judgement. Where's the good Lord Drogheda? Nowhere.

Still there was nobody else looking at the crosses. Nobody to ask about Lord Drogheda.

Carlingford. On the Cooley Peninsula. Fantastic. Fabulous. At the foot of Slieve Foye. To the north, the Mountains of Mourne. On a lough. A castle. Ruined. Once the gateway to the lough. They say that it was here between pints of the black stuff they began drafting the Magna Carta. Tiny narrow streets. Whitewashed cottages. Bars on every corner. Restaurants everywhere. There's even – mamma mia – a Captain Correlli's Italian Restaurant. Oysters on every menu. Why not? They come straight from the lough. Also unending supplies of the local Boyne salmon.

Eat salmon, they say, on 1 August every year and you'll be guaranteed a long life and a happy one. You'll head up-stream and spawn away to your heart's content. The bar and restaurant owners, of course, say eat salmon every day of the year and you'll have an even longer and an even happier life. That's the local catering trade for you. Always thinking of their customers' happiness and well-being.

Eat any other kind of fish, especially the fish swimming around the secret underwater discharges from Sellafield nuclear power station across the water, they say, you'll have problems. Trying to get a fish with three heads on to an ordinary-size dinner plate is almost impossible.

The whole area is a bit like, say, Loop Head in Co. Clare. Except it's the exact opposite. Loop Head is bleak and desolate and rocky. The Cooley Peninsula is wide open and smooth and pleasant. Loop Head is isolated, dramatic, spectacular. Cooley is in summer overrun with holidaymakers and tourists. Loop Head is cold and hungry. Cooley is warm and inviting. Especially at tractor time. Come every August Cooley is host to the international vintage tractor festival. Two thousand tractors. All packed into a 200-acre field. I even found myself discussing the joys of a Massey-Fergus 35X with some whuuumph from Australia who looked like a baggy-trousered boy band cast-off.

Trouble was nobody knew anything about Lord Drogheda.

'It's a hotel, is it? Try the market square. It must be there if it's anywhere.'

'Lord Drogheda. Is he the man who runs the paper shop?'

'Lord Drogheda. Lord Drogheda. Now Lady Drogheda. I've heard of Lady Drogheda. A greyhound. Big in the fifties. Is that the man you're looking for?'

On the other hand I did meet the world's greatest expert on the Cattle Raid of Cooley. The story I knew. Queen Maeve has the hots for this bull. The only thing standing in her way is some teenage lager lout called Cuchulainn, who kills everyone in sight. What I didn't realise was that Cuchulainn was also something of a politician. He could turn around in his skin, put his hands and feet behind him and his buttocks and calves in front of him. And presumably say the first thing that came into his feet.

''Tis as true as I'm sitting here talking to ye now,' says the world's greatest expert.

'You're right there, Pat. You're right. Give the man another drink. If anyone deserves it he does,' says his friend, the world's second-greatest expert.

I bought them both a glass of the black stuff and continued my search.

Dundalk. Big. Bustling. Packed with traffic. The poor relation to Drogheda. World-famous for its engineering and manufacturing skills. They produced the Bubble Car in the 1960s. Surprisingly friendly. No end of people nod and grunt a 'Good morning' or a 'Good evening' at you. The courthouse is four-square, solid, impregnable. St Patrick's Cathedral is unbelievable. It's King's College, Cambridge with an Irish accent. Throw in a few carols, it could be the real thing. The Imperial Hotel. Imperial on the outside. Warm, friendly colonial on the inside. Had a grand time there.

High blood pressure? Something wrong with the old ticker? I went to an Irish doctor once. I told him that suddenly my heart had started beating irregularly. He said, 'I'll soon put a stop to that' and sent me for an X-ray. The lines that show up on an X-ray are called Kerley lines, after Peter Kerley, who was born in Dundalk, discovered them and went on to set up mass X-ray programmes for both the UK and Irish governments.

As for asking about Lord Drogheda, I didn't. People in Dundalk, I very quickly discovered, may be friendly in the street but inside, in a bar or any other public place you ask questions at your peril.

'If the bars start adding water to their beers or even their whiskey nobody is going to question them. Not in Dundalk. Dundalk is different,' a priest whispers to me as I was coming out of St Patrick's one morning. So different, in fact, that all over Ireland there are CCTV cameras. Not in Dundalk.

'Dundalk is different.'

I thought I'd try a meeting of the local Dundalk coursing society. Farmers. All interested in greyhounds. Always good for a chat. So they were. About greyhounds.

'Didyesee the likes of the Duke of Hearts. What a beast. Mighty fine beast.'

'Abbey Brandy. Unlucky. He was just unlucky.'

'Unlucky. Johnny, my boy. He was beat.'

Nobody wanted to talk about anything let alone Lord Whatsisname. They say it's because it's strict IRA, even INLA country. No end of unmarked graves have been found around the town. Much to the disappointment of many I had no intention of adding to them. Especially as my heart had stopped beating irregularly.

But in spite of all the evidence, the total ignorance, the overwhelming indifference, Lord Drogheda existed. I know. I'm eternally grateful to him. He gave me a job on the top floor of the *Financial Times* at an enormous salary when they didn't think I was good enough for a job working in their Surveys department on the first floor for a mere pittance. Worse. After my first interview they wrote telling me not to bother to come back for a second interview. They had just realised I hadn't gone to university. I wasn't a graduate. Push off. We don't want the likes of you here.

The following week came the advertisement for the big job on the top floor. I applied. Had a couple of interviews with the good Lord. Got the job. Had a wonderful time there.

Was there a Lord Drogheda or was there not a Lord Drogheda?

People of Co. Louth. There was. It's because of him that I'm in the position I'm in today.

The Alcohol Counties

Co. Tipperary
Co. Limerick
Co. Longford
Co. Derry
Co. Armagh

Now we're getting to the real thing. The one thing that makes Ireland Ireland. Alc O'Hol. Ireland would not be Ireland without alcohol. So Ireland would not be Ireland without the Civil War. The English Civil War. King versus Parliament.

What was Ireland going to do? Back the pro-Catholic King or the Protestant Parliament? A nation of gamblers, they backed who they thought was the favourite: the pro-Catholic King. If he won, they guessed, he would restore Catholic power to Ireland. But just as they've done many times since, especially at Cheltenham, they backed the wrong horse. The Protestant Parliament won. And the Protestant Parliament did not like the amount of Irish money that poured on to the Catholic King. In 1649 Oliver Cromwell landed in Ireland to take his revenge.

What he did reverberates around Ireland to this day.

He seized over two million hectares of land, over a quarter of the entire country. He shipped thousands of Irish men, women and children off to the Caribbean as slaves. He slaughtered upwards of 2000 maybe 10,000 people. Protestants and even some of the new settlers were not exempt. Deliberately or by accident many were also shipped out as slaves or killed. Others were resettled in the rougher, harsher parts of the world, the wilds of Connemara, Galway, Offley, Sligo.

Cromwell now seized practically every blade of grass in the country and parcelled it out to his backers and cronies, the men who had done the dirty work.

'God alone shall have the glory,' he declared.
The Irish were beginning to dislike the English.

Co. Tipperary
It's not a long way

Famous local resident
Sadler's Wells. The lucky chap

Favourite food
A game bird

Favourite drink
Guinness

Favourite pub
The first pub in Killusty

Favourite restaurant
Any restaurant that serves neat whiskey soup

What to say
If it's yours, I'll back it

What not to say
What's worth backing?

Co. Tipperary is probably responsible for more alcohol being drunk in Ireland than in any other country in the world. Before horse races, trying to decide who to back. During horse races, wondering whether you made the right decision. After horse races either celebrating your win or somebody else's or sitting alone at the end of the bar wondering how the bejesus you're going to survive the rest of the month without any money.

In the old days – remember? – you would go out for a meal. Between every course they would serve soup. Except it wasn't ordinary soup. It was neat whiskey soup with half a pound of butter and six eggs thrown in, brought almost to the boil but not quite – bring it to the boil, it would kill all the alcohol – and served hot. Very hot. Sometimes, if it was a very cold day, they would throw in a couple of pints of beef broth as well to give it the body.

With each course, of course, they drank the real stuff.

Today in Co. Tipp, as we locals say, they might not put away the quantity. But they certainly know how to produce the quality. Horses not alcohol.

For if Ireland is horses and horse racing, Tipperary is the horsiest place of all. Not for racing them. But for producing and training them. Not your ordinary everyday plodders. But your sleek, smooth, super-quality, top of the world, top of the range thoroughbred racers. Look at a car. Any car. You can always tell if it comes from Co. Tipp. There's a sticker in the back window saying, 'My other car eats oats.'

Without Co. Tipp there'd be little good-quality racing in Ireland. Without Ireland there would be little good-quality racing in the world.

Ireland: In a Glass of its Own

Some say Co. Tipp's broad, lush, green, limestone-based central plain, the Golden Vale, is not only the best, the lushest, the richest farmland in the world, it also produces the world's finest dairy cattle, gundogs and greyhounds. Green gold, they call it. But it's the horses that count. Thoroughbreds. Priceless thoroughbreds. Not only are they expensive, they are treated as expensive. The most loved, the most adored, the most treasured second wife

> It's Derby Day. A man makes his way to his seat in the very front row by the rails. He sits down. The seat next to him is empty. He leans over and asks his neighbour, an old Tipperary farmer, if someone will be sitting there.
>
> 'No,' says the old farmer. 'The seat is empty.'
>
> 'This is incredible,' says the man. 'Who in their right mind would have a seat like this for the Derby and not use it?'
>
> The old farmer says, 'Well, actually, the seat belongs to me. I was supposed to come with my wife, but she passed away. This is the first Derby we haven't been to together since we got married.'
>
> 'Oh, I'm sorry to hear that. That's terrible,' says the man. 'Couldn't you find someone else, a friend, a relative, or even a neighbour to take the seat?'
>
> The old farmer shakes his head. 'No. They're all at the funeral.'

couldn't be treated any better. They have the best of everything. The best care. The best attention. The best facilities. There are television cameras on them all the time so that their every movement can be checked every second of the day or night. When they eat. When they drink. When they sleep. The horses. Not the second wives. When they travel, they travel with their own straw, their own feed, their own water, even their own air-conditioning system. Nothing but nothing is left to chance.

The holiest of the holiest is Ballydoyle, at the foot of the Slievenamon Mountains, which has produced more winners over the last 10 years than any other yard in the world. Not your ordinary winners. Your classics. Your Derbys. Your Kentucky Derbys. Your Breeders' Cups. Your 2000 Guineas. Regularly they pocket more prize money than any other training operation in the world. Not just by a couple of pound. But by millions of pounds. That's how successful they are. Some say it's the quality of horses. Some say it's the selection of imitation racetracks they have built so wherever they go the horses feel at home. But everybody says, most of all, it's the lush, green grass of Co. Tipp.

Not only that, it is also turning out tomorrow's winners as well. Just down the road from Ballydoyle is the 5000-acre Coolmore Stud, one of the world's top breeding operations, where tucked away behind the miles and miles of immaculately manicured hedges no more than 20-plus stallions with big grins and happy smiling faces take care of over 1500 visiting mares every year. One stallion, the legendary Sadler's Wells, makes over €20 million a year for a few minutes' work a week doing what stallions do best at €300,000 a time. He is said to have the biggest smile of all. For a rest, they get a trip to Australia or New Zealand where for some reason they switch off. For their final rest they have their own cemetery tucked away behind further hedges. Where, it can be honestly said, they rest in peace.

Look at any horse in any field, especially around Fethard, an ordinary little village, and you could be looking at £1 million of horseflesh or just young Bridget's surprise birthday mount.

Shuffle up to the bar of McCarthy's, the local pub. Chat to the withertongued galumph standing next to you. He could be a stable lad at Ballydoyle, Coolmore or any one of a dozen yards in the area; a vet who is desperately treating the favourite for the Derby; a work rider who is not happy being on the second-favourite for the Breeders' Cup or Bridget's father who's just discovered he's paid twice the price he should have for a bag of bones that will be lucky to make it to the farm gate let alone a racecourse.

''Tis true,' he will say to you. 'Nobody from around here ever goes to meet his maker in the winter months if he's got a promising two-year-old in his yard.'

Prior to Cheltenham, the ultimate, the Mecca, for jumpers in the world, the whole place turns into one huge non-stop horse talk shop.

In practically every pub and village hall there are special preview meetings when the great and the good, the experts, those in the know go through the race card, spill the beans, talk the talk and forecast the winners. Some meetings are free. Some charge. Some charge big money. But a tip is a tip. A good tip that comes across can practically buy you a racehorse. Why else does everyone call it Co. Tipp?

Cool. Professional. Successful. The Irish know their horses better than anyone else in the world. But they are still Irish. I was in Limerick once when 18 runners turned up at the start. They only had starting stalls for 15. Embarrassed? Guilty? Ashamed? Come on, they're Irish. It was an excuse for another glass of the black stuff.

I've also been to races where the commentator has blissfully announced, 'The time of the last race was four minutes sixty-seven seconds.'

Was he embarrassed? Not at all.

'Apologies. Apologies,' he said afterwards. 'Miscalculation. Forgot there were 59 seconds in a minute.'

As for the non-horse Tipp, the largest inland county in Ireland, you'd never think it was so rich, so famous, so important. It's slow. It's plodding. It's way behind other parts of the country. Even the local racecourse looks a touch sad and miserable. Not the way I thought a racecourse in Co. Tipp would look.

Some say it's not just Ireland, it's old Ireland. It's full of old Irish families with what they call bits of land which turn out to be anything between 25,000 and 30,000 acres. Most of them can trace their ancestors back to Oliver Cromwell. Some even further. To St Patrick himself. It's also full of the old Irish way of life. Hunting four days a week. Huge breakfasts. Huge lunches. Huge dinners. Everything needs money spent on it. But why should they worry? Have another glass. It'll do ye good. God bless ye.

About the only thing I've known that's broken their routine was plans to build a giant waste incinerator at Rosegreen. The horsemen say it will destroy their business. The incineration people say it won't.

'A burning issue,' everyone called it.

All over the place there were protest posters decorated with a stark black-and-white skull and crossbones.

Wherever I went, whoever I spoke to told me, "Tis important. We must make a stand on the incinerator.'

Rather you than me, I thought.

Then it was back to hunting and huge breakfasts, and huge lunches and huge dinners and have another glass. It'll do ye good. God bless ye.

Tipperary town, once home to the biggest British military barracks in the whole of Ireland, has got to be one of the most famous towns in the world. Two things, however, surprised me about it. First, it's not a long way at all. About 40 minutes from Limerick. Second, I've no wish to rubbish Tipp but it's the last place you'd want your sweetest girl to be. By the time you got to her her lungs would be coated with diesel fumes. She'd be spitting blood. She'd be no good for anything.

In fact, it's not really a town at all. It's one long street packed, bumper to bumper, with huge 40-ton trucks and lorries ploughing backwards and forwards, up and down, in and out, non-stop, all day, every day. It's so bad that if you're born one side of the street you could be riding a Derby winner before you get the chance to cross to the other side. They say William Hazlitt lived here with his family before moving to America and then back to England. But I don't believe it. He'd never get across the road to get to the bus to take him to the boat to America.

I was there once. I tried to cross to the other side to get to Crankey's for a drink and a mixed grill. It was impossible. I gave up and drove back to Limerick instead.

You think I'm exaggerating. Tipperary town is the only town in the world where because the traffic is so bad bank robbers have to escape by train. I was there when it happened. The amazing thing was half the town didn't think it strange or unusual at all. It could have been worse, they said. Other Irish burglars or bank robbers turn up in a tractor or JCB, wrench automatic bank machines out of the wall or 100-per-cent-secure wall safes out of hotel rooms or get stuck in doors or windows, which can block streets for hours on end. Which, to me, suggests they need more practice.

I was in Co. Kildare when a man was jailed for six months for breaking into a neighbour's house in the middle of the night. The woman woke up and shouted out, 'Who's there?' To which the burglar replied, ''Tis me, Tommy. From down the road.'

I was in Co. Mayo when thieves pulled off the ultimate. They actually lifted a whole lorry load of Guinness.

I was also told the story of a more professional Irish bank robber, who burst into a bank, pulled a gun on the security guard and screamed out, 'Freeze, you motherstickers. This is a fuck-up.'

True or not, it's a great story.

What the other half of Tipp across the other side of the main street thought of the bank robbers escaping by train I have no idea. I still couldn't cross the road.

Even worse, Tipp doesn't have a decent place to stay. The first time I went there I ended up in the Rectory House Hotel ten miles out of town in a place called Dundrum.

The taxi got lost. We stopped outside the old Church of Ireland church to ask the way.

'I'm looking for – cough, cough – Hotel,' I asked one farmer, peaked cap, wellingtons, blackthorn stick. I was still recovering from the fumes after my stay in Tipp. 'Do you know – cough, cough – where it is?'

'Where it always is,' he says.

When I finally got there by going the opposite way everybody told me, the hotel was closed, there was no chef, the taxi failed to turn up the following morning and the owner of the hotel very kindly drove me to Limerick Junction to catch a train that didn't exist. Apart from that everything was fantastic.

The opposite end of the scale is the Rock of Cashel, which I admit I'd never heard of until I stumbled across it. It's fantastic. I drove down the road from Portloise, Co. Laois. I turned a corner. There it was. In front of me. A huge rock that looks as though it was just dumped there in the middle of the wide open plain.

It's Mont St Michel, Carcassonne and the Crac des Chevaliers all rolled into one.

Over 200 feet above ground, for nearly 1000 years the power base of the kings of Munster. From here they dominated or tried to dominate most of Ireland. But it was a problem. They were all born with a limp. I'm not saying they were slow. But when St Patrick – it was here he established the shamrock as the symbol of Ireland – had converted King Cormac and was baptising him into the Christian faith somehow or other he jabbed his crozier straight through the King's foot. The King – can you imagine the pain? – said nothing. He thought it was all part of the ceremony. He and his descendants walked with a limp for ever afterwards. In 1101 enough was enough. The King gave the Rock to the Church. The Church ran the place until Cromwell came calling – and killing. Over 1000 people in all. Give or take 1000 people.

''Tis the work of the Divil,' an old retired rural dean of the Church of Ireland told me. 'He bit a giant lump of a piece out of the mountains and spat it out at Cashel. But missed. That's the Rock. Believe me. 'Tis as true as I'm standing here.'

He was in fact queuing up in Hannigans bar and restaurant at the time. But hey, am I going to nit-pick?

But is it true? I don't know about true. Is the Church of Ireland ever wrong? All I know is, it was the best thing that happened to me in Co. Laois. On the other hand, drive through the Silvermines, close to Thurles, you'll see what they call the Devil's Bit, the missing chunk the Devil bit out of the mountain.

At the top of the Rock are the ruins of a cathedral, complete with all its outbuildings including a tower, 127 steps too high. The cathedral was burnt down in 1495 by the Earl of Kildare. His excuse: he thought the archbishop was inside. Obviously a disgruntled local parishioner unhappy with the length of the Sunday sermon.

Wandering around the Rock is spectacular. The thought of living up there. The sense of security. The views. The surrounding countryside. Fabulous.

At the bottom of the Rock are the ruins of a Dominican friary. Obviously the Earl didn't like the length of their Sunday sermons either.

The Irish should make far more of it than they do. It should be on every leaflet, brochure and postcard they produce. It should be up there with all the other Wonders of the World: Niagara Falls, Angkor Wat, Disney World, Graceland. They should also rename it. The Rock of Cashel is not exactly catchy. It doesn't even give you an idea of its dramatic size, its importance in Irish history, the fact it's the best excuse there is to get out of Co. Laois. My idea: St Patrick's Mount. It's more descriptive. It would set it alongside the St Michael's Mounts of this world. It's also more in keeping with Ireland than boring old Rock of Cashel. All cheques from a grateful nation, please, to Peter Biddlecombe, Everlasting Guinness account, Co. Clare.

Cashel town is a cosy, at home kind of town. Cashel Palace Hotel with all its panelling and plasterwork and red-pine staircase looks like an archbishop's palace. Which it was. Built after the death of the Earl of Kildare. Otherwise it wouldn't still be standing. Many's the time I've stayed there. Very pleasant. Very civilised. Nobody there ever agrees with my idea of renaming the Rock. Just as well I'm not related to the Earl of Kildare. A word of advice. If anyone asks you if you fancy a bit of Cashel blue, take care. It's a lump of cheese. The local park is called Larkspur after the winner of the 1962 Epsom Derby who was trained at Vincent O'Brien's stables at Ballydoyle. See what I mean about horsy?

Just below Cahir, at the foot of the Knockmealdown Mountains, is Ballyporeen, the ancestral home of Ronald Reagan. Was there never an American president that didn't have any Irish ancestors?

After Cahir, Clonmel is my next-favourite town in Co. Tipp. On the River Suir. The town itself, which in 1650 withstood a three-week siege led by none other than Oliver Cromwell himself, is no great shakes.

The Town Hall on Mitchell Street looks impressive. Almost as impressive as the gold mayoral chain. Every time a new mayor is elected he is supposed to add a new link to the chain. Every time a new mayor is elected and adds a new gold link to the chain everyone then starts wondering where he got the money from to be able to afford to buy the gold link or if not where he is planning to get the money from to be able to afford to buy one.

Anne Street is famous for its resident Trollope. Anthony. Post Office inspector and novelist.

Clonmel was also the birthplace of Laurence Sterne, author of one of the funniest unread novels of all time, *Tristram Shandy*. I've tried it myself many times. For some reason I can never get past the bit about the animal spirits escorting the HOMUNCULUS to the place destined for his reception. Or maybe that was page two. It's not for lack of stamina. I've read the whole of Proust, *Ulysses*, even some of St Tony Blair's speeches on Africa. I've even tried it as an excuse not to read Jan Morris. But even that doesn't work.

Some say that it was the thought of meeting Laurence Sterne in the bar of Hearns Hotel that inspired Carlo Bianconi to start the world's first stagecoach service from there to Cahir, 12 miles away. When it looked as though that was not going to be far enough away and that Sterne would give pursuit, Bianconi helped the people of Clonmel get even further away by building up a nationwide transport system covering over 4000 miles a day.

Go in Hearns Hotel today, it still reflects the principles of public transport laid down by Bianconi all those years ago. They cannot make up their mind whether dinner is going to be served in the restaurant or the bar. Order black coffee and the girl, who looks like a retired lap dancer, says to you, 'Will you have milk and tay with it?' and, of course, everything arrives late.

But I wouldn't change it. Clonmel has that friendly, lived-in feel. Some books say it means Cluain Meala, Meadow of Honey, a reference to the fertility of the soil which is ironic because here on 13 May 1827, the height of the famine, a crowd of poor, desperate, starving men tried to steal food from one of the boats sailing up the River Suir from Clonmel to Carrick-on-Suir. The police fired on them. They killed three and wounded ten others.

Ireland: In a Glass of its Own

Today it's one of the great all-round entertainment centres of Ireland. Dog racing. They have their own dog track. Boxing tournaments. Golf. Tennis. Shooting. Fishing. And, of course, horses. Horse shows. Horse racing. Hunting. Friday nights, through the West Gate at the far end of O'Connell Street, turn left, first bar you come to, even the chairs do an Irish jig. Don't whatever you do mention *Tristram Shandy*. It'll kill the whole thing stone dead.

Thurles and Templemore are my other top Tipps.

Thurles has always been known as one of the most prosperous towns in Ireland. A farmers' town. Always busy. A thriving market. Big banking centre. Fairs. A sugar beet factory. A string of big houses that employed more people than the rest of the town put together. The cathedral is said to be a copy of the cathedral in Pisa. It doesn't lean over at a precarious angle. But the congregation does. Even before the bars are open.

They say Thurles is a success because after the Irish were defeated at the Siege of Limerick in 1690 what few survivors there were made their way there, stayed and built the foundations for what it is today.

'The thing about Thurles,' an eager young solicitor told me as we were wandering around Liberty Square, 'is that if a farmer drives his tractor into town you can be assured he'll be wearing his best suit. You won't see that anywhere else in Ireland.'

The tractor will also be the latest model, clean, not a speck of mud on it. Ireland's answer to the SUV.

Templemore is more commercial. Or, at least, it looks it. Huge wide main street. Enormous broad square, the size of a couple of polo pitches. Well kept. Well preserved. If anything Tipperary town should be Templemore and Templemore Tipperary town.

Cahir, as in Don't Care, is a touch miserable. One of the more downmarket heritage towns. It doesn't have the sparkle of, say, Lismore or the buzz of Birr. It's also, like Tipp, full of lorries. I tried to get into Cahir Castle. But it was closed. They said they were making a film there in order to attract more tourists. Well this one's not going back, I can tell you. It took me ages to park. It was pouring with rain. I got caught up with a bunch of Americans.

In any case who wants to see the 10,000-year-old antlers of a giant Irish deer anyway?

I ended up in the Castle Court Hotel instead. Much more fun.

Mitchelstown I don't reckon. I went into their caves once. There was no champagne there. What's the point of having caves if you don't keep champagne in them? A point, I might add, not lost on an undercook who some years back used to work nearby at Kingston College, a home for 'decayed Protestant gentlefolk'. His name: Claridge. They say he left and made a name for himself somewhere in the catering trade.

Carrick-on-Suir should make more of itself. A nice town. Lots of history. A major brewing and wool town in the Middle Ages. Some say the birthplace of Anne Boleyn. Two hundred years ago it was twice the size it is today. Who do they commemorate? Some local cyclist who won some big races twenty years ago.

Much the same applies to Nenagh, home to the man who invented the floating Mulberry harbours used for the D-Day landings, helped found UNESCO and was awarded the Lenin Peace Prize: John Bernal. Trouble is it's always packed with traffic. Somebody should build a floating motorway or something to get rid of it all.

A final Tipp. The one place to avoid: Killusty. It might sound fantastic. But it isn't. It's about as much of a turn-on as one of Andrew Lloyd Webber's greatest hits. Even worse, he lives nearby in Kiltinan Castle. Is he prepared to let his mask drop when he's there and become another one of the crowd? Not at all. He's forever getting his claws into various people. First it was his own gardeners. They were told not to cut the grass whenever he was there. Then it was plans to build a second pub in the village. He didn't want them belting out common tunes all the time like the one about Cats or Draughts or was it Chess? Next? He'll probably be complaining about roller skates.

As they say in the first pub in the village, 'All you can expect from a pig is a grunt.'

With or without a mask.

Co. Limerick
It's in the blood

Famous local resident
The one with the brown paper bag

Favourite food
Twelve inches of the best Afghan

Favourite drink
Guinness

Favourite pub
Dunraven Arms, Adare

Favourite restaurant
Any restaurant where the spoons have a scorch mark
underneath

What to say
I'd prefer a clean needle if you have one

What not to say
It's so easy to become addicted to Limerick

Co. Limerick is not just alcohol. It is, if anything, too much alcohol or rather too much of the new alcohol. In other words, drugs. For, thanks to drugs, Limerick – from the Irish Lim, Believe; Me, me; Rick, it's a wreck, with 52,000 people, another 25,000 in the suburbs, the third-largest city in the Republic, once the most pious town in Ireland, famous for its churches (it had more than anywhere else), its cured ham and bacon and its fine old Georgian buildings – is today probably the roughest, toughest, most deadly place in the country. Well maybe apart from bits of Dublin where they have notched up practically 40 murders in five years.

Once known as 'an ancient city well studied in the arts of war', it's been burnt, looted, smashed to pieces more times than the average syringe is used in a back room in a typical bar on an average Saturday night anywhere in the town, which makes you wonder where this 'well studied in the arts of war' comes from. To me it seems the last thing they are well studied in is the arts of war. But that's Ireland for you.

Come the middle of the eighteenth century it was suddenly all change. The place was rebuilt, refurbished. The city was suddenly peaceful, prosperous. Until the famine. Some say Limerick suffered the worst of all. Then came what they call the Anglo-Irish War.

Robert Graves of *I, Claudius* fame said at the time the place 'looked like a war-ravaged town. The main streets were pitted with holes like shell-craters. Many houses seemed on the point of collapse.'

Today it is known as Stab City. It is *The Sopranos*, *Gangs of New York* and weekends with the family all rolled into one.

Ireland: In a Glass of its Own

In Co. Donegale all the police have to worry about is the theft of the occasional Charolais cross bullock and old age pensioners firing double-barrelled shot guns at grass strimmers. In Co. Limerick its an altogether different matter:

- Sickles and meat cleavers are used in armed robberies
- Scalpels are used by schoolboys to attack other schoolboys in stationery shops
- A sword was used in a row between two first cousins. One of them was struck in the face and lost an eye.
- A semi-automatic was used to murder a man in a packed bar
- A 9 mm luger was found on a 15-year-old schoolboy
- Kalashnikovs are used in drive-by shootings
- Sub-machine guns are used in gang fights.

Old lady, her husband has just died, goes into the offices of the local newspaper to ask how much it costs to put an obituary notice in the paper.

'Ten euros an inch,' she is told.

'The Lord have mercy on us,' she says. 'I'll never be able to afford it. He was six foot six inches tall.'

And it's not just blokes or hoolivans, as they call them, who are at it. It's the women as well. Not for nothing are they said to be 'about as warm as a Kilmallock fire'. In autumn 1691 they fought with broken bottles to defend Limerick against King James. They're still at it.

It's not that the whole town is drug crazy. It's just that a traditional Limerick breakfast is a couple of spliffs dipped in amyl nitrate; lunch, a slab of ketamine; and dinner, as many trips as they can take. Kids are brought up the traditional way. On milk. Laced with heroin. The only thing for young people to do on a Friday night is about 12 inches of the best Afghan.

'The only good thing about being in Limerick,' a policeman who looked as though he was hooked on dried-up Nepalese temple hash once told me, 'is that nobody ever accuses us of planting any drugs anywhere. There's more than enough drugs all over the place without us having to plant them.'

Typical police, I thought. Always doing their best to boost their image.

Another policeman I met took things more seriously.

'If I get killed,' he tells me, 'I have to first present a certificate to the coroner before my wife can get the pension.'

Then I met somebody held in even lower esteem in the community: a bank manager.

'You can always tell a banknote that has been through Limerick,' he says. 'It's got white powder all over it.'

Some experts say that the Stone Age remains at Lough Gur, just south of Limerick city, are not Stone Age remains at all. They are what's left of a once very pleasant part of the city after violence took over just a few years ago.

I believe them. And I'm not the only one.

The Irish Prime Minister, Bertie Ahern, has condemned the goings-on in Limerick as 'totally unacceptable in any civil society'.

The mayor, John Cronin, has appealed for an end to the violence.

The bishop, Donal Murray, has called on everyone to pray for calm.

The Irish Chief of Police, Pat Byrne, has dispatched a 40-strong armed emergency response unit from Dublin and drafted in officers from surrounding areas to try and keep the peace.

Limerick Council has played its part. In order to create jobs, give people a chance to earn an honest living they've decided to build roads all over the place and then in order to stop people flooding into Limerick to make matters worse or even Limerick people flooding out across the county to stir up even more trouble, they've refused to open the roads up for traffic.

The first road they built never to be used: Limerick to the port at Foynes. Built in 2002 at a cost of €4.4 million. Two years later, it's still not open to traffic. Creative, I will admit, although I would have thought it would have been better to build swimming pools full of penicillin. But what do I know?

Industry and commerce, huffing and puffing with righteousness, is also playing its part to support the forces of law and order. The banks have issued their staff with – water pistols. Not ordinary water pistols they say, but water pistols with a special additive that glows yellow under UV light.

The Lord save us. What good is that going to be against a couple of sickles, a meat cleaver and a bunch of scalpels?

Voluntary and charitable organisations are also throwing their weight behind the drive to make Limerick a safer place for its inhabitants. Gay leaders are going around making offers they can accept. Instead of risking three greyhound puppies found abandoned on the streets of Limerick falling into the wrong hands, Limerick Animal Welfare paid over €150 each to send them to a charity, Greyhound Friends. In Boston, Massachusetts.

As for the man, as opposed to the greyhound puppy, in the street, he's just got to get on with it and hope it's not his name written on the next bullet.

Wander around People's Park. You're likely to come across people carrying boxes of home-made firearms. Whatever you do, don't bump into them.

A spot of retail therapy? Don't be surprised if you find the shop manager lying on the floor, in a pool of blood, stabbed in the neck. It wouldn't be the first time.

A cup of coffee to calm the nerves? Check the coffee spoon. Most authentic Limerick coffee spoons have a scorch mark underneath. A word of advice. If you don't want to risk being taken for a stranger don't whatever you do drink the coffee. Snort it up like everybody else.

Fancy a meal? Stay away from fast food restaurants. One restaurant in Ennis Road was the scene of practically all-out war between two rival gangs using the latest sophisticated weaponry: everything from snooker cues, golf clubs and steering locks to baby chairs, brushes and signs saying 'Warning – Wet Floor'.

A drink? Go into any bar or club. There are more bouncers than punters. Because they are scared what will happen to them if they're on their own.

Go into upmarket bars like Boru's in the Southcourt Hotel, Raheen, which all seem to be full of cailini deasa na hEireann in bondage pants, bleach stains and talcum powder. A serious, sombre, now terrified member of the Limerick establishment who looked as though he had just spent three weeks in a dentist chair told me he was there once when just before closing time the barman, all nice and polite, asked one of the spalpeens if he would kindly put out his cigarette. The guy leant across the bar and beat him up. He told me he was amazed. It was usually the women who caused the trouble.

I've even been in bars smelling of hen night vomit on a Friday night or rather 2 o'clock of a Saturday morning full of zoot suits when they started calling time and some of the suits have objected and started threatening everybody in sight. I didn't care. Every time somebody objected, for some reason or other, the barman gave me another glass of Guinness. Probably because he recognised I was from over. When I wanted a cognac I asked for a cognac not a yak, a Hennessey not a Hen-dog. It's amazing how little things like that can give you away. For my part, the Guinness I was pouring down my throat, they could have gone on and destroyed the whole place as far as I was concerned.

The morning after, there's nothing better than a stroll around the city, take in the sights, soak up the local atmosphere. Providing, of course, you're wearing your bulletproof jacket. Buttoned up to the neck.

Wander around Rhebogue and you are forever stepping over one hunting rifle complete with telescopic sights after another not to mention the occasional pump-action shotgun. Sawn-off shotguns are not popular in Limerick. People don't feel they are getting the full value for their money. There are also about as many .38 bullets all over the street as there are cans of Guinness in any other town in the country.

Try Garrowen. If you don't run into a gangland killing you'll probably run into preparations for one. The only consolation is that victims of gangland hits in Garrowen can be stabbed 18 times

– and still survive. There's a cheap joke there somewhere. But I'm not going to risk it.

Amble around Moycross or Cliona Park. In the old days the houses were virtually destroyed by their tenants. Windows were boarded up. Rubbish was strewn all over the streets. Today it's different. The houses are being destroyed by outsiders. There are more bullet holes than walls. How some of the houses are still standing God only knows.

Try the Kilalee area. Everyone is trying to Kilalee everyone else. Hardly a day or rather night goes past without shots being fired into one house or another.

I'm not saying violence is a problem – Heaven forbid – but even Limerick County Courthouse is not safe. I tried to get in there once. There was practically a riot taking place in the hallway between relatives of a local man who had just been given a life sentence for murder and relatives of the murder victim. One of the ushers told me the leader of one of the gangs had just told the magistrates he had no fixed address and his mate had told them he lived in the flat above. If the rioters looked rough the lawyers were a thousand times worse. Eyes that looked as though they could only sparkle if you shone a torch through their ears. A smarmy grin that said they had just stolen a MAC-10 machine gun as a present for their probation officer. And that was just the women. (Me? I've never had a problem with lawyers. Yet.)

Limerick prison. That's not safe either. One half of the prisoners are forever attacking the other half. When they get bored both halves attack the prison officers. As if that's not bad enough nail bombs are forever being lobbed over the perimeter walls and prisoners' and prison officers' families abducted and beaten up.

In fact it's so bad that even parts of Limerick no longer want to be associated with Limerick. Why else would Limerick Junction be in Co. Tipperary rather than in Co. Limerick?

'God save us,' a fully weapons-grade policeman tells me, 'I'd say there are more arms hidden in Limerick than in the whole of Northern Ireland. David Trimble should come down here. He'd soon realise he's got nothing to worry about up there.'

It was so dangerous, he said, that the police no longer walk around in pairs but by themselves. They are scared of walking around with another armed policeman in case he thinks he hears something, loses his nerve, shoots and they both get killed. As for visitors and tourists, he said, we should be alright provided we stuck to the safe areas, did nothing stupid and had luck on our side. But, he added, he had heard there were plans to put up signs all around the city boundaries saying, 'Don't worry. We'll get you next time.'

The cause of the violence? Most people blame it on drugs. Not the buying and taking of them. But the selling, the wheeling and dealing of them, who controls which patch, who wants to control somebody else's.

Not me. I blame it on Frank McCourt. Come on. Look at the facts.

Before he published *Angela's Ashes*, Limerick was nothing like it is today. My God, you could even walk down Rutland Street to Patrick Street to O'Connell Street along the Crescent and into Quinlan Street without a bulletproof vest. The biggest problem you faced wasn't finding somewhere to park but worrying whether the horse would still be there when you got back.

I don't know about *Angela's Ashes* but most people I know in Limerick would prefer to have Frank McCourt's ashes on a shelf in the living room rather than Angela's.

They love the way he can recall word for word conversations that took place when he was just three years old when most people can't remember what somebody said to them three minutes ago.

They treasure his fond memories of open sewers running down the middle of the street, practically every kid in his class going to school barefoot and – get this – boys dodging off into the countryside whenever they felt like it. How? By yellow cab?

They wonder in amazement at how, great farmer that he is, he maintains that Limerick cows not only stand still while being milked by young, inexperienced cowhands but that they also stand still long enough for young kids to lie underneath them so that they can drink the milk straight from the cow.

Come on. Pull the udder one, Frank.

It might be a good story. But look at Limerick today, you wouldn't risk running across Rutland Street unless you had so much armour on you couldn't walk let alone run.

Outsiders however and especially Americans swallow the story whole. I was once in the *Angela's Ashes* exhibition in Pery Square which some people say is the finest Georgian architecture in Ireland. Outside Dublin. There they've rebuilt the original McCourt homestead.

'Is it genuine?' I asked one old bag of bones, who looked as though she could have been Frank's grandmother.

''Tis. 'Tis. As genuine as can be. But without the smells,' she says.

As I was coming out – I was getting thirsty – I bumped into your usual pack of Americans. All baseball caps, shorts, two cups of Coke in each hand and thighs with different postcodes. You know the type.

'Gee,' the leader yells, the way they do. 'This is amazing. I didn't realise Limerick went back beyond the childhood of Frank.'

'Er. Yes,' I said nervously. 'First came the Vikings.'

'Gee. Mr and Mrs Viking. Were they his grandparents?' he says all ogle-eyed and sweating Coca-Cola.

'No. No.' I tried to maintain my half-Irish-half-English diplomatic phlegm. After them came the Normans.'

'No. Don't tell me,' he screams.

'They were the grandparents. Us old colonialists are not so stupid as we look.'

I didn't even blink.

'No. No,' I said looking him straight in whichever eye was not twitching at the time. 'They were the King St Johns. They built the castle. That's where the McCourts started. That's also where many people in Limerick would like to see them end up.'

'Because he wrote such a great book? Right.'

'Because he wrote the book,' I said.

'Gee, a real historian,' he yells. 'Pleased to meet you, sir. Have a great day.'

Off he barges into the exhibition.

One of the gang now comes up to me. He looks as though the

biggest thing in his life is his overdraft. I thought he was going to try to apologise for his leader, the way the occasional sensible American tries to apologise for his humpty hill head of a president. Instead he tries to talk books. He told me he admired Frank but his favourite author was 'Warren Peace'.

The only consolation is that nobody has written a book about Limerick's big anti-Jewish pogrom at the turn of the twentieth century: priests calling down the fires of hell on 'rapacious Jews', boycotts of Jewish businesses, violence. My God, would that cause trouble.

On the other hand Frank hasn't done so bad.

When I first went there, Limerick was calm and quiet and peaceful. I wanted to do all the tourist things. Visit the castle built by King John in 1210. Take a look at St John's Cathedral and its spire, the tallest in the country. Worship at the home of Terry Wogan. I ended up learning all about greyhounds. On the bus on the way in, I started talking to the world's greatest greyhound expert. Or rather he started talking to me.

'Ye want him to run. But ye don't want him to win. Feed him chocolate cake. It'll slow him down. But' – he taps the side of his nose and pulls up his overcoat lapels as if to hide his face – 'it'll never show. Never show up if they examine it. Mark my words.'

He followed me around the whole time I was there. I hardly saw a thing.

Twenty lines cost me I£120.

The next time I went back I was with an aunt. We got the bus from Ennis, Co. Clare to Limerick station. She wanted to do some Christmas shopping.

'Is there a B&Q in Limerick?' she asks the driver as we got off.

'No,' he says. 'But there's two *i*s, an *l*, an *m* and a *ck*.'

'God bless you,' she says.

Which, if anything, proves women never ever listen to any directions anyone gives them. Correction. They never ever listen to anything.

While she went off to do her shopping I thought I'd take a look at the Hunt Museum. Which it wasn't. I thought it was going to

be all about the hunt, horses, dogs, foxes. That kind of thing.
Instead it's all deeply cultural. Over 2000 historic and semi-historic
bits and pieces collected by a certain John and Gertrude Hunt.
American, of course. Some of the stuff was a bit, how d'ye say,
like a coin which was said to be one of the thirty pieces of silver.
Although I must admit I liked their collection of rosaries downstairs in the basement.

The nearest I got to a real hunt was in St Saviour's, the Dominican
church near the railway station. I was trying to avoid going into
Costello's Tavern where I knew I'd get caught and wouldn't be
able to get away till the new year. I went in the church which was
opposite. There was the traditional Christmas crib. In the crib was
a fox. For a moment I thought I had been in Costello's.

'And why not?' a jolly old lady who looks as though she had
been a nun before she had been led astray says to me. 'Who threw
Herod's hounds off the scent so that the Holy Family, God bless
them, could escape to Egypt? The gold, the frankincense, the
myrrh were fine enough. But the leisure-loving dog fox helped
them make good their escape. God knows where we'd be today
if it wasn't for the gift of the fox.'

I tell you. I was in Costello's soon enough after that.

Twenty lines cost me I£70.

Since then I've been back a million times. To change buses. To
catch the train to Dublin. For meetings at the university. At the
science park. Whatever the reason, I always go prepared. A pack
of mescaline in one pocket of my bulletproof jacket. Acid and
screamers in the other. A sniff of cocaine tucked away inside my
safety helmet. A 9 mm shillelagh under my arm.

Twenty lines now cost me about €30.

Usually I stay at the Royal George or the Railway Hotel. Once
as a dare I stayed at Adare Manor. Which it wasn't. It was fantastic.
It was like staying in a cross between an abbey, a castle and one
of these super-modern houses. The dining room was like the clois-
ters of an abbey with plate-glass windows all along what would be
the open side. There was a massive oak staircase with carved ravens,
and a gallery, the second-longest in Europe.

''Tis Ireland's very own Versailles,' one of the barmen told me.

But, again, drugs are everywhere. The supply of them. The effect of them.

Whatever hotel you go in there are people looking for drugs.

'Glory be to God,' one very smart, very helpful doorman tells me. 'We have one young gentleman from Arabia. He wants drugs. And he is prepared to pay big-time. One thousand euros. Maybe more. We get a pack of Aspros, crush them up, give them to him in a roll of paper. We tell him it's the finest. Jesus, Mary and Joseph, I tell ye he's over the moon. 'Tis a grand trade, it is.'

As for the effects of them, I was in the Adare Manor once just before Christmas. I was having breakfast. Into the restaurant comes this hard-nosed, very successful businessman. He's as white as a sheet. He collapses into the chair opposite me. He swears he's seen camels wandering along the busy Limerick-to-Ennis dual carriageway.

'My God,' he says. 'I know the Three Kings decided to take the long way home. But there's no way I thought that meant going via the Two Mile Inn.'

Too many sniffs?

The camels, it turned out, had escaped from a circus visiting the city.

The amazing thing is you can go in and out of Limerick a million times, nobody mentions the real big man of Limerick, the giant of Irish politics, the other American president, Himself, Éamon de Valéra, the General de Gaulle of Ireland. Same height. Same presence. Same nose. Go into any bar in Co. Limerick. People will talk to you about Frank McCourt, Terry Wogan, the increasing violence in today's society especially among women playing the once gentle game of camogie. You'd have to go into a million before anyone mentioned de Valéra. Then for all they know about him you'd think he did nothing but spend his days hanging upside down by his feet in lonely church belfries.

Even when you drive out to Bruree where he was brought up and went to school after returning from New York when he was only four, you have to search to find where he was born. Three times I drove past the tiny cottage a mile outside the village where he lived, the original Dev Res, before I realised what it was. There were no big boards. Just a tiny sign saying de Valéra's Cottage. Not even President de Valéra's Cottage. It was also the scruffiest-looking cottage in the street. All the others had been rebuilt, refurbished, repainted. Poor old Dev. He was really out in the cold.

Twice I had to ask before I found the De Valéra Museum and Heritage Centre in the town itself. First I was told to go to the ruined castle next to the church. Then to something called the Old Corn Mill standing on a ledge above the River Maigue. Finally I found it.

The John F. Kennedy Presidential Library it is not. Neither is it the Jimmy Carter Presidential Library which is half-empty for the want of anything important to say about him. Instead, it's about the size of a public toilet. A small public toilet. Inside there was a collection of this and that, a lock of his and his granny's hair, a rosary, a pair of spindly glasses, a bunch of letters, some medals, the trunk the family used when they came back to Ireland. The whole thing was about as exciting as looking at the great man's underpants. Then – whoosh – it was all over. A fussy old biddy who looked as though her thyroid was on the blink threw me out.

'Now come along, come along,' she insists. 'I have to be going to the doctor. I have no time to be standing here watching ye mooching about.'

I must admit, half-Irish hoodlum that I am, I felt like glassing her. But, of course, half-English gentleman that I am, I didn't.

But a commemoration of a great man it is not. In fact, if they'd have hung out a pair of the great man's socks it would have attracted more attention. In fact, the whole thing makes you wonder why the poor man bothered. If he'd have stayed in Bruree, become a teacher, married a local girl they would probably have made more of a fuss of him than they obviously do now.

Which is surprising because if any country knows how to build heritage centres and museums about nothing at all, it is Ireland. They are all over the place. Some serious and sensible. Some crazy. You wonder how they got the money.

On one of my travels, I ended up in Adare which with its neatly clipped thatched cottages everyone says is the prettiest village in Ireland. Except they're not all cottages, they're houses. They're not all neatly clipped, some have got lumps of grass growing out of them. It's not a village, it's a busy little town and commuter soft spot for both Limerick and even Dublin. But, hey, that's Ireland.

I was staying at the Dunraven Arms, which is more a hunt museum than the Hunt Museum. If you're going out with the Limerick Foxhounds you stay at the Dunraven Arms. That way you know if you're eating your last meal on earth, it will be a good one.

Which is something you don't know if you are staying in Limerick town.

The other advantage is that if you're going out with the Limerick Foxhounds, dangerous though it is, you don't have to wear a bulletproof jacket. With or without the top button done up.

Co. Longford
Nuts. Nuts. Nuts.

Famous local resident
Grey squirrels

Favourite food
Bacon and squirrel (grey) pie

Favourite drink
Guinness

Favourite pub
Any without any squirrels (grey)

Favourite restaurant
Any serving bacon and squirrel (grey) pie

What to say
You mean it doesn't run up trees?

What not to say
But I like them. They're lovely

For me, Co. Longford is an alcohol county because it drives you to drink. Not the happy-go-lucky, not a care in the world, tanksbetoGodI'llbehavinanotheronewidye school of drinking. But the Oh my God, I don't believe it, what on earth possessed him to do that? style of drinking. In fact, if it wasn't for Co. Longford there would be less aggravation, less inconvenience and more peace in the world. Because it was in 1913 in Co. Longford that the Earl of Granard released a dozen American grey squirrels on his estate at Newtown Forbes. They were oversexed. They were over here. They didn't give the poor, honest, hard-working, family-loving red squirrel a chance. As a result, they didn't have to be overpaid. They were more than happy to do what they wanted to do without even thinking of payment. Like all things American, they took over, wiped out the competition and destroyed the environment and thought they were doing everyone a favour.

Today, as a result, the damn things are all over the place. About half a million of them in the loft of my house tearing the place to bits. Am I allowed to gas them, poison them, blow them to Kingdom Come? No I am not. My wife is founder, president, throbbing conscience of not just the Grey Squirrel Conservation Society but also the Grey Squirrels Must Live in the Lap of Luxury Conservation Society. Their breakfast must be served on the dot at 7.23 a.m. My breakfast? I can whistle for it. Nuts. They get them by the sack. At one time I reckon I was shelling out for every nut in Africa. Are there any nuts left for me to nibble with my hard-earned snifter of an evening? What do you think? What's even worse are the hundreds of millions of feeders, plastic tubes, canisters and God knows what dangling from every branch of every tree in sight. In some cases you can hardly see the trees.

Thanks a million, Your Earlship. Next time you have a good idea, forget it.

For everybody else, however, Co. Longford doesn't seem to be an alcohol county at all. People seem to be happy to go with the drift. They're slow. Maybe a touch old-fashioned. Behind the times. Out of date.

> Church needs a new organ.
>
> Parish priest decides to raise money by promising that anyone who gives €100 or more can choose the first hymn to be played on the new organ.
>
> The new organ is installed.
>
> Priest asks a little old lady sitting in the front row, the only person in the parish who gave over €100, what hymn she would like.
>
> 'Glory be to God,' she says. 'My time has come. I'll be having that big blond brute in the back row.'

It's the only place in the country where I've seen a whole stream of traffic wait quietly without making a fuss or sounding a horn as a whole convent of fat, old nuns tried desperately to clamber out of the back of a tiny car which had stopped for no apparent reason in the centre of Longford town blocking traffic in both directions. When the nuns finally got out, they blocked the pavements as well. Nobody said a word. In Dublin, nuns would have been dragged from the car and thrown in the Liffey. In the wrong part of Belfast, they would have been lynched. If there were enough trees still standing strong enough to take the weight.

Similarly, the countryside. It's pleasant. More shandy than champagne. Deep rolling plains. Bright green pastures. Woods. Lakes. Bogs. The River Shannon flowing through the middle of it. It's got history. Prehistoric sun worshipping. The fighting Farrells. The ancient kingdom of Annaly. St Patrick. Again. The great rebellion. Cholera. Oliver Goldsmith. Again. Lord Longford. Prison visitor extraordinary. I'd have thought it was bad enough being in prison without having Lord Longford popping in for a quick chat and a prayer every ten minutes.

When the French surrendered in Co. Longford after they had fought their way across country from Killala, Co. Mayo, they were treated the way only Co. Longford would treat them. Pleasant. Civilised. Gentlemanly. They were put on board ship to be sent along the Grand Canal to Dublin. The Co. Longfordians even allowed them to play the 'Marseillaise' as the boat pulled away. The French, of course, complained they were only allowed to play it once. You know how they complain about everything.

Co. Longford has got some smart little towns, well fairly smart towns, Ballymahon always seems empty perhaps because they say it was the inspiration for our Oliver's 'Deserted Village'. Others disagree. There's Ardagh with its Swiss clock and Swiss-looking houses. Ruth, who does all my typing, is so house-proud she keeps a newspaper on the floor underneath her Swiss cuckoo clock. There's Clondra with its millstone and millpond. The oh-so-tidy Newtowncashel with its outdoor bogwood sculptures and obsessions with waste paper. Goldsmith would never have written 'The Deserted Village' there. They would have complained about all the scrap paper scattered around all over the place as he scribbled away trying to find something to rhyme with

> A man he was to all the country dear
> And passing rich at forty pounds a . . .

On the other hand, my God, Co. Longford gets on your nerves.

Longford town could be nice, pleasant, friendly. It's on the River Camlin. It's got an enormous grey limestone cathedral which can be seen for miles around. It's also got a greyhound racing track. Open Mondays and Fridays. But it's a mess. First time I went there

I wondered where I was. I thought I'd made a mistake, took a wrong turning and ended up in the middle of nowhere. Then I saw the Chinese Medical Centre, the only chinks in their armour. They told me how to get to the Longford Arms Hotel. At least nobody inside looked like Lord Longford which was surprising. I thought if anyone was behind bars, he would be there to chat them up. Hidden away in a corner though I spotted one Old Man of the Sea or rather of the River who was studying a very yellowed copy of *Popular Fishing*.

'If it's a God-fearing wake you're thinking of organising, this is the place to come.' The barman nods toward the Old Man.

The place/plaice to come! Is this a Co. Longford let's be pleasant/civilised/gentlemanly joke? No it's not. The barman then promptly disappears. I stand there looking at the bar. I almost asked the Old Man of the River if he had another copy of *Popular Fishing* I could read while I was waiting. In the end I gave up and went to a bar down the street.

It's much the same in Lanesboro. But more so. It's in a beautiful position. On the Shannon just where it flows into Lough Ree. It's also apparently pretty big on fish. Catching them more than eating them. Not that I know anything about fish. It could be another Kinsale, all fancy restaurants, a couple of upmarket hotels. Instead it's a disaster, I mean, disappointing.

Dominating everything is an enormous bog-standard peat-fired generating plant. When I went there I won't say it was belching out clouds of smoke but I will admit I did think instinctively for a moment of becoming a cough-cough environmentalist. A couple of pints in the Life Belt bar down by the river soon put a stop to that. But it wasn't an Irish pub. It was a fishing pub. Nobody was talking about horses, hunting or even what was running at Punchestown on Saturday. They were talking about fishing, fishing, fishing. Why the River Drowes is the best river in the world for salmon. The day the first salmon of the year was caught. Its weight. How many salmon they catch every year. The one that got away. The big fish they couldn't catch either. The usual kind of thing.

'Eat salmon from the River Boyne,' one old schoolmasterly type with half-rimmed glasses tells me, 'you'll pass all your examinations.'

Not the examinations I want to pass you won't.

Co. Longford

Another Old Schoolmaster of the River tells me the river always rises higher at full moon.

'You try it,' he says.

I'm thinking of long, gentle rolling seas, luxury cruisers, the setting sun, a glass of champagne, a couple of . . .

'Fill a dish full of water at full moon,' he goes on. 'In the morning it will be all over the dresser.'

You can bet your life there's nothing more I'm just dying to try than that.

'You don't want to be listening to him,' says another old boy who looks more like a golfer than a fisherman. 'He's a ramboozler.'

If a ramboozler is someone in the Life Belt bar in Lanesboro on a Friday night with crazy ideas, he was your ramboozler although I must admit that wouldn't have been my definition of a ramboozler.

A twitch, I always thought, was a twitch. A loop around a horse's nose to keep it under control. Not at all. According to the great ramboozler, it's a fish swimming around the body just under the skin, flapping its tail.

God help me. I felt like swimming up-stream and spawning away. Give me horsy talk any day or night of the week.

Lanesboro itself looks and feels about 20 years behind the times. Which in itself is not so bad. Quaint even. Trouble is most of the old farmers drive their tractors as if they were driving a pony and trap. I thought it was because they missed their pony and trap. Wrong. It's because of their respect for the road.

If there was any justice in this world, roads wouldn't be tarmaadam they'd be taredgeworth. For as sure as little pebbles smash windscreens especially if the car in front is being driven fast by a woman over a newly taredgeworthed road, the whole idea of a road surface was developed by Richard Lovell Edgeworth from Edgeworthstown, Co. Longford. Because he realised Co. Longford was such a fun place to live, he invented first of all a bicycle in order to try to escape. Then when that didn't work, a sail-powered horseless carriage. Which didn't work either.

Then it struck him. The state of the roads. They didn't work because the roads were a mess. What he needed were long, smooth stretches of road. Long smooth stretches of road would enable him to escape. You and I would have given up there and then and gone off and had a Guinness. Not Edgeworth. He had better things in mind than hanging around in the bar at the Longford Arms Hotel waiting to be served. He decided to build the ideal road. First it had to have a camber so that the rain would drain off to the sides. Second, it had to be smooth so he put small stones on top so that each time anything ran over the top of them, it would embed them in the surface. Third, it had to have proper foundations. It was no good throwing a couple of stones on top of a bog and hoping for the best. To prove the point, he built a road around his estate. All the facts and figures he then put into a book, *An Essay on the Construction of Roads and Carriages*.

Three years later in 1813 what happens? John McAdam built his famous road in Bristol.

Scottish genius? A coincidence? A straight lift? You tell me.

I know what they say in the pubs in Co. Longford. When they're not talking about fishing.

Although last time I was there, there was almost as much talk about Africans being banned from shopping centres as there was about fishing.

Ireland was coming to terms with being a multiracial society.

Two women, both African, both now Irish citizens, had just been charged at the local district court with shoplifting. Even before they had been tried to see if they were guilty or not – a minor detail – the judge was warning them they would be deported if they caused any more trouble. Where to? Their home country? Ireland? As if that wasn't bad enough, he also said the majority of shopping centres in the area would ban coloured people if this type of behaviour did not stop.

Nobody I spoke to thought there was anything wrong about it

'But the judge was assuming they were guilty before the case had even started,' I would say. 'That is wrong.'

''Tis wrong? Why is it wrong?' they would say. ''Tis the truth. The absolute truth, I'm telling ye.'

'But it's not the truth. You can't say somebody is guilty unless they've been tried and . . .' I would continue.

'But they were.'

'You don't know they . . .'

'I think they should all be banned. All of them. I tell ye. All of them.'

'But you can't blame everybody because one or two . . .'

'He's not blaming anyone. He says he wants them banned. He's entitled to his point of view as much as the next man.'

'But he can't say that. It's not . . .'

'He said it.'

'But he shouldn't have.' I finish my glass of the black stuff. 'Whatwillyebehavin'?'

'A pintthanksbetogod.'

'Carry on like that they'll ban you from the majority of pubs . . .'

'They can't. I've done nothing wrong.'

'Neither did the two women.'

'That's different.'

'Of course it's not different. It's the . . .'

'The Lord help me. Is it a liar ye are calling me? Because if ye are I'll . . .'

Another full, free and frank exchange of views in a pub in Co. Longford. It almost made me feel like talking fishing.

Afterwards a rather too elegant hayseed in a green beret, who looked as though he was a world champion at room roulette, shuffled up to me. He told me he was something to do with the Backstage Theatre. He didn't have to. I guessed it straight away.

Co. Longford people, he says, are not 'stubborn, mindless racial bigots'. They are 'genuine, honest, unbiased, a friend to all especially their friends from overseas'. They only pretend they are 'stubborn, mindless racial bigots' to keep the place to themselves. To stop outsiders from moving in.

'Africans?' I wondered.

'Dubliners,' he says. 'We don't want Dubliners moving in. The government has launched a big drive to bring industry to Longford. We can't say No. But we can do what we can to stop people from coming in. That's why we're the way we are.'

He brought me a glass of Guinness. I agreed with him.

I told you Co. Longford drives me to drink.

Co. Derry
By any other name

Famous local resident
Hmmm. Hmmm

Favourite food
Hmmm. Hmmm

Favourite drink
Guinness

Favourite pub
Hmmm. Hmmm

Favourite restaurant
Hmmm. Hmmm

What to say
I just love being in Co. Derry

What not to say
I just love being in Co. Derry

If you're going to Derry you need alcohol. That's it. Plain and simple. If you're going to stay there you need as much as you can get. Day and night. Day after day. Night after night.

I've been there lots of times. During the height of the Troubles. During the lull. During – fingers crossed – the peace.

During the height of the Troubles you were scared to even pick the glass up off the top of the bar in case you dropped it on the floor, it smashed and everybody threw themselves under the tables. Last man standing was dead.

During the lull, I drank half pints of Guinness on the basis that if nerves got the better of me and I dropped the glass on the floor, it wouldn't make such a loud smash and maybe two or three of us might be left standing afterwards.

During the peace, I could hardly get into a bar to get a drink there were so many people in there.

But before, during or after I admit I still didn't dare call it anything. It was the town with no name.

Say Londonderry. If you're talking to a Protestant he'll put his bowler hat down on top of the bar, buy you a drink especially if he is a Provincial High Sword Bearer, 20 degrees and upwards, and go on for hours and hours about how the London was added to the name Derry by royal charter, by the personal decision of His Majesty the King at the beginning of the seventeenth century when the city was handed over to the London trade guilds for development and how it would take an Act of Parliament to reverse it. If he's a Catholic he'll either turn and run, punch you in the face or go on for hours on end about Yes it's true that London was added to the name Derry by royal charter at the beginning of the seventeenth century when the city was handed over to the London trade guilds for exploitation, an Act of Parliament is neither here nor there, if they wanted to change it they could change it

> Woman walking along the beach at Magilligan. Sees a bottle in the sand. Picks it up. Starts rubbing it. A genie appears.
>
> 'Glory be to God,' she cries. 'I've got three wishes.'
>
> 'Not at all. Not at all,' he says. 'I'm only a one-wish genie.'
>
> 'In that case,' she says taking a map of Northern Ireland out of her handbag, 'I'd like to wish for peace in Northern Ireland. Peace between the Catholics and the Protestants. Peace between the Republicans and the Loyalists. Peace between Gerry Adams and Ian . . .'
>
> 'Hang on. Hang on,' says the genie. 'I'm only a one wish genie. I can't do the impossible. Have another wish.'
>
> 'OK,' says the woman, 'I'd like to get married. I'd like to marry a man who is nice and kind, caring and understanding, who'll help with the washing-up, do the shopping, not complain when my mother comes to visit us, not sit in front of the television all day, yelling and . . .'
>
> Says the genie, 'Let's have a look at that map again.'

and anyhow there are hardly any Protestants left apart from a handful in Waterside so what's the problem?

Say Derry. It's the same. But reversed. If you're talking to a

Catholic he'll put his balaclava helmet down on the bar, buy you a drink and go on about Derry being the end of the famous Civil Rights March in 1969 when 40 people from both sides of the Great Divide set out to walk the 75 miles from Belfast to Derry to champion civil rights and how at Burtollet Bridge Loyalists scared that civil rights would spell the end of their dominant position in Northern Ireland attacked the unarmed marchers with crowbars and lead piping. It was the start of the latest generation of the Troubles. If you're talking to a Protestant he'll put his bowler hat on top of the bar, smash you in the face and go on about Londonderry being famous for its spiced mince and black puddings.

Say Londonderry/Derry and your friendly local murdering psychopath will immediately buy you a half pint, gently punch you in the face, tell you how Londonderry/Derry was once the white shirt capital of the world and how they made all the plain white Italian-cotton shirts for Marks and Spencer.

Say Derry/Londonderry and your friendly local murdering psychopath will tell you sadly that Derry/Londonderry is no longer the white shirt capital of the world but the world capital of fancy £80 designer shirts favoured, ironically, by the heights of the British establishment.

The marketing department of the council ignores everybody and everything and calls the place Derry/Londonderry/Daire, the Irish word. But then marketing departments are nothing if not provocative.

The local Protestant newspaper, the *Londonderry Sentinel*, went a stage further and proposed that it be renamed Oakland. But it was April Fool's Day, I think. In Londonderry. As well as in Derry.

The killer argument is, of course, that the whole thing is a lot of nonsense. The Protestants have always called Derry Derry. Why else would the famous Protestant marching society be called the Apprentice Boys of Derry if they didn't call it Derry? But I wouldn't advise using it. Not that it means you won't leave the place with your kneecaps intact. But because you'll get another history lesson.

The Apprentice Boys of Derry commemorate the 13 apprentices who for six months in 1689 kept at bay the besieging forces

Ireland: In a Glass of its Own

of the Catholic King James II. In any case in the 1980s Chris Patten, at the time minister for Northern Ireland, agreed Londonderry Corporation should be renamed Derry City Council although he stuck with Londonderry as the name of the city. Who says he's not a good Catholic boy?

Some people have avoided the problem altogether. They call it Stroke City on the basis that if you live there long enough and keep stressing yourself out about what you call it sooner or later you'll end up by having a stroke.

Bill Clinton when he came calling as US president called it 'Derry. County Londonderry.' But then Bill Clinton always had problems with the use of English: I did not smoke grass, I did not have sex with that woman, I believe Al Gore would make a great president.

The county's world-famous signature tune, however, is still known as the 'Londonderry Air'. Well let's face it, 'Derry/ Londonderry/Daire Air' isn't exactly something the Radio 3 rejects on Classic FM could get their tongue round.

In the old days it was worse still, say haitch instead of aitch or aitch instead of haitch you could end up getting killed. Haitch to a Protestant meant you were a Catholic. Aitch to a Catholic meant you were a Protestant. When I say the old days I mean as far back as June 2002.

The way I get round the problem? Simple. I say, Mwaughhherry. Which may or may not be cowardly but at least I haven't upset anyone, caused any trouble, ended up dead or worse still spilt any Guinness on the floor.

Yet in spite of everything Mwaughhherry is the basis, the starting point, the measure for everything in Ireland. Geographically speaking. When the Ordnance Survey wanted to start mapping the whole country they drew a straight line nearly 10 kilometres long in the sand on the beach at Magilligan, home to Ireland's only grown-up sand dunes. From there they measured everything else.

This immediately made many people both sides of the Derry/Londonderry divide want to throw up. A local doctor offered his services. His name: James Murray. His helpful proposal: milk of magnesia. He invented it. He also incidentally discovered a way of making artificial phosphate fertiliser. Enough said.

330

But why Magilligan beach? Because it was flat? Because it went on for ever? Because it was close to sea level? Because from there they could link up with Scotland and into all the main UK maps? Don't you believe it. It was because someone in Ordnance Survey had a sense of humour. Drawing all those lines and little pictures of windmills must get to you one day. The sensible thing to have done was draw the line through the middle of Mwaughhherry itself. It's big. It's impressive. It's shaped like a compass. It's also going to last a darn site longer than any line drawn in the sand by a civil servant from London.

The second city of Northern Ireland. The Gateway to the North-West. Big. Imposing. On the banks of the River Foyle. The only completely walled city in Ireland. You can walk the whole way round the outside, come through one of the gates and then walk all the way round the battlements at the top. Each circuit, one mile. I've seen some walled cities in my time. Carcassonne. Old Jerusalem . . . Mwaughhherry is up there with them. The grandest walled city in the world. In the rain.

When Amelia Earhart landed here in 1932 after flying solo across the Atlantic she thought she was in Paris. Which says a lot about Americans. It also, of course, says a lot about the local Mwaughhherry accent. But as a tribute to her knowledge of the world, her skills as a navigator and her uncanny ability, like all Americans, to make friends wherever she went the good people of Mwaughhherry have ever since seen the city walls as a tribute to her and all her fellow Americans. Thick.

Up to 20 foot in some places, wide enough for five Americans to march side by side proclaiming their dedication to freedom, liberty and justice to all the peoples of the world unless, of course, they think otherwise. People from anywhere else in the world, they could march ten maybe even fifteen side by side.

In 1688–9 during the siege which lasted from 18 December to 12 August the following year 30,000 people took refuge behind the walls of the city. Nearly a quarter of them died of starvation before they were finally relieved. It might have happened over 300 years ago but to the people of Mwaughhherry it's still as real as if it happened yesterday. They talk about it. They sing about it: 'The

Sash My Father Wore', 'Dolly's Brae', 'The Orange Lily' and the so-called rip-roaring crowd stopper 'Kick the Pope'. They march about it. Some of them even drink to the health of King Billy and wish the Pope in hell. In some parts of the county they still burn effigies of Lundy, the traitor, they say, who tried to open the gates of the city to the Catholics. Whatever they do, they do to the sound of drums. In fact, they're so obsessed with drums you'd think they were born with them in their ears.

Try to shout to some of the old people over the sound of the drums. They'll tell you they still late at night hear the muskets, the cries of the victims of the siege and see the mysterious ghostly horse-drawn funeral processions. Being brought up with a skeleton on the city's coat of arms can't help. I thought it was something to do with the state you're in either before or after a two-week stay eating and drinking in the local restaurants. Not so. Apparently it's all to do with Norman de Burgos, who briefly owned Mwaughhherry in the early fifteenth century. Again it doesn't say much for Mwaughhherry if that's the way he is remembered. Although I suppose better that than the poor schmuck who worked hard all his life so that his beloved wife could make whoopee with her toy boy once he's gone.

From the top of the wall you can also see why Mwaughhherry has had its problems. Everything is clearly divided up, sectioned off, segregated this way and that, up and over, inside out and back to front.

Wandering along the top of the wall one morning in the rain I came across an old boy who looked as though he could have been a battle-scarred victim of either side of the divide. Catholics, he told me, used to deliberately burn turf and all the rubbish they could find in their fireplaces at home just so the smell and the smoke would drift across to the Protestant houses further up the hill.

Another old boy joined us who again could have been on either side.

'Stuff and nonsense,' he says. 'The last thing the Catholics did was burn the turf. They loved it so much they did. They could be forever seen carrying bags of fertiliser from one side of the city to the other.'

Co. Derry

Inside the walls, it's simple. In the centre is the city square which like all city squares in Ireland is called the Diamond. On the Diamond is an enormous shopping centre. South-west is the courthouse, which looks as if it could do with some R & R, and St Columb's Cathedral, the first Protestant cathedral built in the whole of the UK after the Reformation. It's not difficult to tell. No collection plates. No posters for Lourdes. No notices saying the Sisters of Charity have cast off clothing of all kinds and will be in the church hall after mass for those who are interested. In the east window I noticed St Patrick and St Columba are on the same level as Matthew, Mark, Luke and John. Don't ask me to write captions for what the Big Four are saying when they see themselves raised to the same dizzy heights as St Patrick and St Columba.

Outside I couldn't help but notice a gravestone: 'In affectionate remembrance. David Irvine. Printer of this City. Born 25th December 1831.' Affectionate remembrance? Of a printer? You mean no misprints. No late deliveries. No invoice way over the estimate? Something is wrong somewhere.

St Columb's Cathedral is, however, far more famous than that. It was the wife of one of the bishops of Mwaughhherry who wrote the ever popular 'Once in Royal David's City', which went round the world as a result of the massive launch publicity it received. Her husband, Dr William Alexander plugged it for all he was worth. I'm told there is a somewhat less than reverent version called 'Once in Loyal Gerry's City' but I have yet to discover it although I once heard 'Gerry and the Peacemakers' sung late at night in a not very reverent setting.

The rest of the walled city is backstreets. Or at least I think it is. It always rains so much whenever I go there I hardly have a chance to set foot in the place.

Once I was sheltering from the rain in a bar. I started talking to a pile of old rags with a limp and a walking stick. He was the world's greatest expert on the Victoria Cross. Eleven Irishmen won the VC during World War II or World War Eleven as George W. Bush would call it. Eight from the Republic. Three from Northern Ireland – two of those Nationalists. Soldiers from the Republic also

333

won 780 other medals, more than many countries which counted themselves Allies.

'So why do people think the Irish were on the other side?' I asked.

'Because we were neutral,' he says. 'Or at least officially neutral.'

Another round of the black stuff.

'So what about the total number of Irishmen who've won VCs?'

He took out his wallet from his inside jacket pocket. Opened it on the bar. Took out a mass of little bits of greasy paper, rummaged around and then finally seized one, about half the size of a postcard.

'Two hundred and ten,' he says. 'One hundred and ninety were born Irishmen, nineteen were born of Irish parents. Two hundred and ten.'

'Two hundred and nine,' I said.

'More than any other nationality apart from the English. More than the Scots. More than the Welsh. So who says we were Nazi sympathisers?'

Another round.

'What's more the very first VC was awarded to . . .'

'An Irishman,' I guessed.

'An Irishman,' he repeats, slapping the top of the bar. 'Charles Lucas. In naval action. In Finland. 1855.'

'And the youngest?'

'Andy Fitzgibbon. China. 1860.'

There was only one way to celebrate.

Outside the confines of the city walls, Mwaughhherry is the Cork of the North. Seven days, even seven nights a week. Including Mondays.

I've spent wet, miserable Monday evenings in various fun spots all over the world. A wet, miserable Monday evening in Mwaughherry is unlike any other wet, miserable Monday night anywhere in the world. The place is heaving. The bars are packed. The restaurants are full to overflowing. The music is thumping. The vomit is flowing. I've seen whole gangs of guys and whole gaggles of girls happily throwing up, boozing, throwing up and boozing again as if for all the world it was a

Friday night and they were in Ibiza rather than Strand Road, Mwaughhherry.

One girl who was wearing a big smile once slobbered all over me something about it being her hen night.

'But hen nights are Fridays,' I said.

'Not all all,' she blurts in my face. 'People get so drunk on Fridays it's disgusting.'

With which she slumped to the floor of the wherever I was, opposite some hotel that was being rebuilt somewhere near the quayside.

Saturday nights are a million times worse. Or better, depending on what you are looking for. Wander down the Strand Road you'd think the Troubles had started all over again. The place is packed especially around the junction with Great James Street. People are fighting. Stones are being thrown. Everybody's cheering. If anyone is making Molotov cocktails, they are now putting olives in them. The police are standing by wondering whether the best thing is to ignore it or go in batons flailing.

If Mwaughhherry knows how to party it's thanks to the clergy. Augustus Hervey, Earl of Bristol and Bishop of Derry, travelled the Continent, which is why there are now so many Hotel Bristols all over the place, came back to Derry where – when he wasn't organising steeplechases between his clergy on Saturdays and condemning gambling on Sundays – he tried to have himself crowned King of Ireland. If only he had. What a party they would have had. What a country they would have had.

Early mornings it's different again. Security patrols in their dark grey Land-Rovers cruising the streets. Huge murals everywhere. If the IRA ever wanted to raise funds they should send their artists overseas on contract to the likes of Castro or Gaddafi. They could make millions. What wasn't covered by giant murals was covered by graffiti.

The riverfront is a bit miserable. That fantastic view of the old walled city is blocked off by three multi-storey car parks and the back of a supermarket. Old warehouses along the edge of the river were knocked down and replaced by a dual carriageway. Now there are plans to liven it up. Not by building along the banks of

335

the river. They can't. There's no room. There's also that dual carriageway. Instead they want to extend the river bank over the top of the river and build practically a one-mile stretch of new buildings on stilts on both sides.

I'm sorry but I couldn't leave Mwaughhherry without taking a look at the Saville inquiry in the Guildhall which is examining second by second the events of Bloody Sunday, 30 January 1972 when 13 civilians were killed and 13 wounded during a civil rights march.

First thing that struck me was the location. It's supposed to be an independent inquiry but it couldn't be taking place in a more Protestant environment. The Guildhall is like a first attempt at a post-Reformation cathedral. All huge open spaces, stairs and stained-glass windows proclaiming various Protestant glories. I'd have gone for something far more neutral. Second, the name of the inquiry, 'The Bloody Sunday Inquiry'. It's hardly objective is it? I'd have chosen something neutral like, say, 'The 30 January 1972 Inquiry'.

Then there's all the so-called security checks to get in. It's more like We're the BIG STATE. You're the tiny, insignificant nobody. Open your pockets. Take your shoes off. We're not letting you in here until we are absolutely guaranteed you're one of us. Correct me if I'm wrong but I thought one of the points of the inquiry was to show that the state was not the BIG STATE, could not just go around doing what it wants to do and that we tiny, insignificant individuals do, at least, have some rights. Although I will admit the fact that most of the security guys look like Para rejects, both mentally and physically, was a touch reassuring.

'No. No. It is not a camera. It is a telephone. No. There is no microphone in there. That is a pencil.'

But there you are. Nobody takes any notice of me.

The Inquiry, the longest-running inquiry in British history, is also costing an absolute fortune. Anything between £125 and £150 million. On top of that there's the money spent by the Ministry of Defence defending its reputation. Say, another £25 million. From time to time there's the occasional criticism. The money would be better spent on improving schools, cutting hospital waiting lists. But most people seem to accept that it is better to have it than not to have it and that now they've got it, it's better for it to finish its job than cut it short.

'How can you put a price on human life? How can you put a price on justice?' a relative of one of the victims killed on Bloody Sunday says to me as I make my way in.

From the public gallery up in the rafters, it looks more like Mission Control than a judicial inquiry. There are row upon row upon row of desks facing huge computer screens. Instead of men in T-shirts there are men in suits. Admittedly Irishmen in suits.

'Will ye give me a short?' one smart-looking pinstripe suit yells up to the public gallery. 'Right across the street.'

What on earth he was talking about I have no idea. Obviously all to do with the Protestant environment.

In the gallery, the talk is more gossip among friends, some of whom have not missed a day since it started.

'That's Sir Louis. Not looking too good today.'

'Fourth down. Andrew. Good guy. Met him the other night. No flies on him.'

'Over there. By the edge of the stage. They say he is also free-lancing for *The Times*.'

'Hey, there's Siobhan. Did ye see what she's wearing or rather not wearing today?'

Outside in the bar opposite the conversation is even more inter-esting.

One old boy in a suit much too big for him told me he was there on Bloody Sunday.

'They were after us. They knew what they were doing. They were in full battle dress. They were out to eliminate all the top IRA men in Derry,' he says.

Other old suits joined us.

'I saw soldiers in suits, in denims, in car coats. They were waiting for us. When we got there, wham, they hit. Then they disappeared.'

'To be sure it was organised. It was planned.'

'They knew who they were after.'

'You could see them go for the leaders.'

'They wanted to get them. Wipe out the leaders. That's always the objective.'

'You knew it was going to happen. As soon as the army said the civil rights march was illegal, you knew it was going to happen.'

I met an earnest, eager young man. Anorak. No suit. He told me he had been investigating the events of Bloody Sunday since almost the day it happened. He had been threatened by everybody. The Loyalists. The Republicans. The Loyalists who don't want to be Loyalists. The Republicans who don't want to be Republicans.

In another corner, a big London lawyer was complaining loudly about the extent and influence of the IRA, how even buying books on Amazon.com meant he had to contribute to the funds of the IRA.

'There it is,' he was bellowing over his gin and tonic. 'Shop at Amazon. A portion of what you spend supports the IRA.'

I was going to tell him it stood for International Reading Association. The whole world knows that. But I didn't have the heart. I though it better for him to maintain the integrity and objectivity of the British system of justice. If lawyers started speaking the truth where would we be?

I then met a tall, thin, white-faced man. He looked as though he had been wearing a balaclava helmet all his life. He told me he came from Claudy, about ten miles from Derry. A car bomb went off there 30 years ago killing nine people including an eight-year-old girl and two teenage boys.

'Who was responsible?' I asked.

'We'll never know,' he says.

'Why?' I wondered. 'Didn't anybody claim responsibility?'

'No.'

'Isn't that unusual?'

'Not when the man behind the killing was a local priest.'

'Priest.'

'Priest.'

His theory: the local priest, Father Jim Chesney, was a member of the Provisional IRA. The authorities knew. But said nothing. After the bombing he was moved to Co. Donegal.

'But that doesn't make him guilty.'

'After the bombing there was a meeting between Willie Whitelaw at the Northern Ireland Office and Cardinal Conway. How many meetings were there between Willie Whitelaw and Cardinal Conway? How many took place immediately after a bombing? How many resulted in the local priest where the bombing took place being moved to Co. Donegal?'

'Errrrr.'

Outside Mwaughhherry there are nothing but more ups and downs.

For ups there's, to the south-east, the Sperrin Mountains on the border with Co. Tyrone and to the west the heights of Slieve Gullion.

For downs there's Coleraine, a harbour town, once big in the linen business, strict Scottish Presbyterian country, one of the cleanest, smartest market towns in Ireland. But somehow detached, void, an area of vast consuming emptiness. Which is probably not surprising seeing as the first man to discover what we call black holes came from Coleraine, Alexander Anderson.

Wonder where he got his inspiration.

Claudy also seemed to have an emptiness. The effects of the bomb have long since disappeared – or, at least, the physical effects of the bomb have long since disappeared. Today it's as typical as any typical Irish village. Shy. Quiet. Reserved. Two churches. One old. One new. But nobody wanted to talk about anything. Not in Dan's bar. Not in Brendan's bar. I didn't talk about anything either.

In Bellaghy on the border with Co. Antrim, however, they wouldn't stop talking.

About how Jane Ross wrote the famous 'Londonderry Air'. She was coming out of the hairdressers' in Limavady, a nice, quiet, Georgian town. She bumps into a poor passing fiddler. He is so impressed by how she's had her hair coloured in red, white and blue like the Union Jack, he says, Glory be to God, is that the Londonderry Hair? In return she gives him a few notes for a meal. The rest, as they say, is musical history.

About Magherafelt, the biggest town in South Mwaughhherry,

how at one time you could hardly move for security towers and all kinds of security bits and pieces but today it is one of the safest places to live in Northern Ireland – and one of the most expensive. The average price of a new house was over £75,000. It was fast becoming the fun centre for mid-Ulster.

About Bellaghy itself. I thought it was famous as the birthplace of Northern Ireland's greatest poet, the Nobel Prize winner Seamus Heaney, whose poetry nobody can ever remember. Wrong. Whisper it not but they say that throughout all the Troubles this was where both sides used to meet in McKenna's Bar to maintain contact, exchange information and damn the English to Kingdom Come for the way they were ruining Ireland.

OK, so now you understand what makes Mwaughhherry tick. Not like a bomb. Like a clock. A final question. You're in a bar. It's the end of the evening. The band plays, 'The Soldier's Song'. Do you stand, sit or remain hanging on to the floor in case you fall off?

Remember. Your life could depend on it.

Co. Armagh
From Armalite to Armagh-lite

Famous local resident
That man in camouflage

Favourite food
Anything Armagh-lite

Favourite drink
Guinness

Favourite pub
Shorts, Crossmaglen

Favourite restaurant
Any restaurant in any bar in Camlough

What to say
Not at all, I don't mind being stuck in this traffic jam for another three hours

What not to say
I'm looking for some long bullets

When it comes to alcohol, lush, beautiful Co. Armagh is a yes/no county. Yes, you definitely need it. No, you mustn't have too much. When I first went to Co. Armagh it was Bandit Country. Drink anything, do anything was dangerous. You needed all your wits about you. And more.

Take a wrong turning. You could end up in the middle of one of the biggest chains of military observation towers in Europe since the collapse of the Berlin Wall.

Walk across the wrong field. You could stumble into no end of surveillance equipment, infrared cameras, directional microphones capable of penetrating concrete and picking up conversations inside offices, homes and empty farm buildings. Whether they could also pick up sounds below ground level in cellars, in bunkers or in arms stores nobody knows or if they did would say.

Throw a stick for the dog. It could come back with a roll of Semtex.

Open the wrong farm gate the wrong way, you could set off a booby-trap bomb or, as the army calls them, 'an improvised horizontal explosive device'. Your wife could be counting the insurance money and be on Copacabana Beach with her toy boy by lunchtime.

Co. Armagh, especially South Armagh, was so dangerous the military didn't even dare travel by road. Everywhere they went, they went by helicopter. So did everything to do with them. It was said that even their waste was removed by air. Now if one of those helicopters crashed, it would give a whole new meaning to the Muckish Mountain.

Ireland: In a Glass of its Own

To the Catholics, it was the heavy-handed actions of a foreign power. To the Protestants it was security. To others it was either the safest or the most dangerous area in the whole of Europe. Depending on whether you feel having more military on your doorstep than blades of grass is a good thing or a bad thing.

Today, of course, it's nowhere near as bad.

In the old days they used to say Armagh, the Gap of the North, the Orchard of Ireland, the smallest of the Six Counties, was short for Armalite rifle. Now they say it's short for Armagh-lite, a nice place. Not heavy on the booze. To a few, it's known as The Fews. Because there are now few British troops crawling all over it.

Everybody has their theories about Armagh. To me the two extremes are Drumcree and Crossmaglen.

Drumcree. For years it was famous for Orangemen, the Star of David accordion band, marching, barricades, umbrellas, 'You're blocking our way,' 'Hear, hear,' 'No surrender,' 'Walk on through,' riots, injured policemen and protesters. Sometimes the riots even spread as far as Belfast. Of all the 3,500 odd parades which took place every year this was always the biggest – sometimes as many as 30,000 people would be present – the nastiest, most vicious, most deadly in the country. Thousands of Orangemen and their supporters would march two miles from the centre of Portadown, the Aberdeen of Ireland, past the Corcrain Loyalist estate to Drumcree parish church with its grey steeple and two Union Jacks for a service to commemorate the Battle of the Somme. In church they would pray to the God of Peace and Reconciliation. Afterwards they would insist on marching back past St John's Catholic Church along Garvaghy Road. Catholic residents along Garvaghy Road would object, protest, tear the place apart.

But no more.

The year I was there the only people who suffered and were severely burnt were the Protestants who skipped the church service, fell asleep in the sun and got a bad dose of sun burn. Not that everything is all peace and light and big kisses in the sunset. The problems are still there.

Protestants and Catholics still have to be separated. Admittedly only by anti-spit screens but that's better than 3,000 riot police and half the British army.

The Protestants say their policy has succeeded. They still have the right to march along the Queen's highway, attend the Queen's church and march back again. They have not been banned. They have not been stopped by illegal, anticonstitutional, Catholic behaviour.

Catholics say the Protestants still have their march but it's nothing like it used to be. It's not so large. It's not so inflammatory. It's not so anti-Catholic.

Others say it's because the two communities are now more divided than ever. Both sides now have their own territory. Nobody trespasses on anybody's patch any more. Catholics have moved out of Protestant areas into the Garvaghy area. Protestants have moved into the houses they left behind. There's no more fudging. It's now black and white or rather red, white and blue and green, white and gold.

Wander around the bars, the word is all is peace and quiet because of South Africa.

'South Africa?'

'Sure to goodness you know what's happening.'

'Err. No.'

'The Government. 'Tis flying everyone out to South Africa. That's what they're doing. Giving them a holiday. Letting them lie in the sun. No doubt giving them money to spend as well.'

'Err.'

'Of course, they say it's to learn from South African reconciliation experience and all that. Do what they do in South Africa and all our problems will be over. Yeah. It's the free holiday they're after.'

'Yes. Well . . .'

'You wait. You'll see when they stop giving them all their free holidays in South Africa the trouble will start up all over again.'

As far as Crossmaglen – short for Cross ma glen and I'll kill ye – is concerned I've always thought if it wasn't the home or even the capital of the IRA, it felt like it. When I first went there there were IRA signs and Irish flags all over the place. There were political signs and slogans by the side of the road. The road signs didn't say Men at work, they said Sniper at work. Everywhere there were also signs of the British army at work. A sprawling army/RUC barracks that stopped just short of the Gaelic football pitch. Steel barriers. Aerials. A huge watchtower with four masts. Bulletproof glass. Anti-blast shields. Cameras on top that could swivel 360 degrees. Helicopters hovering overhead. The visitors' book in the local bar was the only visitors' book I've seen anywhere in the world where everybody signed their name. But not their address.

The landlord of one of the local bars was said to have the inside track on what the British Government was or was not planning. A relative of his was said to be a leading member of the Government.

Today it's all changed. It's even recommended in one tourist brochure I saw as the place to go for food and music. The IRA signs and the Irish flags are still there. But they're not so clean. Not so smart as they used to be. A bit tatty around the edges. About the only political sign you see says Keep Right. All the steel barriers and aerials have gone. The watchtower is empty. It looks as though it is either being dismantled or falling apart. In Short's bar the only thing they were talking about was whether they should join some new local Stop Smoking Support Group. I didn't hear or see one helicopter the whole time I was there. What I did notice though was that everybody, especially the women, walked up and down the street as if they're in a military band. Left. Right. Left. Right. Arms swinging up and down. Odd. Very odd. Is it genetic? Is it in the potatoes? Is it the time they spent marching up and down in various pipe bands when they were kids? Could be a big research project for some minger who can't keep their nose out of other people's business. Like a full-time colonic irrigationist.

In between the two, Drumcree and Crossmaglen, there are a million different shades of opinion, a thousand ways of looking at things, hundreds of opinions and some interesting places with some interesting bars.

Talk to anyone about Armagh. They'll tell you it's the oldest town in Ireland. It's got two cathedrals and two archbishops, an English street, an Irish street and a Scotch Street.

St Patrick's is the Protestant one, the one where Swift wrote *Gulliver's Travels*. Or big chunks of it. You can see how busy be must have been. It's a bit dull. Sandstone exterior. St Patrick's is the Catholic one. Twin spires. Gothic or at least imitation Gothic. Inside it's all mosaics.

It's not so bad now but in the old days if you were going cathedral-crawling it was best to make certain you visited the right one first and the Protestant one second. Thackeray loved the place. Because, he said, sermons in the cathedral lasted no more than 20 minutes.

The Catholics say the Catholic one was built by St Patrick himself. The Protestants . . . you know the story.

The Mall in the centre of the city looks like a racetrack, which it once was and should be again. It's green. It's open. It's jam-packed with traffic. It takes as long to get in there as it does to get into Epsom on Derby Day and as long to get out of as it does Aintree on Grand National Day. It's perfect.

I like Armagh not because Scotch Street was full of Scotch – it wasn't – but because this is where, a momentous moment in my life, I discovered the true age of the planet. It all began on 22 October 4004 BC. A Sunday. That's according to Archbishop Ussher who was born in Dublin and became Archbishop of Armagh in 1650. Other people have tried to calculate the day the world began. The Venerable Bede made it 3952 BC. Isaac Newton, who was no particular slouch when it came to mathematics, made it 3998 BC. At the drop of an apple Ussher's opinion was the one everybody accepted. It was printed in all English bibles up until the late nineteenth century. The reason it was accepted? It was based on the Bible. Not on anything as newfangled as mathematics. He counted all the begats in the Old Testament, guessed the age of each begatee, added them up, hey presto, 22 October 4004 BC. Armagh-zing. Especially as Armagh is sitting on top of the Ring of Gullion, a volcanic crater over 60 million years old. Which was responsible for, among other things, the Giant's Causeway, the Mountains of Mourne, a couple of loughs and Greenland and

– thankfully – North America breaking away from Europe.

Did I question the discrepancy of a mere 59,993,992 years with one of the clergy? No way. Have you ever tried discussing anything with any of Northern Ireland's clergy?

What I did do was go to Armagh Planetarium, built in the grounds of Armagh Observatory. There I thought I was bound to find someone who could explain to me how if the world was created in 4004 BC Armagh was sitting on a volcano 60 million years old. They were about as much help as an Armalite rife in keeping off the rain.

'Excuse me, I wonder if . . .'

'Can ye not see we're closed? We're completely rebuilding . . .'

'Yes, I know. But I just wondered . . .'

'We're giving the place a facelift. We've stripped everything back to the concrete. We've pulled all the wires out . . .'

'Yes. Very interesting. It's about the beginning of the world.'

'I haven't got time to be worried about trifling matters like that. I've got to get this job done by next Tuesday.'

'There's a discrepancy of about $59\frac{1}{2}$ million years. That's fairly important.'

'Dis-crep-pan-sy or no dis-crep-pan-sy, will ye leave the building? I've got work to do.'

The Lord have mercy on us. These people are trying to see if there's life on other planets. For the planet's sake, I hope there's not. Can you imagine being on Mars trying to cope with a friendly, cooperative astronomer from Armagh?

I decided to try Portadown. In the old days, of course, when there were orchards all over the place and it was one of the biggest shirt-making towns in Northern Ireland – at one time they were turning out 40,000 shirts a week – it was known as Portaup. Now it's very Portadown. Orchards have been uprooted. Factories have been closed. The whole town is flat. The people are serious, severe. Buildings are somewhat austere. The bars are not exactly a bundle of laughs. What the Lodges are like God only knows.

Lurgan, another one-time centre of the Irish linen industry, was a bit Portadown as well. Its long, broad main street looked as though it was going nowhere. Not that it hasn't had its problems in its time. Founded by an Englishman, John Brownlow from Nottingham. Site of the first meeting of the Society of Friends in Ireland in 1653. Visited by John Wesley himself in 1778 to open their first Methodist church. Obviously it takes time to get over a string of things like that.

Camlough is much more fun. But then it would be. It's in the *Guinness Book of Records* for having more pubs per head or, I suppose, per pair of livers of population than any other town in Europe. I reckon it's also got more Irish flags flying from more Irish bedroom windows, roofs, telegraph poles and flagposts than anywhere else in the 6,000- or 60,000,000-year history of the world. They also had giant reproductions all over the place of those three letters which I think stand for It's Really Armaghzing.

I went into one bar. An old-fashioned bar. It was full of smoke. Most people were talking about how the local line-dancers got on at the World Championships in Tennessee.

'God help us, if they haven't won, 'tis a fix.'

The most reasonable of them was venting his spleen presumably on the basis that an unvented spleen could cause no end of problems.

'Those Yanks. Ye can't trust them. Ye can't trust them.' The second-most reasonable man in the place was clenching his sphincter for all he was worth.

The barman, who looked as though he was embarrassed by the views – they weren't extreme enough – asked me if I was there for the local lough.

'The local lough?' I've been to some strange places for some strange reasons in my time but nobody has ever asked me that before.

'Has got magical powers, it has,' he whispers. 'Ye have a sore or an ache, 'twill cure it for ye, it will. 'Twill cure it for ye, it will.'

'Magical powers, God help us,' the most reasonable man butts in. 'It couldn't make all those watchtowers of the British army all around it disappear could it?'

Suddenly into the bar burst a bunch of has-been bimbroglios, who looked as though they did nothing all day but sit-ups, inhale deeply and exfoliate. They looked as though they wanted to celebrate their so-called liberation. They called for red wine all round. Not the full bottles. Those tiny quarter-bottles. Each paid for themselves. Some liberation.

We all shuffled out of the way like mad. I ended up in a corner with a group of all shades of reasonable men in all types of combat jackets and heavy boots discussing what they called the 'military situation'. To listen to them you'd have thought they were living in the middle of the Somme.

'Mines. Be careful. They're everywhere.'

''Tis a minefield we're living in. A minefield, I tell ye.'

'They have the country destroyed, they have.'

'Only the other day. I swear to God I saw a mine. I sent the dog in after it.'

'So was it a mine?' I ask.

'No it wasn't and more's the pity. Was the neighbour's dog I had with me. Keeps going for me chickens, God damn it.'

'Chickens. The fox got all my chickens last night.'

'The bastard.'

'Don't know how he did it. They were all in the freezer at the time.'

The conversation drifted towards decommissioning. Should the IRA decommission their weapons? When should they? How should they?

A little old lady joined us. She looked as though at one time she had been a pill-popping cat's meow whose thyroid had given up on her.

'Decommissioning,' she says. 'It frightens me.'

'You mean if the other side starts up again you'll have nothing to defend yourself with?' I said.

'Not at all,' she says. 'I'm afeared of walking across the fields and disappearing into all that concrete. My. Can you imagine? It would be the death of me.'

Off she totters for another botox.

'And if it was filled with gold, me ould darlin',' one of the group shouted after her.

She didn't take any notice. She was already out of range.

On my way out I noticed the bottle blondes were all moaning

because, newly liberated women that they were, they didn't know which way to twist the metal cap off the top of their tiny quarter-bottles of red wine. Forever the gentleman, I twisted the tops off for them. None of them as much as batted a detoxed eyelid let alone thanked me. Probably because they couldn't.

If Camlough is in the *Guinness Book of Records* for its number of pubs per head of population, Loughgall should be in there for being so neat and tidy. By the way, will the person who threw away that cigarette packet outside the old football ground please pick it up and take it home? Loughgall is also apple country. Talk to anyone in Loughgall they'll tell you everything you didn't want to know about apples. In all the old legends they're listed with the oak and the ash as trees 'noble of the wood'. In the eighteenth century country doctors prescribed them to 'comfort and cool the heat of the stomach'.

Today there are apple trees all over the place. In summer, they have apple blossom festivals. They even have apples painted on all their lamp-posts. I'd need more than an apple to cool the heat of my stomach if I went back there in the summer.

I didn't stop in the local pub. I thought it would be too neat and tidy for me. And full of apples. But I did meet an old boy outside who looked as though he'd eaten too many apples in his time or was Northern Ireland's Chief Masonic Provincial High Sword Bearer. I asked him if it was the same pub where the Orange Order was founded after the Protestants beat the hell out of the Catholics in a nearby village a million years ago. He didn't know. But he knew why Loughgall had been voted the Best Kept Town in Ireland.

'They were searching for left-over bombs and booby-traps,' he says. 'They did such a thorough job they won the Best Kept Town Competition. They'll never win it again though. Believe me.'

They had also been searching for bombs and booby-traps in Newtownhamilton as well. To dismantle and destroy. The big army observation post was still there. But it was looking distinctly derelict. All the CCTV cameras were still there. But they didn't look as though they were working. If they were I'm in big trouble. All I was doing was asking this local farmer how he fiddled the sheep subsidy from the Department of Agriculture. Honest.

Ireland: In a Glass of its Own

The only other thing I did was go in the local antique shop and ask if they had any recent military antiques for sale.

Oh yes and I also spoke to a guy who looked a bit of a sociopath. He was wearing a baseball cap, glasses, a pair of old trainers. He was hobbling down the road on a stick. He told me he had injured his leg in the war. I didn't ask which war.

He pointed to the old observation post with his stick. An ordinary stick. What looked like a National Health Service stick. Not your typical Irish blackthorn stick.

'I'm glad they're gone, thanks be to God,' he says. 'It's not politics. It's Big Brother. Nearly twenty years we've been living with them spying on everything we say and do.'

He jabbed his stick down on the pavement.

'Helicopters. Helicopters. Helicopters. That's all we used to hear. All day and all night. It was not fitting I tell you. Helicopters. Helicopters. Helicopters. It makes a change to be able to hear yourself think. It was September 11 that did it. The IRA realised they could no longer go on without the support of the people. Bringing everything down now means they keep the support of the people.'

I didn't quite see the connection between September 11 and the IRA. But there you are.

We hobbled into a bar.

He told me why Armagh and South Armagh in particular was known as Bandit Country.

'Because there were bandits all over the place?' I wondered nervously, trying not to look at the leg and the stick.

'A misunderstanding,' he says. 'A British misunderstanding. Another British misunderstanding.'

Merlyn Rees was Northern Ireland Secretary at the time. A tiny man. Welsh Labour. Little experience if any of government. His expert advisers on the ground were telling him wherever you went in Armagh you're bound to find long bullets. Turn a corner, long bullets. Outside a cottage, long bullets. In the centre of a village, long bullets.

Up leapt the minister in the House of Commons to his full 5 foot 1½ inches.

'Bandits,' he shrieked. 'Bandit country. It's nothing but Bandit Country.'

The civil servants who were present, like the civil servants who later were present when other Labour government ministers decided to build the Millennium Dome, invade Iraq, name Dr Kelly, kept quiet. If a minister decides a minister decides. Except in the case of Bandit Country, like so many other cases, the civil servants were right and the minister was a government minister. For in South Armagh long bullets is the name for grown-ups boules.

Block off a road two or three miles long. Select two cast-iron balls, 18 centimetres in circumference, weighing 28 ounces. Nominate two contestants. Their objective: to throw the ball the length of the road with the fewest throws. Whoever does it in the fewest throws wins. Watching the match, there can be anything between 10,000 and 20,000 people and 100,000 bookies. It's as much a gamble as a government minister making the right decision. People gamble on not just who is going to win, but the number of throws, the time, the length of individual throws, whether the guy in the truck who has been held up for 3 hours because of the match will crack, get out of the cab and smash how many people in the face. The size of the bets? Anything from a couple of quid up to once, I was told, over £20,000.

Since then I've tried many times to actually get to watch a match. But to date, no luck. Although once, I remember, I was held up for hours on end by this crowd spilling all over the road yelling and cheering and placing bets all the time.

What it was all about I have no idea.

Thank goodness.

The Finings County

Co. Galway

Come 1660 the English Civil War was over. Cromwell was pushing up the daisies. England was once again a monarchy. Charles II was on the throne. He was pro-Catholic. But not too pro-Catholic. Not too showy about it either. In Irish history this period is known as the Finings. The Irish thought everything was going to be fine. The war was over. Fine. Cromwell was dead. Fine. England was once again a monarchy. Fine. The King was a Catholic. Fine. But not too Catholic. Fine. It's also known as the Finings because, to the Irish, fine means thin, slender, oh so delicate and fragile and that for a short period of time that was what Irish hopes were for good relations between the two countries. Which was just as well because it was about to go nuclear.

Charles II was succeeded by his brother, James II. He was much more openly pro-Catholic. Used to eat fish on Fridays. Drink VAT 69. First in, last out of church on Sundays. That kind of thing. He packed the English courts with Catholic judges. He put as many Catholics as he could into Parliament. He gave all he could important government jobs.

The Protestants didn't like it. They didn't think it was fine at all. But as he was 50 years old they did nothing. He would soon they reasoned, be dead and gone, He would be succeeded by one of his Protestant daughters from his first marriage. Except his second wife, a Catholic, produced a son. Who says fish on Fridays doesn't make a difference?

In Ireland the King's deputy was doing the same thing: giving all the good jobs to the Catholics. Again the Protestants didn't like it. But they did nothing. Until they heard that James was sending a Catholic regiment to be stationed in Derry. There was uproar. A group of 13 apprentice boys, apprentices in starting a revolution

355

to bring down a king, grabbed the keys of the city, locked the gates and refused the regiment entry.

James did what any king would do faced with such revolutionary action by 13 mere apprentice boys. He ran away. He fled the country for France. The French welcomed him with open arms. Some said it was because they were Catholics. One Catholic king was helping another Catholic king. Others say, Non. The French may be Catholic but first of all they are still French. They were merely supporting James as a way of diverting the attention and more importantly the troops and the navies of England and Holland, the other Protestant nation in Europe, from what they were doing elsewhere. The French, perfidious? Jamais. But that's not all. The French also reasoned that if they helped the Irish, the Irish would have to help them. If they ever decided to invade England.

The Protestant Parliament invited the Protestant William of Orange, husband to Mary, one of James's two Protestant daughters, to be the English king. I don't know about Luther but the ties between the Protestant nations in Europe were getting tighter.

James now sailed from France to Ireland to try and get his throne back through the back or rather the side door. He landed in Kinsale in March 1689. He marched north to Dublin. The Irish Parliament welcomed him with open arms, recognised him as king and started grabbing back all the land seized from them by the Protestants.

James now headed for Derry. The Protestants refused to budge. James decided he had no alternative. He was going to starve them out. Thus began the famous or infamous Siege of Derry. For 15 weeks, 105 days, from 5 April to 28 July 1689 he bombed them and he starved them. Give or take a couple of days. Not forgetting the adjustment between the old calendar and the new calendar.

Derry refused to crack.

The French tried to persuade James to take it out on Dublin. Burn the place down. What they couldn't burn down would be killed off by disease and dysentery.

James refused.

On 12 July 1690 William of Orange – King Billy as he is known

356

in Northern Ireland – landed at Carrickfergus just north of Belfast. With him he had 36,000 men. He was a Protestant, a Dutchman, backed by the Catholic King of France, the Catholic King of Spain and the Catholic Pope himself. He was there to fight his uncle and father-in-law, the Catholic King of England and Ireland. If that wasn't too Irish for you.

The Irish, nation of gamblers that they are, again backed the wrong man. William won. James lost.

The battle over, the Pope broke open the last pitcher of wine left over from Cana, invited Ian Paisley round for a snifter and they both went out on the town. Or, at least, that was the equivalent of what happened. Pope Innocent XI ordered St Peter's to be lit up like a Christmas tree and drank a toast to the health of the Protestant William of Orange. Because by leading the English to victory over a Scottish king on Irish soil William, a Dutch king, had done what the Pope himself could not have done: secured the unity of Catholic Europe.

William's victory, the Battle of the Boyne, is even today engraved on the soul of every Protestant throughout Northern Ireland. They march for it. They fight for it. A number have even died for it.

Some say the battle was one-sided. William was destined to win. He had right on his side. Others, of course, say it could have gone either way. At one stage one of James's men, Patrick Sarsfield, the first Lord Lucan, came close to killing King William. They also blame James for retreating too soon. He was on high ground. It was easy to defend. Instead James upped and ran and practically didn't stop until he reached Waterford where he got a boat to Kinsale and from Kinsale to France. He was never to return. To either Ireland or England.

What was left of his army – 20,000 infantry, 3500 cavalry – headed across country to Limerick. Behind its solid Norman walls they thought they would be safe. King William gave chase. But he couldn't breach the walls. He called for heavy artillery. Lucan guessed what was happening. Late at night with 800 cavalry, he crept out the back door of the castle, made an enormous detour through Co. Clare and across the wilds of Co. Tipp and came out behind the heavy artillery on its way to King William. In the middle of the night they struck. The soldiers they killed. The big guns they destroyed.

King William failed to storm Limerick Castle.

At last, you would have thought the Irish would be safe. Not so. You've forgotten the military skills of the French. They decided to give chase. Across a desolate bog west of Athlone. In open combat. They were cut to shreds.

The war was over. The two sides signed the Treaty of Limerick in 1691. The Protestants had won game, set and match. The Catholics weren't even left with the chalk. Those that could, left, led by Lord Lucan. Some say had he led the war against King William after the Battle of the Boyne, Ireland would never have had to endure the sufferings it's had to endure, the never-ending fight for freedom. A skilled professional soldier, an expert on guerrilla warfare, he would have driven the English from their shores. Ireland would have been Irish.

Others, of course, say the opposite. In spite of everything it wasn't an Irish v English war. It was a French v English war. Lord Lucan had no alternative. He had to do what the French said. And the French are never wrong.

All the same when he sailed out of Cork harbour there were no end of Catholics throwing themselves in the sea because they couldn't face what they knew was coming.

The Fining period of Irish history was over.

Co. Galway
The oyster in the pearl

Famous local resident
The hanging mayor

Favourite food
Oysters

Favourite drink
Guinness

Favourite pub
The American Bar, Aran Isles

Favourite restaurant
The one selling minced Irish lamb and Moroccan
vegetables on an Italian pizza made in Ireland

What to say
More, please

What not to say
Well, if the Prime Minister doesn't, why should I?

Finings are a clarifying agent. They help to cleanse and purify anything from a bottle of champagne to a pint of Guinness. That's what Co. Galway does. It cleanses and purifies. The heart. The mind. The soul.

Wander around Galway city. It does the heart a power of good.

Drive around Connemara which even to an addled broken-down old travel addict like me has some of the most beautiful scenery in the world. It stimulates the mind.

Take a trip to the Aran Isles. 'Ciúnas gan uaigneas'. Silence without solitude. It's good for the soul. It's of this world. But not part of this world. It's like something detached. A monastery with a coffee bar.

Then there's the thrill of bumping into the ferocious O'Flaherty's of Galway late on a Saturday night not to mention experiencing the delights of their famous local delicacy, the crubeen, a pig's trotter. What else?

Most parts of Ireland still believe in life after death. Here they believe in life before death.

Galway city practically straddles the fast-flowing River Corrib, which thunders its way from Lough Corrib, all 68 square miles of it, the largest lake in the country – more than 150 foot deep, over 200 islands, it even has its own lighthouse – and out to its famous Bay.

It is known as the City of Tribes, not because of the different forms of dress and decoration worn by the 12,000 odd, in some cases very odd, students attending University College, Galway, many of whom are so starved they look as though they would be

more than prepared to eat one another, but because of the different
tribes who used to hang around the place in the sixteenth and
seventeenth centuries, like the Athys, Blakes, Bodkins, Brownes,
D'Arcys, Ffonts, Ffrenches, Joyces, Kirwans, Lynches, Martins,
Morrises and Skerretts. Not to mention the occasional O'Connor.
But not the Cromwells. Oliver reckoned Galway and Hell were the

---

Galway races. Owner says to jockey, 'Whenever you
come to a jump, say One, Two, Three. Jump. He'll
jump. No problems.'

Jockey thinks it's stupid. Comes to first jump, doesn't
bother. Horse thumps the fence. Second jump, jockey
nearly comes off. He thinks, 'It's stupid but I'd better
say One, Two, Three. Jump.' After that every fence
they come to he says, One, Two, Three. Jump. They
sail over it. They win the race.

Afterwards in the winners' enclosure, the owner
congratulates the jockey.

'What happened at the first two fences?' he says.

'Dunno,' says the jockey. 'The horse must be deaf.'

'Deaf,' says the owner. 'He's blind.'

---

only places suitable for the Irish. But like everything else he said
and did he was totally wrong.

Galway city was always a busy, bustling town. It was well into
its stride before the Normans landed in the thirteenth century and
turned it into a busy, bustling port as well. While the rest of the
country were still drinking their Guinness, the Galwegians, as they
are called, were the first to discover wine. The Spanish used to
ship it in by the boatload. Hence the Spanish Arch where it was

unloaded. The Spanish Palace on top of the arch has been long since destroyed. You know what these Saturday night parties are like on litres of cheap Rioja. But that's not all they brought with them. Some say the local Connemara ponies are descendants of Arab horses, also brought in deliberately by the Spanish, but which escaped en route to the butchers.

Other foreign visitors were luckier. Christopher Columbus dropped by for a quick visit to the Collegiate Church of St Nicholas of Myra. Whether it was before or after his disastrous voyage to discover America, opinion is divided. Most people tend to feel it was before. Had he dropped in afterwards he would never have been allowed to escape alive, Galway being the birthplace of Lynch law.

Years ago a Lynch was lord mayor of the town. His son murdered a Spaniard who was in love with an Irish girl. The mayor upheld the law which is something Irish politicians don't always do nowadays. He sentenced his son to death. The local people went wild. They began rioting and tearing the city apart. The mayor did what any loving, caring Irish father would do in the circumstances: he tied a rope around his son's neck and threw him out of the window. Not surprisingly for years afterwards Galway city had a terrible reputation. It was grey. It was miserable. It was boring. It was nothing but warehouses, narrow streets, dead bodies hanging out of windows. It was also cold. Bitterly cold. Sons of loving, caring Irish fathers no longer wanted to go anywhere near the place.

Today it's probably the most international city in Ireland. It's not only got Moroccan cafés, Italian pasta restaurants, Spanish bars, Kashmiri curry houses, a cake shop selling homemade lemon meringue pies called Goya and pubs with their sales slogans in Latin, it's even got a FFRENCH ROUNDABOUT. *Ooui. Ooui. C'est. VRAI.* A FFRENCH ROUNDABOUT. Lord mayors have stopped throwing their sons out of the window with ropes around their necks although no doubt many have been tempted to do so especially if they bring home a Galway special: minced Irish lamb and Moroccan vegetables on an Italian pizza made in Ireland.

With over 12,000 students wandering around all over the place even though they only take up the space 6,000 students would from any other university in the country, it's often difficult to tell who is a student and who is a busker. But when the Galwegians recognise a busker they recognise a busker. I can remember when one of them, a sword-swallower and trick cyclist known as Johnny Massacre who operated along Shop Street, was killed in a road accident a few years ago, there was practically a shrine built to his memory on his regular spot by Nally's Barber Shop. People left cards praising him to the skies. 'Johnny. The streets won't be the same without you.' One even said, 'Now you can make the angels laugh.'

Who wants to be a half-starved student when a busker gets treated like that?

The only other local institution ever likely to be accorded such love and respect: the famous Galway hookers, so called because they're big. They are powerful. They are strong. And they go on and on practically for ever. In and out. Backwards and forwards. Carrying peat from Galway across to the Aran Islands. Without regular visits from the hookers, the distinctive sailing boats you see sashaying it up and down Galway Bay, the islanders would have been in big trouble. When the hookers were not doing what they were destined to do they also carried beer, cattle, building materials not only to the Islands but along the Galway coast. Now like most hookers in most towns of the world, they are only of interest to the tourists.

For the real thing, until very recently, the only place to go was the dance hall at Salthill, an old-fashioned beach resort a bit like Bournemouth in black and white just outside the city, which was once labelled years ago as one of the wickedest places in Ireland although at the time the Irish idea of wickedness was probably no more than glimpsing the heel of a grandmother's shoe drying out in front of a peat fire.

But Salthill or no Salthill, I like Galway city. It's always busy. It's always bustling with excitement. It's a heaving, thriving, lively town. Lots of bars. Lots of bookshops.

I like wandering around Eyre Square in the centre of town. A couple of drinks in the Great Southern. A nod to the statue to that famous revolutionary Liam Mellows. Who? That's right. He led the Galway Rising at the same time Padraig Pearse and James Connolly led the Easter Rising in Dublin in 1916. Don't worry. Not many Galwegians have heard of him either.

After that I take a turn through the maze of narrow lanes, tiny streets, back alleys, across the sprawling pedestrian-only areas full of Irish shoppers, as opposed to normal shoppers.

'If we hadn't spent those €3000 before Christmas,' I once heard an auld Irish woman scream at her poor, long-suffering husband, 'just think how much money we'd have to spend now.'

She had the kind of mouth that was crying out to be bricked up. If there had been enough bricks around.

''Tis right ye are,' said the poor man. 'We're as far off from Christmas now as we ever were. If we're here to see the next we'll be lucky.'

Dominating everything is the cathedral with its copper dome and thick, heavy grey limestone walls. They tell you it's built on the site of the old jail. If that's the case they must have had more criminals in jail in Galway than probably in the rest of Europe put together. It's enormous. In fact it's so big the entrance is in Galway time, the sanctuary and high altar are in Vatican time.

For all that, it is very practical. It looks as though it was put together with building blocks. There's very little fancy decoration if any. They should sell it to the Lutherans and use the money to build something more, well, Catholic. Not that it's neglected. Many's the time it's packed to overflowing. Not just on Sundays. Often as many as 20,000 people – yes, 20,000 people – attended services here on a single weekday. Weekday.

Outside is the Salmon Weir bridge under which shoals of salmon make their way upstream in the spawning season to Lough Corrib. Never again will the good people attending the cathedral have to rely on some kid with three loaves and five fishes for a decent meal. It's all there. Under their very nose.

I also like to take a look at Lynch's Castle on Abbeygate Street where the lord mayor threw his son out of the window. Perhaps not surprisingly today it is a branch of the Allied Irish Bank. Go in there today. Sometimes I get the impression they would love to treat their customers the same way Lord Mayor Lynch treated his son.

'Please. Could I change some dollars into . . . ?'

'Wait. Not here. Over there by the window.'

'Yaaaaargh.'

It's the same in the ultra-tiny Nora Barnacle Museum in Bowling Green, the home of James Joyce's wife, which from what I've read, is not how I imagined her. It must be the smallest museum in the world. It's so small you can hardly open a copy of *Ulysses* without the covers banging against both facing walls. I wish I'd never gone there. Until then I always thought Joyce was, like the rest of us, a serious, sober writer dedicated to nothing but his craft. Oh yeah. There was a letter from him to Nora saying he was looking forward to going to Galway with her where 'the image of your girlhood will purify again my life'. You expect us to believe that. A barnacle she was not. She is supposed to have given him the time of his life, practically made him go blind and hluff pradolt Collinwrilakkas, as I think he said in *Finnegans Wake* somewhere.

Galway Bay, the most famous of all the famous bays in Ireland, is a must. I go there to watch the sun go down. There's nothing better than a good sunset to cheer me up before heading off for the bars. Other people go there to visit Claddagh, the oldest fishing village in Ireland only because when the Anglo-Normans claimed Galway city for their own they forgot to include Claddagh. Hence its claim: the oldest fishing village in Ireland. Not that it's history people are interested in. They are invariably after the famous Claddagh ring depicting a heart with two hands clasped together, they say, in love. Before marriage it is worn with the point of the heart facing the fingertip. After marriage, the other way round. Not me. Nothing would persuade me to go there. First, the two hands are not clasped together in love. They are wrestling with each other. One to keep the heart pacemaker in place. The other to wrench it out. There's no need for me to say whose heart it is. Second, wear the ring this way before marriage and that way after. So what? Before marriage, everything is one way. Afterwards, it's exactly the same. Not that I've got anything against marriage. Marriage is OK. It's the living together afterwards that's the problem.

Co. Galway

As for the best time to go visiting, opinion is divided. Everybody, however, is agreed it's during the Galway Arts Festival, when there are even more street entertainers or students in town. Although how they have the gall way to hold an arts festival when they once not only banned all Shaw's books but threatened to burn them as well, I have no idea. It's a bit like Lynch's Castle sponsoring a conference on child abuse.

The only reason they get away with it is because, I'm sure, it's so well done. It's not your conventional arts festival. It's more like an Edinburgh Festival performed in the streets rather than in dreary church halls and up dubious back passages. The entertainments are not just a quick tap-dance or a bit of fancy juggling. Sometimes there are full theatrical productions. The performers also come from all over the world. I've seen Australian plays, Icelandic dancing, German singing, Spanish yodelling and a one-legged American taking part in an arse-kicking competition or something. I once saw some kind of postmodernist nonsense on stilts which came from some local wood yard.

There's only one problem. I can never understand a word they say. That's not true. I understand what they say. I can never understand what they mean. I once watched a bunch of Australians rolling around on the pavement screaming their heads off about terrorists, Al-Qaeda and Ground Zero. It was only later over a couple of pints of Guinness in the bar with the Latin slogans that I discovered that terrorists were teachers, Al-Qaeda were parents and Ground Zero was something about untidy bedrooms. Even then I still didn't understand what all the screaming was about. Must be something to do with the lack of food.

True artists, however, say Forget the Arts. The only time to go to Galway is for the Oyster Festival in mid-September when nobody gets a wink of food or a bit of sleep. Much, much more fun. That's even if you don't see the legendary, the one and only Willy Moran, world champion oyster opener, opening oysters with his hands. Behind his back. Just the thought of it is almost too much. A dozen small, tangy, salty, meaty Clarinbridge oysters from south of Galway Bay. A couple of pints of thick, rich, creamy Guinness. Fantastic.

'Till I came here,' some flop sweat American with the jits once told me, 'I always thought an oyster was someone who keeps using Jewish words and phrases.'

Yeah. And I always thought people were innocent until they were proved guilty.

I once met the world's greatest oyster expert. An Englishman. A greasy Brillo-pad haircut. A fading Prince of Wales check suit. I was in some upmarket bar in London. He could tell the difference between a Crassostrea virginica and a Crassostrea angulata at a hundred paces or so he claimed. He would go on about the shapes, the sizes, the taste, how long they had to be opened before you could eat them. Twenty minutes, he insisted, was the maximum. I admit I was impressed. Until he insisted they were always best accompanied by Chablis. Then I lost him. There is nothing but nothing better with oysters than Guinness.

In the old days – only 34 people turned up for the first oyster festival in 1954 – the Irish wouldn't be seen catching oysters let alone eating them. If they were unlucky enough to catch one they'd throw it straight back so it would go towards helping the poor, starving French who were forced to eat them instead of some great, squashy lump of boiled bacon which tasted like a strangled sweaty flip-flop and cabbage which looked like dollops of pus with gangrene. As for lobster, that was nothing more than a giant, bloodshot water spider. Not that they didn't touch it.

'The Lord have mercy on us,' one of my old uncles, God rest his soul, would say, 'it's better than a poke in the eye from Agnes Murphy's 50p bits.'

Not that there weren't others in the parish who would have preferred the poke in the eye from Agnes Murphy's 50p bits.

After the oysters, there's the racing.

In the old days Galway was the start of the season: the Galway Races, the Limerick Junction Races, the Dublin Horse Show and back to Galway again for the shooting and fishing. Now so important is it it's practically racing all the time. So too the drinking. What else would the bar at the racetrack be the longest probably in the world meashurik a fantashtist foo thunder an then fleet flong.

But be warned. Whether you go to the Arts Festival, the Oyster bash or the Racing, the weather, as they say, can be variable. I'v been there in the middle of summer when there's been practically monsoons. Roads have been flooded. The place plunged into darkness. Similarly the winds. They can lift you off your feet and hurl you at the sides of the beer tent.

''Tis a demon they are. A demon,' I remember one fragile old curmudgeon, who looked as though he was in a rush to finish his drink before the hearse arrived, mumbling away to himself as a group of us picked him up from the ground and tried to steady him. Not that anyone believed him, of course.

The best escape, for peat's sake, is to take a bog trot to one of the wettest of all the wettest places in Ireland. Connemara. Over 3000 acres of glorious, spectacular bog which stretches all the way from Lake Corrib to the Atlantic. Lowland bog. Upland bog. Bog covered in dark, purple heather. Bog dotted here and there with the occasional tree. Wild, barren, desperate bog. Maybe two inches of soil on top. Nothing more. Maybe up to 20 foot deep. At the bottom of them, boats, bodies, tree stumps, known as bog oak although in most cases it's pine rather than oak. It's the bog standard for bogs all over the world.

It is, they say, heaven scent.

It's one of my favourite places in the world. But, however much I like it, I never go there for long periods of time. Two or three days on the bog is, I think, more than enough for anyone.

If you're going, go there soon. The rate the bog is being dug up – over 5000 acres a year just to keep UK gardens happy – it won't be there much longer. It will be spread an inch thick all over the Home Counties. That's only in Connemara. In other parts of Ireland it's disappearing even faster. Go to the National Turf Cutting Championships in Carburg, Co. Kildare. You can see it disappear before your very eyes. I often think it's a laugh the way these do-gooders and environmentalists and vegetarians go on about growing their own food when half of them are destroying the Irish peat bogs in the process. I once tried to explain it to a menopausal has-been in the middle of a career meltdown. But she was only interested in whether the plastic bag the peat came in was able to be recycled into artificial hips for stray dogs picked up in Athens before the Olympic Games.

To reach Connemara some people go north out of Galway city and head inland. I head south and make for the coast road and the sin city of Salthill which nowadays is not to be sneezed at. If you're an O'Wrinkly, if you find the likes of Bournemouth too racy, Salthill is for you. It's the kind of town where retired reverend mothers would go to hang out and relax without fear of being upset by too much reality; where most people settle their hotel bills in postal orders. In advance. And where trying to pay by credit card is like trying to rob a bank. I know. I tried. Paying by credit card. Not trying to rob a bank.

From Salthill all the way to Carna, it's tiny villages, bays, headlands and lobsters. In Galway city they tell you this is a big Irish-speaking area. Don't you believe it. The only Irish I've come across is the old trick in the bars of putting the signs – Toilet, Men and Women – in Gaelic. It never makes any difference to me. I go into the first corrugated-iron hut out the back that I come to. Even the Aran Islands is more English-speaking than Irish-speaking. It's so English-speaking I know more Irish than the people I stay with. And that's only two or three sentences which were drummed into me when I was a kid. A bunch of shamrock the size of an oak tree clamped to the lapel of my school blazer. The Life of Kevin Barry stuck in my jacket pocket. So many cold lumps of pig fat jammed into my satchel there was no room for any books. Still I was the only kid in the school who knew the words of 'The Wild Colonial Boy'.

Not that they're not doing their best to try and preserve a language nobody wants to learn. Families with children at school can apply for special grants to help them learn the language. Build a house in an Irish-speaking area and you get another grant. Start up a business and you get yet another. The government has even produced an Irish-language phrase book for Irish policemen full of useful, handy, everyday Irish phrases like *locadh ar tana bus*, parking in a bus lane; *bobghaiste*, a booby trap; and the ever-handy *eactra tamhaigh*, a shooting incident. Not that Gaelic is the ideal language for the police or the criminal fraternity. Because there is no simple word for Yes or for No.

Years ago when everybody spoke Gaelic I can remember driving

370

across Connemara in the middle of winter. There was nothing but snow and ice and a thick heavy mist. I got hopelessly lost. I stopped to ask an old bluggy earwagger with a clay pipe sitting on a stone wall where I was.

'Excuse me,' I said. 'Do you speak English?'

'Yes,' he says, 'if you speak Irish.'

My last trip I ran into one of the local Language Police.

'Irish is important, is it?' I asked her.

'It is,' she says. 'It's our culture. Our heritage. Our history.'

'Your national anthem,' I say. 'The single most important statement of the Irish nation. Was it written in Irish?'

'No,' she says. 'English. It was only translated into Irish sixteen years later.'

'The president,' I say. 'The one single leader of this great Irish nation. Can she speak Irish?'

'She can't.'

'The Prime Minister?'

'He can't.'

'Any other minister?'

'They can't.'

'MP?'

'They can't.'

'Every document, every bit of paper, every cheque, every advertisement issued by the government must also be issued in Irish?'

'They must.'

'Even though nobody in government can read it?'

From the coast I head, like General de Gaulle on a weekend off, for Cashel and the Cashel House Hotel and then across the rich, green grass to Lough Derryclare and the Twelve Bens. The Lough Inagh Valley is the best of the best. Every time I go there it gets better and better. The hills. The rocks. The colours. The emptiness. The silence. The absolute stillness. Sometimes I read the sheep. If they're facing north, it means good health. South, it means illness. West, you're heading for a long, slow, steady decline. East, death. An old Irish saying. Other times I ponder one of the great questions of our time: How did the frog come to Ireland? Was it St Patrick? When he did the deal with the snakes did he take frogs instead? Was it the Frogs themselves? Or rather the Normans. When they invaded did they bring with them frogs as well as rabbits? Were they here all the time? People had better things to drink about than go out looking for frogs? It almost makes me feel human and at one with the world. Steady now, I'm not getting soft. I did say almost.

To the east is Oughterard which claims it is the Gateway to Connemara. Why I don't know. Sure it's got the hotels. It's on Lough Corrib. It's a big fishing town. Everyone you meet talks fishing. Most are local guides. Even the local children get time off school to prepare and sell flies to visitors.

Moycullen further down the road seems a better bet. It may not be so big or as striking. But all the same you step out of the back door and you're right in the middle of wild, desolate countryside.

Even Maam, if it wasn't for that strange-looking statue in the middle of town, would be better. It's called Maam Cross now as a sign of their displeasure at not being called the Gateway to Connemara. Quite right too.

I was in Maam once when I came across two old Connemara farmers, as fine as you'd meet in a day or two. One of them tells me the only way to cook a steak to perfection let alone a slice of Connemara beef or lamb is on the flat of a shovel.

'Not at all. Not at all. Don't ye listen to him,' says the other, waving his blackthorn in the air. 'In the name of God, the only way to cook a steak to perfection is on the flat of a shovel used for digging out the bog. 'Tis beautiful I tell ye. 'Tis beautiful.'

'With a glass of poitín afterwards,' they both add.

To the west, it's a long, slow run through more fantastic scenery to Clifden although sometimes I go the long way through Roundstone, a tiny fishing village, a couple of lobster boats and a handful of pubs, which not only serve oysters but are firmly convinced it's against the law to close until one or two o'clock in the morning. Anything earlier, they think, is an affront to their human rights.

I vaguely remember sprawling all over one bar. 'So what time do you close then?'

'Another pint of Guinness is it?' slurs the barman, as decent a barman as you'd find anywhere in Ireland. ''Tis yer only man.'

'Hit tish. Hit tish,' I shaid, I mean, I said.

I can then vaguely remember him telling me Sir Roger Casement, spy, traitor, pervert or, depending on your point of view, patriot, champion of human rights, martyr was from around these parts. Spent a lot of time on one of the islands off the coast.

'People shay they've sheen his ghooost,' he shays. 'Heard him coughing. Hin the 'otel hof the Hisles.'

'A ghost cough. How can a ghost cough?'

'Zzzzzzzz'

The following morning while I was having a quick, light tradi-tional Irish breakfast, half a dozen eggs, a bucket of potatoes, about three mile of black pudding and two pints of Guinness, the old lady running the b. & b., who was as different as different can be, warned me to beware of 'wayward sods'.

'You mean in the bars?' I wondered.

'Not at all. Not at all,' she says. 'Outside. Across the fields. Wherever ye are going.'

A wayward sod turned out to be a patch of grass that makes you lose all sense of direction and wander off all over the place.

''Tis true. 'Tis true,' she says. 'I'm not telling a word of a lie.'

As I was leaving she warned me to be extra careful.

'The Lord save you,' she exclaims. 'There's a fairy mist coming up.'

I didn't dare ask her what that was.

From there it's on to Ballyconneely and the memorial to Alcock and Brown, who in June 1919 made the first non-stop flight across the Atlantic and have been commemorated in thousands of racist and semi-racist jokes ever since. After taking off from St John's, Newfoundland, over 16 hours later they landed just south of the memorial in the middle of a peat bog. At first, it is said, they were so confused they thought they were in a country which had just been liberated by a president who claimed he was a man of peace. After that they each told each other the first Alcock and Brown joke. After nearly 100 years their time has still to be beaten taking into account the time it takes now to check in, security, Emigration, passport control, delays at the gate, landing, waiting for walkways that have to be specially built to unload the passengers, more security checks, Immigration, Customs. Waiting for your luggage to arrive. If you're lucky.

Clifden, a busy little town right on the edge of the Atlantic, attracts all sorts. Little girls, because it's home to a Connemara Pony Show, the third weekend of August. In Ireland, don't forget, weekends start on a Thursday. The largest display, they say, of the tough, tiny Connemara ponies in the world, no doubt because there is nowhere else in the world where you would find so many Connemara ponies. Wives, so they've got something else to complain about. Happy, relaxed, middle-aged men because for most of them Clifden is written on their heart if not on their prostate.

For it was a Clifden-born surgeon, Sir Peter Freyer, who first developed the technique for removing enlarged prostate glands. First, slice through the bladder. Second, a quick flip in the prostate. Snip. It's all over. Three minutes max. Time for a pint of Guinness. To make certain everything is in working order. The good doctor is buried in the Church of Ireland graveyard. You can't miss it. It's the enlarged one. Every night you can see his happy patients drinking his health in the bar in the Alcock and Brown Hotel as well as in every other bar in town. Not to mention telling even more racist jokes.

As for the church itself that can't be missed either. Especially by lightning. There are two churches in Clifden: a Catholic one and a Protestant one. Which one always gets struck by lightning? So we're all equal in the sight of God. Yeah, just as the Americans believe we're all innocent until proved guilty.

From Clifden I sometimes head out to Claddaghduff where there's nothing better than sitting in Acton's Restaurant, a mountain of seafood in front of you, a pint of Guinness in your hand and the Atlantic roaring outside. Further on is Cleggan and boats to Inishboffin Island which is great if you like birds. To look at, I mean. The alternative is to head straight to Letterfrack. They call it an old Quaker village. But I've never come across one the number of times I've been there.

Co. Galway

Kylemore Abbey is, as they say, a holy sight. The drive around the lake. The setting. But I always think there's something odd about the place. An Englishman goes there on his honeymoon. He has such a fantastic time he builds a mock-Gothic convent to commemorate the event. Come on. There's something not right somewhere.

Killary Harbour is more straightforward. It's Norway comes to Ireland. It's not a harbour at all. It's more like a fjord. Eight miles long. Large enough, they say, to take the whole of the British navy although judging by what's happening to the British navy at the moment there'll soon be enough room in there for the US and Russian navies as well. The entrance is almost blocked by islands. What sea there is is full of dolphins. Either side it's dominated by Mweelrea, the highest mountain in Connacht, to the north and Maumturks to the south. They're Norwegian names for tall, steep hills.

Ludwig Wittgenstein, the one-time cult philosopher who nobody ever read, largely because the one book he ever wrote was completely unreadable, had a cottage here. He used to say that logico-philosophico speaking, it gave him an empirical, scientific dimension where, given the tautology of language as much as in logic and mathematics, he experienced a complete multiplicity of perspectives. In other words, he used to spend hours on end staring at the harbour letting the seagulls shit all over him. Clever guy. Bertrand Russell said it was because he was locked in contemplation of deep philosophical problems. Wittgenstein said it was because he was bored rigid with Russell who, he claimed, was suffering from loss of problem. Whatever that means. Today the spot is honoured for all posterity with, of all things, a youth hostel.

Some people rave about the border between Co. Galway and Co. Clare in the south. They say it's one of the most lonesome regions in Ireland. I think the north is better. Especially around Leenane, which I think is fabulous. I keep promising myself one day I'll stay there for a month. Maybe more. Something to look forward to.

Where I won't stay is the Aran Islands. Life must have been

grand there for the 4000–5000 years until that great English Irishman Yeats started interfering. Bleak. Desolate. Wind-blown. Precious little soil, turf, trees or anything apart from stone walls. No gates. The gates are gaps in the stone wall. What turf they've got had to be imported from Connemara. Even the thatch for the roofs has to be imported. In the old days from Galway. Today from Eastern Europe. It was, they say, a 'divil's patch of land'. But they had the essentials. A police station. Two jails, one for men, one for women, both rarely used. One real pub. A cemetery which goes back to the time of Adam. But no McDonald's and no hospital.

In the old days they lived off practically nothing but kelp, seaweed to you and me, which dried and burnt was a valuable source of soda used for making soap, glazing pottery and even making gunpowder, and sat around all day in armchairs, surrounded by huge standing stones looking like beehive huts, a collection of Celtic crosses and no end of old churches, the central heating going at full blast, tucking into TV dinners and moaning about Yeats making game, as they say, with their traditional way of life. If he had not interfered with John Millington Synge, who was having a high old time of it in Paris and hooshed him to give it all up and go to the Aran Isles and write about the people there they would be unknown, unheard of and completely undisturbed. Today, however, there's boat after boat after boat, plane after plane after plane of people tramping all over the place as if for all the world they were traipsing over the Galapagos Islands gawping at booby birds whose accents they cannot understand either.

Not that there weren't any warning signs. When Synge's first play about the Aran Isles opened at the Abbey Theatre, Dublin there were literally riots. Both inside and outside the theatre. The only way the play could be performed was under police protection, 70 inside the theatre and 500 outside, because from the moment the word 'shift' was used to describe a nightdress everybody knew that was the end of the Aran Isles. Tastes shifted. From then on strangers would be heading there in droves.

Last time I was there you could hardly move without some glop-schot barging into you and making you spill your Guinness all down your front. Before Yeats stuck his oar in the only visitor was the occasional pilgrim. For some reason or other it ranked along-side Jerusalem and Rome as a place of pilgrimage.

Today it's non-stop tourism. Over 200,000 tourists a year. Up to two or even three thousand a day in the summer. Landing on the beaches. Clogging up the tiny airport. I was with a tour guide once who was lecturing a group of baseball caps with severe personality bypasses about Cromwell, why control of Aran meant control of Galway Bay, control Galway Bay and you controlled the world. He could have been talking about Iraq for all they understood. Not that they probably understood anything about Iraq either.

I decided to make my own way. Which is not as difficult as it seems. The whole place is about the size of Galway Cathedral. There are hardly any roads. What roads there are are about wide enough for a couple of bicycles.

The rest of it is fields, tiny, pocket-handkerchief-size fields surrounded by the same dry-stone walls. Still without any gates. If they have to move cattle from one field to another they knock down part of the wall, push the poor creatures through the gap and build it up again afterwards. There are practically no farm buildings. The cattle, because they get far less rain than on the mainland, stay out in the open the whole year round. But more important than anything the Aran Isles is about the only patch of ground in Ireland over ten yards square which does not have a full-size golf course. Glory be.

The big attraction is the remains of some kind of ring fort over 1000 years old called Dun Aengus, Dun Eochla or Dun Duchathair depending on who you talk to. Otherwise known in the tourist industry worldwide as somewhere to dump the punters while I can go off and have a smoke/drink a pint/pick up some more dumb, innocent, unsuspecting tourists Nothing else. This is Ireland, don't forget.

I climbed to the top of whichever it was through field after field, over stone wall after stone wall, across muddy track after muddy track. What a surprise. Unbelievable. There at the very top, the highest point on the island, they were making live, naked sacrifices to the gods. First, the old women. Then the virgins. No, no, I'm kidding. This is Ireland, after all. The two old donkeys at the bottom, in the fancy shed where I bought my ticket, however, believed every word I told them.

'My God,' said one of them who looked as though she could have been St Patrick's mother-in-law. 'They never told us anything about that, I'll get on to the local supervisor.'

You can't help but like them, can you?

All there was at the top was a sign in Irish then underneath it the words 'Do not damage this monument', which can only mean they expect first, Irish-speakers to damage their monument and then English-speakers.

Finally my taxi arrived. We stopped every $3\frac{1}{2}$ minutes to talk to long-lost friends the driver hadn't seen for at least a full 20 minutes. Which was an improvement on the old days. In the old days they would stop at every bar they passed for a drink. But the donkey never complained. He usually knew the way back better then the driver.

The rest of the time I spend on the Aran Isles I spend in the American Bar overlooking the bay, which looked as though Synge had stayed there as well. Old. Dusty. A million years behind the times. Of course, I had to ask, 'So why is it called the American Bar? It's nowhere near America.'

'Because,' said the girl behind the bar who looked as though she could be 70 going on 17, 'it's the first bar you come across if you leave New York and head east.'

Well, of course, why didn't I think of that?

After that the rest of Galway was a bit like one of Yeats's famous No plays. Yes, it was different. No, it wasn't fantastic.

The Yes places. Tuam, I arrived there late one evening. There were a couple of old carthorses charging up and down the main street. Nobody took any notice. Nobody even braked and drove slowly past them. Nobody seemed to care.

Neither did the horses. Luckily. In Ballinasloe there were even more horses running around which is obviously why it wasn't called Ballinafast. But then it is home to the oldest horse fair in Europe where in the old days the old kings of Connacht used to ford across the River Suck – why it's called the Suck I have no idea although I have heard many theories – on their way to have drinks with the high king himself at Tara. The fair itself was no dog and pony show. In an average year during the nineteenth century they would sell every week 5000 horses, 20,000 cattle and over 100,000 sheep. Marengo, Napoleon's horse at Waterloo, came from here. Although I suppose that's no recommendation. So too cavalry horses as well as most of the horses that pulled the gun carriages during the First World War.

The biggest No place was Gort, between the Slieve Aughtry mountains and the Burren. At one time it was virtually the literary centre of the world. Here came the likes of Shaw, Douglas Hyde and, of course, the grand dandy of them all, Yeats. Not to admire the famous nine and fifty wild swans on the lake at Coole House. But to pay homage at the feet of Lady Augusta Gregory, the happy-gogutsy Virginia Woolf of the Celtic Revival and destroyer of the environment whose husband caused no end of unnecessary suffering during the famine by introducing the Gregory Clause to the Poor Law Act which forced anyone owning more than a quarter-acre of land to choose between the land and starvation or the workhouse and a couple of crumbs; who moved easily from being one day a unionist and the next day a nationalist and who airily dismissed Synge's masterpiece *The Playboy of the Western World* as a battle between 'those who use a toothbrush and those who don't'. My God, can you imagine the wonderful conversations they must have had over their dinners of roast swan? Which is why there are only nine and fifty left.

In the grounds is the famous autograph tree. Because my Lady Augusta believed so much in books and the importance of the written word guests were asked not to sign the guest book and add some bland, anodyne, pathetic comment when they left but to carve their name on a tree. The amazing thing is the likes of George Bernard, Sean O'Casey, George Moore, John Masefield, Augustus John, Oliver St John Gogarty and others all did as they were told. Out came their Boy Scout pocket knives and away they went. I would have told her what to do with her tree. Which obviously explains why I was never invited. That and, I suppose, by the time I'd finished carving my full name there would be no tree left.

When Yeats came alone she served him the best of her late

husband's wine cellar 'bottle by bottle' and then when he staggered upstairs, jammed the bottom of his bedroom door with no end of thick, heavy rugs so that, she maintained, he could work away on his poetry in silence. Oh yes. I can think of one or two other reasons, after all it was said she was the kind of woman who would never dream of retiring to bed with a limp excuse.

Towards the end of his life Yeats lived nearby in Gort in Ballylee Castle, which he bought with two cottages and a walled garden, for as much as £35. The castle is long gone. But the town is worth a look. Especially the cathedral. Now look at the Round Tower alongside it. No. It's not the Guinness. It's out of true. About two feet out of true. Ireland's Leaning Tower of Pisa? Wrong. The Leaning Tower of Pisa is Italy's Round Tower of Gort.

Many's the time when travelling by bus between Ennis and Galway I get off at Gort for a couple of hours, wander around. Have a glass or two. But I'm not impressed. Thackeray said it looked like it wondered how it got there in the first place. Or something like that.

My jolly, non-drinking football fanatic of a solicitor in Ennis, Co. Clare once told me, 'Gort! Lord have mercy on me. If I ever ended up in Gort I think I'd top myself.'

I think I would as well. Especially if, for all their fine ways, Lady Gregory, Yeats and the rest of the precious gang were there hacking tree after tree to bits.

But Leenane. I could live in Leenane.

The Nitrogen County

Co. Offaly

Some people think nitrogen is an essential element of life. But not too much of it. Take it neat and you're dead. It's only safe when mixed up with something else. Then the whole thing is transformed into proteins. Usually it's found in plants and animals. Sometimes it is generated in thunderstorms and brought down to earth in rainwater. Don't you believe it.

Nitrogen, as every serious drinker knows, is responsible for one of the truly great mysteries of our time: why the bubbles in a beautiful, freshly poured pint of Guinness float downwards instead of upwards. It's something to do with the bubbles on the outside clinging to the glass causing the bubbles on the inside to float up and push down the bubbles on the outside. The technical term for it is an Eire lift. Check it for yourself. As if you need an excuse for another drink.

Less serious people, people with time on their hands, able to hang around in laboratories instead of the more serious centres of research, where dedicated enthusiasts watch bubbles defy the law of gravity for hours on end, maintain nitrogen is a gas. Too much of it, they say, is dangerous. Used the wrong way, it's dangerous. Used by the wrong people, it's dangerous.

The nitrogen period of Irish history started with the Protestants pushing the Catholics further down the glass, went on to include the French Revolution and the French trying to start their own Revolution in Ireland and ended up with the Famine caused by, whichever way you look at it, the complete disregard of the nitrogen circle: the continuous circulation of nitrogen between living organisms and the environment, soil, air and water.

With the Catholic King out of the way, once again the Protestants turned the screw. Anything Catholic or even slightly Catholic was banned: Catholic religious orders, Catholic bishops, Catholic schools. Catholic priests could stay providing they took an oath never again to support the Catholic Stuarts. Catholics wanting to enter Parliament had to deny everything a Catholic believed in. Which limited numbers dramatically. Intermarriage was practically banned. Catholics, regardless of whether they were next in line or not, who became Protestants could inherit their fathers' wealth and estates. Catholics who married Protestants lost everything. Protestants who died could leave everything to their eldest son. Catholics who died had to break up their estates among all their children.

It was not all one-sided. There were equally strict laws for the Protestants. They were banned from speaking Irish, wearing Irish national dress, marrying the Irish or going to see *Riverdance* three nights running.

Did the Protestants feel guilty crushing the Catholics? Not at all. If God had meant them to be kind to the Catholics, they said, He would not have allowed them to conquer them. The isle of saints and scholars had become the Protestant nation. Protestants living in Ireland were Irish to the English and English to the Irish and to themselves oppressed colonialists, who like their American cousins wanted independence and liberty.

Catholics were either very, very poor or very, very rich. The very, very poor lived in practically hovels. They had little education. The only time they could hear mass was when a priest secretly celebrated mass. To survive they formed secret societies with codes and passwords to attack, maim and even kill anyone who they thought was overexploiting them, overcharging them or just taking the Michael out of their handwriting.

The very, very rich Catholics were known as Castle Catholics because it was obviously their contacts with the Castle and the rich Protestant landlords that accounted for their wealth. A fatal mistake on the part of the Protestants, say the O'Machiavellis among the Catholics. If, like other colonialists in other parts of the world, the Protestants had ruthlessly cleared the land of everybody living on it when they took over they would have had none of the problems they have had. But no. They insisted on doing it the English way: keeping the locals to do all the rough work for them. Of course, after a while the locals became useful, then helpful and finally indispensable.

But on the Protestant side all was not Love thy neighbour as thyself. The Church of Ireland Protestants couldn't stand the Presbyterians. The Church of Ireland was the establishment. The Presbyterians were the Puritans. During the Civil War they were at each other's throats. Now Presbyterians were not allowed to sit in the Irish Parliament or hold government office. They did, however, have a stronger legal right to own land, the Ulster Tenant Right. They also had their own share of secret societies and terror groups.

With the Americans causing more trouble for the British, the Protestants couldn't have been Ballymena. If the British were now not only at war with France and Spain but America as well, Ireland they claimed had no alternative but to defend itself against all-comers. The English were trapped. They had no alternative but to agree. The Protestants established the Irish Volunteers. Ireland now, at last, had the right and the means to rule itself at home without the aid of the British. Not that the British let go of every-thing. They still kept some juicy fruits to themselves. As they do. They still ran the government. They still handed out the contracts. They still distributed the brown envelopes. They still scattered awards and honours in return for votes in the Irish Parliament. Ireland was still under the English. Just.

But while the Protestants were manoeuvring with the English, the Catholics started manoeuvring with the Protestants. If Ireland had to defend itself, it was only right that the Catholics should share their part of the responsibility. To do this some of the harsher anti-Catholic legislation would have to be repealed. If they were sharing their part of the responsibility, they should have the right to vote. What could the Protestants say? The Cat, short for Catholic Emancipation, was out of the bag.

Et maintenant, mes amis, the French Revolution. The French Revolution was many musicals to many people. To the Irish, who still think the main player was a sad case called Les Miserable, it was simple. It was reason v. faith. It was philosophers, intellectuals, troublesome young men against the power, the might, the faith of the Church. Hardcore Catholics, therefore, were against it. Softcore Catholics, Protestants, the workers, the poor farmers were for it on the basis that anything but the present set-up was bound to be better. The French were prepared to help their friends. Not because they necessarily wanted to help the Irish. But because it was a way of getting at the English. Their plan: Land a large force of French troops in Ireland. They could overthrow the Protestant government and then zut alors march très rapide across country and take England.

1796. Just off Bantry Bay in Co. Cork a French invasion force is gathering. To add Tone to the occasion they brought with them an Irish Protestant, Wolfe Tone. Suddenly they are immersed in fog. The ships scatter. Wolfe Tone, more flat than when he arrived, sails back to France and the life of O'Reilly in Paris while his fellow countrymen continued to suffer. Not the first major French military disaster. Not the last.

The English were now paranoid. Because Wolfe Tone and the French had tried to invade the south, they decided with impeccable English logic to disarm the north. Troops burned homes, flogged and murdered whoever they came across whether they had arms or not. Tortures were public. Victims were tied up, a metal cap clamped on their heads, inside molten pitch. Then the pitch would be lit. The terror was so bad that the commander-in-chief of the army resigned in revulsion at what was happening.

In various parts of the country Catholic farm workers and peasants rose up in horror. They were led by not only a Protestant but a Protestant aristo, Lord Edward Fitzgerald, younger brother of the Duke of Leinster. Even though he had served with distinction in the British army in the American colonies, he was refused promotion because of his sympathies for the French Revolution. He threw in his lot with the rebels. He took his seat in the Irish Parliament in Dublin. He preached rebellion. He was the Most Wanted on England's Most Wanted list of rebels. On 18 May 1798 he planned to overthrow the Parliament in Dublin and seize power. But he was betrayed. He was arrested. His supporters however, did what any supporters of any attempted coup would have done if their leaders had been arrested. They went ahead without them.

23 May, they marched on Dublin. The authorities – surprise, surprise – were waiting. The whole thing fell apart.

25 May, the authorities got wind of a similar uprising at Carlow. The English cut them to shreds.

26 May, in Wexford where another uprising was planned the Irish heard news of what was happening in Carlow – and still decided to go ahead. The same thing happened. But worse. The torture, the killings were so bad they turned a local priest, Father John Murphy, into a warlord. He was so incensed when the English burnt down his church that there and then he turned rebel. Better to die a thousand deaths than submit to the English, he proclaimed. Suddenly he was leading an army of over 2000 men.

27 May, they were attacked on Oulart Hill. They decided to set up camp on Vinegar Hill. But it wasn't your typical, strict, iron-disciplined, paint the grass green, military camp. It was an Irish military camp. Off went some of the troops armed with nothing but pitchforks to plunder nearby Protestant homes. Back they came with carpets, chairs, tables. Off they went again. Back they came with cattle to be slaughtered, roasted and eaten in the sun. Thousands more flocked to their ranks. Local families even turned up to enjoy the fun.

29 May, the English army, now many times its original size, marched down to Forth Mountain. They occupied the town. They turned towards Wexford.

1 June, it all began to go wrong. Most of the Irish were forced back to Vinegar Hill. The remainder tried to take Arklow and were cut to pieces.

21 June, Vinegar Hill was lost. The survivors fled. They were pursued by English troops and ruthlessly butchered, tortured, murdered. The ringleaders were deported. Some say as many as 20,000 men were killed – more than those who lost their lives during the whole of the French Revolution. Survivors spoke of the scale of the massacre, how the walls of the windmill at the top of the hill were splattered with the blood and brains of the brave rebels; how for years afterwards the soil had a springy feel to it

because of the number of bodies heaved into shallow graves beneath it; how the courthouse in Enniscorthy was burnt down with 80 wounded rebels inside; how a barn in Scullabogue with 120 Protestants inside was also burnt down in revenge and how the town of Gorey was completely destroyed, the people with it.

But nothing was solved one way or the other.

The Catholics still wanted rid of the English aristos. The English aristos refused to oblige. They decided to dig in. Except to an uprooted English Protestant aristo digging in meant building bigger, stronger, more impressive buildings. They built huge mansions. They built the General Post Office in Dublin. Or rather the poor, downtrodden Catholics built them for them. Better to keep them employed building big buildings. Less likely to cause trouble. What? Wrong. The more the English relied on the Irish the bigger the problem became.

The French were far more practical – and pragmatic. They decided they had had enough of Ireland and, through Ireland, England. They decided instead to invade Egypt. But the English were not to know that.

Question: England is scared of the French. They think they might invade. What do they do to defend themselves? Answer: They merge with Ireland. Under the terms of the Act of Union 1801 the Irish Parliament merged with the English Parliament. Irish MPs moved in with British MPs at Westminster. The Irish aristos loved it. They were now with the grown-ups. The Irish Catholics hated it. They had less influence than before. They were an ever smaller minority in an ever growing Parliament.

1802. At last England and France were at peace. But what did the ever pragmatic French decide to do? Invade Ireland. Around 1000 men landed at Killala, Co. Mayo. They didn't need any more. As soon as they landed, they reasoned, the way the French do, the whole world would rise up and come to their aid. They didn't. The French were outnumbered twenty to one by the English. The best thing, they decided, was to surrender. Well, let's face it, they've had plenty of practice.

Two months later they decided to try again. It's known as learning by experience. This time nine battleships made their way

The Nitrogen County

to Donegal. Again they brought Wolfe Tone with them. But before they even reached sight of land they were spotted by the Royal Navy. Only three survived. Wolfe Tone, resplendent in French naval uniform, was taken prisoner, charged and sentenced to death for treason. Just before he was to be executed, he committed suicide. The first of the legendary martyrs, admittedly a Protestant one, for Irish freedom was born.

He wasn't the only one. Waiting in the wings: Robert Emmett, the son of a government doctor. With rumours and no doubt some pretty dodgy intelligence rife that France was planning to invade England – Napoleon was supposed to be lining up over 2000 ships and 700 barges along the Channel – Emmett decided this was the time to attack. His target: Dublin Castle, seat of the government. The date: 23 July 1803.

16 July, the whole plan blows up in his face. A bomb-making factory run by his men in Dublin explodes. The authorities are on to him and his supporters. With that impeccable Irish logic, he decides to go ahead anyway. Horse-drawn carriages loaded with arms and explosives as well as ladders for scaling the walls of the castle are supposed to make their way secretly across town. Someone fires a shot by mistake. The horses bolt. They now have no arms, no explosives and no ladders. But still they decide to go ahead. On foot. About 100 of them. As they are about to reach the castle, along comes a coach carrying the Lord Chief Justice and his son-in-law. They are dragged from the coach and butchered. Everybody flees. Emmett is arrested, tried, sentenced to death. His death is a messy business. The English botch the hanging. He is decapitated. The scaffolding is covered in blood. Emmett becomes another legendary Irish martyr.

Now come the Terry Alts, one of the most bizarre protest movements you can imagine. Hundreds, sometimes thousands, of people would turn up, spades and pitchforks on their shoulders, and march military fashion led by a piper through a town, out into the surrounding country and deliberately dig up somebody else's whole five- maybe ten-acre field for them. They said they were doing it so farmers could grow more potatoes. The farmers said they were destroying valuable pasture for cattle, most of which was shipped out to burden the tables of the English rich. The authorities didn't like it. The leaders were condemned to death. Others were transported.

A Catholic protester who was not so quickly put down was the Great Dan, Daniel O'Connell, a lawyer, an Irish lawyer. To a fan, who wrote to him asking for his autograph, he replied, 'Sir, I never send autographs, Yours, Daniel O'Connell.' His objective apart from not giving autographs: Catholic emancipation. Equal political rights as Protestants. The Catholics had been promised it as part of the terms for going along with the Act of Union. They had not got it. They wanted it.

O'Connell, one of the first of the great men of Ireland, organised huge marches, meetings, demonstrations. He got the Catholic Church on his side. He also insisted on non-violence. The British ran scared and gave in to his demands – 27 years later. O'Connell was hailed throughout Ireland as the Emancipator, the Great Liberator.

Having won the battle he now wanted to win the war. He wanted the Act of Union abolished altogether. The threat from the French, the reason it was created, no longer existed. He also wanted the Irish Parliament back in Ireland. But before he could move, virtually the whole country was destroyed by the famine, not only Ireland's but many claim Europe's greatest natural disaster. Ever. What had once been the granary of England was reduced to nothing. Literally, nothing. In 1845 practically three-quarters of the potato crop was destroyed in a matter of days. In 1846 the whole crop was destroyed. Again in 1847.

The cause of the famine: according to the Irish, the English. They had squeezed the Irish so much, so many had been uprooted and driven to new parts of the country; so many had been forced to live on smaller and smaller plots of land. Small plots of land meant intensive cultivation. Intensive cultivation broke down the nitrogen circle. It meant blight. No crops. Starvation. Death. QED. Others blamed the Americans, a fungus, Phytophtora infestans. A few, even the weather.

If the Irish are, as they say, the children of God, He had a funny way of showing his appreciation. At the start of the 1840s there were about eight million people living in Ireland, more than had ever lived there before or since. By the end of the famine less than half remained. Over one million died. Over two million emigrated. To Britain. To America. To work for whoever would take them. To work in the new mills and factories being thrown up as a result of the Industrial Revolution. To work for themselves. To build up their own fortunes to ensure they would never have to suffer a famine ever again.

The government couldn't cope. The scale of the disaster was too much for them. Although, fair's fair, they did what they could. They refused to ban the export of Irish crops which instead of going to feed starving Irish men, women and children went to fatten up English horses so they could be beaten by Irish horses in races all over Europe.

As if they hadn't suffered enough the Irish claimed the hated English paid out twice as much money as compensation to slave owners in Africa as they spent on Irish famine relief. Even worse. Instead of spreading the costs evenly across taxpayers throughout the whole of the country since England and Ireland were one, they made only the Irish taxpayers carry the costs. On top of that – it gets worse and worse – as soon as the Irish started objecting to the way they were being treated the English called a halt to an £8 million public work scheme designed to inject jobs and money into the Irish economy.

Irish horses, however, were doing well. They swept the board at the Steeplechase de Paris and at the Grand National. Said one racing commentator, 'These were the famine years in Ireland. But the performance of Irish horses both at home and abroad were the one bright spot in an otherwise desperate period.'

Priorities. Priorities.

Co. Offaly
Offaly nice place. Offaly nice people

Famous local residents
The Galway Blazers

Favourite food
Anything that's burnt

Favourite drink
Guinness

Favourite pub
Dooley's Hotel, Birr

Favourite restaurant
Dooley's Hotel. But be careful. The food might be burnt

What to say
Do you have a Galway blazer to go with my Offaly slacks?

What not to say
Drink up lads. We'll burn the place to the ground

Tell an Irishman you're from Co. Offaly he'll call you, maybe not to your face, a Biffo. A Big Ignorant F . . . from Offaly. Why, I don't know. To me it's an Offaly good county with Offaly nice people. In fact, Ireland couldn't exist without Co. Offaly. It's its heart. It's its centre. It's one of those vital ingredients. Like nitrogen. It's a breath of fresh Eire. With it, you're alive. Without it, you're dead.

Co. Offaly is named after the O'Connor Faly chiefs, who lived in an extinct volcano and erupted from time to time with terrifying consequences. Especially for the O'Molloys, the O'Carrolls and the MacCoughlans and anybody else who got in their way. But not for long. Co. Offaly very quickly became known for people who were Offaly clever.

For over 500 years from 700 to 1200 Clonmacnoise – from the Irish *Clon*, 'We'; *Mac*, 'Don't believe in making'; *Noise*, 'a lot of noise about the place' – was not just somewhere across the River Shannon, it was also one of Europe's greatest centres of learning. Better than Rome. Better than Paris. Better even than some of the backstreets of Dublin especially down near the docks where they seem to know a lot about a lot of different things. How do we know? Because Clonmacnoise was attacked and raided and plundered again and again and again. By local Irish kings. By the Vikings. By the Anglo-Normans. By local rebels. It was even attacked by other local churches who thought it was getting too big for its gaiters. And I mean attacked. In one of the more violent attacks over 200 men lost their lives. Which, you must admit, is more than on the average Thursday-night Whist Drive to raise funds for the church roof.

In the end it could take no more. From the thirteenth century onwards it started going downhill. From being at the top of the ecclesiastical candlestick it became a small, poor church in one of the smallest and poorest areas in the country. In fact, it was so small and so poor it not only missed out on the big church-building boom of the fifteenth century apart from the doorway and bits of vaulting here and there, it also practically missed the Reformation. While everything around it was being seized and destroyed, it remained firmly in Catholic hands. Cromwell, however, was a different story. At first, it was the focus of opposition.

Big international space conference.

The British delegate announces that Her Majesty's Government have decided to send a spaceship to Mars.

Big cheers all round.

The American delegate announces that the US government have decided to send a spaceship to Jupiter.

Big cheers all round.

The Irish delegate announces that the Irish government have decided to send a spaceship to the sun.

Stunned silence.

'But the sun. The heat. How will you overcome that?' asks the conference chairman.

'The Irish government is not stupid,' says the Irish delegate. 'We're going at night.'

Catholic bishops from all over Ireland met at Clonmacnoise to urge everyone to stand up and fight. But in vain. Cromwell overran the place as he did the whole country. Clonmacnoise was again attacked, plundered and left in ruins.

Today it is still in ruins. But beautifully preserved. Well manicured. Lovingly cared for. More private nursing home than local council old people's home. It's also much bigger, more spread out than you'd expect. When I read the books I got the impression it was a couple of ruined old churches and a heap of stones. In fact, it's the leftovers of a whole town: a castle, a cathedral, eleven churches, a round tower, no end of crosses and an old graveyard. But no dovecotes. All monasteries used to have them. Not as a symbol of peace but as a source of meat during those cold, chilly winter months.

I asked a fat old sack of peat with a walking stick why there were no dovecotes. She wasn't interested. She kept ranting on about Clonmacnoise being Church of Ireland instead of Catholic. Not only that but the Anglican Dean of Clonmacnoise didn't even believe Christmas was Christmas or the Son of God was the Son of God. 'Jesus, Mary and Joseph,' she cried, 'how can a clergyman, any clergyman believe the Son of God is not the Son of God?'

Fair point. It must be a lot like claiming Henry VIII is the supreme, sovereign head of the church.

I went back to pondering what to me is the great mystery of Irish monasticism. How come if Ireland was so full of so many holy monks and nuns, the Irish managed to survive at all? I mean somebody must have been busy doing something to keep them all going.

As I was leaving, this woman barges into me. She is so fat all you had to do was stick an apple in her mouth, she'd never be allowed near a synagogue ever again. She grabs me by the arm and gives me that dewy-eyed look.

'Glory be to God,' she says. 'My prayers have been answered. I'm a virgin again.'

Well excuse me if I don't break open a bottle of champagne, light the candles and put on a Val Doonican record.

Birr was altogether different. If Clonmacnoise drew man's attention to heaven, Birr, which has everything Kilkenny lacks, drew man's attention to the heavens. For all but 30 years of the nineteenth century the world's largest telescope was not in America or Russia or even France. It was tucked away at the back of a garden in Birr, Co. Offaly. But it was no mere plaything of a rich man. It was where with the aid of the telescope, man was able for the first time to measure the surface temperature of the moon. The Americans, of course, doubted it. They sent up their own man, Neil Armstrong, to check it out. He merely confirmed what Birr had told them over 100 years before.

But why were the Irish so interested in the moon? An old Irish astronomer I met wandering around the garden told me the moon was more useful than the sun.

'The moon,' he says, 'shines at night when you need the light whereas the sun shines during the day when you don't need it. Tanksbetogod.'

But far, far more important in the history of the world than any telescope is Dooley's Hotel in the centre of town. For as any sensible man knows who's got his liver in the right place, this was where one of the greatest drinking sessions of all time took place. Back came the shy, quiet, reserved members of the Galway hunt – no, not rhyming slang for Galway traffic wardens – after a day out chasing foxes. Straight into the bar. Guinness after Guinness. So eager were they to show their appreciation for a grand day's hunting they burnt the place down. In their shy, quiet, reserved way. Hence the name for which they will be known until the end of time: the Galway Blazers.

Go into the bar today, it's still the same. Maybe not so many blazers. More sports jackets and anoraks. But the talk is still the same.

'Three days on. Three/four days off. That's the way to get the best out of a horse.'

'Badger fat. That's what I use to keep my tack clean. Old man used it before me. His old man before him.'

'A power of foxes. I tell ye we hunted a power of foxes.'

'If ye've got a good groom, keep him. A good groom is more difficult to find than a good wife.'

'A horse that goes hunting three days a week, I tell ye, ye should feed him 16, maybe 18 lbs of oats a day. Plus one or maybe two handfuls of boiled beans . . .'

'The sweet smells. They do be rising.'

'. . . except the day before he goes hunting. They'd be too difficult for him to digest.'

'In that case ye need a rubber or metal gag, a vulcanite pelham or, best of all, a three-ring KK bit. That'd control the beast. That'd put ye in charge.'

'Whatever happened to the auld stirrup cup, will ye tell me? 'Twas grand. Now 'tis all plastic cups. Not the same at all, at all, at all.'

'Envy. That'll eat away the hills, to be sure.'

'I tell ye. It wouldn't take many of them to make a dozen.'

'Aye. Ye're right there. Ye're right there.'

'Now, ye listen to me. I don't care what ye say. Fox hunting is cruel. It can ruin a horse's legs.'

'Ye're right there. Ye're right there.'

'He's well bred for it.'

'Ye going out again tomorrow?'

'To be sure. To be sure. The Lord God Himself couldn't stop me.'

'What'll ye be having?'

'The same again, God bless ye. I have a terrible tooth for the porter. Ye are a true gentleman. A true gentleman. That's what ye are.'

I always wonder what the Galway Blazers would have done if they hadn't had a good day's hunting. Probably stayed for a week, redecorated the place and stuffed themselves on stale spinach roulard.

Birr, they say, was founded by St Brendan in the days when any woman caught serving beer was immediately sentenced to three days in the stocks. Today it looks as though most of the women spent most of their time in the stocks. It's pleasant. It's civilised. It's a string of Georgian buildings, squares, tree-lined malls, river walks, a castle. It's a mini-Bath with an Irish accent.

If they tell you it's also the centre of Ireland agree with them even though late at night in every bar in the country someone is also claiming his home town is the centre of Ireland, if not the world and 'if you're not believing me' they will threaten to do all kinds of things to you.

You think I'm kidding. In the Vatican in Kildare a couple of days' riding from Dublin I once met a seasoned old mitherer with a lonely face who was adamant that Westmeath Hill, just down the road near Knockcosgrey was the centre of Ireland. But then he also told me . . . a leprechaun was a shoemaker to the fairies; to ward off hunger throw a cake against the oven door on New Year's Eve; always keep a handful of sticks from an ash tree in the cow house. It keeps all the cows good milkers whereas even the tiniest white thorn twig means no end of bad luck. As if that wasn't enough, he once played Gaelic football on the runway at Heathrow Airport. Judging by the look of him, it was when Heathrow Airport was nothing but a collection of ramshackle old buildings and a patch of grass. Say, about five years ago.

The centre of Birr is, obviously, the castle, originally family home to the O'Carroll family and since 1620 family home to the Parsons family. It has witnessed one revolutionary breakthrough after another: a suspension bridge, the creation of a lake, a water-fall, a luminous sundial so that they could tell the time in the dark, and some herbaceous borders. In 1840 the third Earl of Rosse, who like most earls was obsessed with heavenly bodies, installed a telescope. I don't know what he was looking for but he was transfixed by what he saw, a whirlpool. Inside the whirlpool, a nebula.

Since then there has been no stopping them. The various earls have turned their land to one thing after another. They've created the largest gardens in Ireland; the highest box hedges in the world, so high they rate a mention in the *Guinness Book of Records*, and a collection of box hedges in the shape of crossed Rs for Rosses. Yuck. The third earl even invented a steam turbine engine which went on to power such famous, such successful liners as the *Mauritania*. Say no more.

Today, however, along with many other famous castles – Ardgillan, Balbriggan; Avondale, Rathdrum; Ballinlough, Westmeath; Belvedere House, Mullingar; Abbeyleix, Laois and

Barmeath, Dunleer – it is being threatened with closure. Not because its star is waning. But because of crippling insurance bills.

In another part of Co. Offaly, while the Earl's telescope was concentrating on heavenly bodies, another telescope was pointing the other way. Into the bodies themselves. Into the very nature of matter itself. With equally stunning results.

In Clareen, George Stoney discovered what he called the electron, the first elementary particle ever discovered. The whole basis of atomic physics, atomic energy, quantum physics. In terms of the history of the world almost as important as the creation of Guinness itself. As if that wasn't enough to draw the world's attention to the genius of Co. Offaly, George went on to also develop a musical shorthand, which even today you find people use to scribble on the back of programmes to stop them falling asleep while the fat lady is still singing.

But if Co. Offaly had the brains it also had the spirit of adventure. The two they combined in Tullamore, Irish for Tulla, Have some, More, more, which makes a big fuss about being a once thriving Grand Canal port town. To me, it looks as though it has never recovered from the Big Party they had when Charles Bury inherited Tullamore's famous brewery way back in 1785, sent up a hot-air balloon to celebrate, the balloon got caught on a chimney, crashed to the ground and burnt down practically half the town. Brewers don't throw parties like that any more.

To tell you how bad it is the local MP Brian Cowen, when he was minister of health, tried to do the town a favour by moving the National Disease Surveillance Centre there. But staff objected. There was no way they wanted to take their diseases even to Tullamore. The minister had to back down. A rare event in Irish politics.

Tullamore's only redeeming feature is not its brewery but its distillery. It's the spirited home of Tullamore Dew whiskey and the ever so sweet, sticky Irish Mist liqueur which I normally cannot stand unless I've got a cold coming. Then I go to bed with a bottle of Irish Mist. In two hours it's gone. I've still got the cold, of course. But I feel much better. Alongside the distillery there used to be an ice-cube-making plant but, I was told, it closed down years ago. The old boy who knew the recipe collapsed and died.

The Tullamore Dew Heritage Centre, however, almost puts you off the drink altogether. It's all very modern and slick and bursting with European Union money. A bit like Peter Mandelson on heat. But my innate good manners, my loyalty and my lifelong devotion got me through although one day I'm determined to get my own back. I shall turn up when I'm not driving, wander up and down the Grand Canal until I feel a cold coming on and then promptly sink a bottle of their Irish Mist. Talk about through a glass darkly. In my case, it'll be through a glass mistily.

Perhaps it's no surprise, therefore, that to the north of Tullamore tucked away in the remains of Durrow Abbey are two stones: the Headache Stone and the Backache Stone although why anyone would be interested in stones that give you either a headache or a backache I cannot imagine. I know people who can switch on a headache or a backache without looking at a stone. Luckily I don't seem to get them. But if I wanted to get a headache or a backache I can think of far more pleasant ways of getting them than sitting on a couple of stones in the middle of a churchyard somewhere in the middle of Ireland. In the rain.

There is, however, a local theory that the headache stone and the backache stone have got something to do with the French. Which I wouldn't argue with. In the seventeenth century the French were all over Co. Offaly. Most of them were French Protestants, Huguenots, fleeing the persecutions of Cardinal Richelieu and his crack messieurs. Co. Offaly, with its strong Protestant sympathies, was a safe haven.

In Portarlington, for example, the local church, St Michael's is still known as the French church. Many of the gravestones are in French. One vieille carcasse, whose face was so black she looked as though she nibbled nothing but lumps of coal, told me that until very recently church services were often conducted in French. It could, of course, have been in Latin. The Irish are not always the most perceptive people in the world.

Where the French are, the Trollopes are invariably not far behind. Every one of them to a man eager to take one to bed with them. The English, naturally, prefer thrillers. Anthony was for a time Post Office Surveyor at Banagher on the Shannon although to be fair he didn't think much of it. After he moved on he is supposed to have said, 'Who has had a happier life than mine?' Which to me seems unlikely. I didn't think he could say anything in less than six volumes.

But that's not the only local literary connection. It was also here that the nasty Arthur Bell Nichols, her father's curate, proposed to the desperate Charlotte Brontë and later married her. But it wasn't to last long. To get away from him, she died a few months later. If it was in a nineteenth-century novel about clergymen and their daughters nobody would believe it.

Banagher today could hardly produce a short story let alone a six-volume novel. It's full of boats, boats and people walking around with a fish dangling at the end of a bit of string.

In Corrigans Lounge one evening I asked a real alter kocker with a trilby, yellow waistcoat and rubber suit what he knew about there being a Trollope in town. But the conversation got bogged down. He told me some story about Leap Castle over near Clareen being haunted.

'You should go there,' he keeps telling me.

'But why?' I asked him. 'A ghost is a ghost is a ghost.'

'But bless my soul, this ghost is different.'

'Different?'

'It's got smelly feet.'

'Smelly feet?'

''Tis true. I swear on my mother's grave. Yeats said so. So it must be true.'

Oh yeah. Yeats also said Innisfree was peace and quiet. Not when I went there it wasn't.

Up the road in Clogham it was worse still. For Clogham is practically nothing but bog. Not black bog but red bog.

'So what's the difference between black bog and red bog?' I once asked an old farmer who looked and smelt very, well, effluential.

I stumbled across him along by the Gem garden centre, where a thief had just strolled in and, as bold as brass, stolen not the company's takings but their guard dog, a massive 12-stone Rottweiler.

He took a long draw on his pipe.

'A black bog,' he says, 'is black. A red bog is red. Good day to ye. God bless.'

Offaly clever the people in Co. Offaly.

The Widget County
Co. Cork

The famine over, the big problem still remained: the tiny widget of Protestants in a full can of Catholic Guinness. The widget Protestants saw themselves as a vital, integral part of the package. The Catholic Guinness were convinced they would be better off without it. The atmosphere became decidedly chilly. If not exactly Ice Cold.

The British Parliament which was composed largely of landowners decided the only way to solve the problem was to come up with a fair and equitable way of dealing with the land. Keep the land in the hands of the Protestants. Make it easier for the Catholics to rent it. Oh yes, and throw in the occasional long lease as well. But surprise, surprise, the Catholics were not interested. For some strange reason they wanted to own the land in their own homeland. To champion their cause: suddenly out of the blue appeared Charles Stuart Parnell. Ireland being Ireland, he was not a Catholic but a Protestant and a landowner. But he hated like a Catholic. He hated English landowners. He hated English rule. He did everything he could to disrupt the British Parliament. In the end the great Mr Gladstone gave in. The only way to solve the problem of Ireland, he agreed, was Home Rule. Allow them to run themselves like Australia, New Zealand, Canada. Except for defence and foreign affairs. Britain would be responsible for those. He had no real alternative. Parnell, after all, used to end meetings with the immortal line 'Gentlemen. It seems unanimous that we cannot agree.' Catholics were for it. Protestants were against it – especially the Protestants in Ulster. For them Home Rule Meant Catholic Rule. Gladstone and Parnell, however, pushed it through the House of Commons. But the Tories in the House of Lords threw it out.

In Ireland, however, things were stirring if not foaming.

In 1848 Young Ireland, a romantic, middle-class group of bar-stool freedom fighters, bubbled up to the surface. But like all romantic middle-class operations it very quickly went flat again.

The Fenians, however, were something different. Named after a gang of ancient Irish warriors, they saw themselves as new Irish warriors. Many of them were battle-hardened warriors of the American War of Independence. They had fought for American independence. Now they were determined to fight for Irish independence. Which they did. By causing chaos. In Canada. In 1866 they seized an empty, desolate island off the coast of New Brunswick and declared it an Irish republic. Excuse me. But are we on the same planet? The Canadians retaliated. They attacked with deadly maple syrup bombs. The Irish fled to the States. Last I heard they were still stuck trying to get through Immigration in New York.

But for all their numbers, the funds at their disposal, their so-called military experience and discipline, the Fenians didn't seem to make the impact they could have done. Partly because they were riddled with informers. Read the history of the Fenians. Practically every other one seemed to be an informer in the pay of the British. Partly because they seemed to take so long to decide to do anything. Then when they finally decided, every other person seemed to tell the British and everything was called off.

Take their raid on Chester Castle. The plan: to break into the armoury. Come the morning of the attack – surprise, surprise – the guard was suddenly doubled at the castle. Local volunteers were called up. A guards regiment was on its way from London. The signal was given to cut and run. What then followed is almost unbelievable. The Fenians who were casually wandering around Chester in their hundreds waiting for the signal to go were suddenly dumping their weapons all over the place and making like casual for the ferry boats back to Ireland where they were met by police only too keen to know why they were coming back home with no luggage.

The Fenians in the States then decided to have another go. They raised what they called a fighting force to invade Ireland, seize it from the English and declare it independent: one ship, 40 men and 8000 rifles. When they arrived off the west coast of Ireland they couldn't find anywhere to land. Some men scrambled ashore to look for food. One of them welshed on them to the authorities. The rest scrambled back aboard. The ship headed back to the States. Mission unaccomplished.

The Fenians, however, made one major contribution to modern life. They invented the terrorist bomb. On 14 December 1867 they risk everything on a burke. They try to spring one of their members, Richard O'Sullivan Burke, out of Clerkenwell prison, close to the centre of London. Instead of just blowing a hole in the wall for him to escape they use so much explosive they don't just practically demolish the perimeter wall they also destroy houses across the street as well as injure 120 people including two girls aged seven and eleven.

Then came the famous or infamous Phoenix Park murders, which yet again proved the Fenians didn't use a little bit of Common.

Lord Frederick Cavendish, favourite of the Liberal Prime Minister, the legendary Mr Gladstone, and England's newly appointed supremo in Ireland, decided after a heavy day in the office to take a stroll in Phoenix Park, Dublin. Alone. Not a bodyguard in sight. Which shows you how qualified he was for the post of England's supremo in Ireland. He is spotted by another burke, his senior civil servant, Thomas Henry Burke. He races after him. He no sooner catches up with him than they are surrounded by a group of men, wrestled to the ground and killed.

Tony Geraghty tells the story in his book *The Irish War*, which was highly praised for its 'honest and accurate analysis'. Though on page 309 he says Cavendish and Burke were surrounded by 'six or seven others' and on page 310 'five of the group were hanged and five others imprisoned'. Makes you wonder what an inaccurate analysis would be.

Now came one bombshell after another.

The leader of the Irish Party at Westminster, Charles Stuart Parnell, was negotiating a peace deal with Gladstone. Tenant farmers were protesting against the ever-increasing rents they had to pay their greedy absentee English landlords even though the amount of money they were making out of farming was getting less and less. Parnell said he would get them to call off their increasingly violent protest movement not to mention the terrorist campaign led by the mysterious Captain Moonlight, who roamed the country by night burning down houses and farms, if the government introduced legislation pegging rents for 15 years, providing loans to tenants wishing to buy their farms and stopping tenants from being evicted if they fell behind with their rent.

Parnell offered to resign his seat as an MP in protest at the murders. Gladstone was against it. Others were not so easily persuaded. MPs demanded a Parliamentary commission to find out whether Parnell was in any way linked with the murders directly or indirectly. He was cleared. *The Times* said he was guilty. He sued for libel. He was cleared.

But what brought him down was divorce. He was named in a divorce case brought by one of his closest colleagues in the Irish Party, Captain O'Shea. Parnell had been living openly with his wife, Kitty. Public opinion swung so violently against him, he had to resign. It was the end.

The Home Rule Bill when it finally came to Parliament was defeated by 30 votes.

The Irish were back to square one. Or rather back to bombing. Between March 1883 and February 1885 thirteen bombs went off in London without any warnings or calls to any radio stations. Between Westminster and Charing Cross. Between Edgware Road and Praed Street. At the Tower of London. At London Bridge. The police established the Irish Special Branch. To mark its launch, the Fenians let off a bomb at their convenience. In a public toilet. Immediately below Scotland Yard.

Inevitably this made the Protestants restless. It also made the Ulster Protestants who were violently opposed to even the thought of Home Rule violent. The Orange Order began recruiting volunteers for its own military struggle.

Problems were getting worse.

For the next 20 years, however, it was virtually an Irish stand-off.

The poor Irish Catholics could sense victory was in sight. Admittedly a long way away. But it was now a distinct possibility. Their numbers started increasing. The Pope also insisted that any children born of a mixed Catholic–non-Catholic marriage should be brought up as Catholics. The Catholics said it was a move to protect the Catholics. You can guess what the Protestants said.

The rich Anglo-Irish Protestant aristos could sense the same thing. Before long they would be able to leave Westminster and run their own show again.

Up in the north, the Ulstermen thought, well nobody actually knows what an Ulsterman thinks, but it didn't seem to be the worst.

27 July 1912 the whole thing blows up.

The Tory Leader of the Opposition, Bonar Law, sees Home Rule edging closer and closer. The Liberal government, he thundered, did not have a parliamentary majority for Home Rule. They only had 271 seats in the House of Commons. The Tories and Liberal Unionists together had 273. The only way the Liberals could push the measure through was with the 84 votes of the Irish nationalist MPs who were depending for their funding on supporters in the US. Corrupt, he called it. Resistance to Home Rule should now be pushed 'beyond the restraints of the constitution', he said. There are things 'stronger than parliamentary majorities', he said.

Some people would say that was incitement to arms.

Unionists saw it as a call to bowler hats. Within six months they had not only formed the Ulster Volunteer Force and had over 100,000 men under arms they were also busy importing all the arms and ammunition they could find without the slightest bother from either the local police or local army units.

Down south the Irish decided they had better do the same. They formed the Irish Volunteers and enlisted around 75,000 men not to mention the usual untold number of double agents who were both for the British and for more extreme Irish protest movements such as our friends the Fenians

Every man, woman and child across the country was dreaming of dying for Ireland. And it wasn't just the Guinness talking. Early morning. Stone cold. Half-sober. All the old heroes would be recalled. Their actions. Their glories. The way they had fought and died for their country. Wolf Tone. Lord Edward Fitzgerald. Daniel O'Connell. Charles Stuart Parnell. Molly Malone. The Irish never let the facts get in the way of a good story. Those who didn't fancy dying on the battlefield or halfway up a back alley saw themselves fighting and dying for the Church. By the hands of ungrateful natives and savages. In faraway nations. Under blistering sunshine. In the backstreets of Liverpool.

Things were also moving on the British side.

The British army based in Ireland decided they didn't want to get involved. If there was going to be an Ireland v Ireland fight they wanted out.

The Irish in London, however, wanted to get involved.

Finally they made it. British Liberals broke the stranglehold of the British Conservatives on the British House of Lords. Irish Home Rule was set for September 1914. But Ireland being Ireland what happens in August 1914? War. Not against the Ulster Protestants, who had signed a solemn pledge to fight to the last man to defend themselves against Home Rule. Nor was it against the Ulster Volunteers, a Protestant army led by Sir Edward Carson who – Ireland being Ireland – was born in Dublin. But World War I. Something always gets in the way.

The Irish, however, continued their war. Both sides beefed up their armies. Both sides smuggled in weapons. From Germany. Talk about even-handed. Many decided to fight for the British. The Ulster Volunteers to a man. The Irish Volunteers split. The majority were in favour. Fighting for the British they thought would stand them in good stead. When the war was over, the British would be grateful and grant them Home Rule. The minority were against. They didn't believe the British would ever be grateful to anyone let alone a Catholic Irishman fighting for Home Rule. They set up their own army, the Irish Republican Army. Their enemy: the British.

In the United States, an Irish-born British diplomat, who was an expert on rubber trees in both Africa and South America, was trying to enlist the aid of the Germans. Sir Roger Casement wanted the German Ambassador in Washington to give him all the Irish soldiers in German prisoner-of-war camps. The Germans agreed. They allowed Sir Roger to go off and talk to the Irish prisoners of war themselves at a special camp in Limburg. Out of over 2000, he could only find ten prepared to fight and die for the auld country.

The Widget County

From then on things just got worse and worse. The Germans landed him secretly along the Kerry coast. He was immediately picked up by the police, jailed, tried for high treason by the British – one of the main witnesses against him was one of the ten men who said they would be prepared to die for Ireland when he met him in Limburg – found guilty and executed.

Meanwhile the Irish war continued.

May 1915 the decision was taken. The Irish Republican Brotherhood decided they were going to seize key points in Dublin. Throughout the country other rebels were going to seize other key points. All they had to do was hold them long enough until the German arms and ammunition arrived to enable them to fight off the inevitable onslaught by the British. Except the arms and ammunition never came. They had been seized by the British. What's more the Irish rebels were now spending more time plotting among themselves than they were plotting against the English. One group wanted one way. Another group another. One group even took an advertisement in the *Sunday Independent* telling its supporters not to fight. How's that for keeping secret a plot to overthrow your country? But they went ahead with the uprising anyhow.

Easter Monday 1916. Practically the whole of Dublin was at the races. The rebels killed an unarmed policeman single-handedly guarding Dublin Castle but instead of storming in and establishing themselves in the seat of government they went off and seized other far less symbolic buildings. They seized three buildings in Mount Street. They seized Boland's Flour Mills. They seized the Four Courts. They seized St Stephen's Green. And, of course, they seized the General Post Office.

In wonderful, gripping, striking Irish prose they proclaimed an Irish republic.

The British troops moved in immediately. Their sole objective, regardless of how many lives it cost, regardless of how much damage it caused: seize back the General Post Office. Which they did ruthlessly, mercilessly. The Irish rebels never stood a chance. They were romantics not soldiers. They were outnumbered, outfought, outmanoeuvred. They had few weapons and even less idea how to use them.

When it was all over, the British were just as ruthless. Thousands were arrested. Some were court-martialled and shot. Others were just shot. And all this without the help of David Blunkett.

Whichever way you look at it, the Easter Rising has got to be a glorious failure. It did more harm than good. It made matters a million times worse. It achieved nothing. Except for one thing. It created martyrs. Many of the rebels who were shot became national heroes, written, spoken and sung about even today. It also kept alive the dream of Irish independence.

The British tried to keep things quiet. But they reckoned without the Kerry brothers. The British had just built three transatlantic cable stations on a tiny island off the Kerry coast. It was run by the Ring brothers. The Ring brothers were all fiercely loyal Fenians. Guess who told the Americans and then the world what the British were doing to the Irish? It was in honour of the brothers and their actions that the famous scenic circular tour of Kerry is even today called the Ring of Kerry.

Now it was a whole new ball game or rather game of hurling. In the outside world, the news created uproar. In Ireland, it created still more martyrs, patriots, the stuff of legend, the heroes of songs still sung today.

November 1918. The big war was no sooner over than the fight was on again.

The general election of 1918 saw the birth of a new political party, Sinn Féin, Ourselves Alone known to their friends as the Shinners. They wanted out of the British Parliament. They wanted an Irish Parliament in Dublin. They won almost three-quarters of the Irish seats in Parliament. When the British refused their demands, they went ahead anyway and formed their own Parliament, the Dáil in Dublin. Fenians claimed they were the true government. The IRA, some of whose members were members of the Dáil, some were Fenians and some were neither, claimed they were the first to proclaim an Irish republic – a republic of the whole of Ireland.

One side claimed it was elected, backed by a majority of the electors, politically legitimate, prepared to accept a divided Ireland

The other, unelected, supported by a minority, prepared to use force but not even over their dead bodies were they prepared to accept a divided Ireland.

Confused? So were the British government. They decided to ignore everything and go to war. To the Irish it was the Irish War of Independence. To the English, it was the Anglo-Irish War. To any impartial onlooker it was a vicious, unnecessarily bloody and brutal war that should never have taken place.

The Irish had practically nothing. Apart from the secret, stop-at-nothing Fenian Brotherhood and the Irish Volunteers.

The British had the Black and Tans, so called because of their uniforms, some of the roughest, toughest, nastiest, dirtiest fighters there have ever been. Many of them were soldiers. But many of them, it was also said, were prisoners released from jail and seconded to the Black and Tans for their, how do you say?, special skills.

'Lord have mercy on us,' I remember one of my old uncles telling me. 'The only good thing about them was we weren't kicked around by a bunch of eejits in khaki shorts and pith helmets.'

Neither side won. Neither side lost. Everyone just seemed to collapse from the exhaustion, the senseless killing. In December 1921 both sides agreed to a deal drawn up largely by Lloyd George. Ireland would become not a republic but a Free State. They would be self-governing. A bit like Canada. As for the border with the North, Lloyd George was vague. The Irish had finally after 800 years thrown off the yoke of the British. What more did they want?

They wanted to know the border. Where it was going to go. Which bit was South. Which bit was North. Some didn't even want any border at all. Ireland was one. Ireland should stay one. This time though it was Irish v Irish, the Irish Civil War. Again, Ireland being Ireland, more Irish were executed for treason by the Irish during the Irish Civil War than were executed for treason by the British during the Irish War of Independence.

Finally on 6 December 1921 the Free State supporters gained the upper hand. The Irish Free State was a goer. It was in the British Empire. It had dominion status. Northern Ireland was separate. It remained part of the United Kingdom. But why six counties? So, the Catholics said, the Protestants could count them on the fingers of one hand.

But still it didn't stop there. The southern Irish continued to fight amongst themselves. Some were for the Free State. Some were against it. But they fought the Irish way. During the riots of 1932 young Pat McKechnie, like other boys and young men, was out on the streets hurling bricks and cobblestones at the police. Except he didn't throw the stones like everybody else. He put the stone in the palm of his hand. Pulled his hand back to his shoulder. Took two or three huge leaps. And hurled it at the police. The head constable on the other side, who was also coach for the national police athletics team, spotted this. As soon as the riot was over he ordered a special snatch squad to find and arrest the boy and bring him to the police station immediately. Which they did. The head constable signed McKechnie up there and then for the national police athletics team and packed him off for training. Within a year he was champion shot-putter for Ireland. Within two, of the whole of the UK. Within four years, he was at the Olympic Games in Berlin. Only in Ireland. In the end the name 'Irish Free State' was dropped. In its place, it became Eire. The leader, the first Taoiseach or Prime Minister was Éamon de Valéra, born in New York, son of a Cuban father and an Irish mother, as tall as the Empire State Building. To most, he was the perfect first president of Ireland. A strong Catholic. Austere. Frugal. Irish-speaking. A believer in self-sufficiency. The basic things of life. More than anything, he was fair. No violence. No extremism. Above all no religious bigotry. No hatred of Protestants. In fact twice during his 50 years as Prime Minister, Irish presidents were Protestants.

For 50 years he dominated Irish politics. For 50 years he moulded Ireland to his dream as the 'home of a people who valued material wealth only as a basis of right living, of a people who were satisfied with frugal comfort and devoted their leisure to the things of the spirit; a land whose countryside would be bright with cosy homesteads, whose fields and villages would be joyous with sounds of industry, the romping of sturdy children, the contests of athletic youths, the laughter of comely maidens, whose firesides would be the forums of the wisdom of serene old age.'

But it was not to last.

The widgets were breaking free.

Co. Cork
Ye can't keep them down

Famous local residents
Somerville and Ross

Favourite food
Black pudding

Favourite drink
Guinness

Favourite pub
Every one

Favourite restaurant
Every one

What to say
'll have the à la carte

What not to say
'm with Fergie

In the old days of my drunken youth the only thing stopping me getting at the Guinness was a cork. Not just an ordinary cork. But one of those corks somehow connected with a bit of reinforced wire to the top of the neck of the bottle. Now it's a widget.

Much the same applies to Cork. It's the only thing stopping me from getting at the rest of Ireland. Because in many ways I'd be more than happy to see out my days in Cork rather than go sniffing around the rest of the country.

Ireland's third-largest and dirtiest city, built like Rome on seven hills, with the most impossible lilting Irish accent, has everything to offer. But be warned. Don't try and find any information about Cork on the Internet. A whole string of hardcore porn websites are for some reason or other using the name Cork City. Latch on to them and you could be on to more than a Corkin' good time. Well, until the police come knocking on your door.

Founded by a sixth-century Irish monk and hermit, they say it's Ireland's cultural capital. Not that you'd notice. There are no famous theatres, no famous museums, no famous art galleries, no famous opera houses. I can't even think of any famous Cork writers. Well apart from Fergal Keane, if you call a BBC television news reporter a writer. Cork, he maintains, was his first puking grounds in his rough, tough, hard-bitten, hard-drinking days before he saw the light, became St Fergal and started writing letters to his son and talking to his long-dead father.

What Cork does have, however, is water. Through the middle of it flows the River Lee or rather two main streams of the River Lee. It's not exactly Venice. More Amsterdammerung with more

415

than its fair share of quays and bridges. With so much water running through its veins – come heavy rains or a storm and the streets are more like full-blown streams or rivers – it's perhaps not surprising it's also the anti-drink capital of Ireland because it was home to Father Theobald Mathew, founder of the Pioneers, who taught Ireland to put the Cork back in the bottle and made people promise to never again take a drop of the hard stuff. And a big success he was too. In fact, a 100 per cent proof success especially for a country known for its love of the drink. Maybe not so much today as it used to be. But his influence is still there. The first year he started, he enrolled an unbelievable 150,000 people.

Man goes into a restaurant in Kinsale.

Waiter says, 'You can have whatever you like so long as you pay in dollars.'

Man says, 'I've always wanted to have elephant ears and onions.'

Waiter says, 'No problem.'

He goes away.

An hour later he comes back.

Man says, 'See. I knew you'd have problems getting the elephant ears.'

Waiter says, 'No. We've got the elephant ears. It's the onions we can't find.'

Which is a sobering thought. At its peak there were probably as many miserable, boring old non-drinkers as there were happy-go-lucky, laughing, joking, carefree drinkers in the country.

Co. Cork

When I first started being dragged across the Irish Sea, I'm not saying the place was full of hardened drinkers. It was just that wherever you went at whatever time of day or night it was measured out in pubs and pints of Guinness.

'The Market? Now we'll have to go past Lynch's, O'Brien's and Ryan's to the cross. There's no way we can pass them by without dropping in to say Hullo and have a spot of refreshment. From Ryan's it's . . .'

And so on.

Going to mass on Sunday morning was the same. But in reverse.

'We'll have to stop at Agnes's on the way back. A quick call at Johnny's. Can't see Johnny without seeing . . .'

Just as well the Irish didn't believe in Evensong. We'd never have had enough time to get back home before we'd have had to leave again.

Sometimes those who looked like heavy drinkers, huge, built like an ox, able to lift a horse out of a ditch single-handed were the non-drinkers and the weak, lily-livered, squeamish types in suits and shiny shoes, the drinkers.

I can remember the old days when St Patrick was still in short trousers. You'd be at the creamery at 7 o'clock in the morning. You'd no sooner have offloaded the couple of churns from the ass and cart than you'd be in the old grocer's shop next door taking your first glass of the day. At 10.20 you'd be off to town. You'd call in at Coffey's, in the village grocery store, on the way. There hidden behind a long, musty lace curtain at the far end of the counter would be the parish priest already well advanced in his spiritual life.

'The drink. It is my greatest enemy. But unfortunately we have been commanded to love our enemies,' he would say. 'I'll have a large one, God bless you.'

On the way back you'd call in at Mary's or Joan's or Nora's or whoever. You'd no sooner darkened the door, proclaimed to all and sundry, 'God bless this house' than there in front of you would be a bottle of Guinness and a glass, depending on where you were, either sparkling clean or smeared with God knows what.

Today, of course, it's different. There are no ass and carts. There are still non-drinkers around but not so many and not so young as I remember. I have an uncle, fifties, heavy smoker, worked hard all his life, who drinks nothing but milk. Take him in a good restaurant, he'll drink glass after glass of milk through the meal. Others are the other extreme. Hitting the bottle breakfast, lunch and dinner. I know a young magger, mid twenties, serious, again hard-working. He's practically dying of the drink. Worst of all are the reformed drinkers, especially the members of Alcoholics Anonymous. They shuffle up to you. 'How's your Uncle Bob?' they say, the secret code for members of the Irish AA. Then they practically drive you to drink with their long, boring stories about how they gave up the booze before it gave up them; how they'll never lose the taste of it; how they've still got to force themselves to go into bars just to prove to themselves they've got the better of it.

In between, most people are like me. Normal. Average. Sensible. Who only drink so that people don't think we're boring old alcoholics. Able to last, at least, twenty or thirty minutes without touching a drop. And then zonk, zonk, zonk. My favourite spot o Cork City: Barrack Street. It's got 25 pubs, more pubs than any other street in Ireland. Apart from all the others that have go more. The Duke of Wellington and the Duke of Marlborough used to hang out there. So it can't be all that bad.

But if Cork is known for its pubs, it's also known for its potholes. Cork is the pothole capital of Ireland. How do they know? Cork City Corporation has a computer record of not only each one bu how many people have fallen into each one. The top score: 1 people. When I rang Cork City Corporation to find out where i was so that I could avoid putting my foot in it I was told the official who could help me was off sick. With a broken leg.

The first time I went to Cork, it was like going back in time to when they used to stuff a dirty rag in the neck of a bottle and hope it did the trick. It was full of old-fashioned shops. Woodfor Bournes – how un-Irish can that be? – was full of coffee beans long wooden counters, a huge steel drum inside the main doc and what they called, glinkeens, silly scatterbrained girls wh looked as though they would have been happier milking the cov than making the coffee. Kids at mass on Sundays were dressed i bright velvet caps with gold tassels, fancy coloured shirts, big fawn boots and purple stockings signifying something or other pagan or irreligious or just illegal. Headlines in the *Cork Examiner* used to proclaim, 'No chaos at Irish airports'.

Cork, they used to say, was inhabited by Irish Gascons. Friendly, charming, every inch as Irish as the next man. Except the next man was a Gascon, cynical, twisted, bitter, completely untrustworthy.

There seemed to be plenty to see. But none of it was very interesting. Again and again I would be told the city was attacked by the Duke of Marlborough; it was the birthplace of William Penn of Pennsylvania fame; home to the Irish navy; final departure point of the *Titanic* and centre of search operations for the *Lusitania*, which was torpedoed off the Old Head of Kinsale by a German submarine on 7 May 1915 with the loss of 1198 lives.

One of my old uncles used to call Corkonians fidgeters. They were forever on the move he used to say, up and down, fidgeting around all the time. An old aunt would drown herself with holy water before setting foot inside the place, bless herself a million times and warn everyone in sight to take care. Cork, she would declare, was a city full of Protestants.

Today, of course, it's all different. All the old stores are gone. Groceries are no longer delivered in brown paper packages all wrapped up with string. Brown Thomas in Patrick Street has been voted, it proclaims, 'Department Store of the Year'. Oh yeah. The table and glassware department didn't look 'Department Store of the Year' to me, unless, of course, it was 1899. Young men go out for fish and chips and don't come back. They are shot and killed as they walk home. Undertakers no longer publish funeral notices giving the address of the deceased in case burglars break into their homes and ransack the place while the family is at the funeral.

'If a Corkman starts smiling at you, beware,' a Dubliner once told me. 'It means the knife is already in your back.' As for Corkwomen, he said, 'They have a face like a cow's arse.'

On the west coast, they have a different opinion. Corkmen, they say, are the Texans of Ireland. They are forever boasting or bragging about something. On the other hand Blarney Street is still not only the longest street in Cork but also in Ireland and from the top you can still look down on the 'flaat o' deh city'. I mean the flat of the city. The Protestants are, of course, still there. There is even a 'Huguenot Quarter' which I thought was going to tell the story of Protestant Cork. All I could see were cafés and bookshops and a drunken old busker slurring away to his heart's content in Rory Gallagher Place. He was celebrating, he told me, because he had just ripped off the Irish railways. He had bought a return ticket Cork–Dublin and come back by coach.

St Finbarr's Protestant Cathedral wasn't much better. I thought I was letting myself in for some Cromwellian masterpiece. It seemed to be nothing but statues and gargoyles and plaques to British officers lost in the Punjab. Best thing of all was the floor plaque to Elizabeth Atword. She was discovered hiding behind a curtain during a meeting in the local Freemasons' lodge. Instead of throwing her out on her neck, the good Masons decided there was no worse humiliation for her than to stand her on a chair on one leg, a leather skirt around her and enrol her as a member of the Irish Grand Lodge. She is the only young woman ever to become a Mason. No end of old women, however, are Masons.

Even the restaurants are not what they used to be. I went to Otter's at The Kingsley at Victoria Cross. All they were serving was organic food. Not an otter in sight. I headed for Lovetts Restaurant. For me, it's one of the best restaurants not only in Cork but in Ireland. Had a fabulous meal. But no Delamain. Still Lovett.

My other favourite spot is the bus station down by the river. Many's a happy, rain-drenched, sweaty hour I've spent there waiting for a bus to take me to wherever. As if that's not bad enough I always manage to get stuck with some mumper of a baseball cap who looks as though he took his sun baths in the dark. The last one I couldn't avoid meeting told me it was his first time in Ireland.

'Goin' to kiss the Blarney Stone?' I says.

In spite of everything I thought I should try some polite conversation.

'I dunit. I dunit,' he grunts.

'But you said this was your first time in Ireland.'

'Sure.'

'Then how . . . ?'

'I did it on the Net.'

'On the Net?'

'Yeah. There's this website. It shows you the Blarney Stone. You lean over backwards and kiss the screen. It was great. I've now got, whatdidtheysay, the gift of, err, eloquence. And it only cost me ten bucks.'

'Ten bucks?'

'Yeah. You had to send ten bucks for kissing the Blarney Stone. That's only fair isn't it?'

Duh.

I kissed the Blarney Stone years ago. All I can remember is that there were no jokes then about getting AIDS. Not like today. In any case, it never made any difference to, uhh, my eloquence.

Why Blarney Stone? Because the castle was built by Cormac MacCarthy, Lord of Blarney and Queen Elizabeth I is supposed to have complained to her secretary, Stone that he never kept his word, 'This is all Blarney, Stone. What he says he never means.' Which coming from a queen and a woman is something.

After the bus station, the railway station is another favourite.

I'm queuing up for a ticket to Dublin. In front of me is this fuzz-pop who looks as though he's just been buried alive.

'Where are you going?' the man in the ticket office says to him.

'To lunch,' he says.

The train is late. The porter tells me it's in 'suspended loco-notion'.

Finally the train arrives. The loudspeakers announce, 'Ladies and Gentlemen. We apologise for the delay. This is because we are ten minutes early.' I clamber on board. Sitting opposite me is this upper-class ditz who looks as though agents have been queuing up for years to handle her.

The ticket collector comes along. He asks for our tickets.

'Young man,' she says in an obviously well practised plummy Dame Edith Evans voice, 'I am not showing you my ticket. You're not properly dressed.'

He shuffles on down the carriage.

She looks at me and winks.

421

Ireland: In a Glass of its Own

Outside Cork, the rest of the county, the biggest in Ireland, is foreign territory. Largely because it's full of foreigners. Especially Dutch and Germans who told me they had not come for the peace, the quiet, the solitude, the scenery or to spend three days a week out with the local hunt. They had come because they worked out in the late '70s when the whole world was expecting a nuclear war that Co. Cork was the best place to go to escape a nuclear blast. Although in some cases, they told me, a nuclear blast would have been preferable to the Irish blast that greeted them.

'The Irish. They are nice for visiting,' a hard-eyed, straight-down-the-line klutz who was obviously to the spanner born, told me. 'But living with them, they are different. We come here. We buy a castle. We spend lots of money. We give jobs to local people. Are they happy? No. They criticise. They don't like the materials we use. They don't like the style. They don't like the colour. OK, I say, next time I let your castle fall down. Go to hell.'

The Irish are nothing if they are not fair. They also criticise the foreigners who come in and build all those wonderful, small modern bungalows with their cheap plastic pillars, metal gates, sweeping iron railings, strange-looking lions and eagles perched on top of precarious gateposts. Why they should do that I have no idea.

'Will ye look at them? Will ye look at them?' I am buttonholed one evening in a bar by an old farmer who looks as though he could melt down a whole menopausal hotline. 'And all on some of the best farmland in the country.'

North Cork is Mallow, once a famous spa town, which in its time attracted the fun crowd such as Charles Wesley and Sir Walter Scott. Wesley went there religiously. Sir Walter when he had a touch of consumption. With all that water flowing through the town, inevitably it attracted more than its fair share of waterholics. 'Beauing, belling, dancing, drinking, / Breaking windows, damning, sinking, / Ever raking, never thinking, / Live the Rakes of Mallow.' In spite of everything, the locals will tell you they invented steeple chasing. From the steeple of Butterant Church to the steeple of St Leger Church, a distance of four miles, Edward Blake challenged his next-door neighbour in 1752. The prize: the 23 volumes of

John Wesley's favourite hymns. How they ever got the horses up on those church towers I'll never know. What they won't tell you is that because of all the steeplechasing the land is now so soft and marshy, they're thinking of renaming the place Marsh Mallow.

It is also home to the Irish Post Office's funny address office.

I know because whenever I go there everyone tells me the story of the little old lady who writes a letter to God. She tells him she is so poor, she has no money, she would like to have €100 so that she could spend it all entertaining her friends at Christmas.

The letter ends up at the funny address sorting office in Mallow. The postmen feel sorry for her, collect €96.50 between them and send it to her.

The following week comes another letter from the little old lady. She thanks God for the €96.50. The remaining €3.50, she says she assumes was stolen by those theivin, miserable bastards in the Post Office.

I like going to see the ruins of Kilcolman Castle. To me it's a tribute to female gratitude. For eight years Edmund Spenser worked on *The Faerie Queene* as a homage to Elizabeth I. All that time and effort you'd have thought she would have given him a castle in much better condition as a thank-you present. Go there at night-time. They say you can hear Ireland's only ghost fox hunt. Horses and hounds canter across the park. From Ballydineen to Glou-na-Goth, across Wilkinson's Lawn, through Byblox, over the ford at Shangh-agha-Keel to Aghboobleen, Watkin's Glen, the Old Deer Park, the Horse Close and on into the park itself. My God. I bet there's no lack of spirits there.

Fermoy, however, is more my kind of town. Tiny. Compact. Lots of bookshops. Castlehyde Mansions, just outside the town, is another matter. Chicago-born Irishman Michael 'Lord of the Dance' Flatley has taken it over, blown over US$20 million doing it up and turned it into his own little bit of Ireland complete with a two-climate-controlled wine cellar – one for the white wine, one for the red wine – a Roman spa and an African safari room. I once tried to check into the Castlehyde Hotel nearby. I was told there were no rooms available. President Clinton was expected at any minute.

'You're kidding me,' I said.

The goodfornobody girl at the reception desk grinned sheepishly.

'They're permanently booked,' she says, 'in case he should drop by.'

To the east is Youghal, pronounced Yowl, like a peacock stuck on a barbed-wire fence. I once got a bus from Waterford to Youghal. I asked the driver to let me know when we were there.

'No problem,' he says. 'You get off the stop before me.'

It was here in the garden of Myrtle Grove, which he named after his wife, Sir Walter is said to have planted the very first potato in Europe. His wife, of course, thought he should have planted it somewhere else. I don't know about you, but to me it conjures up a wonderful picture of that great Elizabethan adventurer, seafarer, explorer and, of course, writer reduced to the usual pathetic wimp cutting the grass and looking after the garden at weekends.

It is also the site of the first after-dinner cigarette. It is said that after a hard day in the garden as the old sea horse was having his first Irish fag, the maid came into the room, saw all the smoke, rushed out and immediately returned with a bucket of water which she hurled all over the two of them. Hence the strange prounciation of the town's name.

After that everything else is an anticlimax so I won't bother mentioning that Youghal also used to be famous for lace and heavy-duty cast-iron pottery, the likes of two-gallon jugs and almighty flowerpots for transplanting real live oak trees. To some people it's like Derry by the seaside. The city wall looks as though it could have come straight from up North. So too the houses along the gently curving Main Street. I couldn't tell you. Whenever I go there it seems to do nothing but rain. Not like stair rods More like scaffold poles.

Once, while I was trudging through Youghal in the middle of yet another storm, some cheery little hobbit wrapped in water proofs assured me it wasn't just raining it was 'spillin' out of the very heavens themselves, tanksbetogod'.

'Not at all,' another passing hobbit joins in. ''Tis just a damp poem it is.'

Yeah. Like *The Faerie Queene*. Whenever I read it, it brings tears to my eyes. All that work and all he got was broken-down Kilcolman Castle.

Along the coast is Cobh, pronounced Cove as in Once this was a booming, prosperous town with one of the busiest ports along the south coast but it is now covered in dust. Serves them right. As far as I can discover they've done everything they can to help people escape the place. The world's first yacht club was launched here before yachts were even invented and ocean racing introduced before oceans had ever been trained to race. The first steamship to cross the Atlantic left from here before there was anywhere to go. And the *Titanic*, this was its last port of call before it set off on its last fateful voyage. Why they keep on about it, I don't know. I would keep quiet about it if I was them. It certainly didn't make me feel like leaping aboard ship and sailing anywhere. Not even in one of their local, traditional 26-foot yawls powered not by a sail but by a towel. A towel? It conjures up all kinds of images. But don't worry. In Cove, pronounced Cobh, a towel is a sail, pronounced sale.

Come out of Cork airport and turn right and you head south for Kinsale, pronounced fabulous but fabulous food and restaurants. The first time I went there I asked the taxi driver how far it was from the airport.

'I'm not telling ye a word of a lie, sir,' he says. 'It's a good fifteen miles as the crow flies. But for you, ten.'

Ireland, they always said, had the best food in the world – until they cooked it. I can remember the old days of bacon boiled until it was as grey as a battleship, mountains of overcooked vegetables, buckets of rice pudding so thick and so stodgy it could block the River Shannon from flowing into the sea, and it took until Tuesday afternoon before you finally got the smell of fish out of the house only for the smell to come back again the following Friday.

I could never make up my mind whether I'd suffer more by eating meat on Fridays and going to hell or eating fish and having to put up with the smell for half the week. I compromised on cruibins or pickled pigs' trotters. There was definitely no meat on them and they smelt worse than fish.

Ireland: In a Glass of its Own

My God, the meals they used to slop up in the old days. They weren't exactly a grub fest. Stew that looked like an anal probe gone wrong and smelt like it as well. A – I don't know what it was – that looked like pigeon droppings. Something called the 'baste of a cow' although to me it looked like the worst of it.

'Here eat this,' my mother would say throwing the plate down on the table. ''Tis farm-fresh.'

Farm-fresh. I'd say it was farm-fresh. It looked and tasted as if it had just been scraped up off the farmyard. Even the sandwiches she made, the size of doorsteps, tasted better if you ate them in the paper bag. Ours was the only house in the street where when meals were served the dogs ran away from the table. No wonder the women would never sit down at the table and eat their food with everyone else. They were too ashamed to be associated with it.

The restaurants were no better. Although credit where credit is due. Many's the time I can remember seeing waiters and waitresses sampling the food as they brought it to the table, obviously determined to ensure it met their strict standards. Once I can remember, years ago, we asked for a jug of water to drink with the meal. That tells you how long ago it was. The spotty, greasy girl, whose thighs were so thick they had separate postcodes, brought the glasses to the table, took a sip from each of them and waddled back to the kitchen, if that's what they called it.

Did anyone complain? Not at all.

'Poor cratur,' says my old aunt. 'Must have been dying of the thirst.'

But it wasn't always the trainee staff. Sometimes the trainee customers were just as bad. Once I remember I took half of Ireland out to dinner. Everything is going fine until we all sit down around the table.

'Will ye have a cocktail?' says this middle-aged trolley dolly who had so much peroxide on her moustache my eyes were running.

'God bless you,' says one of my uncles. 'I'll be having an Irish cocktail, thanks be to God.'

Everybody else joins in. I order a couple of million Irish cocktails. Off goes the trolley dolly on three wheels.

About three days later, back she comes.

'Begging your pardon,' she says. 'But what's an Irish cocktail?'

''Tis half of whiskey,' says my uncle. 'With another half added.'

The drink taken, my uncle is now regaling the whole restaurant with his tales of yore. His wife, like wives all over the world who see their husbands enjoying themselves, keeps trying to quieten him.

'Will ye be quiet,' she says. 'You're taking inordinate portations. You're an alcoholic you are, an alcoholic hoor.'

'Not at all, woman,' he says, 'Not at all. I don't go to meetings.'

We get to the main course, some half-dead slops which wouldn't have been worthy of even a bucket.

''Tis the best I've ever had,' says another one of my old uncles. He pushes the plate to one side. 'I'll be having the rest after my dessert.'

Everybody else then does the same. Suddenly a table that was big enough for half of Ireland is now half the size. There's no room for all the plates piled high, three-quarters-piled and half-piled with whatever it was. We end up by taking over a second table, the sweet trolley and a window ledge. In spite of everything, however, it was a grand success. Everybody talked about it for weeks on end. To their doctor.

Another occasion I keep trying to forget was in Clonmel, Co. Tipp. I'm in a not particularly downmarket restaurant. There were only two or three stains on the table. For no reason at all, this gork of a kid waddles up to my table and starts rearranging the plates: some he puts on the floor, others he takes back to his parents, who are obviously non-smoking, non-drinking vegetarians, obsessed with e-numbers, with stale spinach roulard running down their chin. They do nothing. My instinct was to push my thumb through the top of the kid's head, let it play with the steak knife or give it a dose of the olive oil. I resisted the temptation. I ordered another bottle of wine, two large cognacs and sent the whole bill to the liberfreak's parents. I wish now I'd pushed my fingers through the top of its head.

Today it's all changed, nowhere more than Kinsale which unusually for an Irish town has more restaurants than bars. Serious eating

and drinking restaurants. Not your typical weddings, family celebrations and any excuse for a booze-up restaurants. They even
have one or two restaurants which throw a hooley if anyone dares
to even hint that maybe, perhaps food should play any kind of
part in a balanced diet.

The French, of course, are responsible. They first discovered
Kinsale on a bitter winter morning in 1601. Then the Spanish. They
landed there under Don Juan del Aquila and saw off the O'Neills
and the O'Donnells. Go for a walk. They say you can still find the
bones, if not the bones some of the old musket bullets fired in
the course of the battle.

The following year the English fought back. It was one of the
most decisive battles in Irish history. Ireland would never be the
same again. It was the end of Gaelic civilisation. The English were
in. The Irish were out. The English language was in. The Irish language
was out. From then on it was going to be landowner and peasant,
loyalist and rebel, Protestant and Catholic. To rub the Irish Catholic
noses in it even more the English shipped out all their Irish oak trees
to repair the roof of their Protestant English Westminster Abbey.

The first governor of the first English fort in Co. Cork, Colonel
Warrender, had an obviously feisty daughter called Wilful. Wilful
marries Sir Trevor Ashurst. The wedding ceremony over she
decides she would like nothing more than some of the wild flowers
growing on the rocks below the fortress as a posy, the way young
brides do. Sir Trevor hesitates to climb down and get them for
her, obviously eager to conserve his energies for duties yet to
come. Instead a young sentry offers to climb down and fetch them
providing Sir Trev. stands in for him while he is gone. Off goes
the young sentry who, of course, slips and falls to his death. Sir
Trev. in the sentry's hat and coat grows tired of waiting and falls
asleep. Along comes Colonel Warrender who thinks he is the
sentry and promptly shoots him for falling asleep on the job.
Which must have been the last thing he intended. The Colonel
realises he's shot his own son-in-law of just a couple of hours,
shoots himself. Wilful realises she has been responsible for the
death of three innocent men all for the sake of a bunch of flowers,
throws herself off the cliff.

It would make a good opera if it wasn't so funny.

Talking of strange stories, it was also from here in 1703 Alexander Selkirk sailed around the Cinque Ports, was shipwrecked on the almost deserted island of Juan Fernandez in the Pacific and ended up as Robinson Crusoe. Not that anybody would feel it worthwhile turning it into an opera let alone a book. Not enough action.

Only a few years ago Kinsale was a huddle of streets, back lanes and what they used to call 'antique pathways'. With no water supply. Today, it's big-time. It's five stars. It's the gastronomic centre of Ireland. Full of fashionable, very fashionable restaurants. Tell anyone a few years ago you could eat better in Ireland than you could in many places in France, they'd have thrown their berets and striped sweaters in your face. Not any more. Kinsale is up there with the best of them.

The best thing of all, the Irish being the Irish, the restaurants compete not to see who can attract the best possible guests but who can turn them away. One restaurant I stumbled into, no booking, no reservation, no nothing was boasting they had just turned away Fergie, the Duchess of Thing for no other reason than that she was Fergie, the Duchess of Thing.

'Don't you be worrying yourself now,' says the waiter. 'We've turned away lots of important people as well in our time.'

Not that it hasn't been a struggle. When they first started, all the locals were against them. They thought it outrageous to devote so much time and money to lobster and champagne. What's wrong, they said, with the usual bacon and cabbage? Or even an Irish stew?

'They used to tear the claws off the crab and throw the rest back in the sea,' one French-Irish chef told me.

Now it's venison with cherry poteen jus, oyster sausages, fish poached in milk, carpaccio of wild salmon from the River Blackwater, so thin it's like a skin graft, duck, blackened shark with banana ketchup, hand-reared mutton and pork from the restaurant's own farm. I eat the lot. As far as I'm concerned cutting out cholesterol does a fat lot of good.

I was in a traditional Irish restaurant once in Kinsale. I could tell it was traditional. All the Irish were sitting there in their hats and coats. The waiter asked me if I wanted olive bread. I said, 'Yes. Please. Make a change from white sliced.'

He says, 'Green or black?'

Not that the menus don't have an Irish flavour.

'There are a lot of game birds in the area,' an Italian chef told me.

Obviously another one of its attractions.

The prices also seem to match their menus. Pubs and bars are good value. But try any decent-looking restaurant with tables and chairs, an Australian serving at table with torn jeans and tattoos in all kinds of unlikely places and you're looking at €200 maybe €300 for two. That's just the basic three courses plus an ordinary bottle of wine. Hit out at a salmon hand-caught in the restaurant's private lake by a brown bear with an Irish accent you'd need a second mortgage or at least one of those scam Irish companies which helps you avoid paying VAT.

The most expensive meal I think I ever had in Ireland was not, however, in Kinsale. It was in Dublin. Near St Stephen's Green. It was all Georgian splendour and crisp white tablecloths. As I was going in I heard a big hoogle-head of an Irish businessman with a thick Caribbean tan say, 'Nobody comes here any more. You can't get a table.' Trouble was the place was run by a herd of Australian dinks and porkers in upmarket torn jeans with even more intricate tattoos on parts of the body you normally only ever see referred to on menus, who judging by their colour had been overdosing on betacarotene additives. It cost me one arm and two legs. But it was worth it. Every time the food arrived from the kitchen the Australian students would whisk it behind the serving table, take a big mouthful, rearrange the food on the plate and serve it to a grateful customer with an even greater flash of their tattoos. At the end of the meal I asked one of the tiny Irish wait-resses – she was obviously not getting her share of the food from the punters' plates – if I could have a black coffee.

'Will ye have milk and tay in it?' she says.

Obviously continuing a great Irish tradition.

West Cork isn't just West Cork. It virtually sees itself as a complete, entire, self-contained world in its own right. Ask someone from Mallow where they are from and they will say Mallow. Ask someone for Youghal and they will say Youghal. Ask someone from, say, Ballinspittle, and they will say West Cork with as much pride as Texans used to boast they were from Texas until they discovered George Bush was from there as well.

West Cork is not really West Cork but North-West Cork, West Cork, South-West Cork and everything in between. Ask a Corkman where, for example, Clonakilty is and he'll tell you either where it always has been or in West Cork even though the whole world can see it's on the south coast. If he's from Clonakilty himself, he'll go on and on about their black puddings or drisheens which they maintain are the best in the world. Better than French black pudding. Better than Spanish black pudding. Better than Greek black pudding. I must admit I'm inclined to agree. That black pudding pizza I once had in Clonakilty is something I shall never forget.

But whatever they call it, everyone agrees West Cork is poor land. Nothing but bogs and mountains apart from the bit around Bandon, Clonakilty and Skibbereen. The reason, they tell you, is the English. When the English crushed the Irish at the Battle of Kinsale, they swept across the country murdering and killing as they went. The Irish fled their homes and farms and made for the woods and the bogs. The English took over their homes and farms. But didn't know how to work them. The countryside never recovered.

West Cork was also one of the worst-affected areas hit by the famine. People in their thousands just lay down and died. Others dragged themselves and their families in desperation to Clonakilty hoping to find food, relief, room in the workhouse. Others struggled on to Cobh to try and board a ship and escape to America. Which makes it even more ironic that today it's known for its good food and restaurants.

My starting point is always Kinsale. Well, why not? Any excuse or another game bird.

First stop is Ballinspittle, home of the famous moving statue of the Blessed Virgin. Moving? Only because it wanted out of a place with such an absurd name as Ballinspittle.

431

Ireland: In a Glass of its Own

From there I take the coast road. I don't know why but along the coast houses used to be furnished with deckchairs marked 'A Deck', 'B Deck' or 'C Deck', cupboards and wardrobes with ships' names all over them and the wildest variety of boots and shoes anyone could imagine. Once or twice, I've even been offered far better wine and cognac than they have even in Kinsale. And always a grand vintage. Funny that. Apart from their famous black pudding, Clonakilty is also the birthplace of that other famous Irish legend, Michael Collins, whose guerrilla war against the British forced Lloyd George to the negotiating table. Some say he won the war against the Black and Tans but then lost it at the negotiating table when he signed the Anglo–Irish Treaty giving independence to the 26 counties and an opt out to the six Protestant Ulster counties. The Irish then split. Within weeks they were fighting each other. Half for the Treaty. Half against.

Glandore is paradise on earth. It's peaceful. It's quiet. It's got fantastic views over the sea as well as the countryside. It's got a whole string of big, expensive houses. It's also got two harbours: Adam and Eve. Adam, they say, is fine, hard-working, pleasant, willing to tackle anything. Eve is problems, ruins everything, never prepared to take the blame, was the first woman in history to eat her husband out of house and home. But then what do you expect? She was created on a Friday afternoon.

Skibbereen is known as the Wigan Pier of Ireland. Why, I have no idea. It's friendly. It's pleasant. You can understand what people say. There are no miserable retired Malayan policemen moping around. To me, however, it's Irish R.M. territory, the land of Somerville, Edith Somerville and Ross, Martin Ross, the two greatest writers in the English language. They're not just funny, they're hilarious. They are every funny writer in the world and more. The characters are fabulous. The situations are absurd but believable. The language, the style is beautiful. *Hamlet*? Forget it. *The Faerie Queene*? Are you out of your mind? Dr Johnson? Come on. Are you talking literature or literature?

When Somerville was not riding out with the West Carbery Hunt twice a week, breeding and breaking in hunters and sending them off to her cousin, Mrs Sylvia Warner, in Boston to sell at a grand price she was scribbling short stories about the life and riding times of Major Sinclair Yeates, an Irish Resident Magistrate. These she sent to Ross. Ross changed, amended, approved them. The result: the most hilarious series of short stories ever. Even funnier, even more hilarious than the British government's justification for invading Iraq.

Not everybody, however, agrees with me. A few say – steady now, this could be something of a shock – Skibbereen is not funny/hilarious at all. Long gone are the days when you'd put three shovels in a corner and ask an Irishman to take his pick. Skibbereen is serious, boring, mathematical. It saw the invention of the computer. Well why not? Skibbereen has never been one to flinch from its international responsibilities. The local newspaper, the *Skibbereen Eagle* once famously warned the Tsar that they would be keeping a close eye on his actions. A local accountant with the unlikely name of Percy Ludgate invented a machine that could do everything a computer can do. His genius was recognised immediately by the British government. During World War I he was one of a group of experts charged with the awesome responsibility of supplying oats to horses out in the front lines.

From the high-tech world of Skibbereen I head across country to Bantry Bay, one of the largest natural harbours in the world.

People moan about the oil tanks on Whiddy Island, right opposite Bantry. But in fairness, which is something I hate being, they don't really make that much difference. First, you can barely see them. They're practically buried. Second, the rest of the scenery is so spectacular you hardly notice them. Thackeray raved about the place when he was there. 'Were such a bay lying upon an English shore, it would be the world's wonder,' he said. It's still the same today. They also serve fantastic mussels.

From Bantry I head for the Cork, sorry the West Cork side of the Beara Peninsula, as in I cannot beara the other two. This is the best one.

I start off at Glengariff, a long, thin, almost anorexic town.

At Adrigole you can either turn right over the mountains or stick to the coast road. I always stick to the coast road. Through Curryglass on to Castletownbere with its fishing boats and processing plants. I can smell it a mile away. This is O'Sullivan country. Practically everyone you meet is called O'Sullivan. On to Ballydonegan and its grand beach. Then the old copper mine at Allihies which was run by Cornishmen because they had the experience and the Irish did not. Now the road zigzags like mad. Go too fast you could be over the sheer drop and a memory in no time at all. At Eyeries, I take the road to Kenmare which is not in West Cork at all but in Co. Kerry. But it's a good place to stop.

That's the sea coast route. Sometimes if I'm pushed for time I take the inland route. From Kinsale – well, why not? those game birds – I head back to Cork city and then strike west to Bandon, short for Abandoned, which even today is a tiny Protestant enclave where they used to say even the pigs were Protestant. Not any longer. They're sliced rashers in a million BLT sandwiches by now. Bandon was once a thriving mini-industrial town. It had cotton mills, a corduroy factory, a woollen mill as well as several big rope makers. But technology changed. They failed to keep pace. From 2000 weavers in the mid-1800s, within ten years there were just 30. They were driven to drink. Within practically another 10 years they had three distilleries, four breweries as well as a whole host of companies supplying the drinks business. But then – shock, horror, especially in Ireland – the drinks business collapsed. Their next phase of expansion: pawnshops. By the end of the nineteenth century they had over a dozen of them.

But whether you take the coastal route or the inland route or just pig out in Kinsale, you're bound to have a Corkin' good time. I always do.

The Soft, White, Creamy, Frothy Counties

Co. Dublin
Co. Antrim
Co. Clare

The one. The ultimate. The pinnacle. That soft, white, creamy froth that makes the black stuff the black stuff. In some places in the world I won't mention they actually do everything they can to avoid serving it with the froth on top. But then Americans are like that. Not in Boston. There they are civilised. Well, almost. But in the likes of Vermont or North Dakota or the sophisticated heights of Billings, Montana, 207-year-old tanorexic Trixie the barmaid, I mean, the senior social liquor consumption coordinator, actually apologised for it.

'Gee I'm sorry, sir. I tried to avoid getting that stuff on top but I couldn't help it. What is it? Some kind of scum. If you like I can change it for a Coke. Compliments of the house.'

Thank you. And drop dead.

On the other hand I've been in bars in Africa, across eastern Europe, even in the middle of Mongolia where they've served the perfect pint. Not always, I will admit, as smooth, as silky, as in Ashford Castle, Co. Mayo. Sometimes they haven't given it as long to settle as they do in Ireland. But nevertheless the answer to any prayer. Especially if you've just come back from three months dragging yourself across the Sahara, three weeks drowning your sorrows in vodka on the Trans-Siberian Express or three minutes with the in-laws. Sometimes there's just not the slightest drop dribbling down the outside of the glass. Sometimes there's not a shamrock etched in the froth or better still the barmaid's telephone number. No, Trixie. Thank you very much. Just the black stuff, please. Thank you.

The counties Dublin, Antrim and Clare are like that. They're the froth on the top of the pint. But there's nothing frothy – unimportant, irrelevant, insignificant – about them.

Dublin has to be one of the best capital cities in the world. There's a lot to be said for the likes of downtown Phnom Penh and the back streets of Ashgabat, I admit, but Dublin still beats the lot of them. Not just on a Friday or Saturday night. All the week long. All the year round. From 17 March through to 16 March.

Co. Antrim is one of the great undiscovered delights of Ireland. It has the scenery. The drama. The people.

Co. Clare, I admit, I have a soft spot for. My mother came from there. From Ballynacally. It was the first place I went to in Ireland. I have uncles and aunts and cousins and the Lord knows who else, all over the place. I've criss-crossed it a million times. Each time with as much fun as the previous.

The history of Ireland is the same. They've had all the agony and the heartache. Now they're experiencing the froth.

If there's a time when you can distinguish Ireland without the froth and Ireland with the froth it's 1959 when it became the modern, present-day Republic of Ireland.

Before it was inward-looking, farming-orientated, very much Church-dominated. In schools, children studied the three R's. Reading. Riting. Religion. Ireland had endured the hard stuff for too long. They needed the froth. Poor de Valéra. Out went his dream of Ireland as a land whose countryside would be bright with cosy homesteads, the home of a people living the life God desired men should live where nobody earnt more than £1000 a year, where 'the sturdy children, the athletic youths, the comely maidens' would be satisfied with frugal comfort, make their firesides 'forums for the wisdom of serene old age' and devote their leisure to 'things of the spirit' in a nation that has stood alone 'not for one year, or two, but for several hundred years against aggression; that endured spoliation, famines, massacres in endless succession; that was clubbed many times into insensibility, but each time on regaining consciousness took up the fight anew; a small nation that could never be got to accept defeat and has never surrendered her soul.'

The Soft, White, Creamy, Frothy Counties

I can remember the old days. Dinner was lunchtime. Supper was dinner time. And breakfast was half a bottle of whiskey and a drop of hot water to keep out the cold. The bars were so filthy they threw sawdust on the floor to brighten them up, The sawdust was, of course, the previous night's furniture. The nearest thing to a slimline tonic was to drink your Guinness in halves. To keep it chilled, you'd put a bottle in a sock and dangle it for hours on end in a ditch or a stream or the mighty River Shannon itself. Walk down the street. Everyone but everyone would be greeted with a ''Tis a grand day, glory be to God.' A doff of the cap. A quick salute. Catch a train. Get a seat. It wasn't so much a matter of getting from A to B as keeping somebody else's chewing gum warm and soft and pliable. If you told lies, you'd get a spot on your tongue. A cut or a burn would be cured with the lick of the tongue – provided the tongue had first licked the back of a lizard. Saturday nights unless you chanced upon Dessie, who was a great gas, the only excitement in town was standing outside the funeral parlour, hoping to get an invitation to view the body. The first sign of summer was being able to buy a newspaper at 8 o'clock in the morning, being able to check out of a hotel before 9 o'clock and hearing that delightful sound of the dustbin men on their early-morning round about 12 noon. Except hear it first in your left ear and it meant you'll have nothing but bad luck; in the right, you'll probably win the pools. But how you can make your right ear the first to hear them let alone tell which ear heard them nobody could tell me. Crows were another matter. See any number of them standing on the roof of your house, it would be the Holy Rosary virtually non-stop for days on end because crows on the roof meant there was going to be a death in the house before long. Although, again, nobody could tell me how long long was. Then when you died your soul would fly out of your mouth like a bee. Fairies, however, were a far more important matter. To stop them from kidnapping you and carrying you off, the only possible hope was to keep the house full of dirty washing. Well that's what my mother said and I always believed what my mother said. Well, up to a point.

I was once in Ennis, Co. Clare. I was leaning up against the door of the newsagent's at around nine o'clock in the morning.

'Goodness me,' I said when the old scratchankle finally tottered down and opened the door. ''Tis easier to get in to see the Pope himself than to get through the door of your shop to buy a copy of the *Irish Independent*.'

You have to speak like that in Ireland otherwise they pretend they don't understand what you are saying.

The old biddy looked straight in my bloodshot eyes.

'Let God have his way,' she says.

A similar thing happened to me in Birr, Co. Offaly. Another newsagent's shop. Again it's gone nine o'clock.

'When God made time,' the broken-down old fox-hunter says, 'he made a lot of it.'

Not that the Irish are superstitious. Drop the wedding ring on the floor or, strangely enough, if an old dog licks a bride's ring it will mean bad luck. Work any week of the year with a Friday in it, bad luck. Get married any day of the week, bad luck.

When Sean Lemass took over as Prime Minister or Taoiseach from de Valéra he gave them the froth of their life. A new modern Ireland. New modern ideas. He opened Ireland up to the outside world. Ireland became Oireland. Paddy became Paddywhackery. The crucifix on the wall gave way to iodine tablets. While the rest of the world was concentrating on the Cold War, the Bomb, nuclear proliferation, the government in a bid to ensure salvation for the Irish people from nuclear attack distributed one iodine tablet to every household in the country even though medical experts maintained the tablets were only beneficial to children; they would only protect you from iodine absorption and no other aspect of nuclear fallout and what good was one tablet per household anyway? On the other hand, I suppose, one shouldn't criticise. It was better than in this country where the chairman of the Health Protection Agency, Sir William Stewart maintained that if 'we are to combat the avoidable spread of infection there is no substitute for regular hand washing'.

The result, the Irish economy boomed. Out went the ass and cart let alone the pony and trap. In came the Celtic Tiger. Ireland became the greatest country in the world created by the love of God and an unending supply of funds from the European Union.

The Soft, White, Creamy, Frothy Counties

Down came all the old traditional thatched cottages. In came modern Spanish-style bungalows. With electricity.

'Dandruff in the hairy armpit of the Glen' were the immortal words of Cathal O Searcaigh, in his famous poem 'A Runaway Cow'.

The larger bungalows turned out to be hotels equipped with all the latest facilities including no end of high-tech computerised safes with every built-in security facility imaginable – except they were invariably so small you could pick them up, put them in your briefcase and wander out with them without anybody noticing.

Farms went bust. Families left the land. In came new, modern industry. Suddenly God-fearing little old ladies who when they had married had sat up all night waiting for their sexual relations to arrive or as they had got older were contemplating a hysterectomy because they didn't want any more grandchildren were devoting their lives to satisfying the ever-increasing worldwide demand for Viagra. Take a deep breath anywhere within 100 miles of Ringaskiddy, Co. Cork, it was said, and not only were the criminals likely to become more hardened, old men suddenly were no longer liable to fall out of bed. It was not only the bedroom doors that had knobs on. The only things unaffected by the factory were the local badgers. They were already rampant.

I didn't follow every twist and turn but to some the fumes were symbolic. To others they were heaven scent. Not only did their attitudes harden, they also stiffened their resolve. More than anything they brought a new meaning to the not too Irish phrase hard at work.

One evening in a nearby bar, I met one young sore back who looked as though he suffered from chronic fatigue syndrome. He told me he worked for a 'mighty grand conglamourate'. When he first started at the factory he was invited to tea by every spinster and not a few married women in the parish. When the house was empty, of course. But the demand was there no longer.

'It has fallen off,' he told me. 'The Lord have mercy on us.'

For his sake, I hope the Lord has mercy on him.

I asked him if he had thought of suing.

''Tis an idea,' he says. 'D'ye tink it will stand up in court?'

We were joined by one of his mates who looked as though his future was all behind him. As a result of working in the factory, he told me he was now homophobic.

'To me,' he says, 'women are like churches. I'm glad they're there. But I don't particularly want to go in them any more.'

I made a limp excuse and left.

The Sean Lemass revolution rolled on. Out went the family rosary. In came television, refrigerators, cars. In spite of their new-found wealth some say the Irish deliberately left their messy, dirty, untidy litter all over the place, grass uncut, hedges scraggly, thorn-bushes wild, gates coming off their hinges, houses desperate for a lick of paint. It was part of their culture. In the old days if they cleaned the place up, made everything neat and tidy then along would come the wicked English landlord or worse still his agent and put up their rent. Admittedly today there are no English land-lords but it takes them a long time to get out of the habit of keeping everything scruffy and dirty.

But what amazes me is that today there are fewer and fewer farms, the farmers are supposed to be making less and less money but the roads are choked with more and more tractors. It doesn't make sense. The only reason I can imagine and I say this as someone who has driven the length and breadth of the country a million times, is that unknown to us the Irish National Farmers' Union is running some secret competition to see which farmer can collect the longest possible tailback behind his tractor. That farmer doesn't just get his EU subsidy but a bonus to enable him to build yet another Spanish-style bungalow complete with garage – for his tractor. His four-style kiss-and-tell Mercedes, he leaves outside in the rain and the snow.

Thanks to EU subsidies, both official and unofficial, things may not have turned out quite the way they planned. Gaelic is still the 'first national language', at least according to the Constitution, but it is only spoken by around 20,000 people in and around Connemara in the far west and in Dublin by taxi drivers on Friday nights looking for an excuse not to go to the airport.

Irish politicians and diplomats are now strutting their stuff on both the European and the world stage. They are pressing the flesh, wheeling and dealing, brokering deals, getting locked in their own embassies for weekends on end unable to escape and printing a series of stamps to commemorate the enlargement of the European Union and moving Cyprus a couple of hundred miles to the west just so it would fit their design. 'Cartographer's licence', they called it. Yeah, what would they have called it if Cyprus published a series of stamps and moved Eire a couple of hundred miles to the east or, worse still, to the north?

Not that it would ever be front-page news in Ireland. In Ireland front-page news is a 75-year-old statue of St Columba having its head knocked off by vandals and the local priest appealing for its return and again six days later it being returned in a plastic bag mysteriously left for passers-by to discover in a nearby garden. When they do print a political story it is either to reassure people that the introduction of a new distribution system by the Post Office means that Christmas cards are guaranteed to arrive by 2 January at the latest or, as in the case of the once prestigious *Irish Times*, a major policy statement by the minister of finance, Mr McGreevy, in banner headlines on the front page. Except his name was spelt McCreevy. Social stories tend to be stories about breast cancer accompanied by photographs of the journalists appearing topless. What photographs accompany the articles about testicular cancer I shudder to think.

Not that words are important. Words mean what they choose them to mean. Neither more. Nor less. All over the country vans and lorries are advertising Duff Products. Coffe is someone who is Coughed upon. Gargoyle is an olive-flavoured mouthwash. Willy-nilly means the poor man will not be contributing to the country's population growth. A convenience store is one that never opens. Distances are measured in kilometres. Speed limits are displayed in miles per hour. Warning signs are written back to front: Down Slow, Lane In Get. Wheelchair cabs are considered buses and charged almost double the toll rate for taxis. Ambulances with seriously ill patients on board are clamped at Dublin airport. Caesarean operations take place on women after they've given birth. For over 30 years the government illegally charged old people staying in public nursing homes. Patients are buried before death certificates are issued. Bus Eireann, the national bus company, officially announces bus crashes injuring eleven people, two seriously that never took place and a BMW man is a part-time farmer from the Border, Midlands and West Counties making a fortune out of subsidies from the European Union.

But in spite of everything, Ireland is still a Christian country. Traditional Christmas cribs are still on display in the windows of betting shops in Listowel, Co. Kerry, in February. Marriage is still considered so sacred that front-page advertisements in newspapers offer to send by return of post '3/4-inch heels, really beautiful, satin toe shoes, size 3–8 to brides getting married in Barbados'. Ask an Irishman the time, he'll still say, 'Between going to mass and coming back.'

At least I think its still Christian. Gone are all the old simplicities. Priests no longer talk about things such as work, it's a 'poetic of growth'. Landscape is no longer landscape, it's the 'ultimate where'. Animals no longer live in the open, they live 'outside the politics of human intention'. If a species disappears, 'we diminish the vocabulary of our own unconsciousness'.

My God. The Penny Catechism was nothing like this.

But of all the countries I've visited in the world – so far, a meagre 190 – Ireland is still, in spite of everything, my favourite. To its success and prosperity I'll for ever raise my glass. Of Guinness, of course. Anything else would be an insult. I love it. It's the best pint of Guinness in the world.

God bless.

Co. Dublin
The joyciest of all joyciest joycities in the world

Pope lands at Dublin airport. Met by big car and chauffeur.

'Tell you what,' says the Pope to the chauffeur, 'Ireland is a safe country. I'll drive. You sit in the back.'

Pope is doing 100mph along motorway to Dublin. He is stopped by the police. Policeman calls Police HQ.

'I've just stopped this car speeding to Dublin,' he says.

'Book him,' says Police HQ.

'But I think it's someone important,' says the policeman. 'I think its . . . God.'

'God,' says Police HQ. 'What makes you say that?'

'Well,' says the policeman. 'He's being driven by the Pope.'

Co. Antrim
Big Ian's territory. He thinks

Famous local resident
Big Ian

Favourite food
Whatever Big Ian eats

Favourite drink
Guinness. But don't tell Big Ian

Favourite pub
My God. Never go near such dens of iniquity

Favourite restaurant
Whichever one he says

What to say
I agree. I agree. I agree

What not to say
You hit me again, I'll call the Pope

The froth always rises to the top. And Co. Antrim, a late joiner to the Six, which promotes itself as 'an area of amazing contrasts' – they can say that again – will always rise to the top. For spectacular landscape and scenery, Co. Antrim is – shh, it's a secret – up there with the likes of Co. Kerry, Co. Galway and the Comeragh Mountains in the north of Co. Waterford. Some say it has one of the loveliest coast roads in Europe. Better than anything France or Italy or even Croatia has to offer. It's just that people don't know about it.

It's also home to Ireland's one and only dinosaur – no, not him; their first armaments factory; one of their greatest archaeological sites; the deadly, soul-destroying banhe, the red-headed fairy woman who from what I can gather is a cross between a guardian angel and a mother-in-law who does nothing but follow you around all your life moaning and making things worse. And, of course, to bigotry, hatred and violence. Because – another secret Co. Antrim tries to keep to itself – it's also home to Belfast which I always think is unfair. Belfast being, well, Belfast, it should be either on its own or shared between Co. Antrim and Co. Down. The burden is too much for one county to bear.

To Catholics however, Co. Antrim – short for 'And trim your hair. You're not coming in a Protestant church with your hair down to your shoulders looking like . . .' well, never mind – was always known as the Black North. Which is wrong. They should have called it the Tartan North. But there you are, nobody listens to me. The best job a Catholic could look forward to in Co. Antrim, they used to say, was pulling down a Protestant church and being paid for it.

To Protestants it was known as – I have no idea. I can hardly understand their accent let alone what they are saying. Fit, I know, is foot. Shae is shoe. Staived your aankle is sprained your ankle. Sut doon is sit down. Beekin in the soon is baking in the sun. Tatie-hokers is potato pickers. And whuskey is whiskey. So, 'I put ma fit in ma shae. I staived ma aankle. I had to sut doon, beekin in the soon with the tatie-hokers drinkin the whuskey' means – I don't know what the hell it means. Read it again with a slow booming voice. You'll see what I mean.

> Gunman leaps on top of another man, puts a gun to his head.
>
> 'Are you a Catholic or a Protestant?'
>
> The man doesn't know what to say in case he says the wrong thing. He says, 'I'm a Jew.'
>
> The gunman says, 'Are you a Catholic Jew or a Protestant Jew?'
>
> Man says, 'No. No. I'm just a Jew.'
>
> Gunman says, 'Great. I'm the luckiest Arab in Belfast tonight.'

Whun I furst, I mean, when I first went to Belfast at the height of the Troubles, there were bars and grills all over the place. Everybody looked and dressed the same. Drab. Miserable. Everywhere there were bricked-up houses. Barricades. Broken glass. Rubbish. Litter all over the place. Kids playing in the rubbish. Flags flying everywhere. Union Jacks. Irish flags. Wherever you looked there were mysterious strangers from all over the world. It was like eastern Europe at the height or rather the depths of the Cold War. Correction. It was worse than eastern Europe at the depths of the Cold War. It was the UK. It was peacetime. Ordinary people were saying and doing the most unbelievable things to each other and to each other's families. Meetings would take place in dark, empty, mysterious rooms and hallways and even that room where women bang and crash about trying to warm up the packets of frozen food for a meal. I lost count of the number of times I was collected at Belfast International Airport and immediately driven deep into the countryside. To tiny, mysterious places. In strange-looking villages. Where everyone spoke in a pronounced whisper and had a strange habit of continually looking over their shoulders.

''Tis shocking. 'Tis a terrible business the war,' one old man with a deep fearless accent used to bawl at me. 'But 'tis better than no war at all.'

He would then reel off lists of who was Catholic, who was Protestant, like it was the Northern Ireland football results:

Stormont Castle. Porters: 31. Protestants: 30. Catholics: 1.

Ministry of Agriculture. Porters: 109. Protestants: 105. Catholics: 4.

And so on.

Protestants were the same. Well, almost. I remember one Grand Master of one very Grand Lodge. If he wasn't, he looked like one. The bowler hat looked as though it had been on his head since the day he was born. If not before. The black suit. The shiny boots ready to crush anything that came their way.

'Protestants must employ Protestants,' he would roar. 'One Catholic employee is one vote less for the Protestants.'

His sidekick, who had a smaller head but a bigger bowler hat, blamed it all on the press.

'Until they came along and started putting it on their front pages and in their news bullytins, we never had any problems,' he shouted. 'They have a lot to answer for.'

He was right. On the flight back, I picked up the local newspaper. There was an advert, 'Wanted. Man and woman to look after two cows. Both Protestant.'

Even at the sordid commercial level there was rivalry between the two sides.

Catholics were selling British army maps to Belfast showing all the Protestant areas, the homes of all the big Protestant trouble-makers, suspected snipers' locations and ammunition stores.

Protestants were selling British army maps of Belfast showing all the Catholic areas, the homes of all the big Catholic trouble-makers, suspected snipers' locations and ammunition stores.

Both sides were also offering guided tours, quick chats with the local neighbourhood sniper, in-depth briefings with the head honchos.

I didn't bother. I was getting all my information on the 07.25 train from Buxted arriving Victoria 08.50, 09.15, 09.25, 10.43 or whenever. In fact, I think one train has still yet to arrive.

Throughout the height of the Troubles there was hardly anything I didn't know about the British government's secret activities in Northern Ireland. And I mean secret.

Most days of the week when I wasn't being forced to drag myself around the world desperately trying to earn a living, I would travel up to the office by train with an old military man – 'HHC. You know, what!' – who was a barrister and part-time judge. He would complain about being picked up from his home at night by car, flown to various places in Northern Ireland to preside over one court after another and flown back again early the following morning.

'Secret courts?' I would casually ask him.

'My dear chap,' he would bellow back at me.

'But did you hear the evidence before you pronounced sentence?'

'My dear fellow.' He would practically burst a blood vessel. 'You don't understand. We all went to Oxford together. We've all been barristers together. I read the evidence. I know that if old Jeremy says that's the case that's the case. No need to go over it all again. I make my decision. That's it.'

By now, of course, half the carriage would be awake and pretending to read their newspapers.

'So why do they use you?' I would ask. 'Why don't they use local judges?'

'Local judges, local judges,' he would bluster. 'Local judges wouldn't have the courage to pass the proper sentence. That's why they need an outsider like me. Objective. Dedicated to the truth. Sense of justice.'

As the Troubles got worse, the less I used to see him. Unfortunately he also became increasingly deaf. As a result when I did see him he was not only passing on secret, confidential information to me but to the whole carriage as well.

'Poor old Maurice. They got him. Higgins was lucky. They attacked his house. Missed him. Donald was also lucky. But it's shaken them I can tell you.'

'You'll be busy then?'

'Off again tonight.'

'No rest for the wicked.'

'You must come and have lunch with me at the HHC when I get back.'

Maurice was Sir Maurice Gibson, Lord Chief Justice of Northern Ireland. Higgins was Sir Eoin Higgins. Donald was Donald Murray, a Northern Ireland judge.

'Frightful fuss the other night. The Redcaps caught Maurice with one of his little boys. They'll keep him on though. Best man for the job, what?'

This time Maurice was Sir Maurice Oldfield. Some said he used to run MI6. Some said he was the original Smiley of John le Carré fame. Mrs Thatcher appointed him security coordinator for Northern Ireland. He was the man, they say, who first established the behind-the-scenes links between the British government and the IRA throughout the whole of the Troubles. It was said if he had a preference for anything it was for the rough trade.

'Met old Jimbo the other night. Couple of pints in the mess. He's in something called FOO or FROO or FRUIT or something. Having a splendid time. Thoroughly enjoying himself.'

'What's it? Something to do with the courts, judges. That kind of thing?'

'No. Frightfully secret. Research.'

'You mean spying.'

'Yes. He's got all these military types. They're trying to identify the real troublemakers. The leaders. They want to look after them.'

'You mean guard them, protect them . . . ?'

'Talk of starting a laundry.'

'What, for the military?'

'No. The public.'

'The public?'

'Reckon it will enable them to detect traces of explosives on people's clothes. Good idea, what.'

'Look. Are you free next week for lunch, what?'

FOO, FROO, FRUIT was FRU, the mysterious army research unit that reports say worked alongside the RUC Special Branch and selected different targets and then turned the other way if anything happened to them.

'Ashford. Been to Ashford. Very interesting.'

'You mean Leeds Castle. Yes. I know, I've been . . .'

'No, the Intelligence Corps. They're at Ashford. They're teaching their chaps to speak with Irish accents. Top of the morning to you. Thanks a million. That kind of thing. Damned good some of them. They also showed me how to break into a car. They call it a Slim Jim. You can be in in a couple of seconds. Damned good, what. Now how about lunch?'

Ashford was the secret home of the Army Intelligence Corps. They trained military intelligence officers as well as military intelligence liaison officers.

Then there was the occasional ominous note in his conversation.

'Not staying up in town for the next couple of weeks are you?' he would bellow secretly across the carriage.

'Wasn't planning to. Why? Any reason?'

'No, just thought I'd ask. Maybe later we'll have lunch or something at the HHC.'

Within weeks bombs would be going off all over London.

Towards the end he became very weak, very doddery. He shrank to about half his size. He still wore the same black suit, black bowler, carried the same black umbrella.

'Just do the odd job now and then,' he would say.

Go back to Belfast today and it's all changed. The bars and grills are no longer on the front of heavily armoured army trucks driving slowly down the middle of the street. People no longer wear bala-clava helmets, flak jackets and big boots although many of them would be doing themselves a favour if they did. People still pour in from all over the world. But they're no longer surgeons, burns specialists, physios and experts on rebuilding kneecaps.

Not that Belfast is short of expertise. When it comes to break-throughs in medical technology and violence Belfast leads the world. Wilhelm Röntgen discovered X-rays in December 1895. Two months later Dr Cecil Shaw used X-rays in Belfast to detect the location of a bullet in the hand of a man who, of course, said he shot himself by accident while cleaning the gun. On 28 February 1896 the *Lancet* printed the radiograph of the man's injury. You couldn't make it up could you?

Belfast, however, is now a party town. Every night. All night. Hen nights. Stag nights. Any night of the week excuse to party nights. It's even better, some people slur, than Dublin. I didn't disagree. It might be all boozin' and everything else but you still don't do you? Don't want to give those doctors any more work to do, do we?

My first visit to Belfast, I remember, was straightforward. I was all set to fly direct. The obvious thing to do. Then, I don't know why, I thought it would be better to build myself up to it. First I thought I'd do the countryside. Then Belfast. Go to Belfast first I might never want to leave it even if it was only half as good as they said. Or, of course, I might never be able to leave it.

It was the right decision. Which is rare for me. So I keep being told. Co. Kerry has the Ring of Kerry. Co. Antrim has the Antrim Coast Road. Over 30 kilometres of cliff-hugging coast road. Tiny villages. Breathtaking views. On a clear day you can even catch a glimpse of Scotland. Fabulous. Stop off at every bar you come across. You'll never want to go home again.

Inland the Glens of Antrim are a series of nine valleys. But these are not the narrow valleys you find in Scotland. They're Northern Ireland valleys. Big. Imposing. Wild. Further inland it's not quite so interesting apart from Ballymena, sorry I should have said **BALLYMENA**, home to the **BIG MAN HIMSELF. THE SHY. THE QUIET. THE UNASSUMING MR PAISLEY. LEADER OF THE IRISH FREE**

Ireland: In a Glass of its Own

PRESBYTERIANS or BIG IAN AS HE IS KNOWN AROUND HERE. From the moment you drive into town YOU KNOW THAT IT IS HIS COUNTRY. For flying on the lamp-posts are UNION JACKS, THE OFFICIAL FLAG OF OUR OWN DEAR MOTHERLAND, FOR WHICH WE WILL STAND AND FIGHT, GIVE OUR BLOOD AND OUR LIVES TO UPHOLD AND PRESERVE.

Now whenever I get the chance I drive up from Derry and take the coast road all the way round to Belfast. Out of season it's slow, quiet. Apart from Sundays when THE BIG MAN IS PREACHING. And if THE BIG MAN IS PREACHING, everybody BUT EVERY-BODY, EVERY ONE OF THE QUEEN'S LOYAL CITIZENS, THE LENGTH AND BREADTH OF THIS GREAT GOD-FEARING COUNTRY OF OURS NOT ONLY KNOWS ABOUT IT BUT CAN HEAR HIM AS WELL.

Others start from either Portrush, Portstewart or even Coleraine. Forget it. They're boring. Portrush is nothing but holidaymakers, b. & b.s and happy caravan parks for all the family. Excuse me while I throw up. It's called Portrush because at 9 o'clock every morning there's a rush to the port to sit on the sand and at 4 o'clock every evening a rush back from the port to the b. & b., a quick rub of the flannel and off to Don Giovanni's for an exotic plate of pasta. Portstewart is a bit more upmarket. Whenever I go there there are always lots of blokes walking round dressed in rubber. They say it's for the surfing. All I can remember of Coleraine is the railway station and people asking me the time of the next train to Dublin or Belfast. Why me? Do I look like a railway porter? An Irish railway porter? A Northern Ireland railway porter? Either way I treated everybody equally and politely. With all the efficiency of the German railways, the Dublin people I sent to the Belfast platform. The Belfast people I sent to the Dublin platform. Serve them right. Fancy thinking I'm a railway porter. What is it with these blowheads?

Out of Derry, my first stop is always Bushmills and the – hic – oldest distillery in the world. It was started in 1297 when a wee dram was anything but a wee dram. But it has only been legal since 1603. Some people say that's what ruined it. It was much better before the government got their hands on it. Which is invariably the case.

454

Co. Antrim

At Bushmills, I'm always treated with respect. Especially at the Bushmills Inn. From the outside it looks like a slightly upmarket Scottish bed and breakfast. Inside it's spectacular. They allow me to drink my coffee standing at the bar. Others have to take their coffee and sit either in the bar or in the lounge.

'The bar is for glasses. Not for cups,' I heard one arch Flora MacDonald of a barmaid with a bar-code hairstyle upbraid one very mild, pathetic, un-German couple. Off they scarpered towards Poland, spilling their coffee as they went. Not me. There I stood, slugging it back, desperately trying to sober up a little before hitting the road again. Obviously Flora recognised class. Either that or she must have thought I was the porter from Coleraine railway station and didn't want me mixing with their proper guests.

I have yet to stay there. Never enough time. But it's on my list. So, too, is a bottle of Bushmills 16 years old. When I do I just know it will be, as they say, a livsadventure from moonshine and shampaying down to clouts and pottled porter. If I can remember it, that is.

Like Dr Johnson, I'm in two minds about the Giant's Causeway. It's 'worth seeing', he said. But not 'worth going to see'.

The good doctor, it seems to me, never said anything. He always declaimed.

Thackeray, who was much more fun, said it looks like the beginning of the world. Others say it is Ireland's most spectacular coastline.

To me it looks like piles. Geological piles. Which, in turn, would mean Co. Antrim/Northern Ireland is the . . . No maybe not. I never said that.

To the unimaginative, to women, to the English, it is 38,000 six- and eight-sided columns of lava left over from an old volcano.

To the Irish, the most rational people on earth, they are stepping stones of the giant, Finn McCool, the giant as opposed to the lesser Finn McCool who scooped out the land creating Lough Neagh and hurled it into the sea creating the Isle of Man. It was supposed to be his stairway to the love of a giantess on Staffa island in the Hebrides. But like most Irishmen, the intention was here but it was never consummated. He gave up before he had hardly begun and went off to have a giant glass of McCool, as opposed to Ice Cool, Guinness.

But the big question remains. Where did the giants come from? From the Republicans or from the Loyalists?

We should be told.

From 1882 until 1949, the world's first hydro-powered tram took people up to the Causeway. This was followed by the world's first hydro-powered tramway and the world's first hit-and-run driver.

On a World Heritage Site scale of one to ten I reckon the Giant's Causeway is worth about minus three and a half. It's no Grand Canyon or Victoria Falls. It's not even a grand, prestigious Lady Di Memorial fountain in Hyde Park. It works. It's also so small. The whole area only covers about seven acres, the size of an average bar.

You trudge about 20 years along the coast, down to the edge of the water. If you don't look carefully you could easily miss it. The photographs make it look dramatic and stunning. You'd think the stones are the size of the Empire State Building. Not at all. They're about the size of a giant lead pencil.

Fair's fair, the National Trust, which owns and runs the place, tries to make it interesting. There's a 'Guess which picture we can see in the rocks today?' competition. Which shows you how desperate they are to make it interesting. On what they call Portnaboe you're supposed to see a camel; on Stookans, your granny; in the Middle Causeway a wishing chair; east from the Causeway Stones, chimney pots; in the middle of Port Noffer, a giant's boot and in the cliff face above Port Noffer, the organ. Not the Giant's Organ. The pipes of an ordinary church organ. This is Ireland, don't forget.

I told our guide I could see looming over everything **BIG IAN** which he didn't think was funny. Down in his little notebook went my name no doubt to be sent off to **THE BIG MAN HIMSELF** so that **HE CAN PERSONALLY DENOUNCE ME** from his **PULPIT** on **SUNDAY** after **SUNDAY** after **SUNDAY**.

In spite of that I was glad I went.

First because it confirms my impression of Irish builders. Millions of years after starting building it, it still isn't even halfway finished. Now I know the usual trick. Start one job so it's yours. Go off to the second. Maybe a third. Run them all together. That way you hang on to two/three jobs instead of one. What I want to know is what other jobs are these giant Irish builders doing that are so important that after thousands of years they still haven't been able to come back to finish off the Causeway.

Second, I loved the signs or rather signage as they call it nowadays all over the place: 'Footsteps damage wildlife and the soil. Please stay on marked paths.' The land has survived no end of giants. What damage can a pair of size-eight boots do to it? How big is the wildlife anyway that can be damaged by a pair of size-eight boots? If it can be damaged by a pair of size-eight boots that's not wildlife. Wildlife is an elephant or a hippopotamus. A pair of size-eight boots are not likely to do them much damage. In any case I can't remember the last time I saw an elephant or a hippopotamus in Ireland.

Third, the leaflet they give you when you begin – to them – your perilous descent to see the stones. To the rest of the world, it's just a pleasant walk by the seaside. Now call me innocent if you must but do visitors to the Giant's Causeway – a World Heritage Site, National Nature Reserve, Area of Special Scientific Interest – actually need a drawing indicating to them what is waterproof clothing and what are sensible shoes? Admittedly the drawing is of a woman but I can't for the life of me believe even an Irish woman needs a pretty little drawing to be told what is waterproof clothing and what are sensible shoes.

From the Giant's Causeway, next stop is the North Antrim Cliff Path: The Harp. The Spanish Organ. Hamilton's Seat and the remains of Dunseverick Castle, once home to Conal Caernac, famous wrestler, swordsman and – are you ready? – the man who not only saw Christ being crucified but also removed the stone from the sepulchre on Easter Sunday morning. These Irish. They get everywhere.

Inevitably, Ballycastle where the Irish Sea meets the Atlantic is an anticlimax. Let's face it, after Conal Caernac and Dunseverick Castle everything is an anticlimax. Even Torr Head, the most northerly corner of Northern Ireland, just 12 miles from Scotland was an anticlimax. In the old days it is said the Scottish settlers would think nothing of rowing the 12 miles across the sea on a Sunday morning to go to church in their own homeland. On the other hand they could just have been trying to get away from **THE** Reverend **IAN PAISLEY**, **THE BIG MAN** although they could no doubt **HEAR HIS SERMON FROM OVER THERE**.

There was no way I was going to row 12 miles across the sea to go to church especially in Scotland but I did think of going out to Rathlin Island where Robert Bruce saw the spider. But the boats were so slow and so in between, the place would have been covered in cobwebs by the time I got there. I decided instead to go and treat myself to a Guinness in the House of McDonnell. Or it could have been the Central Bar. I can't remember.

Cushendall, the heart of the Glens of Antrim, the meeting place of the glens Glenaan, Glenballyemon and Glencorp, which has obviously got American overtones, is a picture-postcard village. Houses all along the harbour. All brightly painted. As if they were waiting to have their photo taken for yet another picture-postcard guide to Ireland. The whole place is, again, owned by the National Trust. But, strangely enough, here they allow you to walk on the wildlife and the soil. Maybe the place is run by a man. Out across the sea you can see the Mull of Kintyre. On a quiet night you can hear the noise they're making as well.

Just outside Cushendall is Glenariff with its waterfalls. They're all right. But I'd prefer a Guinness falls any day. Then on through Camlough, Glenarm, Ballygally and Larne. Thackeray praised the road from Glenarm to Ballygally and Larne to the heavens. But then he was probably smashed out of his mind. He couldn't remember a thing. The size of an old-time Boston policeman, six feet, three inches tall, he had a huge belly, an equally huge appetite for both the drink and the food. As a student at Cambridge he was known for sitting at tables 'covered with bad sweetmeats, drinking bad wine, telling bad stories, singing bad songs over and over again'. But it put him in good stead for the career he was to pursue with such dedication: eating and drinking. And I mean eating and drinking. He would drink six bottles of wine of an evening and still remain sober. Even after an evening putting away the port and the punch he would say it tasted 'like so much milk and water'.

What he would have thought of Larne, I shudder to think. It's an in-and-out port. In comes the boat. Straight out go all the passengers in their cars heading no doubt in many cases for far less interesting places. On the other hand it did inspire a local doctor, Sir Ivan Magill to invent anaesthetics. Must be a connection there somewhere. He worked with another doctor, Harold Gillies, who helped to rebuild the shattered faces of injured soldiers. He also developed special techniques which made chest and heart as well as lung operations easier and safer for both the patient and the surgeon.

Just outside Larne was Ireland's first arms factory. Over 8000 years ago they were making arrowheads. Thousands of them. Over 7000 years ago they were making stone axes. Thousands of them. It was something to kill for. Edward Bruce, brother of Robert, came here to be King of Ulster. It only lasted three years. But three years is three years. Later with Home Rule on the horizon Edward Carson and his Ulster Volunteers shipped in over 20,000 German rifles and ammunition. It was all illegal. But nobody noticed it. Nobody said a word. Everybody was looking the other way. Funny that.

Carrickfergus Castle on the northern shore of Belfast Lough is so called because it was here that Fergus, founder of the Royal House of Scotland, got Car, carried away by the waters in the lough and rick, ricked his neck and drowned. You can't miss it. King John didn't because he called in there a number of times. William the Bruce didn't. The Earl of Essex didn't. He used it as his base when he planned to colonise south and east Antrim. William of Orange didn't. It was his stopping-off point on the way to the battle of the Boyne.

Carrickfergus itself, however, is well worth missing. It could have been a nice, small, pleasant historic town. It isn't. It's suburban sprawl. Belfast commuter sprawl.

If there was any justice in this world Lisburn should be called Linentown. Although whenever I go there there always seems to be a distinct lack of linen or, come to think of it, any kind of clothing at all. Prisoners at Maghaberry high-security prison always seem to be staging one naked protest after another.

Just as William of Orange was conquering Ireland for the Protestants and making Catholics' lives a misery, the opposite was happening in France. The Catholics were making Protestants' lives a misery. Many fled to Ireland. The Irish had been making linen since St Patrick got his first misshapen badly styled old-fashioned shirt but the Huguenot refugees who settled around Lisburn showed them how to do it properly and commercially. Before long there were factories all over the country. By the end of the 1870s Ireland was home to the biggest linen-making industry dans la monde.

Not any more. If the customers haven't fled, many of the workers have. Because of the Troubles. Because of the fear of redundancy. Better they wanted to get out at a time of their choosing rather than at the time of some remote banker sitting in London. Or because of carpal tunnel disease, when the tiny bones in the wrist seize up, blow up or, in extreme cases, the whole of your arm drops off.

'You'd never believe the number of people who worked in the mills who got carpal tunnel. I reckon more suffered from carpal tunnel than suffered from the IRA.'

I met one lump of blubber who looked as though he fantasised about goldfish. He looked like a 15-stone man in a 30-stone body. Most of the weight or rather flab was swishing around his middle like a giant rubber tyre.

'Thirty years I sat on the machines. Destroyed me. My wrist couldn't take it any more. Had to get out before they seized up altogether.'

'So what are you going to do?'

'Find something.'

He did. Years later I was in Douglas in the Isle of Man. There had been a big storm. The hotel I was booked into was cut off. Roads were flooded. Trees were all over the place. Usual problems. Instead I checked into a small hotel near the airport. There was my friend with the rubber tyre still round his waist.

'Offer came up. Decided to go for it. Lots of people here from

460

across the way. Can't live in peace there. But you can live in peace here.'

'How's the wrist?'

Stupid question. He was pouring three pints of Guinness, serving two customers, wiping the bar down, handing out plates of sandwiches and ringing up the till all at the same time.

'Not a problem. Not a problem. Must be the sea air. Will ye have a Guinness before your meal?'

On the other hand instead of Linentown they could call it Ghosttown. Because so many factories have closed down. Because so many people have left. Because wherever you go they keep telling you nothing but ghost stories.

I had a meeting once in Market Square. We were talking about the town, ghosts, old women standing in front of fires, soldiers marching through the kitchen, mirrors smashing of their own accord, old men being hurled from their beds.

'You should go up to Piper's Hill.' I was talking to this perfectly sensible businessman in a bar one evening. I say perfectly sensible. He spent the whole evening picking up the napkins off the bar and stuffing them into his mouth. 'There was a royalist piper standing on the top of the hill during a battle in the seventeenth century. Had his head blown off by a cannon. The head rolled all the way down the street into the town. Go and talk to virtually anyone who lives along Piper's Street. They'll wowhawh wa whoohwoo.'

I did. They did. They took me out to the site of the infamous Long Kesh high-security prison just outside of town. This was where Bobby Sands and nine other hunger strikers starved themselves to death back in 1981.

'Forget your Piper,' they told me 'This is where the real ghosts re.'

The whole bleak, desolate 380-acre site complete with watchtowers, known to Republicans as Long Kesh to Loyalists as the Maze, is up for grabs. The government is wondering what to do with it. Leave it, say the Republicans. People can come here to remember, the way people go to the Somme or to Flanders to remember. Factories, say the Loyalists. Or shops. Or anything.

I told them that in Tehran I once went to Bobby Sands Street where there was a Bobby Sands snack bar. They thought it was wonderful. I thought it was sick.

They then told me they were going to convert Ian Paisley.

'Convert Ian Paisley?'

'Yes. We're going to take him down to Lansdowne Road at the next match and kick him over the crossbar.'

Just outside Lisburn, I tried to find Magheragall. But I had problems. My compass was playing up. Which was odd because the first man in the world to work out how a compass works came from Magheragall. Joseph Larmor, later Sir Joseph Larmor, discovered the earth had a magnetic field and that compasses always lined themselves up with it. Except mine.

I then drove slowly along Lough Neagh which boasts its own monster – don't they all? – to the county town of Antrim. To me Antrim is a shy, quiet, nervous little town as if it's in awe of **THE BIG MAN UP THE ROAD**. I've been there a number of times and I honestly can't remember anything about it apart from lots of wire mesh, road-closed barriers, empty streets and Viscount O'Neill's Bar and Grill. I didn't have my bowler hat with me so I didn't dare go in. The books go on about a monastery and a round tour with walls three foot thick that is now all in ruins. Obviously built to shield the noise of Belfast International Airport nearby. Now whether the people pouring through the departure gates in their hundreds of thousands and heading off to anywhere has got anything to do with **YOU KNOW WHO** I'm too frightened to ever think.

OK. I can't put it off any longer. The little puddle of froth at the base of my spine is now the size of the Irish Sea. Deep breath. Earplugs at the ready. Over the top. Ballymena here I come.

Surprise, surprise. It's nice. It's pleasant. It's friendly. It's not dominated by **BIG IAN** at all.

Now I've got that out of the way – can't risk falling out with **THE BIG MAN** – the truth. It's worse than I thought. **MUCH WORSE**

I checked into the Galgorm Manor Hotel on the outskirts. The girl at reception insisted I paid for everything **IN ADVANCE, NOW IT'S OUR RULES**.

'So you don't . . .'

'IT'S THE RULES, SIR. IT APPLIES TO EVERYONE.'

'To everyone.'

'I AM AFRAID IF YOU DON'T LIKE IT, SIR, YOU CAN . . .'

'OK. OK.'

My eardrums are beginning to melt. I meekly hand over my credit card. At least, I thought, things can't get worse. They did. The place was scruffy. Every time I tried to put any of my threadbare clothes on a coat-hanger, the coat-hanger fell off the rail. My clothes spent the night on the floor. The restaurant was closed. I had a congealed meal in the hotel bar. St Patrick had just as bad a time of it when he was there. As a boy he looked after the swine on the plains of Ballymena. He didn't stay at the Galgorm Manor, however. He didn't have a credit card. Lucky man.

The following morning I drove slowly into Ballymena itself. Very slowly. I tried to park. Every time I tried I was pounced on and told there was No parking, Parking was not allowed, Park there and you'll be condemned to 50 million years in **HELL**.

My first meeting I was three minutes late. On the way there I spotted a shop selling what I thought would be an essential piece of equipment for my stay in Co. Antrim: earmuffs. The bowler-hatted pillar of the local establishment was going to give me the full inside story on the biggest problem currently facing local town councillors. Drink. They had decided that drinks should not be served at town council meetings which had come from abroad. Abroad being from across the border in Co. Donegale. They should come from local, domestic suppliers. But when I got there, he'd gone. To his next meeting.

'But,' I said to the lard butt of a secretary, 'he told me he could spare me an hour. That means he's left 57 minutes earlier than he expected.'

She looked straight through me.

'WELL. HE DIDN'T WANT TO BE LATE,' she screamed.

If there were enough bricks in Northern Ireland, I'd have bricked her mouth up.

I made for the nearest bar. I was going to stay there all day. But I was warned Ballymena has a strict anti-drink policy. Stagger out of a bar late at night and you're in for the shock of your life. You're likely to be met by a nice kindly old lady handing out not just tea, coffee and hot chocolate but also Wagon Wheels. For free.

They say Ireland's one and only dinosaur was found in Ballymena, I don't believe it. The place is full of them. They're weird. Call me suspicious if you must, I swear they all look like either a potential or a retired policeman. They even act like policemen. They walk up and down slowly, dodge in and out of alleyways and feed raw meat to their pet pit bull terriers while walking down the street.

'So are they all retired policemen?' I asked a retired policeman who looked as though he wasn't the retiring type.

'Probably,' he said. 'You find they tend to disappear for a few days at a time. Then come back with a few cuts and bruises and enough money to buy a new car. What else could they be?'

As for trying to talk to them, the truth, they say, is stranger than diction. Not in the case of Co. Antrim, it isn't. It's the same. It's like trying to chat up **THE BIG MAN DURING ONE OF HIS SHORT 3½-HOUR SUNDAY SERMONS. WHEN HE'S CALLING DOWN THE WRATH OF ALMIGHTY GOD** upon anyone **WHO DISAGREES WITH HIM**.

'Excuse me, I wonder if . . .'

'YOU'RE NOT FROM AROUND HERE.'

'No, I'm . . .'

'NOT CATHOLIC ARE YOU? THE POPE. MRS POPE. ALL THE BABY POPES.'

'I'm actually looking for . . .'

'OLD RED SOCKS THAT'S WHAT WE CALL HIM.'

As for the town itself, it's practically an Ian Pais . . . sorry, I mean **AN IAN PAISLEY THEME PARK**. He is everywhere. His church and all the surrounding overspill buildings take up practically the centre of the town. I reckon it's the only town in the whole of Ireland which boasts more churches than bars. Everywhere there are fresh, clean, bright Union Jacks. On lamp-posts. On telegraph poles. On specially erected flagpoles the height of a house. When there are not Union Jacks there are posters, religious posters. Practically every street has a sign saying One Way which I suppose could be either a religious slogan or a political one. Or both. Practically every shop sells photos of Lady Di, King Billy keyrings, and red, white and blue chocolates made by a farmer from Co. Tyrone.

From somewhere deep inside the town I was told **HIS MINISTERS** run a big mailing campaign aimed at persuading Catholic priests throughout England and Wales to defect and join them. You've heard of the Nigerian scam letters. These are Ian Paisley scam letters. Send your name and address, join us, you will get your reward in heaven. Strange as it may seem they have had a big effect on Catholic priests the length and breadth of the country. They brought joy and warmth to many of them. They threw the letters on the tiny fires in their chilly houses for a little bit of extra warmth during the cold winter evenings when they were wrestling with their sermons for the following Sunday.

The only thing I knew which would cheer me up was a visit to the Moravian Cemetery just down the road in Gracehill. I'd come across the Moravians before. In Malmesbury, Wiltshire, one of my favourite villages. But I had never seen them before in Ireland. A mixture of strict Calvinism and not so strict Methodism, they first arrived in the early eighteenth century. At first they boomed. They had over 200 churches. Now they're a good few pews short of a church. The thing I like about them is their attitude to death. In order to ensure that they can at least rest in peace in the next world they insist on not being buried with their wives. All the good, holy, hard-working, honest God-fearing men on one side of the cemetery. Women on the other. Makes sense to me.

They used to do the same thing on the tiny island of Inishmurray, Co. Sligo until as recently as the 1940s. Why did they stop? I'll give you one guess.

Having seen Ulster's belief in the strict division of people in death, I was now ready to see Ulster's belief in the strict division of people in life: Belfast.

First things first. Belfast is in a fabulous setting. On the River Lagan – as in Lagging behind the times – which flows into Belfast Lough which then flows into the sea. Three sides are either hills or mountains depending on whether you think mountains begin at 30,000 feet like Mount Everest or, as in Belfast, 30,000 inches. On the fourth side are the giant now rapidly rusting cranes of Harland and Wolff, the once great shipyard that they insist on reminding us built the *Titanic*, the world's largest liner, weighing an unbelievable 77,000 tonnes. If I was them I'd keep quiet about it. But no. They think it promotes their reputation worldwide. Which, of course, it has done. They haven't built a ship there for years.

The two cranes are known in this city which is so conscious of its religious knowledge and faith as Samson and Goliath. Why not Samson and Delila or David and Goliath I have no idea. Founded by a Yorkshireman, Sir Edward Harland, it was once the largest shipyard in the world, employing over 11,000 men responsible for over 10 per cent of the world's ships. If you go there, a helpful suggestion, they like nothing better than to be reminded that the Ark was built by amateurs and the *Titanic* by professionals. They always enjoy the joke. Honest.

But Harland and Wolff were not their only, err, success. Belfast which in its heyday doubled in size every ten years, was also home to Shorts, so called because of the number of shorts served in the boardroom before lunch. The oldest aircraft company in the world it started when it took 16 hours to fly from London to New York compared to today when it can take whole weeks to check in, go through security, answer a string of damn fool questions nobody has any chance of verifying before you get anywhere near the plane.

Belfast has also had its share of geniuses: John Bell and John Dunlop. John Bell is the man who proved Einstein wrong. First Bell said measure the polarisation of one photon, you'll immediately know the polarisation of the other. Second, E does not equal mc^3 but mc^2. The inflatable John Dunlop invented the world's first inflatable rubber wheel. A vet by profession, he invented the pneumatic tyre because his son was forever complaining about the rough ride he was getting from his tricycle. To shut him up, Dunlop came up with the pneumatic tyre. An Englishman would have clipped the kid around the ear, chucked the damn bike over the wall and left him to get on with it. Such was Belfast's reputation that one of their greatest visitors arrived in 1963 and has been making whoopee ever since: the yellow-bellied New Zealand flatworm.

Outsiders always claimed Belfast was five, ten years behind the times. The people of Belfast disagreed. They always maintained it was nowhere near as bad as that. It was ten to twenty years behind the times. The Ulster Museum once turned down the offer of a striking Renaissance painting of the Madonna and Child on the basis that the Madonna wasn't wearing a wedding ring. There's no end of Presbyterian churches that refuse to sing the hymn 'Jerusalem' because they say it's about a foreign country: England. Come Christmas, however, they all agree on their favourite carol: 'A Cartridge in a Pear Tree'. It gets worse. The *Belfast Newsletter* once published a letter from a woman who was so worried in case her pet budgie was breaking the strict laws of the Sabbath by jumping on to his swing on a Sunday that she said she had 'made a practise of disconnecting his swing each Sunday and not putting it back in to use until Monday morning.'

Today it's still behind the times.

In the bad old days Catholics and Protestants used to live or try to live side by side. No longer. The Protestants have moved out of Catholic areas, Catholics from Protestant areas. It's more segregated now than it has ever been. Surveys show that an unbelievable 98 per cent of public housing is divided along religious lines. That's not all. The segregation is now so strict that it even extends to which side of the bridge you walk on. Take Albert Bridge. After 11 o'clock at night Protestants walk on what they call the Maysfield leisure side, Catholics walk on the other side. Walk on the wrong side you could end up under it. The Peace Wall is still there, Belfast's answer to the Berlin Wall and now I suppose the Israeli wall built by Sharon to keep out the Palestinians. Over 40 foot high. Covered in graffiti. Scorched by firebombs.

The Protestant areas are still very Protestant. I saw giant murals, 20 foot high, the size of a house, of King Billy, of flags of 'C' Company of the 2nd Battalion, the Ulster Defence Association. There's one for the Ulster Freedom Fighters showing three masked men all wielding guns. Another promising death to three IRA gunmen. Another with a gun that seems to point directly at you wherever you are.

'It's our *Mona Lisa*,' a pit bull terrier covered in tattoos told me.

Even the kerbstones are painted red, white and blue. If everywhere in the United Kingdom was as Loyalist as this the Queen would never have another *annus horribilis* again.

Late one evening I was even taken to what I was told was the most famous Protestant shrine in Belfast: the home of Johnny 'Mad Dog' Adair. He wasn't there to welcome us. He's now moved to a much bigger house further down the road: Maghaberry Prison just outside Lisburn.

I was in Short Strand area during the Queen's Jubilee celebrations. Shopkeepers were warned not to serve Catholics. There were signs all over the place saying 'No Short Strand taigs on our roads.' A Catholic church was burnt down together with some houses. A group of Loyalists burst into the College of Further Education in Tower Street and started grabbing students and demanding, 'Are you a Catholic or a Protestant? If you're a Catholic, you're going to be shot.' Charming.

The Catholic areas are still very Catholic. They, too, have their giant murals, also the size of houses. They also have about a couple of miles down the Falls Road, Milltown Cemetery, which is virtually a shrine to Republican martyrs: the hunger strikers, the Gibraltar Three.

Late one evening I was taken to a tiny estate, just 14 streets at the top of a triangle where the Newtownards Road meets Albert Bridge Road. It's completely surrounded by a 15-foot-high security fence. Inside are Catholics. Surrounding them are Protestants. Inside the Catholics were preparing to defend themselves. They were knocking down walls and piling the bricks up as ammunition. Children were collecting all the empty bottles they could find. The women were making petrol bombs. Outside the Protestants were doing the same. It was unbelievable.

Over the years I've been in a number of houses, Catholic as well as Protestant. They all had photographs of Clinton's visit to the North. Both sides expected great things from him. Both sides were disappointed.

Co. Antrim

I've also heard every view and counter-view, every opinion and counter-opinion expressed by everyone from undercover agents to members of the FRU, 14 Company or, on occasions, 22 Squadron SAS. Among the more interesting:

Decommissioning. One prematurely old man who spoke like a whisper in chapel told me he didn't believe the story about the IRA concreting over their arms bunkers.

'Now you think about it,' he says. 'They say they are concreting over the bunkers. They're going to need an awful lot of concrete. Where's it coming from? Who's supplying it? Where are the lorries? Ireland's a small place. Why have there been no reports of lorries full of concrete going backwards and forwards across the country? The bunkers are on somebody's land. Why has nobody said they've seen the lorries? I tell you they're making it up.'

'What about the press and the media?' another old boy joins in. He looks as though he's been gozzing in his beer. 'The press and the media can say or do whatever they like. Why haven't there been any press reports and media reports about lorries, about concrete, about concrete being poured into great holes in the ground?'

'Another thing,' another old guzzler butts in. 'There can't be any decommissioning, any bunkers, any concreting in. If there was the press would know about it. They would find out. The fact they haven't means either they don't exist or if they exist the press is deliberately cooperating with the government to keep them secret. All of the press and the news media. Keeping secret about every single one of the bunkers. It's not possible. Not possible.

'If the IRA were prepared to decommission their arms why didn't they just hand them in, why didn't they just tell the authorities where they were without going to all the bother about concreting them in? It doesn't make sense.'

British troops. A woman I met one Sunday morning coming out of church. She had a row of nice even teeth. Numbers 1, 3, 5, 7, 9 and 11 were missing. She told me how they welcomed the British troops when they first arrived in Belfast.

'When the British troops first arrived we thought they were here to protect us. We used to take them out cups of tea and sandwiches. Then we realised they weren't here to protect us. They were here to protect the Loyalists against us. But it didn't make any difference to us. We still took them out cups of tea and sandwiches. Except the tea was full of laxatives and the sandwiches were full of broken glass.'

Contact with the enemy. I had a meeting once with a big company just outside Belfast. Meeting over we went for lunch. I sat next to the production manager who looked as though he built the *Titanic* with his bare hands.

'We had some good times even in the midst of all the bad times,' he says. 'We had this agreement, both sides, that we had to have a neutral area, a contact zone, where we could meet and talk if we had to.'

'You mean like Churchill and Hitler sitting down and chatting about the war while both sides were busy killing each other?' I said.

'We're not Germans,' he says. 'We're Irish. We're civilised. In any case there were things we both agreed on that had to be sorted out.'

'Like what?'

'Like the British.'

'So where did you meet then? Where was this neutral ground?'

'Bellaghy,' he says. 'On the border between Antrim and Derry In McKenna's on the High Street.'

'Did the British know about it?'

'We didn't go out of our way to tell them.'

'But they must have.'

'If they did they never gave us any indication, no hints, no winks, nothing.'

'Not even Maurice?'

'How do you know about Maurice?'

'You'd never believe me.'

Andersontown police station in west Belfast, once the most bombed and attacked security building of the Troubles, might now shut up shop between 7 p.m. and 7 a.m. the following morning but Belfast is still a violent city. The problems now are drugs, extortion, racketeering, punishment attacks, kneecapping, shooting. It' also racist, some say one of, if not the most, racist capital in Europe.

Drive around. It's there to see. Ku Klux Klan slogans. Swastikas. Chinks Out plastered all over doors and walls. Racist leaflets nailed to doors. Houses are ransacked, bombed, burnt to the ground. Cars are set alight. People are spat at, stoned in the street. In South Belfast, a desperate, run-down area, with Union flags flying from lamp-posts – it is sandwiched between two strong Republican areas, Lower Ormeau Road and Markets Road – I saw a giant mural on the end-wall of a house in Tarvanagh Street showing a menacing white figure in military uniform, a shotgun in its hand, bearing down on the surrounding streets. Alongside it was a poem:

> So when you're in your bed at night
> And hear soft footsteps fall
> Be careful it's not the UFF
> And the reaper come to call.

Fear is in the air. You can feel it. Smile at a foreigner, I was told, let alone say Good morning. At best you'll get a brick in your face. At worst the last thing you'll remember is your house going up in flames.

An estate agent, all pinstripe suit and tiepin, told me he had been warned not to rent, let alone sell, any flats or houses to foreigners.

What's happened, of course, is that as both Protestants and Catholics moved out to their own areas, as houses were left empty and derelict, Asians and Africans moved in. Now both sides are turning against them. It's nothing new. Belfast has always been wary of foreigners. When Liszt visited the city in 1841 a bunch of Protestants surrounded his carriage, cut the horses free and were about to throw him in a nearby ditch when finally sense prevailed. They tried to make out that they thought he was the great Irish Catholic Liberator, Daniel O'Connell. Oh yeah. One's Irish. One's Hungarian. One's a politician. One's a composer. One speaks English. One doesn't.

Although to be fair, Ireland has started at long last to adjust to the influx of foreign residents. There are plans, I understand, to rename Bettytown, Fatimatown; Holy Cross Abbey, Holy Crescent Abbey; Tobercurry, Toberfishandchips.

At the same time I must admit Belfast city is slowly catching up with the rest of the world. It's throwing off some of its Victorian airs and graces. The great towering cranes of Harland and Wolff may be busy rusting away but there are plenty of other, smaller cranes at work building, rebuilding, refurbishing. City Hall in Donegale Square still looks as though it came lock, stock and barrel from an American boot sale. The Old Court House and jail may still be crumbling to dust but it still looks impressive. The new Waterfront Concert Hall is spectacular. It's circular so that nobody can sit squarely opposite anyone else. Total capacity: 2250 people and no doubt 2250 million different opinions. The Grand Opera House is now living up to its name and presenting spectacular, sophisticated productions for Belfast's growing cultural elite such as *The Full Monty* and *Saturday Night Fever*. The Europa Hotel, once the most bombed building in Europe, is now back to normal. All the security barriers have gone although I noticed they've still got those extra-thick heavy curtains in the rooms presumably just in case. When President Clinton is in town this is where he stays. Apparently to make him feel at home they turn his suite into a trailer park. Then they keep up a non-stop supply of goodies to his room. For food, they provide all the hot dogs and pizzas they can find. To commemorate the number of times he has stayed there, I was told, there was a plan to honour the great man by putting up a special plaque outside the hotel saying 'Bill Clinton slept here – alone'.

Last time I was there, there was a questionnaire in the room 'Where did you hear of the Europa Hotel?' it asked. I put down 'Three streets away'.

People are also more relaxed. You now hear them saying things they would never have dared say years ago like 'See you later.' 'I'll see you on the way back.' 'OK. Make it Wednesday.'

In the old days there were two kinds of bars in Belfast: the unsafe ones and the unsafe ones that didn't close on time. Today they're all safe apart from the ones that aren't. My favourite: the Crown Liquor Saloon. As a pub, it's the best National Trust property

I know. No stupid leaflets. No nonsense about where you can walk and where you can't. In fact if it came to calculating who spent more time in National Trust properties, doddery little old ladies who look as though they've dedicated their lives to organic lentils tottering around Sissinghurst on a Sunday afternoon or me, I'd win hands down. As far as spending money is concerned, I reckon they owe me a good few life memberships as well.

The Crown Liquor Saloon is also the best chapel I know. The story goes that the Catholics wanted to build a new church, St Malachy's. They wanted to make it the most ornate church in the country. They brought over the finest Italian craftsmen. To ensure they didn't blow all their money on things they shouldn't spend their money on, the Church gave them only a few pennies a week to live on. The rest they sent back to their families. The Italians did what Italians always do. They made a deal. They refurbished the pub with all the materials destined for the church in exchange for all the booze they could drink. The result: the Crown looks like the inside of a rich, ornate church. The church looks like the inside of a bar.

My other favourites: Bittles Bar on Victoria Square. It's covered with tiny portraits of Ireland's, as opposed to Northern Ireland's, most famous literary figures. Trouble is it's full of lawyers. The Duke of York, Commercial Court, the printers' pub. The Garrick, Chichester Street. The next best thing to the Crown. Don't whatever you do go to Madden's on Berry Street. The tin whistles will drive you mad. For a real upmarket pub, of course, there's the Culloden Hotel, a grand five-star hotel overlooking Belfast Lough. The restaurant, the Mitre, is a touch expensive. But then it's got so many awards, so I guess it's OK. The bar, however, on a good night with the right people makes you forget everything. Including the bill.

Of course, that's the way to enjoy Co. Antrim and Belfast. Forget everything. Start from scratch. You'll have a great time.

Co. Clare
I de-Clare my interest

Famous local resident
Himself

Favourite food
Caterpillar

Favourite drink
Guinness

Favourite pub
The Railway Tavern, Ennis

Favourite restaurant
The one without the caterpillar

What to say
My mother comes from Co. Clare

What not to say
Where did you get that belt?

The first time I went to County Clare I admit it, within minutes I was curled up on the floor, under the table, dribbling and babbling away like crazy.

I was about two years old at the time and because of the German bombing had spent my life up to then either under a table or in an Anderson shelter at the bottom of the garden at home in London. I'd love to have another excuse. But I haven't.

My mother was born in County Clare. In Lisheen, Ballynacally. About six miles outside Ennis, the county town. In your typical rough-built thatched cottage. On the top of a hill overlooking the River Shannon, the longest river in either the UK or Ireland depending on who you talk to. She was the youngest of five children – one boy, the eldest, four girls. Mother. Father. The five children lived in the cottage. Struggled to survive on just 20 acres. But in the end they couldn't. The old story. Somebody had to go. The son stayed to work the land. The four girls were set for America; Springfield, Massachusetts. The two elder ones made it. Minnie and Katty. My mother and Leena were to follow. But there were problems with the paperwork. Instead of sorting it out my mother decided to come to England. She met my father. They married at the start of the war. As a result, I'm half Irish. Luckily, it's the top half. If it had been the bottom half I would have had big problems. The rest, as they say, is downhill.

As the war, known in neutral Ireland as the Emergency, got worse and the bombing increased – we were living in the middle of it – my mother, no doubt prompted by my father, decided to go back home till the worst was over.

Home couldn't have been more basic. But at least there were no doodlebugs. The door was always open. To cats. To dogs. To cattle. To pigs. To anything on three or four legs. Three because my old uncle would always tie up the leg of any animal he didn't want running away. It might not have been exactly animal-friendly. But it worked. It didn't seem to do the animals any harm either. The floor, I seem to remember, was part flags, part sand or soil. But I could be wrong. The walls were solid: three or four foot thick. Outside they were white. Inside they were brown and black with smoke. The fire was the centre of everything. But it wasn't a

---

Mary O'Reilly goes up to the priest after mass on Sunday.

'Father,' she says. 'I have terrible news. My husband has just died.'

'Mary,' says the priest. 'I'm so sorry. When did it happen?'

'Last night,' she says.

'And what were his final words to ye?' says the priest.

'Well, Father,' she says, 'his final words were "Mary will ye please put down that gun?"'

---

proper fire with a grate. It was an outdoor camp fire inside the house. It was lumps of peat, bits of wood – whenever anyone went for a walk, they always brought back bits of wood – bits of anything that would burn. Above it, on one side a kettle as black as soot, various hooks with or without pots and pans dangling on them, an enormous chimney that could have come straight out of Hampton Court. Hanging inside the chimney were lumps of pork or bacon or goodness knows what. Maybe the gun that . . . No, he'd have got rid of it by now . . . On the other hand . . . Opposite the door was the dresser. This was full of plates and cups and saucers that were in better condition than all the other plates and cups and saucers. They were less chipped. Between the dresser and the fire were a mixture of two or three very primitive chairs, in the final state of collapse, a sort of sofa which also served as a bed more times than I can remember and all the usual farmyard junk you can imagine.

Meals were served either on plates straight from the fire or on a table by the window by the door. I say meals. I mean potatoes. With cabbage. With bacon. With bacon and cabbage. With potatoes. I'm not saying we had nothing but potatoes but often I can remember not being able to see anybody for the pile of potato skins on my plate. Afterwards we might have a griddle cake or a scone, or a dollop of something or other heated over the fire.

Off this main area were two rooms and a loft. On one side was the family room. What was in it nobody knew. What people did in it was something that nobody dared even think about. Although the results were running around all over the place. On the other side was, I suppose, the parlour although more often than not it was the guests' quarters. Whenever we went there, however many of us there were, we all stayed there. The air conditioning was fantastic. You didn't have to wait for winter to get cold. It was cold all the time. It was also dark all the time. Even when they lit the candles and the paraffin lamps it somehow made it seem darker still. But more than anything it was full of smoke. No wonder everybody had bad eyesight. They lived in perpetual smoke and gloom. Sometimes just a few seconds and my eyes would be running. As I got older and my glasses got stronger and stronger, to cover my shame and embarrassment, I would invariably say it was nothing to do with the smoke. It was the sooty picture of the Blessed Virgin above the fire. It was so beautiful. So graceful. So lifelike you could swear she also had tears running down her eyes. Which in traditional Irish fashion would usually result in me being offered no end of bottles of Guinness all evening.

Outside there was a small garden, a brick wall, the inevitable stack of peat, more chickens, a stream at the bottom of the first field from which they used to fetch their water first in old wooden buckets until they started catching up with the rest of the world then in modern metal buckets. Alongside the house was a lean-to, a byre, a stable, a shack with piles of straw, a pitchfork and my God is this how backward they are?

But it never seemed to do anybody any harm. If it did the cure was always the gold wedding ring. A bruise. A cut. A sore. A broken leg. Dab it, rub it, lacerate it to shreds with the gold wedding ring. Everybody swore by it. Not me. Even at an early age I can remember realising that whenever the wedding ring was involved it invariably made matters worse. That and the fact it always used to take me hours to scrub all that green stuff off afterwards.

My uncle was virtually a hunchback. He was bent over, twisted, forever wheezing and coughing and smoking a rolled-up cigarette and, of course, hollering away at his long-suffering wife, Agnes, who had a wonderful face like a poem. There were lines all over it.

'Away woman. Away,' he would scream. 'Blathering women. Go near a fire, they have to ruin it. Lord have mercy.'

My mother used to say that when he was a young man he was the handsomest man in Co. Clare. But one day he pulled his back. Everything inside snapped. There was nothing anyone could do for him. It didn't seem to stop him enjoying himself even though everyone said he let his hands go barefoot the whole of his life. He was full of the craic, as they say.

The priest would come to bless the house.

'Are ye ready now?' the priest would say.

'Sure, I am as ready as I ever shall be,' he would reply.

'I mean spiritually,' the priest would say. 'Are you ready spiritually?'

'Sure I am indeed, Father,' he would say. 'I've five bottles of whiskey inside in a crate. I'm as ready as I'll ever be.'

Michael's wife down the lane was pregnant. She should not go to a cemetery, he would say. If she walked across a grave, intentionally or unintentionally, the child would be born with a twisted foot. Then when the child was about to be born, he would say she should wear a shirt, a scarf, a waistcoat belonging to the fathe to transfer the pains of childbirth to the father. He would give a big, wide grin, take a drag of his shrivelled-up homemade cigarette and slap his knee a good few times.

He'd go to a christening. He'd tie a red ribbon to the child for good luck. He did the same thing with cattle. He'd come back full of himself. The child, he'd say, "twas the only one who went anywhere near the water".

He'd go and visit the family of someone who had just died. He'd open all the doors and windows. If the roof was thatched he would make a hole in the thatch so that the soul could easily leave the body and begin its long spiritual journey upwards. To ensure it had a clear run, he would insist nobody should stand or kneel in front of the door, window or hole in the thatch until they reckoned the soul had made it and was on its way. All clocks, however, would be stopped. All mirrors turned to the wall. Any cats or dogs or other household pets thrown out in the yard for fear of the departing soul leaving the body and heading straight for another living creature from where it could cause all kinds of problems. Precautions taken, all the doors and windows would then be firmly closed, to prevent the departing soul from doing a celestial U-turn and heading back down again.

He'd go to a wake. There the body was lying in his Sunday best. His best pair of shoes on him. My uncle would go out for a drink. Back he would go a few minutes later to say his final goodbyes. The body, he would say, was now wearing a muddy old pair of boots. One of the other mourners had done a swap when nobody was looking.

He'd go to a funeral. They were all there waiting for the priest, he would say. While they were waiting they decided to have a glass and a game of cards. Every time they had a glass they put one in front of the body. Every time they dealt a card, they put one in front of the body as well. Who won? The dead body. For weeks afterwards they left food and drink and sets of playing cards on the grave so that the corpse's good luck would continue into the next world.

He'd go to the graveyard afterwards. The coffin, he would say, was so heavy one of the men lowering it into the grave slipped, fell in after it and broke his leg. 'Did cast a terrible gloom over the day's proceedings,' he would add with a big, wide grin, taking another drag of a shrivelled-up home-made cigarette and slapping his knee.

He seemed to know everybody, every second dog and every third horse in Co. Clare. He would walk and stumble miles across fields for a drink. Usually a Sergeant, a squat, high-shouldered, short-neck bottle of Guinness the same shape as the one Mr Boffin dug up among the mounds in *Our Mutual Friend*. He would then settle down in a corner and sing songs and tell stories until the cows left home.

Once we ended up somewhere or other. It was late. It was gone closing time. He asked a policeman where we could get a drink. 'Johnsey's,' he says. We race up to Johnsey's. They say they are closed. There was no way they can give us a drink. We wandered back down the street. Along came the policeman.

'You had yourselfs a quick drink?' he says.

'No way,' says my uncle. 'They said they were closed.'

'Glory be to God,' says the policeman. 'What is this country coming to? No respect for the law.'

Off he ambles down the street.

One evening I remember we were sitting in the cottage talking about shooting. Suddenly my uncle leaps up, grabs his shotgun off the wall and starts firing off more rounds than the rebels fired from the post office in 1917. It was crazy. Worse. It was lunatic. But great fun. The inside of the cottage smelt like the Battle of the Boyne for about two weeks until the smoke cleared.

He also, I remember, always used to wear a belt he said he got from the Black and Tans during the Troubles. I never asked him how he got it. Where he got it. Or if the Black and Tan knew he was giving it to him although I can remember him again and again proclaiming, 'Burn everything English that comes into Ireland Except the coal.'

Maybe that was for the laugh. Maybe not.

Years later I heard that there had been a fierce battle during the Troubles nearby at Rineen Hill near Lahinch. The British troops came off worse. Their bodies were laid out for identification and removal for burial.

Co. Clare

'Pitch your tent there today,' they say. 'You'll be lucky if you're not woken up in the middle of the night by the sounds of the wind and in the morning all your things are not scattered around all over the place.'

Maybe. Maybe not.

Later, after the war was over and I was no longer curling up on the floor under the table and dribbling and babbling away like crazy for the wrong reason, we used to go on holiday to my father's family in Portsmouth. To his mother and eldest sister who lived in a tiny house that could have come straight out of Trollope. An abridged paperback edition. Then after my father died, it was back to Co. Clare.

Most of the time we just used to stay in Ballynacally. Taxis were practically non-existent. If there were any around they were too expensive. In any case those were the days when everybody still went to market as well as to mass on Sunday in the pony and trap. Things, however, were improving. Candles and paraffin were replaced by electric light. All the cooking, however, was still done on the fire, water was still brought in from the stream, one of the dogs was now allowed to run around on four legs. Only one of my eyes watered like mad. The other had given up years before.

For a treat we were allowed to work all day and every day, break our backs and develop enormous blisters on our hands to bring in the harvest. First was the privilege of cutting the hay with enormous scythes. Swing it too slow, too carefully you cut nothing. Swing it too far, too fast you sliced your own legs off. If the Health and Safety Executive could have seen us then they would have raised their hands in horror. Promptly to have them sliced off by one of a million scythes whizzing backwards and forwards in all directions. Having cut the hay there was then the thrill of raking it all up, grain side up, into stooks or little wigwams. Some farmers used to put little hats on top of the stooks. Some say to keep out the rain. Others say to protect them from evil spirits. All the stooks then had to be gathered up into a hayrick. The top of the hayrick they would then thatch to protect it from the weather. Thatching the house was different. That had to be done as near as damn it to a full moon because it was supposed to guarantee strength, a perfect cover and, of course, good luck. When the moon was at its lowest and darkest was the time for castrating calves, which always seemed to me to pose an unnecessary risk for the calves.

The harvest over, it was time to celebrate. Well I say celebrate. People would come across the fields from miles around to dance the night away to no end of – talk of the pluck of the Irish – diddly-diddly music with strange-sounding names like 'The Bridge of Athlone', 'The Walls of Limerick', 'The Siege of Ennis' and something I seem to remember was called something like 'The High Coal Cap' or 'The High Cold Cap' and 'The Siege of Ennis' again, although to me they all sounded exactly the same. In spite of all the warlike-sounding songs, however, there wasn't a note of discord all evening. In fact, there probably wasn't one chord played properly all evening.

To keep our strength up there was no end of slabs of soda bread the size of a gravestone, made from sour milk and soda and buckets of fresh milk, smeared six inches thick with enough cholesterol-inducing home-made butter to keep a decent-size heart-attack hospital going for years. If what they say is true about cholesterol I should have been dead 93 years ago. Which is why I don't bother any more. I should also have been deaf.

When I got older and passed my driving test, I used to hire a car. After it had been suitably doused in holy water more thoroughly than a modern car wash, and the back seat stacked high with slabs of soda bread and churns of fresh butter in case we should step on a patch of hungry grass and be struck down there and then with what my mother called faminism, we went everywhere. Well I say everywhere. The Irish being the Irish first we had to visit Aunt this, Uncle that and no end of cousins where we would be received with a strange frozen formality.

First, I'd be told I was the spittin' image of my father. Even though none of them had ever seen my father.

Then I'd be told I had a 'good drop' in me. A good drop? Guinness? Whiskey? Not at all. Blood. The blood of my mother's family.

Finally, the curse. He'll make a grand man. He'll make his weight in money. He'll be the talk of the county.

Now look at the mess I'm in.

Then there was the meal, which wherever we went was always the same: salad piled high on a plate in the centre of the table. Once I remember on a shiny Sunday we went visiting an old lady from County Wexford who always used to say 'Teach me the salt' instead of the more normal English "Ere. Giss it 'ere, mate.' My mother, all prim and proper, was about to glomp into the salad when – I can see it even today – a large lettuce leaf shivered and out from under it crawled this huge green, staring, throbbing caterpillar. Nobody said a word. We all carried on chatting and gossiping as if it wasn't there. As we left the old lady says, 'I'm glad we enjoyed ye.'

After family came the friends. As good Christians, we had to go and visit school friends, church friends, work friends. If we visited the O'Connors and the O'Reillys we had to go and see the O'Briens. If we were going to see the O'Briens we should also go and see Mrs Maguire's cousin's uncle's wife's brother's great-great-grandcousin twice removed, especially as he was on the pig's back. In other words, rich. If we didn't, what on earth would they think of us?

The result was days on end driving up and down desolate farm tracks, a growing aversion to lettuce which has never left me and precious little time for the important things of life: drinking Guinness. On the other hand I learnt a lot.

Visit any one of the tiny islands off the coast which are virtually forever shrouded in mist. Land on the island the day the mist has disappeared. You'll live for ever.

Never allow a pregnant woman to go to a wake or a funeral. It could mean death to the unborn child.

If you're selling a horse keep spitting on it. It will keep away the fairies, stop them from doing any damage to it and prevent them from stopping you getting the best possible price you can.

Finally, if you've got two cats you need two cat flaps. One for the big cat. One for the small cat. Well that's what cousin Billy told me.

Go back there today and everything is different. Even the caterpillars. They're now organic.

Ennis I can remember when it was nothing but tiny narrow

streets and a chemist's shop that was called a Medical Hall; a butcher that was a Victualler; a pub that was a Grocery; a curate who was a barman and you got farthings in your change. The main street was small and dark and dingy. For some reason we always had to go and see Lollipop, a big, jolly, fat man, who had a watch repairer's shop. He was so fat he used to almost fill the shop. There was hardly any room for watches let alone customers. The only thing he ever did to earn money, my uncle would say, was to lose his baby teeth. But the fuss and the excitement everybody made about going to Ennis you'd have thought the streets were paved with gold.

The cattle market was on the edge of town. Today it's the bus station. We used to go there market days to watch the sales, catch up on the gossip, have a drink. The talk, I remember, was usually politics.

Ennis is a revolutionary town. It was the rallying point for freedom, for independence, for Sinn Fein. The Great Liberator, Daniel O'Connell fought and won the Clare election. He was the first Irish Catholic to win a seat in the British Parliament. De Valéra won Ennis for Sinn Fein and represented it for 40 years. But it was also strangely pro-British. Years ago there was practically a riot when come Armistice Day there was no place for all the old Irish soldiers who had fought on the British side. In the end they marched to the Protestant church not the Catholic church and demanded to have their own service.

I was in Ennis once when an African arrived on an exchange programme which involved swapping local government officials in Ireland with local government officials in developing countries. Everybody was amazed at 'the native' and followed him every-where. Traffic came to a standstill. People rushed out to shake him by the hand. In spite of years praying for and supporting the foreign missions, he was the first black man most of them had ever seen. For weeks afterwards there were agonising debates about whether it was real or whether it would eventually wash off.

Ennis today is a very nice, very pleasant little town. Great fun. Great bars. My favourite: the Railway Tavern. And safe. The police say its the safest town of its size in the country. It's also supposed to be the music – diddly-diddly six chords and a pint of Guinness music that is – capital of Ireland. But I have no idea whether that's true or not. I can't even tell the difference between funky hip-hop home garage music and a strangulated scream in the dark. I'm also strangely deaf to Irish music due, in part, I'm sure, to my upbringing.

After Ennis, of course, the biggest most dramatic change has got to be Shannon, birthplace of those two greatest breakthroughs in modern aviation: duty-free shopping and Irish coffee for the husbands whose wives were doing all the duty-free shopping. Now why can't Heathrow come up with something like that? After all far more people spend far more time waiting for far more things to go right at Heathrow than they ever do at Shannon.

When I first started flying to Shannon it was barely the size of an Irish ten-bob note. Every time the plane landed they had to first get the cattle off the runway. Now it's so big and so grand the likes of Jeremy Irons – think of a mid-life crisis, he's starred in it – are seen, dishcloth in hand, wiping down the tables in the transit lounge and US secretaries of defense use it as a military base away from home in which to address their troops before sending them off to destroy faraway countries on the pretence of bringing them peace and justice. During the Iraq War, when George Bush admitted he was doing everything he could to make the US 'a literate country and a hopefuller one' you could hardly move. Outside there were nothing but massive US Air Force Hercules C-130s, the size of Co. Clare, blocking the runway. Inside the terminal there were nothing but US troops in transit and airport officials rushing backwards and forwards playing patsy with the military bigwigs and banking all the money they were paying them. Down the road protesters were in mouth-to-mouth combat against US troops and their deplcted uranium-tipped missiles and napalm, which incidentally are banned internationally as well as by the UN, passing unchecked through what they say is a civilian airport.

'Jaysus,' your typical butt-thumping red-headed firebrand says to me. 'The fourth of July should be a public holiday here as well as in those godforsaken United States. Except here it should be called Dependence Day.'

It's the same all over. Towns, villages, little huddles of houses that were once covered in dust and cobwebs would today be beautiful if it wasn't for the Americans. Labasheeda, Kilrush, Kilkee, and all the way up to the Cliffs of Moher. Across to Scarvill and Killaloe and back to Bunratty. When I first started going there they were all dull, drab, damp, paraffin lamps and a priest or a nun round every corner. Today they're giving in to the baseball cap.

Kilrush is almost a poor man's Kinsale. It's on the water. It's full of fancy boats. The food, however, is not so hot although dolphins are very popular. The place seemed to be full of people desperate to see them. I should know. I was stuck there once for a couple of hours. The whole town was blocked solid with a funeral. All I could do to avoid the dolphins was to go from bar to bar. The funeral over, the streets cleared, I made for Kilkee and Loop Head.

Kilkee's most famous visitor was Lord Tennyson. Which tells you a lot about Kilkee and its popularity as a holiday destination. It is said by locals that his lines 'Into the valley of Death / Rode the six hundred' were inspired more by visiting Kilkee's famous amusement arcades than anything to do with Cardigan's ill-fated cavalry charge. But I wouldn't know. I know nothing about amusement arcades.

Loop Head is a must. It should be up there with the Giant's Causeway. Not true. It's better than the Giant's Causeway. To me it's one of the top sights of Ireland. The cliffs are some of the most spectacular I've seen anywhere. In fact, they're not cliffs. They're more like huge Atlantic sea sculptures. On a beautiful calm sunny day, it's like sitting in a bar knowing all you've got to do all day is drink Guinness. In other words, heaven. The sea is calm, almost like a mirror. The fields are soft. The grass is green. To the south, you can see Dingle and Mount Brandon. To the north, the Twelve Bens of Connemara and the Aran Islands. On a wild, dark, cold winter's day, it's hell. In other words, like knowing you can't sit in a bar all day and do nothing but drink Guinness.

At the far end is Kilbaha, a tiny bay, and the New Bar, the nearest bar to New York. Perfect for a drink on a good day. Or a bad day. Last time I was there I got into a long, involved discussion with an old Irish farmer who looked as though he was suffering from too many repeats on Discovery Channel. He had this theory about cows. They knew everything. If they sat down it meant rain was coming. If they scratched their ear it meant a storm was coming. Their left ear, it was coming from the east. Their right ear, from the west. If they swished their tails, the sun was going to shine. If they jumped over the moon, you'd had too much to drink.

About turn and head north to the Cliffs of Moher. Doonbeg, Quilty, Spanish Point, Liscannor and Miltown Malbay are all tiny little fishing villages apart from Miltown Malbay, which looks as though the only fish they ever see is on the best Victorian china.

Doonbeg has a reputation for being the soul – or should that be the sole? – of Irish music. But I didn't stay to find out. My diddly-diddly count is already too high. Quilty is big on fishing except they fish seaweed. Go there the wrong time of day, the place smells like a Japanese restaurant full of sweaty pulsating vegans. On a good day it's supposed to be perfect for surfing. On a bad it's supposed to be even better. If you see any seaweed at Spanish Point, so called because at one point it was knee-deep in Spaniards when the Armada was blown off course and swept ashore, it's on top of the roofs. Revisionist historians who probably do nothing but surf the Net claim that Spanish Point is short for 'There they go again, the Spanish pointing in the wrong direction'.

Liscannor I always remember on a bad day. I was in a bar. The wind was howling. The rain was lashing down. The whole place was practically under water. A pale old walnut sitting at the far end of the bar who looked as though he made a living testing laxatives looked up at me and said, 'Would it surprise ye, if I was to tell ye that the man who invented the submarine came from Liscannor?'

No it wouldn't. I'd have thought it was about the only way to get from one side of the street to the other.

''Twas a certain Mr John P. Holland. People said he was Dutch, accounting for his name. But he wasn't. He was as Irish as I am. God bless ye. I'll be having a large one, begging ye pardon.'

Another old walnut shuffles along the bar.

'Of course, it was his second attempt that did it,' he says. 'He thought it would probably work better with glass in the windows. I'll be joining you if I may. Not wishing to be bad-mannered.'

Now the Cliffs of Moher, one of Ireland's greatest five-pint attractions. Over five miles of rough, rugged, desperate cliff gouged out by the Atlantic. Over 600 feet high. The sounds of the sea crashing against the cliffs you can hear miles away, worse than a throbbing hangover. The spray can drench you half a mile away. Far, far more grand, far more impressive and far more spectacular than the Giant's Causeway.

The Giant's Causeway is chemistry gone wrong. The Cliffs of Moher are action, drama, suspense.

Some people like to go there on a nice sunny day, picnic with the family and yell and shout and swear at each other. Not me. I prefer the bad days. A howling gale. Rain coming down like steel reinforcing rods. The wind howling like a pack of wounded banshees. The waves crashing against the cliffs. For some reason I don't understand, the local council want to build a giant underground Cliffs of Moher Visitor Centre complete with audio-visual theatre, exhibition area, restaurant and no doubt a million signs warning of the dangers of going too close to the edge. Why I don't know. The whole point of going there is not to hide underground but to get out into the open, to be picked up by the wind and hurled into the sea, to be smashed against the rocks and spend the rest of your life in hospital. I'd go further. On a good day they should give us our money back. It's no more fun than kissing your sister.

East Clare is different altogether. It's landscape. It's farming. It's fishing.

Just south of Scarriff was born Edna O'Brien. In Drewsborough House. Go into any of the pubs, get into a conversation with the locals and there's no end of speculation about the real identity of Mr Gentleman, the old smoothie who led those two young country girls astray in her first novel, *The Country Girls*. I knew her years ago. She'd just moved to England. She was scribbling away in exercise books on the kitchen table hoping to become a famous novelist. I wonder if she ever made it.

From Scarriff whenever I get the chance I like to drive along

Lough Derg to Killaloe. Some of Ireland's loughs are no bigger than a fish pond. But Lough Derg is the real thing. It's the size of a couple of dozen fish ponds. Not to be confused with Lough Derg up in Co. Donegale which, of course, it always is.

I was coming out of Scarriff once when I was stopped by an old man practically standing in the middle of the road. He must have been late seventies, all in black, a plastic bag in one hand, a blackthorn stick in the other. He looked like an Old Testament prophet with an Irish accent. He told me he was looking for Station Island where every year tens of thousands of pilgrims go to walk barefoot, eat nothing but bread and water, sleep on bunk beds in smelly dormitories and do nothing but pray, pray, pray. He told me he wanted to go there to atone for his sins. You should have seen the look on his face when I told him he was at the wrong Lough Derg. The one he wanted was over 200 miles away. He insisted I dropped him off at the first bar we came to.

''Tis the will of God,' he says. 'If He had wanted me to atone for my sins He would have directed me to the real one. Sure to goodness, He's telling me I have nothing to atone for in my life. I'm a newborn babe.'

Killaloe was always a Sunday-afternoon treat. Best suit. Best tie. Best shoes. Visiting Killaloe was the next best thing to being invited into the parlour by the parish priest for a cup of tea. Or even the Pope himself. It was what was known as a grand town. On the banks of the Shannon. A fine old historic 13-arch bridge, wide enough for a horse and cart. Upmarket bars and tea shops. A nice old cathedral. A town for the gentry as opposed to farmers. That's apart from the holy hoof marks.

Just below Killaloe on the rocks on Friar's Island you can see the hoof marks left behind by St Patrick's horse after he had made a flying 200-yard leap across the river to escape from his pagan pursuers. The only reason you cannot see them today is because of the Germans. No, not because of that. But because after the Irish gained their independence they wanted to build up their natural resources. There was no way they were going to ask the British to help them. Instead they turned to who else? The Germans. In the Germans came, flooded miles and miles of land, turned the whole area into a huge reservoir, built a giant 38,000-horsepower power station, which provided Ireland with all the power they needed and completely transformed the River Shannon between Limerick and Killaloe. Before it wasn't possible to navigate the river because it fell by over 100 feet. Now, it's not possible because of all the boats and cruisers chugging up and down.

An old dog face, who had obviously slipped his lead, told me the whole town was against the idea. Especially the clergy.

'Why? Because of the war?' I wondered nervously.

'Not at all. Not at all,' he says. 'They didn't like it at all when they heard these Germans and their Siemens were coming in.'

I know two English builders who every year spend the summer working and drinking in Killaloe. Not just your ordinary Guinness. But Guinness with a slug of port thrown in for extra flavour. They swear it's heaven on earth. What their customers think when they turn up full of Guinness and port to repair a hole in the roof or rebuild the crooked wall they built the previous year is probably something else.

As far as I'm concerned, however, the real killer Guinness drink is a Depthcharge. Which is not only for real drinkers but also a spectacular drink to order: Fill a liquor glass to the brim with Drambuie. Put the glass into the bottom of a pint glass. Into a pint glass you then pour a pint of Guinness, being careful not to disturb the Drambuie in the liquor glass. Then as you drink the Guinness, the angle of the glass tips the Drambuie slowly into the Guinness. Fabulous. Guinness and port is for English builders and old ladies. A Depthcharge is for men.

Today, however, Killaloe is a very weak shandy. Maybe because it's too motor boats and cruising and sailing and waterskiing and sailboarding. I know Ireland is an island. I know it's surrounded by sea. I know St Brendan and all that. It's just that I don't associate rivers and boats and, Heaven help us, sailboarding with Ireland. Maybe because I've reached the stage in life where nothing lives down to my expectations. Maybe because the local bar had run out of Drambuie and I couldn't mix any more Depthcharges.

From Killaloe I always head back to Ennis via Bunratty Castle, built by Thomas De Clare, the great-great-grandson of Strongbow, the famous Irish cider maker, around 1277. Nice guy De Clare. He pledges lifelong friendship with Brian Ruaddh O'Brien then has him torn in two by horses, decapitated and his body hung up on the castle gates as a sign to tourists that they were open for business. From then on the castle was attacked, set on fire, destroyed, rebuilt, destroyed, rebuilt again, but amazingly spared during the Great Rebellion of 1641. Today it dominates Co. Clare and Co. Limerick because of the noise created by the nightly medieval banquets. Especially if they have the baseball caps in yelling and screaming about their latest colonic irrigation.

Behind the castle is Bunratty Folk Park which is no folk park as far as I'm concerned. Many's the time I can remember visiting Ireland when the whole place looked like that: the old thatched cottage, the fisherman's house, the mansion, the shops, the post office, the pub. My mother used to insist I took her there with no end of aunts and uncles and cousins three times removed. Why I don't know. They lived in cottages like that. They slept in beds like that. They ate at tables like that. Made butter in a churn. Baked soda bread on an open fire. They used to do all that themselves. The old forge. They used to take their ponies and horses to a forge just like that.

'Beautiful. Beautiful,' they would say, the tears streaming down their faces.

Then there's the pub, Durty Nellie's so called because Bunratty farmers were the first to buy a horse-drawn muck-spreader from America. They decided that with the new technology it was only fair that the women did less of the hard work. So the men travelled in the muck-spreader making certain it was doing its job while the Nellies walked behind making certain it was spreading the muck in all the right places.

I had a cousin who used to work there. Every time we went to see him he would meet us across the road. With him he'd bring a plastic carrier bag full of oysters. But no knife to open them with. The number of oysters I've opened with a carjack you'd never believe. You'd never believe what they tasted like either. I don't know how but he also had a good deal going with a friend, cousin or whoever twice removed who worked at the lush, out-of-this-world expensive Dromoland Castle up the road. For half a pint of the black stuff, a handful of dollars or the keys of your car, he could arrange for you to play on their supposedly out-of-this-world golf course. I wasn't interested. To me golf is a stupid game. In the end I wished I had done it. To make up for me not playing the course, he used to bring me more and more oysters. In the end, using the carjack so much the muscles in my arm were as solid as the Cliffs of Moher. If I'd have played golf, every shot would have been 500 yards, no problem.

Last time I was in Durty Nellie's I was having a drink with one of the locals, three-piece suit, trilby, completely unburdened by any form of subtlety. We were getting on famously until somehow or other he discovered my father was English. That was it. Down came the shutters. Up went the drawbridge. Complete shutdown.

'So what's the problem?' I said. 'It was nothing to do with me.'

'The English,' he goes all surly. 'The English. They ruined my family.'

'Ruined your family?' I asked nervously.

'They beat Napoleon at Waterloo. We had a contract to supply Napoleon with horses to help him conquer Europe. You beat him. He cancelled the contract. Ruined us for ever.'

From Durty Nellie's we used to take the back roads and lanes and tracks back to Ennis and Ballynacally. Now there are motorways. But Ireland being Ireland the motorways do not take precedence over everything. They have to take note of the fairies. It's true. I'm not joking. The €90 million Newmarket-on-Fergus bypass had to be rerouted to avoid destroying the famous fairy bush of Latoon, where the Kerry fairies meet with the Connacht fairies to discuss fairy things like the joys of anaesthetic-free dentistry, rational expectation theory and how important is the size of the wand. A fairy fence was built around it to protect it from non-fairy people.

Then what happened? Non-fairy vandals came along in the middle of the night with a non-fairy chainsaw and cut it to the ground. Clare County Council were called in. They called in the police to investigate.

'Will the Gardai find the man who did it?' I asked one fairy with a poodle perm I met in the bar of the Clare Inn who was gagging on an organic lettuce leaf.

'Probably not,' he minces. 'But no matter.'

'Why?' I said. 'I thought it was a big crime to cut down a fairy bush.'

'The fairies will get him,' he says. 'Have no fear. I wouldn't like to be in his shoes, thank you very much. God bless.'

In the old days, everywhere we used to go was a favourite. But some places were more favourite than others. For a while the best place in the whole world was Ennistymon, a grey-stone town on the River Inagh. It suffered desperately during the famine. In 1850 there were over 2500 people in workhouses throughout the town. But not the same 2500. At one workhouse they were admitting 600 people a month against over 900 people dying a month. But it soon climbed back. By the late 1800s it was booming. Its butter market was reckoned second only to Cork's in the whole of Ireland. Today it's famous for the Falls, a 200-metre stretch of waterfalls running though the centre of town. They're not exactly the Victoria Falls. But they have their admirers. Dylan Thomas and Augustus John used to hide up in the Falls Hotel for a spot of R and R. It is said that Dylan Thomas staggered out of one of the local bars one day, a bottle of Guinness in his back pocket. He stumbled and fell. The whole town heard him praying that the soft, warm liquid running down his leg was blood. The nearest I got to any hard stuff was a pot of tea and some cakes whenever I went there in my role as chauffeur and runaround.

Quin was another favourite. Not so much for what was there but for what wasn't there. We'd go to Quin Abbey. There we'd have to stand still and wait and wait and wait to see the lines of ghostly friars going into a ghostly mass.

Best of all was Lisdoonvarna, the only spa town you'll find in Ireland although it's not for its waters that all the old farmers make for it every year. Whatever it can do for their arthritis and rheumatism, they're not interested. They're looking for something to liven them up far more than a couple of glasses of sulphur and iodine. They're looking for a wife although why they are so eager to find a wife always struck me as strange because as far as I know most

Irishmen are convinced that any day of the week is a bad day to get married. And what's more if it rains that's the end of it.

Hence the story of Patrick and Mary who as they used to say at the time have been walking out together for over 30 years.

Suddenly one evening Mary says, 'Patrick. Don't you think that after all these years we should get married?'

Patrick replies, 'Who would have us?'

When we used to go there it was like an old-fashioned dating agency run by a group of elderly nuns. The men were invariably middle-aged to old, lonely, isolated with few if any tricks up their trousers. In their eyes they had that look that said, It's taken me 700 years to get my freedom I'm not going to give it up in 5 minutes whatever she says. Most of them looked as though they'd be happier at home being licked to death by their old cow. They could pull twenty piglets out of their old sow before breakfast but as far as they were concerned fallopian tubes were something to do with the Irish bagpipes.

'I swear to God,' my old uncle once told me, 'the only excitement they look as though they've had in life was pushing a stick up a pig's arse.'

Not that he was a great expert. In the old days, he told me, the only way they could find out if a woman had knock-knees was to listen to her walking in and out of church.

'Now,' he said, 'women wear clothes so short there is no knowing where it is going to end.'

The women were worse. Not one of them would tickle anyone's hypothalamus. Not that anyone knew such a thing existed in those days. They looked like a row of potatoes in an upmarket greengrocer's. Some small and neat and well-scrubbed. Others huge with great bumps all over the place smelling of mud. They all had that look in their eyes that said one thing and one thing only: I can't wait to get my hands on his most prized possession. His post office book.

The number of times I've been there I only once heard the slightest hint of passion. I was having a glass of the black stuff in the Imperial Hotel. Suddenly I heard an old farmer declare, 'Jesus, Mary and Joseph. Will ye look at the body on that one.' I swung round. He was talking about a tractor he'd just seen drive past the window.

Go there today and it's all changed. People who go there go there for a clean break. The sulphur springs are south of the town. The iron springs, north of the town. Rheumatism and arthritis sufferers swear by it. I don't usually tap into this spa business but I must admit even I find it difficult to turn down the opportunity of a foam bath with rosemary.

Now and then you still come across an old farmer, still on the prowl for the one thing in life that will bring him true happiness: a pint of the black stuff. If there are any spare women going he might also be interested in them. But only if the Guinness runs out. The young farmers now do their shopping by post. A local farmer in Miltown Malbay has set up a catalogue dating agency. Just €50 down you can have your own Filipino bride. Brings a new meaning to the term, 'mail order'. Beats all that moping around Lisdoonvarna. Doesn't interfere with the Guinness either.

I went back to Co. Clare after my mother remarried. She didn't want us at her wedding. Why, I never asked her, although I can guess.

After my father died, she went back to work as a nurse. She worked nights. We used to see her when she came home in the mornings as we were going off to school. Then in the evenings when we were coming home and she was going off to work. We virtually brought ourselves up. Whether we made a good job of it I have no idea.

When she retired, she started going back home for her holiday. One holiday she met – if you have tears to shed, prepare to shed them now – her old childhood sweetheart, Christie, the man she promised faithfully she would go back and marry when she left Ireland all those years ago. Instead she stayed and married my father. So much for women's promises. Her childhood sweetheart, however, was now a widower. His wife had died a few years before. The two of them, now in their sixties, started where they left off. Well, almost. After much agonising and heartache, they got married. They couldn't have been happier. The rest of their lives they spent talking about the old days.

'Sure, d'ye remember . . .'

'Wasn't it Michael O'Hare who . . .'

'In those days . . .'

They knew everything and everybody in Co. Clare. Or if they didn't they made a good show of it.

I tried to go across and see them once a year, maybe twice. Wherever I took them they knew somebody, somebody's mother, cousin, uncle or aunt. They'd remember seeing them at school, at market, going or coming out of church. Then as the years went by I would go back because one or the other was not too well, serious, being rushed to hospital. Christie was the first to go. My mother was a widow again. She never really got over it. She started going downhill. She had a heart attack, was in hospital, was no longer able to look after herself. She went into a nursing home. The strange thing was whenever I saw her after that she never spoke about Christie. She always spoke about my father. It didn't make any difference to me. She was happy. But I felt sorry for Christie's family, who had more than cared for her and looked after her especially as she grew older and frailer.

There's a lot spoken about Alzheimer's, what it is, how it should be treated, how it should be prevented, how it should be cured. But to me, as I watched my mother drift further and further away, the more I came to realise it is in many ways a blessing. Think about it. You're getting old. You're falling apart. You're beginning to act and behave and do things you probably would have done in child-hood. The last thing you want is to be able to remember them. Although I will admit more should be done for people suffering from Alzheimer's. They shouldn't be locked away and forgotten. At least once a year we should have a special day dedicated to people suffering from Alzheimer's the same as we have for people suffering from cancer, lifeboats, homelessness or any of the other things for which we have collections. My suggestion: Remembrance Day.

While all this was happening there was the question of Christie's will. Wills or lack of them can cause enormous untold problems between families let alone between second families. Obviously Christie's family were worried in case these English-Irish inter-lopers grabbed a share of the action as I supposed we would have been entitled to do. But I made it clear from the beginning there was no way I wanted any of Christie's money. Christie's money was for Christie's family. Except.

There's always an except. I said that because my mother was in a home we would use first what little money she had to look after her. If her money ran out before she did, we'd start to use Christie's money. In the event, it never happened. She died before her money ran out. We never had to touch Christie's money.

The Burren, Irish for 'Barren', is not so much like death as the preparation for death. It's cold. It's bleak. It's stark. It's desolate. It's empty. It's lifeless. It's about 350 square miles of wild, rocky, desolate, treeless, soil-less moonscape. Huge limestone slabs, the size of football pitches. Weird-looking rocks. A patch of grass. A couple of Irish shorthorn cattle wondering why they drew the short horn and ended up on the Burren and not on the rich, lush grass of Co. Kerry. It's a geological monotony turned into a spectacular natural work of art, buffeted non-stop by the Atlantic wind and rain. It's like they were building a moonscape, laid the foundations, got bored, went and had a drink and didn't bother to come back. One of Oliver Cromwell's sidekicks complained it did not have enough earth to bury a man, enough timber to hang him nor enough water to drown him.

Drive through it in the old days, it was always a risk. A risk the car would break down. A risk if it did, there'd be nobody around to help. A risk that if you did break down you'd be drowned with holy water with everybody praying and splashing themselves before help arrived.

Nowadays the only danger is going there with anyone who knows even the slightest thing about flowers. They'll go on and on and on about the plants. Apparently there are more plants there than anywhere else in the universe. Orchids. Over 20 different varieties. Maidenhair ferns. Mountain avens. Alpines. Gentians. Geraniums. Goodness knows what else. There are also supposed to be a million different butterflies and moths. Great. But what good is that if you're thirsty?

Some say it's all the doing of a glacier. It made its way from the North Pole, liked what it saw, stopped, melted and promptly obliterated everything it had seen with millions of rocks. Others go for the more rational explanation. The man in the moon and his wife were having a row. The wife accused him of letting an old cow jump all over him. He went to hit her with a sledgehammer, missed, shattered a rock and scattered all the debris all over the Burren.

When the end came, it came slowly. She became more and more frail. She fell out of bed. She fell over. She started wandering around the home she was in. Somehow she found her way out of her room, along a corridor, into a lift, down to the ground floor and out in the grounds. She started developing strange ideas and obsessions. Little old ladies she had known for years, she started accusing them of being men.

'You,' she would point at a shrivelled-up candlewick dressing gown with stains all down the front. 'You're a man. What are you doing here? This is for women.'

The dressing gown took no notice.

'I've been given two weeks to live,' he/she told me once, 'I'm taking one in July and the other in February.'

Another old lady in the ward was suffering from Parkinson's disease. Her son turned up one Christmas with a present for her: a tambourine.

Just to shuffle down the corridor, my mother would insist on dressing up in her outdoor clothes. The door of her room had to be locked, barred and bolted as if it was the front door of her home. She started hiding everything away. She began talking more and more about my father. Me? She didn't know who I was.

'You.' She would look at me all concerned and anxious. 'Who are you? Who's your father?'

Once I grinned.

'You should know,' I said.

'You're a son of a bitch,' she says.

She fell over once more, was taken to hospital and then just started to drift slowly away.

As soon as I got the telephone call, I flew across. It was just before Christmas. There was snow and ice everywhere. When I got to the hospital, the nurses told me which ward she was in. I went in. I didn't recognise her. She was so shrunken and shrivelled up. I had to ask the nurses who my mother was.

The last night I sat with her to the end. The family came. Her Irish family that is. We said our rosaries. Slowly they left. She began to grow colder and colder as if she was slowly turning into a block of marble. First, the feet. Then the hands. Then gradually more and more of her body. The breathing became slower and slower and softer and softer. Then nothing. She was gone.

The nurses were wonderful.

'For weeks she lay at death's door,' says one. 'But the doctors pulled her through.'

The funeral was a grand affair. She couldn't have had a better send-off if she had been a bishop. Practically the whole of Co. Clare turned out.

At the undertaker's the previous evening, the family sat around the edge of the room. A few were in black. Most in their ordinary clothes. The coffin was in the centre. Everybody filed past. Some felt her hand. A few kissed her on the forehead.

We all walked behind the coffin as it was taken to the church. People stopped, took their hats off, blessed themselves. After the coffin was placed at the front of the church facing the altar everybody then filed past us all, shaking our hands and saying, 'Sorry for your troubles.' Must have been a good few hundred people.

The funeral took place after high mass on the Sunday morning. There seemed to be more priests there than you see in a week at the Vatican. Not that my mother was particularly religious. It just seemed to happen. Probably because it was a Sunday morning.

''Twas grand. 'Twas grand,' says one aunt or cousin or somebody. 'The shame is you have to die first before ye can have one.'

The burial was to be in the local cemetery, in the middle of the country, miles away from the church. I bought a new pair of shoes for the occasion. My usual townie black shoes had started falling apart. They'd be no good for the mud and the rough ground. I bought my first pair of thick, heavy brown brogues. They were practically a cross between safety shoes with reinforced steel toes and miners' boots. Even then they still leaked.

The church service over we all bundled into cars and followed

501

the coffin. Again people stopped, took their hats off and blessed themselves. Cars kept out of the way. We had the road to ourselves.

Down into the ground went the coffin alongside that of Christie. A few more prayers. Then it was back to Ennis, the Old Ground Hotel and a gossipy, chatty, not very boozy lunch.

'Will ye come and say hullo to . . . ?'

'A grand woman. She was a . . .'

'My God. She'll be missed. She was the . . .'

Since then I go back every year on the anniversary of her death. There's a special mass in the cathedral in Ennis as near as possible to the actual date. Afterwards we go off and have a meal. Nothing riotous. Nobody seems to drink much any more. A glass of wine here. Two Cokes over there. A beer. A glass of milk. I drink two or three glasses of wine and feel like an alcoholic. On the other hand be invited back home with any of the family and I am an alcoholic. Out will come a bottle of whiskey that's been in the back of the cupboard since St Patrick was a boy.

'Will ye have a drop?' they say.

'I will,' says I.

They've no idea of different measures for different drinks. Whether it's a glass of water or the best 16-year-old Bushmills they slosh out a pint measure.

'Will that be enough?' they say. 'Here have a drop more. Will do you good.'

Do me good. Sometimes my liver throbs as much as the back of my eyes.

How long will I keep going back? As long as they will have me. In fact sometimes I think I should go back there for good. Hunting in the morning. Chatting and drinking and laughing the rest of the day. What a country! Could there possibly be a better one on earth?

Cheers.

God bless.